BALANCED SCORECARD
STEP-BY-STEP

BALANCED SCORECARD STEP-BY-STEP

Maximizing Performance and Maintaining Results

Second Edition

Paul R. Niven

WILEY

John Wiley & Sons, Inc.

Library of Congress Cataloging-in-Publication Data

Niven, Paul R.
    Balanced scorecard step-by-step : maximizing performance and maintaining results / Paul R. Niven. — 2nd ed.
      p. cm.
    Includes index.
    ISBN-13: 978-0-471-78049-6 (cloth)
    ISBN-10: 0-471-78049-9 (cloth)
     1. Organizational effectiveness — Measurement.
   2. Performance — Measurement. I. Title.
    HD58.9.N58   2006
    658.4'013 — dc22   2006008526

Printed in the United States of America

10 9 8 7 6

This being a second edition it seems fitting that
I dedicate the book to my "second parents," my wife's
mother and father, Harry and Pat Ackstein.
Thank you both for your love, generosity, and support.

About the Author

Paul R. Niven is a management consultant and noted speaker on the subjects of performance management and the Balanced Scorecard. As both a practitioner and consultant he has developed successful performance management systems for organizations large and small around the globe. His clients include Fortune 500 companies, public sector agencies from all levels, and nonprofit organizations. He may be reached through his Web site at www.senalosa.com.

Contents

Preface

Four years ago I wrote *Balanced Scorecard Step-by-Step* to provide a systematic implementation guide to readers incorporating or considering incorporating the Balanced Scorecard methodology in their organization. My experiences as a Balanced Scorecard practitioner with a large Canadian company taught me that tremendous results are possible with the tool, but to attain those results, you must overcome numerous pitfalls that can derail or significantly damage the implementation effort. I have been amazed and humbled at the success of the first edition, which has now been translated in over a dozen languages. The many e-mails, calls, and letters I have received from readers who have benefited in some way from the guidance offered in the book have been very gratifying and demonstrate that, with a little help, every organization can derive tremendous success from the Balanced Scorecard system.

This second edition contains the same core implementation guidance found in the original volume but has been updated and enhanced to include guidance on a number of topics that were still relatively immature as of the first printing in 2002. The most significant change is my expanded coverage of strategy maps, powerful communication tools signaling to the entire workforce (and beyond) what is critical in executing the organization's strategy. The text also provides new and updated information on the linkage between the Balanced Scorecard and corporate governance, the critical importance of strategy-centered management meetings, and an emerging trend, the Office of Strategy Management. In addition to entirely new sections, you will find the latest thinking on all aspects of the Balanced Scorecard journey, honed from my work as a consultant and researcher.

THE BALANCED SCORECARD

Organizations in today's change-filled, highly competitive environment must devote significant time, energy, and human and financial resources to measuring their performance in achieving strategic goals. Most do just that, but despite the substantial effort and related costs, many are dissatisfied with their measurement efforts. In fact, at any given time, as many as 50 percent of organizations are making changes to their performance measurement systems.[1]

Increasingly, organizations are concluding that while measurement is more crucial than ever, their systems for capturing, monitoring, and sharing performance information are critically flawed. Today's systems in many ways bear a remarkable resemblance to their reporting ancestors. Although the methods of modern business have transformed dramatically over the decades, our systems of measurement have remained firmly mired in the past. At the root of our measurement misery is an almost exclusive reliance on financial measures of performance. These systems may have been perfectly suited to the machinelike, physical asset–based nature of early industrial endeavors, but they are ill-equipped to capture the value-creating mechanisms of today's modern business organization. Intangible assets such as employee knowledge, customer and supplier relationships, and innovative cultures are the key to producing value in today's economy. Additionally, the importance of a differentiating strategy is more important today than it has ever been. Whether you're a high-tech newcomer or an established manufacturing veteran, executing strategy effectively is crucial in an era of globalization, customer power, and rapid change. But the sobering fact is that about 9 out of 10 organizations fail to implement their strategies. What is needed is a measurement system that balances the historical accuracy and integrity of financial numbers with today's drivers of economic success, and in so doing allows the organization to beat the odds of executing strategy.

The Balanced Scorecard has emerged as a proven and effective tool in our quest to capture, describe, and translate intangible assets into real value for all of an organization's stakeholders and, in the process, to allow organizations to implement their differentiating strategies successfully. Developed by Robert Kaplan and David Norton, this deceptively simple methodology translates an organization's strategy into performance objectives, measures, targets, and initiatives in four balanced perspectives: Financial, Customer, Internal Process, and Employee Learning and Growth. Organizations around the globe have embraced the Balanced Scorecard and reaped swift benefits from its commonsense principles. Such benefits include increased financial returns, greater employee alignment with overall goals, improved collaboration, and an unrelenting focus on strategy, to name just a few. To reap those rewards, however, an organization must possess the tools necessary to craft an effective Balanced Scorecard.

---

1. Mark L. Frigo, "The State of Strategic Performance Measurement," *IMA 2001 Survey.*

About This Book

In the mid-1990s I was working with an organization that, like so many others, was about to undergo significant change. The industry structure was changing, competitors appeared more nimble and threatening than ever, and customers were demanding better service with no price increases. A new strategy was developed that, if effectively implemented, would see the organization enhance employee skills, develop new processes, build customer loyalty, and ultimately deliver breakthrough financial performance. But how could the strategy be executed successfully? The organization's chief financial officer investigated the Balanced Scorecard approach and determined it was the right tool at the right time. Acting as the executive sponsor for the initiative, he appointed me to lead a team charged with the responsibility for developing a new management system featuring the Balanced Scorecard as the cornerstone. Two years later his intuition paid off in a big way. Employee knowledge of strategy had increased significantly, internal processes were functioning more efficiently than ever, customer loyalty was on the rise, and despite many adverse factors beyond the organization's control, financial returns were on target.

The organization just described is Nova Scotia Power, Inc. (NSPI), a Canadian electric utility company. As the results demonstrate, its Balanced Scorecard implementation was a great success and has been featured in case studies and shared at conferences throughout North America and beyond, and has earned the organization a spot in the Balanced Scorecard Collaborative's Hall of Fame. As successful as the implementation was, however, it was not without challenges. Our team quickly learned that building a Balanced Scorecard is far more than a metrics project; instead it touches many disparate organizational processes. Building an effective team; generating support and enthusiasm for a change initiative; efficiently gathering and sharing data; and coaching, training, and facilitating are just some of the many exciting and challenging tasks we faced. At that time, Balanced Scorecard literature and support services were at a nascent stage, and we were left to our own devices when grappling with the many issues awaiting us. Although Scorecard literature and related consulting and support products have proliferated in recent years, few if any focus on the wide array of organizational activities that must accompany a winning Scorecard campaign. This book has been written to fill the void existing between theory and application. Since its original publication in 2002, it has guided thousands of organizations worldwide through their Balanced Scorecard journeys.

Organizations embarking on a Scorecard effort must be aware of—and properly equipped with the tools to navigate successfully—the many potential pitfalls associated with an initiative of this magnitude. Based on my experience as a consultant working with organizations around the globe plus extensive research, these pages guide the reader through the entire

Balanced Scorecard process on a step-by-step basis. From determining your guiding rationale for the Scorecard, to testing your mission, to building a Strategy Map, to developing measures and targets, to placing the Scorecard at the center of your management system, to tips for sustaining your success, you'll find all this and more. Let's now take a look at how the book is organized and consider how you can use it to best suit your needs.

How the Book Is Organized

This second edition of *Balanced Scorecard Step-by-Step* is comprised of 12 chapters, spanning the entire Scorecard experience. The opening chapter is designed to familiarize you with the field of performance measurement and provide a solid grounding of Scorecard background and principles. It elaborates on the discussion begun in this preface by examining how the Scorecard solves three fundamental modern business issues: reducing the reliance on financial performance measures, the rise of intangible assets to value creation, and the difficulty of implementing strategy. Chapter Two lays the foundation for the work ahead by examining the purpose of developing a Balanced Scorecard, securing executive sponsorship, creating a team, and preparing a development plan. The core elements of any effective Balanced Scorecard—mission, values, vision, and strategy—are the subject of Chapter Three. You'll discover why each of these elements is crucial to the success of a Balanced Scorecard.

With the Scorecard building blocks firmly in place, Chapter Four explores the world of Strategy Maps, powerful communication tools signaling to everyone in the organization what is critical in executing strategy. You will learn why Strategy Maps are a decisive ingredient to overall Scorecard success and be provided with numerous tips on development and facilitation. Chapter Five provides an in-depth view of what it takes to build measures that act as a faithful translation of strategy, the backbone of any successful Balanced Scorecard. The critical role of target setting and the Balanced Scorecard is presented along with a review of different types of targets in Chapter Six. Ensuring that organizational plans and initiatives are aligned with the Balanced Scorecard and strategy is also given extensive coverage in that chapter.

Aligning every employee's actions with overall organizational goals is the subject of Chapter Seven. This "cascading" of the Balanced Scorecard is critical if organizations hope to enjoy the benefits of greater employee knowledge of, and focus on, key organizational strategies. In Chapter Eight the role of the Balanced Scorecard in the budgeting process is examined. The chapter equips readers with specific techniques to align spending with strategy. The often-challenging topic of incentive compensation is tackled in Chapter Nine, where you will find a comprehensive review of critical compensation planning and design elements. This chapter also reviews how the Balanced Scorecard can play a significant role in the improvement of corporate governance, a vital topic in the post-Enron era.

Frequent reporting of results is critical in gaining support for the Balanced Scorecard as an effective management tool. But should organizations purchase one of the many performance management software packages available or build their own reporting solution? Chapter Ten probes this question and offers several tools to be used when making the decision. The strategy-centered meeting is also explained in the chapter, providing the means to ensure the Balanced Scorecard forms the agenda for your management meeting process. Maintaining the Balanced Scorecard is presented in Chapter Eleven. It carefully reviews business rules, processes, and procedures (including those for gathering data) necessary to embed the Scorecard in the fabric of organizational life and introduces you to an emerging function in modern organizations: the Office of Strategy Management. The important role of organizational change in securing a successful Scorecard effort is presented in the book's final chapter. There you will also discover the top 10 implementation issues and receive guidance on the use of outside consultants when constructing a Scorecard.

Nearly 2,500 years ago the Greek playwright Euripides noted the importance of balance in our lives when he said, *"The best and safest thing is to keep a balance in your life, acknowledge the great powers around us and in us. If you can do that, and live that way, you are really a wise man."* I truly believe the same applies to organizations.

PAUL R. NIVEN
San Diego, California
August 2006

Acknowledgments

When people learn I have written a number of books, among the first questions they ask is "How long does it take?" Since in addition to being a writer I am also a consultant, I typically default to the classic response of "it depends," as many factors contribute to the duration of the process, including: the amount of research required, maturity of the subject matter, experience with the topic, and of course other commitments that life lays in your path. Despite my fence-sitting answer, there is one thing I can say with virtual certainty: If it weren't for the keen insights, generosity of time and spirit, and passion of others, my books could not be written. And so it is with tremendous gratitude and deep appreciation that I thank the following individuals for their invaluable guidance, encouragement, and commitment both to me and to the ideals of the Balanced Scorecard.

I will begin with some of the many clients whose conference rooms and offices I have used as a laboratory for these many years and whose experiences and insights form the scaffolding that allowed these pages to emerge. From Aliant, Jay Forbes and Dennis Barnhart; Amy Kosifas from the Unified Port of San Diego; Norio Mitsubayashi and Stan Romanoff from Brother Industries (USA, Inc.); Marlon Fuentes, Junie Villongco, Jim Mahoney, Bart Johnson, Jake Reyes, Kevin Tirrell, and Leo Casco of Financial Freedom; from Ingram Micro, Krista Arellano and Jim Annes; Laurie Cason of the United States Navy; Ronnie Hepp and Mike Morino from the Recreation Vehicle Dealers Association; Allan Kingston and Regina Korossy of Century Housing; and Dr. Tom Lynch and Vicki Lynn of the Worcester Polytechnic Institute.

Many others have contributed to this book, including my editor Tim Burgard from John Wiley & Sons, Hazel Wiggington and Holly Smith of H2 Performance Consulting, Vik Torpunuri of e2e Analytix, Chuck Salmond of Bearing Point, J. P. Kirton of QPR Software, and Joe and Catherine Stenzel, editors of the *Journal of Cost Management*.

Finally, and most important, I would like to thank my wife, Lois. While I wrote this book she acted once again as first-line manuscript editor, chief supporter, and, through it all, a constant source of encouragement and love.

CHAPTER 1

Performance Measurement and the Need for a Balanced Scorecard

When you can measure what you are speaking about, and express it in numbers, you know something about it; but when you cannot measure it, when you cannot express it in numbers, your knowledge is of a meager and unsatisfactory kind . . . .

—*William Thompson (Lord Kelvin), 1824–1907*

Roadmap for Chapter One   The purpose of this chapter is to provide you with an overview of performance measurement and the Balanced Scorecard system. Although you may be eager to get right to the work of developing your new performance management tool, I urge you to spend some time on this chapter since it serves as the foundation for the rest of the book. When you begin developing a Balanced Scorecard, your organization will rely on you not only for advice on the technical dimensions of this new system, but also on the broader subject of performance measurement and management. You can enhance your expert credibility within the organization by learning as much as possible about this subject. This is especially important if your current function is one that typically does not engage in projects of this nature. Think of this chapter as a primer for the exciting work that lies ahead.

The Balanced Scorecard assists organizations in overcoming three key issues: effective organizational performance measurement, the rise of intangible assets, and the challenge of implementing strategy. We begin by discussing performance measurement and, specifically, our reliance on financial measures of performance despite their inherent limitations. Next we examine the rise of intangible assets in modern organizations and their impact on our ability to measure corporate performance accurately. From there we move to the strategy story and review a number of barriers to successful strategy implementation. With the issues clearly on the table, we introduce the Balanced Scorecard and how this tool can overcome the barriers related to financial measures, the growth of intangible assets, and strategy execution.

Our Balanced Scorecard overview begins with a look back at how and when the Scorecard was originally conceived. Next we pose the question, "What is a Balanced Scorecard?" and elaborate on the specifics of the tool as a

1

communication system (with particular emphasis on the concept of Strategy Maps), *measurement system,* and *strategic management system.* Here you will be introduced to the theory underlying the Balanced Scorecard and the four perspectives of performance analyzed using this process. The chapter concludes with a review of the critical task of linking Balanced Scorecard objectives and measures through a series of cause-and-effect relationships, where you will discover how telling a powerful strategic story will be a great ally in your Balanced Scorecard implementation. Let's get started!

THREE FUNDAMENTAL ISSUES

Welcome to your performance measurement and Balanced Scorecard journey. During our time together we will explore the many facets of this topic, and it is my hope that both you and your organization will be transformed as a result. As I write this second edition of *Balanced Scorecard Step-by-Step,* the concept itself has been with us for just over 15 years. Born from a research study conducted in 1990, the Balanced Scorecard has since become a critical business tool for thousands of organizations around the globe. In fact, recent estimates suggest a whopping 60 percent of the Fortune 1000 has a Balanced Scorecard in place.[1] Further evidence of the ubiquity of the Balanced Scorecard is provided by The Hackett Group, which discovered in 2002 that 96 percent of the nearly 2,000 global companies it surveyed had either implemented or planned to implement the tool.[2] Before we discuss the nature of the Balanced Scorecard, let's examine its origins and attempt to determine just why it has become such a universally accepted methodology.

Whether it's the freckle-faced kid enthusiastically peddling lemonade on a sweltering midsummer's day, the chief executive of a global conglomerate mulling a crucial decision, or a harried public sector manager attempting to do more with less, the common denominator among all is the overwhelming drive to succeed. And while hard work and desire still go a long way, business, as we all know, has changed dramatically in recent years, rendering success more difficult than ever to achieve. In the pages ahead we'll examine three fundamental factors that affect every organization, at times in game-changing ways: our reliance on financial measures of performance to gauge success, the rise of value-creating intangible assets, and, finally, the difficulty of executing strategy. While separate and distinct factors, the trio is bound together by the inspiring ability of the Balanced Scorecard to overcome and maximize them to their fullest potential. Let's begin our discussion with an examination of financial measures of business performance.

FINANCIAL MEASUREMENT AND ITS LIMITATIONS

As long as business organizations have existed, the traditional method of measurement has been financial. Bookkeeping records used to facilitate financial transactions can be traced back literally thousands of years. At the turn of the twentieth century, financial measurement innovations were critical to the success of the early industrial giants, such as General Motors. That should not come as a surprise since the financial metrics of the time were the perfect complement to the machinelike nature of the corporate entities and management philosophy of the day. Competition was ruled by scope and economies of scale with financial measures providing the yardsticks of success.

Financial measures of performance have evolved, and today concepts such as economic value added (EVA) are quite prevalent. EVA suggests that unless a firm's profit exceeds its cost of capital, it really is not creating value for its shareholders. Using EVA as a lens, it is possible to determine that despite an increase in earnings, a firm may be destroying shareholder value if the cost of capital associated with new investments is sufficiently high.

The work of financial professionals is to be commended. As we move into the twenty-first century, however, many are questioning our almost exclusive reliance on financial measures of performance. Perhaps these measures served better as a means of reporting on the stewardship of funds entrusted to management's care rather than as a way to chart the future direction of the organization. And as we all know, stewardship is an increasingly vital issue in light of the many corporate scandals we've witnessed recently and the surge of shareholder value and job losses left in their wake. Let's take a look at some of the criticisms levied against the overabundant use of financial measures:

- *Not consistent with today's business realities.* Today's organizational value-creating activities are not captured in the tangible, fixed assets of the firm. Instead, value rests in the ideas of people scattered throughout the firm, in customer and supplier relationships, in databases of key information, and in cultures capable of innovation and quality. Traditional financial measures were designed to compare previous periods based on internal standards of performance. These metrics are of little assistance in providing early indications of customer, quality, or employee problems or opportunities. We'll examine the rise of intangible assets in the next section of this chapter.

- *Driving by rearview mirror.* Financial measures provide an excellent review of past performance and events in the organization. They represent a coherent articulation and summary of activities of the firm in prior periods. However, this detailed financial view has no predictive power for the future. As we all know, and as experience has shown, great financial results in one month, quarter, or even year are in no way indicative of future financial performance. Even so-called great companies—those that once graced the covers of business magazines and were the envy of their peer groups—can fall victim to this unfortunate scenario. Witness the vaunted Fortune 500 list; two-thirds of the companies comprising the inaugural list in 1954 had either vanished or were no longer large enough to maintain their presence on the list's fortieth anniversary.[3]

- *Tend to reinforce functional silos.* Financial statements in organizations are normally prepared by functional area: Individual department statements are prepared and rolled up into the business unit's numbers, which ultimately are compiled as part of the overall organizational picture. This approach is inconsistent with today's organization, in which much of the work is cross-functional in nature. Today we see teams comprised of many functional areas coming together to solve pressing problems and create value in never-imagined ways. Regardless of industry or organization type, teamwork has emerged as a must-have characteristic of winning enterprises in today's business environment. As an example, consider these three fields of endeavor: heart surgery, Wall Street research analysis, and basketball as played by the well-compensated superstars of the National Basketball Association (NBA). At first glance they appear to have absolutely nothing in common; however, studies reveal that success in all three is markedly improved through the use of teamwork: The interactions of surgeons with other medical professionals (anesthesiologists, nurses, and technicians) are the strongest indicator of patient success on the operating table. When it comes to Wall Street "stars," it's not the individual analyst and erudite calculations that spell success, but the teaming of analyst and firm. Even in the NBA, researchers have found that teams where players stay together longer win more games.[4] Our traditional financial measurement systems have no way to calculate the true value or cost of these relationships.

- *Sacrifice long-term thinking.* Many change programs feature severe cost-cutting measures that may have a very positive impact on the organization's short-term financial statements. However, these cost-reduction efforts often target the long-term value-creating activities of the firm, such as research and development, associate development, and customer relationship management. This focus on short-term gains at the expense of long-term value creation may lead to suboptimization of the organization's resources. Interestingly, an emerging body of evidence is beginning to suggest that cost-cutting interventions such as downsizing frequently fail to deliver the promised financial rewards and in fact sabotage value. University of Colorado Business School professor Wayne Cascio documented that downsizing not only hurts workers who are laid off, but destroys value in the long-term. He finds that, all else being equal, downsizing never improved profits or stock market returns.[5]

- *Financial measures are not relevant to many levels of the organization.* Financial reports by their very nature are abstractions. "Abstraction" in this context is defined as moving to another level, leaving certain characteristics out. When we roll up financial statements throughout the organization, that is exactly what we are doing: compiling information at a higher and higher level until it is almost unrecognizable and useless in the decision making of most managers and employees. Employees at all levels of the organization need performance data they can act on. This information must be imbued with relevance for their day-to-day activities.

Given the limitations of financial measures, should we even consider saving a space for them in our Balanced Scorecard? With their inherent focus on short-term results, often at the expense of long-term value-creating activities, are they relevant in today's environment? I believe the answer is yes for a number of reasons. As we'll discuss shortly, the Balanced Scorecard is just that: balanced. An undue focus on any particular area of measurement often will lead to poor overall results. Precedents in the business world support this position. In the 1980s the focus was on productivity improvement; in the 1990s quality became fashionable and seemingly critical to an organization's success. In keeping with the principle of what gets measured gets done, many businesses saw tremendous improvements in productivity and quality. What they didn't necessarily see was a corresponding increase in financial results, and in fact some companies with the best quality in their industry failed to remain in business. Financial statements will remain an important tool for organizations since they ultimately determine whether improvements in customer satisfaction, quality, innovation, and employee training are leading to improved financial performance and wealth creation for shareholders. What is needed, and what the Balanced Scorecard provides, is a method of balancing the accuracy and integrity of our financial measures with the drivers of future financial performance of the organization.

The Rising Prominence of Intangible Assets

What a difference 50 or so years can make. Writing in the *Harvard Business Review* in 1957, Harvard professor Malcolm P. McNair had this to say about organizations paying excess attention to their people: *"Too much emphasis on human relations encourages people to feel sorry for themselves, makes it easier for them to slough off responsibility, to find excuses for failure, to act like children."*[6] Can you imagine the reaction business leaders would have to this quote if it were uttered today? What was your reaction? If you're like most, you would probably disagree completely with McNair's pessimistic view and instead assert the now-prevailing notion that an organization's people — its "human capital" — represent the critical enabler in the new economy. *Harvard Business Review* editor Thomas Stewart recently captured the essence of this notion succinctly and powerfully when he said, *"The most important of all are 'soft' assets such as skills, capabilities, expertise, cultures, loyalties and so on. These are the knowledge assets — intellectual capital — and they determine success or failure."*[7]

In the previous section we discussed some of the limitations financial measures possess. Given these limitations and the growth in prominence of human capital, both business and investment communities are placing ever-increasing emphasis on nonfinancial indicators of performance. Business leaders are now questioning their almost exclusive reliance on financial data with its historical accuracy and integrity and have begun to look at the operational drivers of future financial performance: customer satisfaction and loyalty, continuous innovation, and organizational learning, to name but a few. On the investor side, Wall Street has made it clear that nonfinancial data matters greatly to valuation and is growing in prominence all the time. A 1999 Ernst & Young study found that "even for large cap, mature companies, non-financial performance counts."[8] One of the study's findings suggests that, on average, nonfinancial criteria constitute 35 percent of the investor's decision. The researchers also found that "the more non-financial measures analysts use, the more accurate are their earnings forecasts."[9] But just what is "human capital," and why is it important to the future of the Balanced Scorecard?

Before terms like "human capital," "intellectual capital," and "intangible assets" entered the business lexicon, there was another metaphor sweeping across organizations: "the employee as asset." Annual reports, press releases, and business literature were awash in statements proclaiming the great value companies placed in their human assets. By recognizing the value individuals bring to the firm, this metaphor represented a great improvement over the "employee as a cost object" philosophy that lay at the heart of the downsizing movement of the early 1990s. But consider the definition of an asset from our accounting studies: an object owned or controlled by the firm that produces future value and possesses a monetary value. Do we employees really fit that definition? Another school of thought has gradually developed that likens the employee more to an investor of human capital than an asset to be controlled by the organization. Author, consultant, and Babson college professor Thomas Davenport cogently describes this new paradigm: *"People possess innate abilities, behaviors, personal energy and time. These elements make up human capital—the currency people bring to invest in their jobs. Workers, not organizations, own this human capital . . . and decide when, how, and where they will contribute it."*[10] The late Peter Drucker would label these investors "knowledge workers" and suggest they hold the key to value creation in the new economy. For the first time in business history the workers, not the organization, own the means of production—the knowledge and capabilities they possess—and they decide how and where to apply it.

CREATING VALUE IN THE NEW ECONOMY

Consulting organizations offer a compelling example of creating value from intangible rather than physical assets. Consultants don't rely heavily on tangible assets; instead they provide value for clients by drawing on relationships with subject matter experts throughout the firm and knowledge from past client experiences to provide innovative solutions. A client engagement I was involved with provides an example: The clients encountered a problem in loading data for their new performance measurement software. Building automatic data interfaces for the software (pulling data directly from source systems throughout their locations) would require significant human and financial resources and was not considered a viable option. The alternative of manual data entry was also deemed unacceptable as it would prove a time-consuming and non–value-added activity for system administrators. Our team was tasked with finding an innovative and cost-effective solution. We convened a team of experts on various subjects: the Scorecard software program, the Balanced Scorecard methodology, desktop applications such as MS Access and MS Excel, and client data sources. The newly formed team brainstormed various approaches that would satisfy the criteria of cost efficiency and very limited manual data entry efforts. In the end we determined our best approach was to build a new data entry tool in Excel. Data owners would enter their individual data in the spreadsheet and e-mail it to the system administrator, who would then automatically upload the information into the software. The spreadsheets were custom designed to contain only those measures for which each owner was accountable. This solution ensured both criteria were satisfied. The new system would cost very little to develop and implement and would eliminate manual data entry for system administrators. It wasn't the physical assets that led to this innovative solution to a client's needs, but instead the skillful combination of an array of knowledge held by the individual team members.

The situation just described is happening in organizations around the globe as we make the transition from an economy based on physical assets to one almost fully dependent on intellectual assets. While this switch is evident to anyone working in today's business world, it is also borne out by research findings of the Brookings Institute. Take a look at Exhibit 1.1, which illustrates the transition in value from tangible to intangible assets. Speaking on National Public Radio's *Morning Edition,* Margaret Blair of the Brookings Institute suggests that tangible assets have continued to tumble in value: *"If you just look at the physical assets of the companies, the things that you can measure with ordinary accounting techniques, these things now account for less than one-fourth of the value of the corporate sector. Another way of putting this is that something like 75% of the sources of value inside corporations is not being measured or reported on their books."*[11] If you happen to be employed in the public sector, you may have noticed that Blair uses the term "corporations" in the quote. Believe me, your organizations are being affected every bit as much as your corporate counterparts. The challenges represented by this switch are not going unnoticed in Washington. David M. Walker, Comptroller General of the United States, said in February 2001 testimony to the U.S. Senate that *"human capital management is a pervasive*

Exhibit 1.1   Increasing Value of Intangible Assets in Organizations

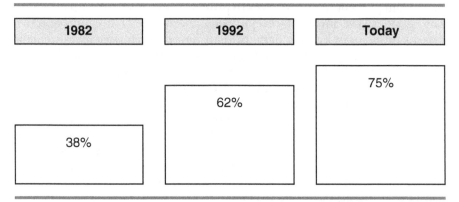

challenge in the federal government. At many agencies human capital shortfalls have contributed to serious problems and risks."[12] U.S. President George W. Bush in his President's Management Agenda echoes Walker's comments and adds: *"We must have a Government that thinks differently, so we need to recruit talented and imaginative people to public service."*[13] In yet another demonstration of the importance of intangible assets, companies are opening the purse strings for intellectual investments. (On second thought, opening the purse strings is a bit like saying World War II was a little skirmish, considering the fact that American companies spend a staggering 36 percent of their revenue each year on human capital–related investments.[14])

This transition in value creation from physical to intangible assets has major implications for measurement systems. The financial measurements that characterize our balance sheet and income statement methods of tabulation were perfectly appropriate for a world dominated by physical assets. Transactions affecting property, plant, and equipment could be recorded and reflected in an organization's general ledger. However, the new economy with its premium on intangible value-creating mechanisms demands more from our performance measurement systems. Today's system must have the capabilities to identify, describe, monitor, and fully harness the intangible assets driving organizational success. As we will see throughout this book, particularly in our discussion of the Employee Learning and Growth perspective, the Balanced Scorecard provides a voice of strength and clarity to intangible assets, allowing organizations to benefit fully from their astronomical potential.

The Strategy Story

Could there possibly exist a more passionately discussed and debated subject on the business landscape than strategy? While military strategy has been with us for millennia and continues to influence our thinking—witness the ever-popular *Art of War* by Sun Tzu—business strategy is a relatively new phenomenon with its greatest contributions arriving in the twentieth century. Despite its brief tenure, the topic has spawned hundreds of books, thousands of scholarly articles, and countless gurus each espousing his version of the holy grail of strategy.

In every facet of my life I've always tried to cut through the clutter and arrive at the essence of an idea, the pearl of wisdom or nugget of knowledge I can use to effectively direct my energies. If I applied that same process to the pursuit of strategy's "one thing" I would surely drive myself slowly mad. You see, strategy is not a subject that can be ripped apart at the academic and practical threads to reveal the one right method or version of the truth. Every reader of this book, if appropriately prodded, could undoubtedly produce a coherent and cogent definition of "strategy." Ultimately we all cherish that spirit of discovery and rightly applaud our diversity of ideas, but practically, it makes the study of strategy a frustrating one. Fortunately for all of us, the one thing that pundits from every strategy corner do agree on is the fact that strategy execution or implementation is far more important than strategy formation.

During my career I've had the opportunity to sit in on a number of strategy-setting workshops and have always relished the spirited debates, the "aha" moments of breathtaking clarity, and of course the ever-present jugs of coffee and gourmet cookies. The freshly minted strategy emerging from these often grueling sessions is a justifiably pride-invoking achievement; however, producing this document is a far cry from actually living and breathing it day in and day out. But to succeed in any business today, that is precisely what we must do—bring the strategy to life with the unmistakable clarity necessary for everyone in the organization to act on it each and every day. Let's face it: We have to execute not only to thrive but simply to stay alive in a business world in which 84 percent of respondents in one recent poll said that competition in their industry had significantly increased in the last five years.[15] And leaders, you know how vital it is to execute your strategy quickly; an oft-quoted *Fortune* magazine study from 1999 found that 70 percent of CEO failures came not as a result of poor strategy but the inability to execute.[16] In fact, a team of researchers recently discovered that companies, on average, deliver only 63 percent of the financial performance their strategies promise.[17]

The good news is that strategy implementation has been proven to boost financial fortunes rather significantly; one study suggested a 35 percent improvement in the quality of strategy implementation for the average firm was associated with a 30 percent improvement in shareholder value.[18] Unfortunately, many organizations fall off the strategy execution track, frequently in dramatic fashion. So why does strategy execution prove so elusive for the typical enterprise? Scorecard architects Robert S. Kaplan and David P. Norton believe the answer lies in four barriers that must be surmounted before strategy can be effectively executed. These barriers are presented in Exhibit 1.2.

Exhibit 1.2   Barriers to Implementing Strategy

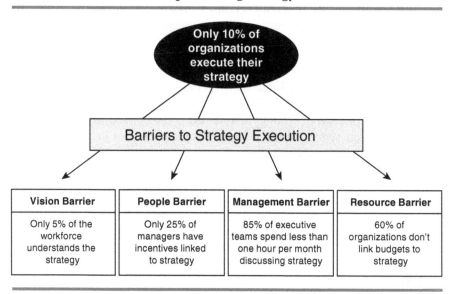

Source: Adapted from material developed by Robert S. Kaplan and David P. Norton.

The Vision Barrier   The vast majority of employees do not understand the organization's strategy. This situation was acceptable at the turn of the twentieth century, when value was derived from the most efficient use of physical assets and employees were literally cogs in the great industrial wheel. However, in the information or knowledge age in which we currently exist, value is created from the intangible assets—the know-how, relationships, and cultures existing within the organization. Most companies are still organized for the industrial era, utilizing command and control orientations that are inadequate for today's environment. Why is this the case when all evidence suggests a change is necessary? Former United States Senator and college professor S. I. Hayakawa introduced a concept known as "cultural lag" over 50 years ago, and it goes a long way in explaining this organizational inertia. Hayakawa states, *"Once people become accustomed to institutions, they eventually get to feeling that their particular institutions represent the only right and proper way of doing things . . . consequently, social organizations tend to change slowly, and — most important—they tend to exist long after the necessity for their existence has disappeared, and sometimes even when their continued existence becomes a nuisance and a danger."*[19] Does this remind you of your company? If your structure is hampering employees' ability to understand and act on the firm's strategy, how can you expect them to make effective decisions that will lead to the achievement of your goals?

The People Barrier   In its 2005 Reward Programs and Incentive Compensation Survey, the Society for Human Resource Management found that

69 percent of companies offer some form of incentive compensation to their employees.[20] Like most people, I'm a fan of incentive plans because of the focus and alignment they can drive toward the achievement of a mutually beneficial goal. However, companies take many liberties when constructing these plans, and often the designs leave something to be desired. For example, it's not at all uncommon for incentive plans to link a cash award with the achievement of a short-term financial target, such as quarterly earnings. In fact, in our meet-the-numbers-or-else culture, this evil twin of the effective compensation plan springs up frequently in boardrooms across the globe. When the focus is on achieving short-term financial targets, clever employees will do whatever it takes to ensure those results are achieved. This often comes at the expense of creating long-term value for the firm. Does the name "Enron" or "WorldCom" ring a bell?

The Resource Barrier   Sixty percent of organizations don't link budgets to strategy. This finding really should not come as a surprise, because most organizations have separate processes for budgeting and strategic planning. One group is working to forge the strategy that will lead the firm heroically into the future, while independently another group is crafting the operating and capital budgets for the coming year. The problem with this approach is that, once again, human and financial resources are tied to short-term financial targets and not long-term strategy. I recall my days working in a corporate accounting environment for a large company. I was housed on the same floor as the strategic planners and not only did our group not liaise regularly with them, we barely even knew them!

The Management Barrier   In a sad yet humorous commentary on modern organizational life, a recent poll of U.S. office workers revealed that 41 percent would rather wash their kitchen floors than attend a management meeting at their company.[21] What exactly is being said at these meetings that employees would rather scrub than attend? Most of the survey respondents would, if pressed, probably report that the management meetings are just plain boring, and in many cases that is undoubtedly accurate. With mind-numbing charts and graphs, sleep-inducing commentaries, and zero conflict, most meetings can be rightly classified as both a waste of time and, unfortunately, a huge lost opportunity. It certainly doesn't have to be that way. When strategy forms the agenda for a management meeting, new life can be pumped into an antiquated institution, instantly changing the dynamic from dull and rote presentations to stimulating debate and discussion on the factors driving the firm forward. We'll return to this stimulating topic in Chapter Ten.

How does your executive team spend its time during monthly or quarterly reviews? If the team is like teams in most organizations, members probably spend the majority of their time analyzing financial results and looking for remedies to the "defects" that occur when actual results do not meet budget expectations. A focus on strategy demands that executives spend their time together moving beyond the analysis of defects to a deeper understanding of the underlying value-creating or destroying mechanisms in the firm.

THE BALANCED SCORECARD

As the preceding discussion indicates, organizations face many hurdles in developing performance measurement systems that truly monitor the right things. What is required is a system that balances the historical accuracy of financial numbers with the drivers of future performance, while simultaneously harnessing the power of intangible assets and of course assisting organizations in implementing their differentiating strategies. The Balanced Scorecard is the tool that answers this complex triad of challenges. In the remainder of this chapter we will begin our exploration of the Balanced Scorecard by discussing its origins, reviewing its conceptual model, and considering what separates the Balanced Scorecard from other systems.

Origins of the Balanced Scorecard

The Balanced Scorecard was developed by two men, Robert Kaplan, an accounting professor at Harvard University, and David Norton, a consultant also from the Boston area. In 1990 Kaplan and Norton led a research study of a dozen companies exploring new methods of performance measurement. The impetus for the study was a growing belief that financial measures of performance were ineffective for the modern business enterprise. The study companies, along with Kaplan and Norton, were convinced that a reliance on financial measures of performance was affecting their ability to create value. The group discussed a number of possible alternatives but settled on the idea of a Scorecard featuring performance measures capturing activities from throughout the organization—customer issues, internal business processes, employee activities, and, of course, shareholder concerns. Kaplan and Norton labeled the new tool the Balanced Scorecard and later summarized the concept in the first of several *Harvard Business Review* articles, "The Balanced Scorecard—Measures that Drive Performance."[22]

Over the next four years a number of organizations adopted the Balanced Scorecard and achieved immediate results. Kaplan and Norton discovered these organizations were not only using the Scorecard to complement financial measures with the drivers of future performance but were also communicating their strategies through the measures they selected for their Balanced Scorecard. As the Scorecard gained prominence with organizations around the globe as a key tool in strategy implementation, Kaplan and Norton summarized the concept and the learning to that point in their 1996 book, *The Balanced Scorecard*.[23]

Since that time the Balanced Scorecard has been adopted by over half of all Fortune 1000 organizations. The momentum continues unabated, with companies large, medium, and small taking full advantage of the tool's profound simplicity and unmistakable effectiveness. Once considered the exclusive domain of the for-profit world, the Balanced Scorecard has been translated and effectively implemented in both the nonprofit and public sectors. These organizations have learned that by slightly modifying the Scorecard framework, they can demonstrate to their constituents the value they provide and the steps being taken to fulfill their important missions. So widely accepted and effective has the Scorecard been that the *Harvard Business Review* recently hailed it as one of the 75 most influential ideas of the twentieth century. Does all this whet your appetite for more? Let's now turn our attention to the tool itself and see what makes up the Balanced Scorecard.

What Is a Balanced Scorecard?

We can describe the Balanced Scorecard as a carefully selected set of quantifiable measures derived from an organization's strategy. The measures selected for the Scorecard represent a tool for leaders to use in communicating to employees and external stakeholders the outcomes and performance drivers by which the organization will achieve its mission and strategic objectives. A simple definition, however, cannot tell us everything about the Balanced Scorecard. In my work with many organizations and research into best practices of Scorecard use, I see this tool as three things: communication tool, measurement system, and strategic management system. (See Exhibit 1.3.) In the next few sections we will take a look at each of these Scorecard uses, but first let's consider perhaps the most fundamental aspect of the Balanced Scorecard: the four perspectives of performance.

Balanced Scorecard Perspectives

The etymology of the word "perspective" is from the Latin *perspectus*, "to look through" or "see clearly," which is precisely what we aim to do with a Balanced Scorecard: examine the strategy, making it clearer through the lens of different viewpoints. Any strategy, to be effective, must contain descriptions of financial aspirations, markets served, processes to be conquered, and, of course, the people who will steadily and skillfully guide the company to success. Thus, when measuring our progress, it would make little sense to focus on just one aspect of the strategy when in fact as Leonardo da Vinci reminds us, *"Everything is connected to everything else."*[24] An accurate picture of strategy execution, it must be painted in the full palette of perspectives that comprise it; therefore, when developing a Balanced Scorecard, we consider these four: Customer, Internal Processes, Employee Learning and Growth, and Financial.

Exhibit 1.3   What Is the Balanced Scorecard?

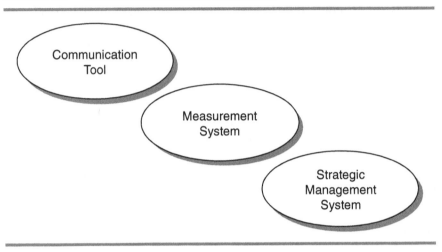

When building your Balanced Scorecard, or later, when it is up and running, you may slip and casually remark on the four "quadrants" or four "areas," but as seemingly inconsequential as this slip of the tongue appears, I believe it has serious ramifications. Take, for example, the word "quadrant": the *Oxford English Dictionary* begins its definition by describing it as a quarter of a circle's circumference. The word reflects the number four and in that sense is almost limiting to the flexible approach inherent in the Scorecard. You may wish to have five perspectives or only three. With its focus on viewing performance from another point of view, the word "perspective" is far more representative of the spirit of the Balanced Scorecard, and I encourage you to be disciplined in the use of this term. Now let's take a brief tour of those four perspectives.

Customer Perspective   When choosing measures for the Customer perspective of the Scorecard, organizations must answer three critical questions: Who are our target customers? What is our value proposition in serving them? and What do our customers expect or demand from us? Sounds simple enough, but each of these questions offers many challenges to organizations. Most organizations will state that they do in fact have a target customer audience, yet their actions reveal an "all things to all customers" strategy. As strategy guru Michael Porter has taught, this lack of focus will prevent an organization from differentiating itself from competitors. Choosing an appropriate value proposition poses no less of a challenge to most firms. Many will choose one of three "disciplines" articulated by Treacy and Wiersema in *The Discipline of Market Leaders*:[25]

1. *Operational excellence.* Organizations pursuing an operational excellence discipline focus on low price, convenience, and often "no frills." Wal-Mart provides a great representation of an operationally excellent company.

2. *Product leadership.* Product leaders push the envelope of their firm's products. Constantly innovating, they strive to offer simply the best product in the market. Sony is an example of a product leader in the field of electronics.

3. *Customer intimacy.* Doing whatever it takes to provide solutions for unique customer's needs defines customer-intimate companies. They don't look for one-time transactions but instead focus on long-term relationship building through their deep knowledge of customer needs. In the retail industry, Nordstrom epitomizes the customer-intimate organization.

Regardless of the value discipline chosen, this perspective will normally include measures widely used today: customer satisfaction, customer loyalty, market share, and customer acquisition, for example. Equally as important, the organization must develop the performance drivers that will lead to improvement in these "lag" indicators of customer success. Doing so will greatly enhance your chances of answering our third question for this perspective: What do our customers expect or demand from us? In Chapters Four and Five we will take a closer look at the Customer perspective and identify what specific steps your organization should take to develop customer objectives and measures.

Internal Process Perspective   In the Internal Process perspective of the Scorecard, we identify the key processes the firm must excel at in order to continue adding value for customers and ultimately shareholders. Each of the customer disciplines just outlined will entail the efficient operation of specific internal processes in order to serve customers and fulfill our value proposition. Our task here is to identify those processes and develop the best possible objectives and measures with which to track progress. To satisfy customer and shareholder expectations, you may have to identify entirely new internal processes rather than focusing your efforts on the incremental improvement of existing activities. Product development, production, manufacturing, delivery, and postsale service may be represented in this perspective.

Many organizations rely heavily on supplier relationships and other third-party arrangements to serve customers effectively. Such organizations should consider developing measures in the Internal Process perspective to represent the critical elements of those relationships. We will examine the development of performance objectives and measures for Internal Processes in greater depth in Chapters Four and Five.

Employee Learning and Growth Perspective   If you want to achieve ambitious results for internal processes, customers, and ultimately shareholders, where are these gains found? The objectives and measures in the Employee Learning and Growth perspective of the Balanced Scorecard are really the enablers of the other three perspectives. In essence, they are the foundation upon which the Balanced Scorecard is built. Once you identify objectives, measures, and related initiatives in your Customer and Internal Process perspectives, you can be certain of discovering some gaps between your current organizational infrastructure of employee skills (human capital), information systems (informational capital), and the environment required to maintain success (organizational capital). The objectives and measures you design in this perspective will help you close that gap and ensure sustainable performance for the future.

As with the other three perspectives of the Scorecard, we would expect a mix of core outcome (lag) measures and performance drivers (lead measures) to represent the Employee Learning and Growth perspective. Employee skills, employee satisfaction, availability of information, and alignment could all have a place in this perspective. Many organizations I've worked with struggle in the development of Learning and Growth measures. It is normally the last perspective to be developed. Perhaps the teams are intellectually drained from their earlier efforts of developing new strategic measures, or they simply consider this perspective "soft stuff" best left to the Human Resources group. No matter how valid the rationale seems, this perspective cannot be overlooked in the development process. As I mentioned, the measures you develop in this perspective are the enablers of all other measures on your Scorecard. Think of them as the roots of a tree that will ultimately lead through the trunk of internal processes to the branches of customer results and finally to the leaves of financial returns. We will return to this important topic in Chapters Four and Five.

Financial Perspective   Financial measures are a critical component of the Balanced Scorecard, especially so in the for-profit world. The objectives and measures in this perspective tell us whether our strategy execution — which is detailed through objectives and measures chosen in the other perspectives — is leading to improved bottom-line results. We could focus all of our energy and capabilities on improving customer satisfaction, quality, on-time delivery, or any number of things, but without an indication of their effect on the organization's financial returns, they are of limited value. We normally encounter classic lagging indicators in the Financial perspective. Typical examples include profitability, revenue growth, and asset utilization. As with the other three perspectives, we will have another look at financial objectives and measures during Chapters Four and Five.

The Balanced Scorecard as a Communication Tool: Strategy Maps

Earlier in the chapter I noted that *Harvard Business Review* had cited the Balanced Scorecard as one of the 75 most influential business ideas of the twentieth century. So how does a management tool ascend to such a lofty position when hundreds of others are relegated to has-been and flavor-of-the-month status? First and foremost, the Balanced Scorecard has been proven to generate results for thousands of organizations in private, public, and nonprofit fields of endeavor. This efficacy would seem a prerequisite of any tool destined to reach the pantheon of business systems. Dig a little deeper, however, and you find another equally compelling rationale for the Balanced Scorecard's continued growth: its continued growth. Perhaps "evolution" is a more suitable description. Brought into the world by Kaplan and Norton as a methodology to tame the power of financial metrics run amok, the Balanced Scorecard soon evolved into a system capable of bridging short-term leadership action with long-term strategy through links to such processes as budgeting and compensation. This discovery heralded a new chapter in its life and beckoned thousands of additional organizations to heed the call. But quite possibly the most powerful evolutionary leap in the Balanced Scorecard's life has been from measurement system to strategy communication device through the advent of the Strategy Map.

The subtitle of Kaplan and Norton's first Balanced Scorecard book is *Translating Strategy into Action,* which is exactly what you'll accomplish by creating performance measures to track the execution of your one-of-a-kind game plan for success. But creating effective performance measures that serve as true barometers of strategy and performance is tough sledding. Just imagine opening the three-ring binder housing your 50-page business strategy with the task of translating the contents into a coherent set of measures that indicate whether you've actually taken the proverbial hill. Even if it's a two-page strategy pamphlet, the chore is an onerous one since even the most well-conceived and carefully crafted strategies are bound to contain at least a portion of ambiguous terms like "customer service" or "product development." Early Balanced Scorecard adopters faced this challenge and found themselves instinctively spanning the strategy/measures chasm with a discussion of *objectives,* or what needed to be done well in order to implement the essence of the strategy. So instead of beginning with "How do we measure this strategy?" they uncorked the process by asking "What do we need to do well in order to execute?" Parsing the task in this way allowed users to add a necessary layer of granularity to the strategy, ultimately rendering the job of measures creation significantly simpler. For example, if the strategy devoted a section to new product development, stressing the need to bring new products to market at a faster rate than competitors, this narrative was translated into the simple objective of "Accelerate new product development," which may be accurately measured by the new product development life cycle.

As with any esoteric business tool, the Balanced Scorecard has a lexicon all its own, and I've distinguished between two key terms in the last paragraph: "objective" and "measure." This is a critical distinction and one you must master if you hope to create a Scorecard that accurately describes your strategy and brings it to life for those charged with the responsibility of executing it on a day-to-day basis: your employees. An "objective" is a succinct statement, normally beginning with a verb, describing what we must do well in each of the four perspectives in order to implement our game plan. Examples vary widely but could include: "Increase profit margins," "Improve service delivery time," "Reduce emissions," and "Close our skills gap." Strategy Maps are comprised entirely of objectives. Tracking our success in achieving the objective is the domain of the measure, a (typically) quantitative device used to monitor progress.

For those of you who grapple with an issue best by first defining it, let's try this one for Strategy Maps: a one-page graphical representation of what you must do well in each of the four perspectives in order to execute your strategy successfully. We're not taking any measurements in the Strategy Map; there's no tallying of results here. Instead we're communicating to all audiences, internal and external, what we must do well if we hope to achieve our ultimate goals. Hence the description of the Strategy Map as a powerful communication tool, signaling to everyone within the enterprise what must occur should they hope to beat the almost overwhelming odds of strategy execution. So why do we use the term "map"? Why not a more mundane moniker, such as "strategy sheet" or "must-do" list? A map guides us on our journey, detailing pathways to get us from point A to point B, ultimately leading us to our chosen destination. So it is with a Strategy Map; we are defining causal pathways weaving through the four perspectives that will lead us to the implementation of our strategy. We'll return to the exciting world of Strategy Maps in Chapter Four, where you'll discover how to create a document that brings your strategy to life with dazzling clarity and allows you to flex your creative muscles to a degree rarely seen in the corporate world. Exhibit 1.4 presents a sample Strategy Map.

The Balanced Scorecard as a Measurement System

When Kaplan and Norton initially conceived the Balanced Scorecard, they were attempting to solve a problem of measurement: How do we acknowledge the importance of financial metrics in decision making and business success while also recognizing the rapid rise of intangible assets and their critical importance to the overall recipe for organizational success? Their answer to this quandary lay in the development of measures in each of four distinct yet related perspectives of performance: Financial, Customer, Internal Processes, and Employee Learning and Growth. Kaplan and Norton rightly hypothesized that financial measures will always remain a vital part of any enterprise's attempts to gain an accurate picture of its performance, but those measures must be balanced by indicators demonstrating how those financial yardsticks will be maximized.

Exhibit 1.4   Strategy Map

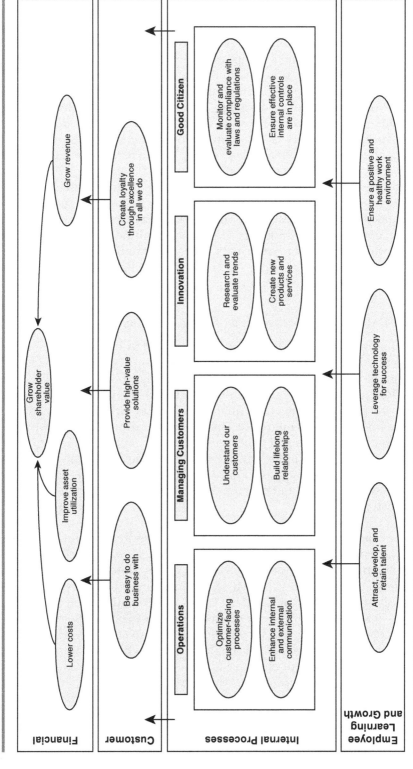

Measures for the Balanced Scorecard are derived from the objectives appearing on the Strategy Map, which itself serves as a direct and clarifying translation of the organization's strategy. These two links in the chain of success remind me of the old song "Love and Marriage": You can't have one without the other. A Strategy Map may prove to be the most inspirational document you've ever produced, but without the accountability and focus afforded by accompanying performance measures, its value is specious to say the least. Conversely, performance measures serve as powerful monitoring devices, but without the benefit of a clear and compelling Strategy Map, much of their contextual value is lost. It would not be an exaggeration to suggest that measurement is at the very heart of the Balanced Scorecard system; it's in the tool's very DNA, and has been from its inception in 1990. Strategy Maps communicate the strategic destination, while performance measures housed within the Balanced Scorecard monitor the course, allowing us to ensure we remain on track. We'll return to the vital concept of measurement in Chapter Five.

The Balanced Scorecard as a Strategic Management System

For many organizations that are highly skilled in the art of the Balanced Scorecard, the system, besides communicating strategy and measuring progress, serves as what Kaplan and Norton have described as a "Strategic Management System."[26] While the original intent of the Scorecard system was to balance historical financial numbers with the drivers of future value for the firm, as more and more organizations experimented with the concept, they found it to be a critical tool in aligning short-term actions with strategy. Used in this way, the Scorecard alleviates many of the issues of effective strategy implementation discussed earlier in the chapter. Let's revisit those barriers and examine how the Balanced Scorecard may in fact remove them.

Overcoming the Vision Barrier through the Translation of Strategy

The Balanced Scorecard is ideally created through a shared understanding and translation of the organization's strategy into objectives, measures, targets, and initiatives in each of the four Scorecard perspectives. The translation of vision and strategy forces the executive team to determine specifically what is meant by often vague and nebulous terms contained in vision and strategy statements, such as: "best in class," "superior service," and "targeted customers." Through the process of developing a Strategy Map and Scorecard, an executive group may determine that "superior service" means 95 percent on-time delivery to customers. All employees can now focus their energies and day-to-day activities toward the crystal-clear goal of on-time delivery rather than wondering about and debating the definition of "superior service." By using the Balanced Scorecard as a framework for translating the strategy, these organizations create a new language of measurement that serves to guide all employees' actions toward the achievement of the stated direction.

Not only is strategy brilliantly illuminated for employees, but the Scorecard can direct its laserlike focus to another topic much in the spotlight these days: corporate governance. Unless you've been living in a cave for the past four years, and with the price of houses in most of the United States that may have been a prudent shelter strategy, you are no doubt well aware of the unethical and often illegal shenanigans that have become all the rage in the corporate world. For most of 2002 and 2003 the *Wall Street Journal* read more like the FBI's most wanted list than a quotidian business journal. Needless to say, all of this malfeasance severely rattled the often chummy cages of the governance world, with cries for reform resulting in the costly Sarbanes-Oxley Act of 2002. The legislation, critics notwithstanding, has made substantial inroads in the fight to establish fair and transparent reporting standards, but it is clear that should boards of directors expect to fulfill their duties, they need additional insight into the value-creating and destroying mechanisms at play within the corridors of their charges. Once again, the Balanced Scorecard rises to this challenge, with board Balanced Scorecards increasing in number and prominence in recent years. In Chapter Nine we will return to this topic of emerging interest and unquestionable importance.

Cascading the Scorecard Overcomes the People Barrier   To implement any strategy successfully, it must be understood and acted upon by every level of the firm. Cascading the Scorecard means driving it down into the organization and giving all employees the opportunity to demonstrate how their day-to-day activities contribute to the company's strategy. All organizational levels distinguish their value-creating activities by developing Scorecards that link to the high-level corporate objectives. By cascading you create a line of sight from the employee on the shop floor back to the executive boardroom. Some organizations have taken cascading all the way down to the individual level with employees developing personal Balanced Scorecards that define the contribution they will make to their team in helping it achieve overall objectives. In Chapter Seven we will take a closer look at the topic of cascading and discuss how you can develop aligned Scorecards throughout your organization.

Rather than linking incentives and rewards to the achievement of short-term financial targets, managers now have the opportunity to tie their team, department, or business unit's rewards directly to the areas in which they exert influence. All employees can now focus on the performance drivers of future economic value and what decisions and actions are necessary to achieve those outcomes. Chapter Nine will outline strategies for the linkage of Balanced Scorecard results to compensation.

Strategic Resource Allocation Overcomes the Resource Barrier   When discussing the resource barrier, we noted that most companies have separate processes for budgeting and strategic planning. Developing your Balanced Scorecard provides an excellent opportunity to tie these important processes together. When we create a Balanced Scorecard, we not only think in terms of objectives, measures, and targets for each of our four perspectives, but just as critically we must consider the initiatives or action plans we will put in place to meet our Scorecard targets. If we create long-term stretch targets for our measures, we can then consider the incremental steps along the path to their achievement. The human and financial resources necessary to achieve Scorecard targets should form the basis for the development of the annual budgeting process. No longer will departments and business units submit budget requests that simply take last year's amount and add an arbitrary 5 percent. Instead the necessary costs (and profits) associated with Balanced Scorecard targets are clearly articulated in their documents. This enhances executive learning about the strategy as the group is now forced (unless it has unlimited means) to make tough choices and trade-offs regarding which initiatives to fund and which to defer.

The building of a Balanced Scorecard also affords you a great opportunity to critically examine the current myriad initiatives taking place in your organization. When I begin working with a new client as a consultant, one of the laments I hear repeatedly from front-line employees is "Oh no, another new initiative!" Many executives have pet projects and agendas they hope to advance, often with little thought of the strategic significance of such endeavors. More worrisome is the potential for initiatives from different functional areas to work against one another. Your Marketing Department may be attempting to win new business through an aggressive marketing campaign, while independently your Human Resources group has just launched a new incentive program rewarding the Sales staff for repeat business with existing customers. Should the Sales team focus on winning new customers or nurturing current relationships? Initiatives at every level of the organization and from every functional area must share one common trait: a linkage to the firm's overall strategic goals. The Balanced Scorecard provides the lens for making this examination. Once you've developed your Scorecard, you should review all the initiatives currently under way in your organization and determine which are truly critical to the fulfillment of your strategy and which are merely consuming valuable and scarce resources. Obviously the resource savings are beneficial, but more important, you signal to everyone in the organization the critical factors for success and the steps you are taking to achieve them. Chapter Eight is devoted to a greater review of this topic and provides guidance on how you can link your budgets to strategy.

Strategic Learning Overcomes the Management Barrier   In the rapidly changing business environment most of us face, we need more than an analysis of actual versus budget variances to make strategic decisions. Unfortunately, many management teams spend their precious time together discussing variances and looking for ways to correct these "defects." The Balanced Scorecard provides us with the necessary elements to move away from this paradigm to a new model in which Scorecard results become a starting point for reviewing, questioning, and learning about our strategy.

Enter the strategy-centered management meeting anchored by Balanced Scorecard results as its agenda. Ushered away are the cudgels of criticism and blame as poor results are paraded in front of head-nodding attendees. They are replaced with a spirit of discovery and learning as strategy takes center stage. In these sessions churlish commentaries focused on defects are replaced by a sincere desire to dig deeper, invest more intellectual energy, and question results as they relate to the strategic journey stretching out in front of the organization. The process is aided significantly by wizard-like software tools that perform all manner of tabulations at the click of a mouse. Snazzy, yes, but these tools are entirely necessary to guide discussions and perform meaningful analysis, as we shall discover in Chapter Ten.

TELLING YOUR STRATEGIC STORY THROUGH CAUSE AND EFFECT

Perhaps the best thing about writing a second edition of this book is the opportunity to update my thinking on certain aspects of the model based on current research, best practices, and, of course, my field experience gained through numerous consulting engagements. Cause-and-effect linkages are one tenet of the Balanced Scorecard that has received a significant amount of my cognitive energy over the past several years, and my view has altered somewhat from what was presented in the first edition of this text. In 2001 I wrote: "What really separates the Balanced Scorecard from other performance management systems is the notion of cause and effect." While I still believe cause and effect is an important consideration when crafting both a Strategy Map and performance measures to appear on a Balanced Scorecard, as with most things, there is a wide spectrum of commitment to the idea in practice. It will serve you well to understand both the advantages and limitations of the idea. Let's begin by leveling the playing field with a discussion of what cause and effect is all about, then transition into what is taking place within organizations adopting the Balanced Scorecard.

Cause and Effect in Theory

The best strategy ever conceived is simply a hypothesis developed by its creators. It represents their best guess as to an appropriate course of action, given their knowledge of information concerning the environment, competencies, competitive positions, and so on. What is needed is a method to document and test the assumptions inherent in the strategy. The Balanced Scorecard allows us to do just that. A well-designed Balanced Scorecard should describe your strategy through the objectives appearing on the Strategy Map and measures you have chosen for your scorecard. These measures should link together in a chain of cause-and-effect relationships from the performance drivers in the Employee Learning and Growth perspective all the way through to improved financial performance as reflected in the Financial perspective. We are attempting to document our strategy through measurement, making the relationships between the measures explicit so they can be monitored, managed, and validated.

Here is a typical example of cause and effect: Let's say your organization is pursuing a growth strategy. You therefore determine that you will measure revenue growth in the Financial perspective of the scorecard. You hypothesize that loyal customers providing repeat business will result in greater revenues so you measure customer loyalty in the Customer perspective. How will you achieve superior levels of customer loyalty? Now you must ask yourself what internal processes the organization must excel at in order to drive customer loyalty and ultimately increased revenue. You believe customer loyalty is driven by your ability to continuously innovate and bring new products to the market, and therefore you decide to measure new product development cycle times in the Internal Process perspective. Finally you have to determine how you will improve cycle times. Investing in employee training on new development initiatives may eventually lower development cycle time and is then measured under the Employee Learning and Growth perspective of the Balanced Scorecard. This linkage of measures throughout the Balanced Scorecard is constructed with a series of if-then statements: *If* we increase training, *then* cycle times will lower. *If* cycle times lower, *then* loyalty will increase. *If* loyalty increases, *then* revenue will increase. When considering the linkage between measures, we should also attempt to document the timing and extent of the correlations. For example, do we expect customer loyalty to double in the first year as a result of our focus on lowering new product development cycle times? Explicitly stating the assumptions in our measure architecture makes the Balanced Scorecard a formidable tool for strategic learning.

Cause and Effect in Practice

Theoretically, the idea of cause and effect is very seductive—it's simple to grasp and promises great rewards in the form of strategic insight when implemented with care. But out in the real world of Balanced Scorecard usage, are companies availing themselves of this option? The answer, it would appear, is no. In one recent study of performance measurement practices, the authors discovered that of 157 companies surveyed, only 23 percent consistently built and verified causal models.[27] This despite the fact that return on assets was 2.95 percent higher and return on equity 5.14 percent higher in those organizations using causal models.

While no conclusive evidence exists to explain the dearth of companies investing in cause-and-effect modeling, here is one possible explanation. Many pundits, particularly statisticians, would suggest it is difficult if not impossible to prove causation between two performance measures. Correlation—either positive or negative movement in tandem—perhaps, but pure causation, stating that one measure drives the other, probably not. For example, let's say you've hypothesized a cause-and-effect link between employee training in the Employee Learning and Growth perspective and the number of manufacturing defects in the Internal Processes perspective. Logically, this relationship makes sense; trained employees should have a higher skill level and thus be able to limit defects on the line. In actual practice, however, problems in manufacturing may result from dozens of factors, including machine failures, supplier quality issues, and computer malfunctions. This lack of scientific rigor may be enough to deter many organizations from pursuing a pure cause-and-effect linkage model when creating their Balanced Scorecard.

What's Really Important Is Telling Your Story[28]

Robert McKee is a man who knows a thing or two about telling a story. You may not know his name, but I'm certain you'll recognize some of the works produced by his students: *Forrest Gump, The Color Purple, Toy Story,* and *Erin Brokovich,* just to name a few. McKee is arguably the world's greatest screenwriting coach, and the 18 Academy Awards, 109 Emmys, and 19 Writers Guild Awards won by his protégés are very solid testimony to that assertion. In a recent interview McKee discussed the very real necessity of introducing the art of storytelling in a business context. As he puts it, *"A big part of a CEO's job is to motivate people to reach certain goals. To do that he or she must engage their emotions, and the key to their hearts is a story . . . if you can harness imagination and the principles of a well-told story, then you get people rising to their feet amid thunderous applause instead of yawning and ignoring you."*[29]

The objectives and measures appearing on your Strategy Map and Balanced Scorecard can tell your *strategic story.* All of the elements you need to create a compelling and dramatic story are present: customers, processes, people, and finances. Your job is to creatively link the objectives in a manner that both tells a spellbinding story and allows you to garner additional insights about your business. To do that, it's not necessary to create complex cause-and-effect models that would make an econometrics professor proud; you simply need the creativity and acumen to craft a story that works on two levels: entertainment and business logic.

Consider for a moment two possible scenarios for presenting corporate objectives to your employee base. In the first case your CEO goes to the front of the room, directs the audience's attention to a series of PowerPoint slides, and dutifully walks them through each chart with exacting precision and detail. My eyes are rolling back in my head as I write that. Contrast that with your CEO telling the story of your company: the strategic destination of financial success, the customer outcomes that will fuel that success, the key processes driving results for customers, and the enabling infrastructure setting the foundation for it all. The linkages among the perspectives bring the story to life, demonstrating that your business is not a series of disparate elements but is actually a powerful and cohesive system that, if working seamlessly, is geared for success.

I've seen cause and effect take many forms. Some organizations draw links between practically every objective appearing on their map. I call these graphical nightmares "spaghetti diagrams." At the other end of the spectrum are maps with virtually no cause-and-effect relationships whatsoever. For those of you thinking you'll probably come down in the middle on this debate and create fairly simple cause-and-effect models, emphasizing the relationships among the perspectives, take heart. Simple modeling certainly does not preclude you from enjoying great success with the Balanced Scorecard. Many leading scorecard adopters exhibit very limited cause and effect among objectives while still garnering tremendous focus, alignment, and improved resource allocation decisions from their work. In my opinion, the key linkages you should consider articulating on the map and in the scorecard are between the Internal Process and Customer perspectives. In many ways the objectives appearing in the Employee Learning and Growth perspective are the enablers of everything you're attempting to achieve; thus they may not warrant one-to-one connections with other sections of the map. However, the link between processes and customers is key, as it is here we signal two major transitions: from internal (employees, climate, processes) to external (customers) and from intangible (skills and knowledge, etc.) to tangible (customer outcomes and financial rewards). Customer outcomes signal the "what" of strategic execution, and Internal Process supplies the "how." Every organization should make an effort to explicitly document this equation, articulating specifically how it expects to transform its unique capabilities and infrastructure into revenue-producing results.

KEEP IN MIND

- The Balanced Scorecard assists organizations in overcoming three fundamental problems: effectively measuring organizational performance, tracking and exploiting the value of intangible assets, and successfully implementing strategy.

- Traditionally, the measurement of business has been financial. However, our reliance on financial measures of performance has come under criticism in recent years. Critics suggest financial measures are not consistent with today's business environment, lack predictive power, reinforce functional silos, may sacrifice long-term thinking, and are not relevant to many levels of the organization.
- Approximately 75 percent of value created in organizations arises from intangible assets. The Balanced Scorecard provides a mechanism for monitoring, evaluating, and fully exploiting these critical drivers of success.
- Successfully implementing strategy is another key issue facing the enterprise. Four barriers to strategy implementation exist for most organizations: a vision barrier, people barrier, resource barrier, and management barrier.
- The Balanced Scorecard balances the historical accuracy and integrity of financial numbers with the drivers of future success. The framework enforces a discipline around strategy implementation by challenging executives to carefully translate their strategies into objectives, measures, targets, and initiatives in four balanced perspectives: Customer, Internal Processes, Learning and Growth, and Financial.
- A Strategy Map is a one-page graphical representation of what the organization must do well in each of the four perspectives if it hopes to execute its strategy. Strategy Maps are comprised of objectives and serve as a powerful communication tool for all of a company's many stakeholders.
- While originally designed in 1990 as a measurement system, the Balanced Scorecard has evolved into a strategic management system for those organizations that fully utilize its many capabilities. Linking the Balanced Scorecard to key management processes, such as budgeting, compensation, and alignment, helps overcome the barriers to implementing strategy.
- Strategy Maps of objectives and Balanced Scorecards of measures can be used to tell the organization's strategic story by utilizing the concept of cause and effect—demonstrating relationships among objectives and measures throughout the four perspectives. Complex cause-and-effect modeling is not a prerequisite to gaining the many benefits offered by the Balanced Scorecard.

Notes

1. From the presentation delivered by Robert S. Kaplan, "Creating Strategy-Focused Public Sector Organizations," September 2004.
2. David P. Norton and Randall H. Russell, "Translate the Strategy into Operational Terms," *Balanced Scorecard Report* (May–June 2005): 1–5.

3. Thomas A. Stewart, *Intellectual Capital* (New York: Currency, 1999), p. xxi.

4. Scott Thurm, "Teamwork Raises Everyone's Game," *Wall Street Journal,* November 7, 2005.

5. Lauri Bassi and Daniel McMurrer, "Are Employee Skills a Cost or an Asset?" *Business Ethics* (Fall 2004).

6. Malcolm P. McNair, "What Price Human Relations?" *Harvard Business Review* (1957).

7. Quoted in 11th Annual Worldwide Luminary Series, "Leading to Greatness" participant workbook, November 2, 2005.

8. Ernst & Young Center for Business Innovation, "Measures that Matter," 1999.

9. Ibid., p. 13.

10. Thomas O. Davenport, *Human Capital* (San Francisco: Jossey-Bass, 1999), 7.

11. Interview on National Public Radio's *Morning Edition,* October 27, 2000.

12. Testimony by David M. Walker, Comptroller General of the United States, before the Subcommittee on Oversight of Government, Management, Restructuring, and the District of Columbia Committee on Governmental Affairs, U.S. Senate, February 2001.

13. Found at: www.whitehouse.gov/omb/budget/fy2002/mgmt.pdf, 2002.

14. Haig R. Nalbantian, Richard A. Guzzo, Dave Kieffer, and Jay Doherty, *Play to Your Strengths* (New York: McGraw-Hill, 2004).

15. McKinsey Quarterly Global Survey of Business Executives, November 2004.

16. R. Charan and G. Colvin, "Why CEOs Fail," *Fortune,* June 21, 1999.

17. Michael C. Mankins and Richard Steele, "Turning Great Strategy into Great Performance," *Harvard Business Review* (July–August 2005): 65–72.

18. Brian E. Becker, Mark A. Huselid, and Dave Ulrich, *The HR Scorecard* (Boston: Harvard Business School Press, 2001).

19. S. I. Hayakawa and Alan R. Hayakawa, *Language in Thought and Action* (New York: Harcourt Brace and Company, 1990), p. 171.

20. Reported in *Synygy Magazine* (Fall 2005).

21. Julia Neyman and Julie Snider, "USA Today Snapshots," *USA Today,* November 15, 2004.

22. Robert S. Kaplan and David P. Norton, "The Balanced Scorecard—Measures that Drive Performance," *Harvard Business Review* (January–February 1992): 71–79.

23. Robert S. Kaplan and David P. Norton, *The Balanced Scorecard* (Boston: Harvard Business School Press, 1996).

24. Michael J. Gelb, *How to Think Like Leonardo da Vinci* (New York: Random House, 2004).

25. Michael Treacy and Fred Wiersema, *The Discipline of Market Leaders* (Reading, MA: Perseus Books, 1995).

26. Robert S. Kaplan and David P. Norton, "Using the Balanced Scorecard as a Strategic Management System," *Harvard Business Review* (January–February 1996): 75–85.

27. Christopher D. Ittner and David F. Larcker, "Coming Up Short on Nonfinancial Performance Measurement," *Harvard Business Review* (November 2003): 88–95.

28. Portions of this section are drawn from Paul R. Niven, *Balanced Scorecard Diagnostics: Maintaining Maximum Performance* (Hoboken, NJ: John Wiley & Sons, 2005).

29. Robert McKee, "Storytelling that Moves People," *Harvard Business Review* (June 2003): 51–55.

CHAPTER 2

Getting Started

Roadmap for Chapter Two   Victor Hugo once said, "He who every morning plans the transaction of the day and follows out that plan, carries a thread that will guide him through the maze of the most busy life. But where no plan is laid, where the disposal of time is surrendered merely to the chance of incidence, chaos will soon reign." If that's a little too long for you to commit to memory, try this one, which was posted on the wall of a former colleague: "Plan your work, work your plan, your plan will work." The point is this: Before we can develop and implement a Balanced Scorecard, we have to diligently plan the campaign ahead. A number of elements of the implementation must be considered long before any objectives are drafted or metrics are debated. In this chapter we'll take a careful look at each of the building blocks of a successful Balanced Scorecard implementation. Specifically we'll explore developing a guiding rationale for your Balanced Scorecard project by answering the question "Why are we building a Balanced Scorecard?"; determining where to begin your efforts; understanding the importance of executive sponsorship and how to secure it; building an effective team to carry out the work ahead; constructing a development plan for the Balanced Scorecard; and, finally, strategies for communicating the Balanced Scorecard. Along the way key pitfalls to avoid and strategies for your success will be provided to ensure your implementation gets off to a great start.

FIRST THINGS FIRST: WHY ARE YOU DEVELOPING A BALANCED SCORECARD?

I can still remember that morning two summers ago. Before the alarm had a chance to shake me from my slumber I jumped out of bed with a great sense of anticipation, stemming from the fact that I was to begin a Scorecard engagement with a new public sector client that day. After a hearty breakfast of grapefruit and toast (my grandfather's favorite), I opened my front door and took a couple of steps toward my car when it hit me—something you rarely feel in Southern California—humidity. Not the stifling, barely drag one foot in front of the other kind of humidity you get in say

New Orleans, but a warm and damp enough sensation for me to audibly utter: "Hmmm, strange." But as it turns out my morning was to get even stranger.

When I arrived at the client's location the standard pleasantries were exchanged, and soon after I was ushered into a large conference room where I was plunked down at the head of the U-shaped table and introduced to the suspicious looking crowd as their Balanced Scorecard consultant. As my host enthusiastically outlined my background I thought to myself: "Two minutes into this and we're off the page already." I was sure he was going to reach a crescendo that would go something like, "Now join me in welcoming Paul as he tells us all about the Balanced Scorecard," but just as the humidity had jolted me earlier that morning his next move caught me off guard as well. He did introduce me, but to my pleasant surprise, then kept the floor himself for the next fifteen minutes as he regaled the crowd with pledge after pledge of his commitment to the Balanced Scorecard: "The Balanced Scorecard is the most important initiative we'll be pursuing this year." "I'm putting the full weight of my office behind this." "I expect you to give Paul your full cooperation as he assists us in this critical endeavor." I could barely contain myself; as we'll learn in the next section on executive sponsorship, this sort of promotion for the Scorecard is pure gold and he was in full oratorical sail with no provocation from me. The only concern I had, one that was coming from that little voice within me, the one that has seen its share of good and bad Scorecard implementations, was the fact that while his cheerleading skills were second to none he never really did come right out and say why the Balanced Scorecard was so important to the organization.

Two months into the engagement, things were sputtering like the engine of my first car. As hard as we tried to engage people, they just didn't seem inclined to get on board with us. Finally, after considering every logical textbook intervention, I simply began directly asking people why they were hesitant to participate. After some gentle prodding the truth emerged. In the absence of a "why" from their leader, the grapevine quickly took over the communication challenge and plugged in "for layoffs" as the reason behind the Balanced Scorecard. That notion spread like wildfire; soon nobody wanted to play ball when stepping up to the plate might just hasten the end of your employment. It took us weeks of communication and education to get the real impetus for the Balanced Scorecard out on the table and grudgingly accepted by a still largely incredulous rank and file. The executive who discovered the Balanced Scorecard felt it was the perfect tool to create alignment around the organization's new customer intimacy strategy, but his failure to state that in terms that everyone could rally around ultimately cost him the hearts, if not the minds, of most of his employees.

Answering the Question: Why Balanced Scorecard and Why Now?

We live in a world that has been characterized as one of "excess access."[1] When I read that pithy little phrase, I suddenly felt as if I was surrounded by a choir of truth singing in beautiful harmony. Everything seems to be at the tip of our fingers, and everyone out there seems to want to keep pushing more things—products, information, entertainment, you name it—our way. Who among us doesn't feel a little overwhelmed, overworked, and overstressed these days? At home and at the office, our senses are constantly being bombarded with attention-demanding stimuli. With time, attention, and energy constituting our most precious of resources, we must be absolutely certain that those things we do allow into our cognitive air space truly warrant our attention. The first and most critical hurdle any new initiative, including the Balanced Scorecard, will face in your organization is: "Why exactly are we doing this anyway?" If you can't supply a powerful and compelling answer to that question, how can you justifiably expect your employees to shove aside a pile of competing demands and priorities the size of Mount Everest to focus on the Balanced Scorecard?

As with any other business tool or system you employ, the Balanced Scorecard must solve a pressing business issue or problem that everyone understands and the importance of which is universally acknowledged. Be forewarned, fashionable clichés like "We're going for excellence" or "We're going to be a cutting edge company" won't cut it with a workforce that has more than likely seen its share of such vague sentiments come and go.[2] To have the Scorecard gain acceptance, it must be seen as a fire hose clearly capable of dousing the flames of trouble at your doorstep. So perhaps the most fundamental question you can ask yourself is "Do we really need a Balanced Scorecard?" To help you answer that question (and possibly save yourself about 250 pages of reading), Exhibit 2.1 presents an assessment guide you can use to determine whether the Balanced Scorecard is right for you.

Asking why we are doing something, attempting to unearth the true purpose, should become second nature to us in every facet of our lives. Regardless of the pursuit, it's critical to peel away the shiny veneer of possibilities and tackle the fundamental question of why something is important to us at this moment. Only then can we sincerely determine whether our full commitment of action is merited. Roger Smith, the former CEO of General Motors, learned that lesson the hard way. Here is a quote from Smith as he reflected in retrospect on his turnaround plans for the automotive giant:

> *If I had the opportunity to do everything over again, I would make exactly the same decision that I made in 1981 . . . to rebuild GM, inside out and from the bottom up, to turn it into a 21st-century corporation, one that would continue to be a global leader. But I sure wish I'd done a better job of communicating with GM people. I'd do that differently a second time around and make sure they understood and shared my vision for the company. Then they would have known why I was tearing the place up, taking out whole divisions, changing our whole production structure. If people understand the why, they'll work at it. Like I say, I never got all this across. There we were, charging up the hill right on schedule, and I looked behind*

Exhibit 2.1   Assessing the Need for a Balanced Scorecard

To complete the exercise read each statement and determine how much you agree with what is stated. The more you agree, the higher the score you assign. For example, if you fully agree, assign a score of 5 points.

1 2 3 4 5   **1.** Our organization has invested in Total Quality Management (TQM) and other improvement initiatives, but we have not seen a corresponding increase in financial or customer results.

1 2 3 4 5   **2.** If we did not produce our current performance reports for a month nobody would notice.

1 2 3 4 5   **3.** We create significant value from intangible assets such as employee knowledge and innovation, customer relationships, and a strong culture.

1 2 3 4 5   **4.** We have a strategy (or have had strategies in the past) but have a hard time implementing them successfully.

1 2 3 4 5   **5.** We rarely review our performance measures and make suggestions for new and innovative indicators.

1 2 3 4 5   **6.** Our senior management team spends the majority of its time together discussing variances from plan and other operational issues.

1 2 3 4 5   **7.** Budgeting at our organization is very political and based largely on historical trends.

1 2 3 4 5   **8.** Our employees *do not* have a solid understanding of our mission, vision, and strategy.

1 2 3 4 5   **9.** Our employees *do not* know how their day-to-day actions contribute to the organization's success.

1 2 3 4 5   **10.** Nobody owns the performance measurement process at our organization.

1 2 3 4 5   **11.** We have numerous initiatives taking place at our organization, and it's possible that not all are truly strategic in nature.

1 2 3 4 5   **12.** There is little accountability in our organization for the things we agree as a group to do.

1 2 3 4 5   **13.** People tend to stay within their "silos," and as a result, we have little collaboration among departments.

1 2 3 4 5   **14.** Our employees have difficulty accessing the critical information they need to serve customers.

1 2 3 4 5   **15.** Priorities at our organization are often dictated by current necessity or "firefighting."

1 2 3 4 5   **16.** The environment in which we operate is changing, and in order to succeed we too must change.

1 2 3 4 5   **17.** We face increased pressure from stakeholders to demonstrate results.

1 2 3 4 5	**18.** We **do not** have clearly defined performance targets for both financial and nonfinancial indicators.
1 2 3 4 5	**19.** We cannot clearly articulate our strategy in a one-page document or "map."
1 2 3 4 5	**20.** We sometimes make decisions that are beneficial in the short term but may harm long-term value creation.
_____	**Total**

Scoring Key:

20–30: If your score fell in this range you most likely have a strong performance measurement discipline in place. The program has been cascaded throughout your organization to ensure all employees are contributing to your success and is linked to key management processes.

31–60: You may have a performance measurement system in place but are not experiencing the benefits you anticipated or need to succeed. Using the Balanced Scorecard as a strategic management system would be of benefit to you.

61–100: Scores in this range suggest difficulty in executing your strategy successfully and meeting the needs of your customers and other stakeholders. A Balanced Scorecard system is strongly recommended to help you focus on the implementation of strategy and align your organization with overall goals.

Source: Adapted from Paul R. Niven, *Balanced Scorecard Step-by-Step for Government and Nonprofit Agencies.* John Wiley & Sons (Hoboken, NJ, 2003).

me and saw that many people were still at the bottom, trying to decide whether to come along. I'm talking about hourly workers, middle management, even some top managers. It seemed like a lot of them had gotten off the train.[3]

Assuming you've used Exhibit 2.1 to assess your need for the Balanced Scorecard, chances are at least one of the reasons for that decision is reflected in Exhibit 2.2, which outlines a number of possible explanations for launching a Balanced Scorecard effort. One of these alternatives for embarking on such a journey, "implementing strategy," warrants a bit of extra attention. This is far and away the most popular rationale stated when I ask clients why they've decided to pursue the Balanced Scorecard, and it's a powerful impetus when you recall from Chapter One that only 10 percent of organizations effectively execute their strategies. Frequently, however, a slight problem will emerge as we begin our work together. When I ask the seemingly straightforward question "Can I see your strategy?" it's not uncommon for the heads of my clients to bow ever so slightly as they whisper, "Well, we really don't have a strategy per se" or "We've got

Exhibit 2.2 Rationale for the Balanced Scorecard

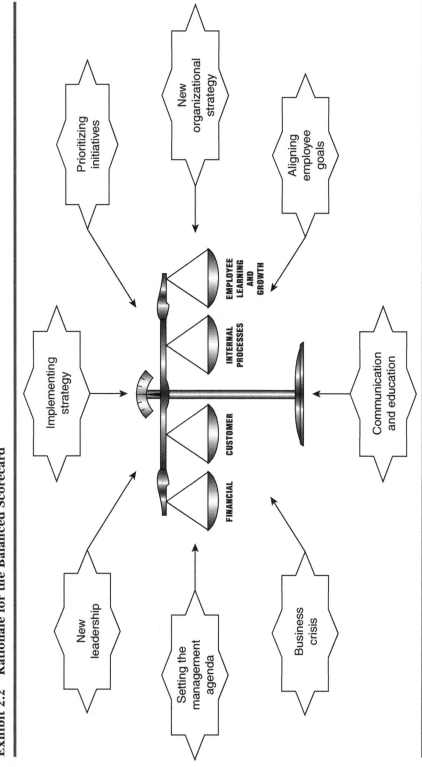

a strategy but it's not written down anywhere." Call me suspicious, but I think some of these clients are actually engaging me and turning to the Balanced Scorecard in an effort to craft a coherent strategy, one they can sell to their employees and, more important, themselves. I call this "reverse engineering" the strategy through the priorities inherent in the Strategy Map and measures. Although you can generate tremendous results from the Balanced Scorecard in this manner, keep in mind that it is first and foremost a tool for translating a strategy, not a tool for creating strategy. If your strategy canvas is currently blank, you may be better served focusing on painting that masterpiece before taking it to the world in the form of a Balanced Scorecard.

Benefits of a Guiding Rationale

For the Balanced Scorecard to succeed, it cannot be viewed as a one-time event. Determining your objectives in developing the Balanced Scorecard will go a long way in securing the evolution of the tool in your organization. Once you've made the decision to go forward, your first obligation is to clearly explain why that choice has been made and what benefits you expect as a result. The more specific, the better—outline in vivid detail the challenges you face from competitors, changing customer tendencies, supplier pressures, stakeholder demands, and so on. Demonstrate to your team why change is not simply an option but an imperative if you're to stay in the game and sustain your success.[4]

When you have a well-understood, agreed-on, and widely communicated rationale for the project, you possess a valuable tool in expanding the role of the Balanced Scorecard. Management and employees alike will view the development of measures in a Balanced Scorecard framework as the first of many stops on the road to a new and powerful management system for the organization. The consensus achieved from an overarching rationale for the Balanced Scorecard greatly assists your communication efforts as you focus and educate all employees on the goals of the implementation. Finally, every implementation loses momentum at one time or another; the practical realities of modern business and its multitude of attendant priorities make that a virtual certainty. The true test is whether you can emerge from these periods of corporate lethargy with renewed vigor and enthusiasm for the task at hand. A guiding rationale for your Balanced Scorecard can serve as your rallying cry, bringing together the entire organization under the banner of why you made this decision in the first place.[5]

WHERE DO WE BUILD THE BALANCED SCORECARD?

Scorecard architects Kaplan and Norton have described the Balanced Scorecard as simple but not simplistic. This is the first of probably several times I will call on that reference as we develop your Balanced Scorecard. While the concept itself is relatively straightforward—balancing financial and nonfinancial measures to drive strategy—the execution of those tasks will involve many difficult deliberations on a wide variety of topics. We just described one such issue when we examined the rationale for developing a Balanced Scorecard. In this section we'll explore another important subject requiring careful consideration, the choice of an appropriate unit in which to develop your first Balanced Scorecard.

Sensing possible resistance and attempting to limit downside risk will lead some organizations to begin their Balanced Scorecard effort at the business unit or department level, piloting the program in an attempt to generate quick wins and enthusiasm for a broader rollout. Such was the case at Canon U.S.A., which began its Balanced Scorecard journey with three relatively small units: Information Technology, Medical Systems, and Logistics. Just as executives had hoped, each group soon profited from the investment, delighting in the powerful articulation of strategy, progress on key metrics, and unification of previously disconnected processes. It wasn't long before 50 percent of the company had turned to the Balanced Scorecard.[6]

Despite the possible challenges, including resistance and logistical constraints, many organizations believe that starting at the top represents the most logical choice, and frequently this is in fact the case. A Corporate Balanced Scorecard provides the means of communicating strategic objectives and measures across the entire organization. The focus and attention derived from these high-level metrics can serve to bring together disparate elements of the organization toward a common goal of implementing the strategy. The measures on the corporate Scorecard then become the raw materials for cascaded scorecards at all levels of the firm, producing a series of aligned measurement systems that allow all organizational participants to demonstrate how their day-to-day actions contribute to long-term goals.

Criteria for Choosing an Appropriate Organizational Unit

Before we jump to the conclusion that a Balanced Scorecard at the highest level is the best choice for you, we should consider a number of criteria for making this important decision. I have found that several elements contribute to the selection of an appropriate organizational unit for your first Balanced Scorecard. Those criteria are shown in Exhibit 2.3.

Let's consider each of these criteria in turn and then discuss a method for using them to make this important decision.

1. *Strategy.* The single most important criteria in making your selection is whether the unit under consideration possesses a coherent strategy. After all, the Balanced Scorecard is a methodology designed to assist you in translating your strategy into objectives and measures that will allow

Exhibit 2.3   Seven Criteria for Choosing Where to Begin Your Balanced Scorecard

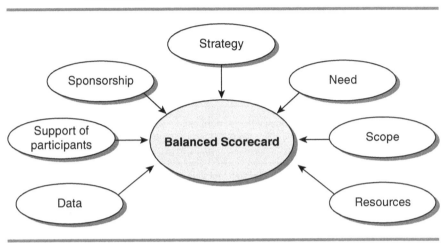

you to gauge your effectiveness in delivering on that strategy. Without a strategic stake in the ground you're very likely to end up with an ad hoc collection of financial and nonfinancial measures that do not link together to tell the story of your strategy. Having said this, the lack of a clearly defined strategy certainly doesn't preclude you from building a Balanced Scorecard. As we discussed in the preceding section, many organizations reverse-engineer a strategy through the Scorecard development process. The importance of strategy to the Balanced Scorecard is examined in greater depth in Chapter Three.

2. *Sponsorship.* In the next section of this chapter we'll take a close look at the vital necessity of executive sponsorship for your Balanced Scorecard effort. Suffice it to say here that if your leader is not aligned with the goals and objectives of the Balanced Scorecard and does not believe in the merits of the tool, your efforts will be severely compromised. An executive sponsor must provide leadership for the program in both words and deeds.

3. *Need for a Balanced Scorecard.* The importance of clear objectives for the Balanced Scorecard program was discussed in the first section of this chapter. Based on that review, does the unit you're considering have an overarching impetus for implementation? Is there a clear need for revamping of its performance measurement system? In an excellent article, Vitale and Mavrinac outlined seven warning signs that could indicate a new system is needed.[7] Their signals for pending measurement change are outlined in Exhibit 2.4. Does the organizational unit you're considering display any of these signs?

**Exhibit 2.4   Signs that You May Need a New Performance
Measurement System**

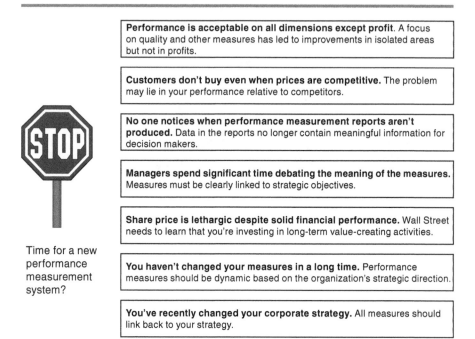

Performance is acceptable on all dimensions except profit. A focus on quality and other measures has led to improvements in isolated areas but not in profits.

Customers don't buy even when prices are competitive. The problem may lie in your performance relative to competitors.

No one notices when performance measurement reports aren't produced. Data in the reports no longer contain meaningful information for decision makers.

Managers spend significant time debating the meaning of the measures. Measures must be clearly linked to strategic objectives.

Share price is lethargic despite solid financial performance. Wall Street needs to learn that you're investing in long-term value-creating activities.

Time for a new performance measurement system?

You haven't changed your measures in a long time. Performance measures should be dynamic based on the organization's strategic direction.

You've recently changed your corporate strategy. All measures should link back to your strategy.

Source: Adapted from Michael R. Vitale and Sarah C. Mavrinac, "How Effective Is Your Performance Measurement System?" *Management Accounting* (August 1995), p. 43.

4. *Support of key managers and supervisors.* There is no doubt that executive support is critical for a Balanced Scorecard implementation to succeed. However, while executives may use Scorecard information to make strategic decisions, we also depend heavily on managers and first-line supervisors using the tool in their jobs. When the Scorecard is driven down to all levels through a process of cascading, the alignment and focus derived across the organization can lead to real breakthroughs in performance. Managers and supervisors make this happen with their understanding, acceptance, support of, and usage of the Balanced Scorecard. Not all members of these groups will demonstrate such a willingness to participate, however. While boisterous and open criticism of new senior management initiatives is fairly rare, managers and supervisors often remain silent or demonstrate muted enthusiasm, which workers quickly interpret as a questionable show of support for the program.[8] When choosing your organizational unit for the Balanced Scorecard, make an honest evaluation of the management team and supervisors you'll be relying on for participation and support.

5. *Organizational scope*. The unit you choose should operate a set of activities across the typical value chain of an organization. In other words, it should have a strategy, defined customers, specific processes, operations, and administration. Selecting a unit with a narrow, functional focus will produce a Balanced Scorecard with narrow, functionally focused metrics.

6. *Data*. This criterion encompasses two elements. First, does this unit support a culture of measurement, that is, would they be amenable to managing by a balanced set of performance measures? While every group within a modern organization should rely on performance measures, for your first attempt you may wish to choose a unit with a history of reliance on performance measures. Second, will the unit be able to supply data for the chosen performance measures? This may be difficult to assess initially since at least some of the measures on your Balanced Scorecard may be new with data sources as yet unidentified. However, if the unit has difficulty gathering data for current performance measures, it may be reluctant or unable to supply the data you'll ultimately require for your Balanced Scorecard.

7. *Resources*. You can't build this new management system on your own. The best Balanced Scorecards are produced from a team of individuals committed to a common goal of excellence (see "Forming Your Team" later in this chapter). Ensure the unit you choose is willing and able to supply ample resources for the implementation. If your experience is like many that I've had, you'll find that people vigorously defend their time, and rightly so.

Exhibit 2.5 provides a simple worksheet you can use to determine the right organizational unit for your initial Balanced Scorecard effort. In this example, Business Unit "A" is being considered for a Scorecard implementation. Plotted along the left-hand side of the table are the seven criteria just discussed. In the next column, I have assigned a score out of 10 for this unit against each of the criteria. The third column represents weights for each of the seven dimensions based on my judgment and experience. You may feel more comfortable assigning equal weights to each of the seven items, but clearly some areas, such as sponsorship and strategy, are imperative to success and should be weighted accordingly. The fourth column contains the score for the unit within each criteria. Under "Strategy," Business Unit A was assigned a score of 10, which when multiplied by the weight for that category yields 3 total points. In the final column I've provided a rationale for the scores assigned based on an assessment of the unit in the context of that specific criteria. It's important to document your decision-making process to validate it with others responsible for choosing the Balanced Scorecard organizational unit. Finally, a total score is calculated and an overall assessment is provided. The overall assessment provides worksheet participants with the opportunity to discuss potential

Exhibit 2.5   Sample Worksheet for Choosing Your Organizational Unit

Balanced Scorecard Project
Organizational Unit Assessment
Business Unit "A"

Criteria	Score (Out of 10)	Weight	Total Points	Rationale
Strategy	10	30%	3	This unit has recently completed a new strategic plan for the next five years.
Sponsorship	9	30%	2.7	New unit president has successfully utilized the Balanced Scorecard with two other organizations before joining us.
Need	5	15%	0.75	Results for this group have been excellent, and they may not see the need for this tool to sustain future efforts.
Support of Participants	7	10%	0.7	Young, energetic management group is willing to experiment with new approaches.
Scope	8	5%	0.4	This unit produces, markets, and sells a distinct group of products.
Data	4	5%	0.2	Despite their success, they have not utilized sophisticated performance measurement systems in the past.
Resources	4	5%	0.2	Unit is understaffed and will have difficulty finding resources for this project.
Total		100%	7.95	

Overall Assessment   This unit scores a very high 7.95 out of 10 and is an excellent candidate for the Balanced Scorecard. The data and resource issues, while not insignificant, are mitigated by the strong leadership of the unit president and the creation of a new strategic plan. Early education initiatives within this unit could focus on the value of the Scorecard as a means of sustaining results for the long term. This may reduce skepticism surrounding the implementation based on the unit's past success.

strengths and weaknesses of the unit, mitigate significant risks, and offer opinions on the viability of this group for the Balanced Scorecard project.

EXECUTIVE SPONSORSHIP: A CRITICAL ELEMENT OF ANY BALANCED SCORECARD PROGRAM

Warning labels are ubiquitous in our modern world; they grace our household products; we find them at every tight turn on the roads we travel every day; and I don't know about you, but I'd be lost if I didn't know the precise "best before" date on milk. I think any conceivable change initiative an organization dreams up—and I mean any type of change—should come with a screaming yellow warning label: Do not proceed without the support of an executive for this initiative! I really should have included this on page one, but I wanted to get you this far before springing it on you. Actually, I'm not telling you something you don't already know. You've seen programs come and go, launched with great fanfare and the best intentions only to be abandoned shortly thereafter due to a lack of executive attention. Of all the things that separate organizations, this is one thing every single public, private, and nonprofit agency shares.

The Balanced Scorecard is not immune to this first law of organizational change, and in fact it may be more susceptible than other less visible organizational interventions. Scorecard architects Kaplan and Norton believe senior management commitment is necessary for a number of reasons:[9]

- *Understanding of strategy.* Most middle managers lack an in-depth knowledge of the organization's strategy. Only the senior management team is able to articulate an ongoing strategy effectively.
- *Decision rights.* Strategy involves trade-offs between alternative courses of action, determining which opportunities to pursue, and, more important, which not to pursue. Middle management does not possess the decision-making power to determine strategic priorities, such as customer value propositions and related operating processes that are critical to the development of any Balanced Scorecard.
- *Commitment.* Although knowledge of the enterprise's strategy is necessary, the emotional commitment of executives to the Balanced Scorecard program is the true differentiating feature of successful programs. Kaplan and Norton summarize this well: "*More important is the time spent in actual meetings where the senior executives debate and argue among themselves . . . . These meetings build an emotional commitment to the strategy, to the scorecard as a communications device, and to the management processes that build a Strategy-Focused Organization.*"[10]

In today's business environment, where many CEOs have achieved icon-like stature and rock star fame—I think Steve Jobs poses for more magazine covers than Tyra Banks—employees are watching more closely than ever for their leaders to signal what really matters in the organization. If senior management provides only shallow and casual support for the Balanced Scorecard, all employees will quickly determine that the project probably isn't worth their time and effort. Employees *"watch what the boss watches"*[11] and know what projects are likely to merit their attention. Writing in their provocatively titled book *Confronting Reality,* authors Charan and Bossidy state:

> *The usual reason for the failure of an initiative is that it was launched halfheartedly, or was beyond the ability of the organization to master. Here's what tends to happen: the leaders announce a bold new program and then walk away from it, leaving the job to others. With no clear impetus from the top, the program will wander and drift. An initiative, after all, is add-on work, and people already have full plates. Few of them can take it seriously if the boss doesn't. Eventually the effort bogs down and dies. . . . Real results do not come from making bold announcements about how the organization will change. They come from thoughtful, committed leaders who understand the details of an initiative, anticipate its consequences for the organization, make sure their people can achieve, it, put their personal weight behind it, and communicate its urgency to everyone.*[12]

Enough of this doom and gloom; let's pull the veil from this vexing topic and consider how you can transform even the most recalcitrant executive into a raving Balanced Scorecard fan.

Securing Executive Sponsorship

After reading the preceding paragraphs, I'm sure you'll agree that senior management support and leadership is a must-have ingredient for a successful Balanced Scorecard program. Unfortunately, gaining the buy-in and support of senior leaders often is easier said than done. Executives at the uppermost ranks in the organization have myriad demands on their time and attention; like the rest of us, they quickly filter out those ideas seemingly not worthy of their valuable resources. Clever people use many techniques to win the support of a senior manager for the Balanced Scorecard. Some of the most convincing methods are discussed next.

- *Look for a good fit.* If your senior management team focuses almost exclusively on financial control systems to run your business, then the Balanced Scorecard probably won't offer natural appeal to them. You need to find senior executives who believe in the value, and indeed necessity, of balanced performance measurement and management. Senior managers who have gone through a strategic planning process designed to help them focus their efforts and define their objectives will also be more amenable to the Balanced Scorecard approach. Find the senior manager who fits this profile and make her door the first stop on your sponsorship tour.

- *Demonstrate results.* Senior leaders are charged primarily with achieving results for the organization. Appeal to this tenet of leadership life by outlining the many successes of other organizations pursuing a Balanced Scorecard approach. Success stories of Balanced Scorecard implementations abound in the business literature and at conference venues around the world. Testimonials from other senior executives are also very convincing, as is this one: *"We've found the concept of the Balanced Scorecard incredibly useful, both as a framework for deciding which things we are really going to try and achieve, and as a way of showing people where we are going."*[13] Finally, the chances are pretty good that at least one of your competitors will be using the methodology, and perhaps even another geographic unit within your own organization. Document their success with the Balanced Scorecard and convince your leaders that you can achieve even better results using this tool.

- *"Survey says."* We all want to feel needed, and you can make your senior management feel very needed in the Balanced Scorecard by sharing a couple of key statistics on the implementations of other organizations. A Best Practices LLC study found that half of benchmark participants' CEOs took part in the process, and senior vice presidents and vice presidents participated 80 percent of the time.[14] In a study conducted for the Balanced Scorecard Report, respondents reported that CEOs, more than any other individuals, were the sponsors of the Balanced Scorecard. Thirty-one percent of the organizations stated the CEO was their sponsor.[15]

- *Is danger lurking?* Take the proactive step of assessing your organization against the seven warning signs of performance measurement problems presented earlier in the chapter. Convincing evidence of issues in several of the categories should catch an effective executive's attention.

- *Educate.* To support any cause or idea, we must first accept it as meaningful or valuable. Meaning and value are derived from a comprehensive understanding of the subject. Senior managers follow the same constructs on their road to acceptance of new change initiatives. What this means to you is that you must provide your executive team with a well-designed and delivered presentation on performance management and the Balanced Scorecard if you hope to win their support. Let's discuss how this event might unfold. Prior to the session, you should consider distributing Balanced Scorecard literature to your executive team. Copies of books like this or good articles on the subject will help your audience prepare for the presentation to come. Regarding the session itself, if possible I would suggest holding it at an offsite location. Keeping distractions to a minimum will prove beneficial for all involved. Having an administrative assistant knock on the door and shuttle an engaged executive out of the room at a pivotal moment can be disastrous to your momentum. Consider using an outside consultant to deliver the actual material or at least participate in the event, for a number of reasons.

First, a well-trained consultant will have delivered countless presentations of this nature and use time-tested material. Second, and unfortunately, many times an outside voice will carry more weight with, and be assumed to have more credibility by, executives than will an internal one. This is a sad but true reality of modern organizational life. Finally, and perhaps most important, you're holding this event because you want to win the support of your executive team. An experienced consultant will have faced similar crowds many times and be well prepared to answer all queries and objections raised by the audience. And believe me, cogent and articulate responses here can translate to real support down the road.

Regarding the actual agenda, I suggest a two- to three-hour event structured in this way: 30 minutes on your organization and why a change is necessary (to keep pace with competitive forces, forge ahead, etc.), 90 minutes on performance management and the Balanced Scorecard. Topics covered should include background information on the topic, a detailed review of the methodology, and case studies and success stories. Spend the final 30 to 60 minutes answering questions and soliciting support for the implementation. Oh, and one final thing, don't forget to feed attendees. I say that only half jokingly. If your culture is one in which food is present at all meetings, don't leave those sandwiches and cookies out of this session.

- *Involve them in the process.* People only support what they help to create. The more involved your senior management is in the Balanced Scorecard development process, the greater the likelihood they will evangelize over and use the tool as a management device. Involvement isn't tantamount to blocking off enormous chunks of time from their tightly guarded calendars; it could be as simple as holding review meetings in which the executive team is offered the opportunity to review Balanced Scorecard deliverables and imprint the process with their own stamp.

- *Link the Balanced Scorecard to something the executive is passionate about.* Any executive is more inclined to lend vocal and active support to an initiative appealing to a core belief or value. Thus it is incumbent on you to find that linchpin and discuss how the Balanced Scorecard can transform it from rhetoric to reality. For example, perhaps she is acutely aware of the power of intangible assets, such as culture and customer relationships, in transforming your business. Discuss the proven ability of the Balanced Scorecard to translate intangibles into real business value. If quality is his first love, demonstrate the idea of cause and effect, outlining the fact that quality is a result of unique organizational elements, such as training and culture, and quality drives customer satisfaction and ultimately financial rewards, all key dimensions of the Balanced Score-card framework.

Sponsorship in Action

If you are a senior executive sponsoring the Balanced Scorecard program within your organization, how do you know you're "walking the talk"? Try this test: When you feel that you are talking up a change initiative at least three times more than you need to, your managers will feel that you are backing the transformation.[16] It takes that much, and probably more, to get the message across to an employee base that is change-weary and con-stantly bombarded from all sides. Employees are looking to you to set the course.

You must utilize every available opportunity to reinforce the importance of the exercise. One of my favorite examples of this stems from a common lament I hear during Balanced Scorecard workshops: the *"What time is this session going to end? I have real work to do"* complaint often lobbed from a disengaged participant. I was once in a strategy mapping workshop at a large telecom company when a vice president tossed just such a verbal grenade into the late afternoon air. I was poised to answer his query in my most restrained manner when I was rescued by the CEO himself. It was as if he were literally riding in on a white horse ready to save the day when he said: *"What could possibly be more important than what we are doing right here and now? We're shaping the tool that we'll use to execute our strategy over the next three years, and frankly, if you don't understand the importance of this exercise, then maybe you don't belong at this table."* The silence that followed was, as they say, deafening. In the intervening moments before the CEO continued, everyone sitting around that table had to dig deep and critically evaluate their commitment to the exercise. Not surprisingly, this implementation was among the most successful I've ever had the privilege to engage in. I attribute that not to my consulting acumen but to the incident in which the CEO clearly demonstrated his passion for the Balanced Scorecard.

YOUR BALANCED SCORECARD TEAM

Throughout much of the twentieth century, a strongly held myth existed in the organizational world: There existed a great man or woman work-ing feverishly with tremendous dedication to solve any and all problems that stood between them and the organization's success. Of course, this myth did not reflect the reality of organizational life. How often during our lives have we heard the phrases "Two heads are better than one" or "None of us is as smart as all of us"? These words remind us of the power of groups to accomplish tasks using the variety of skills and experiences that a collection of individuals possesses. In reality, groups have been coming

together to solve complex problems for centuries. For example, Michel-
angelo worked with a group of 16 to paint the Sistine Chapel—truly a
complex situation! Perhaps the complex, competitive, change-demanding
world of today's organization is exposing the vulnerability of the "Lone
Ranger" myth. Increasingly, organizations are developing self-directed work
teams to solve the problems they face, and many compelling reasons
support this movement. Teams strengthen the performance capability of
individuals, hierarchies, and management processes. They are practical,
and most people and organizations can make teams work. Finally, teams
get results. Your Balanced Scorecard implementation is well suited to a
team approach. No single individual within your organization, including the
CEO, will possess all of the necessary knowledge of strategy, markets, competitors, processes, and competencies to build a coherent Balanced Scorecard.

Choosing Your Team

And with the first pick in this year's Balanced Scorecard draft the (please
play along and insert your company's name here) select . . . drum roll
please . . . . So, who would you choose? What was the first name that came
to mind and why? If you've read the previous sections of this chapter closely
my hope is that an executive's name was at the tip of your tongue, and
who knows, perhaps you played the fantasy scenario out to its ESPN-like
conclusion by disheveling the executive's normally neatly coiffed hair with
a ball cap and handing him an oversized team jersey with a giant "1" on
the back.

As you probably surmised, a critical member of your team is the executive sponsor. This person will take ownership of the Balanced Scorecard and,
based on interactions with the senior executive team, will provide the necessary background on strategy and methodology to guide the team's work.
A critical responsibility is maintaining constant communication with the
entire senior management group to ensure their ongoing commitment and
support of the implementation. The sponsor must also take responsibility
for providing resources for the initiative and influencing other executives
to do the same. The team will require both human and financial resources
and will most likely face competition from other initiatives equally pressed
for resources. Here the executive sponsor must possess the ability to clearly
demonstrate the strategic significance of the Balanced Scorecard and why
it warrants the allocation of scarce and valuable resources. Finally, and most
important, the sponsor must exhibit complete and enthusiastic support for
the Balanced Scorecard in words and deeds. During the implementation
phase, your entire organization will take cues from the sponsor; does he
appear legitimately committed to using this tool, are his words consistent
with actions and policies he supports? Obviously the executive sponsor will
have other duties during the process, but he must commit to regular attendance at team meetings to be seen as a truly committed and credible sponsor.

Now that your number-one draft pick, the executive sponsor, is in place, you are ready to select the core members of your Balanced Scorecard team. In an ideal world, your organization's full executive team would take complete responsibility for developing the Balanced Scorecard, investing the time and energy necessary to produce a product to guide the entire organization. If you're fortunate enough to enjoy this rare situation, I congratulate you; your Scorecard effort is off to a great start. However, a more likely scenario is one in which you have the support of one or maybe two executives (perhaps you are a senior executive yourself), but you require other members of your organization to step up and assist in the effort of crafting your Balanced Scorecard. Don't despair; you can develop an effective Balanced Scorecard without your entire executive team working exclusively on the project. Let's take a look at some questions that will help you form a powerful Balanced Scorecard team.

Who Chooses the Team Members?   The first duty of the executive sponsor is selecting the group of people who will come together to mold your Balanced Scorecard. It is important not to rely on instinct alone. Most executives will reach out to colleagues, soliciting names of top performers and working with Human Resource managers to find potential stars to fill the team's roster. While volunteers are welcome, boisterous promoters are not always the best choice for a team that will require a healthy dose of conflict in order to produce an effective product. Executives also must scan the ranks looking for potential team members who are not reluctant to rock the boat and swim against the common tide during heated discussions.[17]

If We Don't Have the Entire Executive Group on the Team, What Level of Organization Should Our Team Represent?   The obvious, and accurate, answer to this question is the most senior level possible. In the past I've had clients who feel the biggest hurdle to clear in successfully implementing the Balanced Scorecard is the buy-in and support of front-line staff. Quite frequently this is a very pragmatic point of view. To generate staff-level support, they feel that a team comprised of lower-level employees will indicate their confidence in the group to deliver a sound product and simultaneously silence critics who suggest that only the organizational elite have any say in important matters. Philosophically I am all for this approach, but practically I have unfortunately seen it backfire, leaving once-promising implementations in tatters.

There are several problems with delegating the development of your Balanced Scorecard to a low-level staff team: First of all, many people at this end of the hierarchy simply don't possess the deep knowledge of strategy and competition necessary to forge an effective Scorecard. I am not suggesting that front-line associates are not critical to the company's success; in fact, the opposite is often true. For example, a recent article noted the strategic importance of cashiers to a retailer's fortunes.[18] What

I am suggesting is that front-line associates typically are not steeped in the strategy at a deep enough level to contribute meaningfully to the development of a Balanced Scorecard. Another problem often stems from this lack of in-depth strategic acumen: indecision. How do they know the decisions they are making, in this case vital considerations impacting the future health of the company, are the right ones? Finally, we need to recognize that many associates on the lower rungs of the corporate ladder don't want any change, including the Balanced Scorecard, to rock the comfy status quo they've been enjoying for who knows how long. As author William Bridges puts it, "*Simply to turn the power over to people who don't want a change to happen is to invite catastrophe.*"[19]

To prove beneficial, your Balanced Scorecard ultimately must be owned by the senior leadership of your organization, and it is therefore vital to ensure your Scorecard development team is comprised of senior-level people who possess the knowledge, credibility, and decision-making rights to build a tool that will be accepted and, more important, utilized by the ruling body.

How Many People Should Be on the Team?   According to the literature on teams, they can range in size from 3 to 30. Studies of Balanced Scorecard implementations have demonstrated that many organizations use 10 or more people in the Scorecard-building process.[20] To choose the appropriate number of people for your team, be sure that all the areas of your organization that you expect to be using the Balanced Scorecard are represented. If, for example, you're creating a high-level Corporate Balanced Scorecard, you should strive for representation from each of your business units as well as critical support functions, such as Finance, Human Resources, and Information Technology. If your Scorecard effort is beginning at the business unit level, then key functional areas within the unit should have a presence on the team. Remember our earlier admonition: No one person has all the knowledge of strategy, markets, competition, and competencies to build an effective Balanced Scorecard. The knowledge you need to build an effective Balanced Scorecard resides in the minds of your colleagues across the entire organization. Additionally, by involving a number of people in the process, you increase the likelihood they will act as ambassadors of the Balanced Scorecard within their unit, thereby increasing knowledge and enthusiasm for the tool. A group effort is the clear choice for building your Balanced Scorecard, but, if at all possible, I recommend you attempt to cap your team at 10 people or less. Anything larger will present logistical, facilitation, and consensus-building challenges.

Team Members: Roles and Responsibilities

Batman had Robin, the Lone Ranger had Tonto, and Bill Clinton had Hillary—or is it the other way around? Anyway, you get the picture. No one can go it alone. Behind every great and often mythic figure is someone lighting the way forward with unending vigor and unquestionable perseverance. Your executive sponsor needs such a partner if the Balanced Scorecard is to burn brightly within your company. Thus the *Balanced Scorecard team leader or "champion"* is a critical contributor to your success. This intrepid soul will face many challenges, providing solutions that keep the team moving forward. The champion guides the process both logistically and philosophically by scheduling meetings, tracking progress, providing relevant background materials to team members, and offering subject matter expertise on the Balanced Scorecard concept. This individual should provide the thought leadership on Balanced Scorecard and performance management concepts that ensure the team is taking advantage of proven methodologies and best practices. A potentially difficult aspect of this role is balancing the analytical requirements of Scorecard development with the interpersonal skills of team building and conflict resolution. Team members look to the champion to provide both emotional and cognitive support, making the role all the more challenging. Given the demands, the champion must be a skilled communicator, able to liaise easily and comfortably with both executives and front-line employees. Ideally, your champion should provide full-time support to the implementation and be in a position to support the Scorecard's development and linkage to management processes on an ongoing basis. So vital is this role to the DNA of Scorecard success that David Norton has suggested, *"Selecting a program manager (champion) to lead the day-to-day activities of the Balanced Scorecard implementation is the single most important resource decision an organization can make."*[21]

In many ways your sponsor and champion lay the groundwork for the Balanced Scorecard by providing background, context, and concept knowledge. The ultimate responsibility of translating those raw materials into an actual Scorecard falls on the shoulders of your core *team members*. This group will bring esoteric knowledge of their business unit or functional department to the table and provide critical input on Scorecard objectives and measures that apply to their areas. They must also have the ability and opportunity to influence the executive to whom they report in an effort to keep the lines of communication open and flowing two ways. Team members bring challenging issues and questions to their leaders and also attempt to detect and deter any personal agendas that may be advanced to the detriment of the overall Scorecard effort. They balance the precarious issues of representing the best interests of their home area with the overall goal of creating an organization- or unit-wide Balanced Scorecard. As with all implementation participants, they must act as willing ambassadors of the Balanced Scorecard.

It may be easier to pry open the doors of Fort Knox than to have people devote time to this or any other effort, but you must demand a significant investment of that commodity, especially in the early stages of the implementation. Time will be required to complete homework assignments, attend workshops, review output, and liaise with superiors. Any potential team members who are not willing to provide this time must be viewed with caution. While they may carry valuable knowledge of their particular area, you must weigh this against the very negative lack of participation in the effort. Finally, to maximize the performance of team members, I suggest the team share a geographic location. Commitment to the team increases with co-location: having team members work in the same geographic place.[22] In my experience, teams that work "shoulder to shoulder" form stronger relationships both professionally and personally, and these bonds tend to strengthen the team's work products.

The Balanced Scorecard represents a major departure in performance management for many organizations. Strategy, not financial controls, dictates the firm's direction, and the Scorecard creates a powerful new language for employee change. However, like any transformation, this one has its share of roadblocks. I've found the inclusion of an *organizational change expert* on the team can mitigate many of the change-related issues that arise during the implementation. Any major change initiative will bring to the surface a number of concerns from those affected. For example, how will this change affect my routines and processes? What does the organization expect from me as a result of this change? Is this change even necessary? Your organizational change resource person can work with your team and projected users of the Balanced Scorecard to investigate the root causes of any concerns and design solutions to reduce and, it is hoped, eliminate any potentially serious threats to the Scorecard's success. The role is very important but not required as a full-time resource to the team. Draw the change expert in at regular intervals to review progress and issues. I urge you to pay close attention to this topic during your own implementation. You may feel it's "soft stuff," but it's not the technology or the methodology that can cause these initiatives to fail, it's the people every time! Exhibit 2.6 summarizes the roles and responsibilities of your Balanced Scorecard team.

Training Your Team

For the majority of employees within your organization, the team you assemble will be the embodiment of the Balanced Scorecard. If the members don't appear as knowledgeable and credible sources of information, you can be certain that skepticism for the initiative will increase. Some team members may come to the implementation with a background in performance management and Balanced Scorecard concepts, while for others, this may be their first exposure to these topics. Either way, to ensure a level playing field for the entire team, you have to invest heavily in up-front training. I'm a strong believer in the power of training to improve business results, and I'm not alone. Former U.S. Secretary of Labor Robert Reich has said that well-trained and dedicated employees are the only sustainable source of competitive strength. No less eloquent, but definitely more colorful, Tom

Exhibit 2.6   Balanced Scorecard Team Roles and Responsibilities

Role	Responsibilities
Executive sponsor	• Assumes ownership for the Balanced Scorecard implementation • Provides background information to the team on strategy and methodology • Maintains communication with senior management • Commits resources (both human and financial) to the team • Provides support and enthusiasm for the Balanced Scorecard throughout the organization
Balanced Scorecard champion	• Coordinates meetings; plans, tracks, and reports team results to all audiences • Provides thought leadership on the Balanced Scorecard methodology to the team • Ensures all relevant background material is available to the team • Provides feedback to the executive sponsor and senior management • Facilitates the development of an effective team through coaching and support
Team members	• Provide expert knowledge of business unit or functional operations • Inform and influence their respective senior executives • Act as Balanced Scorecard ambassadors within their unit or department • Act in the best interests of the business as a whole
Organizational change expert	• Increases awareness of organizational change issues • Investigates change-related issues affecting the Balanced Scorecard implementation • Works with the team to produce solutions mitigating change-related risks

Peters chimes in on the subject of employee training with this thought: *"Companies that don't encourage employee education of all kinds are dumb!"* Start your education efforts by preparing and distributing a comprehensive primer on the subjects of performance management and Balanced Scorecard. These topics are quite mature and a rich and abundant literature is available. I suggest you include the three seminal articles by Kaplan and Norton appearing in the *Harvard Business Review* from 1992 to 1996. The Scorecard originators have written additional articles on more advanced theories, which you may include as your implementation progresses. There are literally hundreds of other articles and white papers to choose from so narrow your search by including any documents that specifically reference your industry or implementation focus (e.g., corporate-wide versus business unit). A number of good books have been published on these subjects as well, and you should consider providing at least one to each of your team members. Your team will also benefit from attending one of the many excellent conferences on performance management and the Balanced Scorecard. Again, you have the opportunity to tailor your training with your implementation by choosing an event focused on your industry type or implementation plan. They provide a very valuable exchange of ideas, challenges, and solutions.

Forgive the pitch, but I strongly suggest your initial training session be conducted by a consultant or other expert in the Balanced Scorecard field. The last thing your fledgling initiative needs at this critical juncture is someone stammering at the front of the room grasping painfully to provide answers to commonly asked questions. A knowledgeable guide will typically structure a training agenda that includes these elements: background on performance management—drivers of this topic in the modern organizational world; Balanced Scorecard fundamentals including Strategy Maps and performance measures; success stories; and hands-on exercises to apply the learning.

Continuing with the theme of learning by doing, I suggest your team develop a Strategy Map and set of Balanced Scorecard measures specifically for the implementation. The purpose of this exercise is twofold. First a pragmatic reason: The Strategy Map will act as a powerful communication tool to the implementation's stakeholders, and performance measures serve to keep the team focused on the critical tasks at hand. Your team will require yardsticks to gauge their implementation progress, and the Balanced Scorecard provides a powerful means for accomplishing this task. Second, developing the objectives and measures gives team members a unique opportunity to engage in the mental gymnastics required to create an effective Scorecard. Who are our customers? What are their requirements? At what processes must we excel? What competencies do we require? These are all questions your team will be posing to others in your organization very soon, so it is perfectly appropriate that they go through the process themselves. Exhibit 2.7 presents a sample team Strategy Map and set of Balanced Scorecard measures. Notice that here the financial perspective represents a constraint (i.e., budget dollars for the initiative) rather than an overall goal as it would in most profit seeking enterprises. This is a good demonstration to the team of the Balanced Scorecard's flexibility.

Exhibit 2.7 Sample Balanced Scorecard for Your Implementation Team

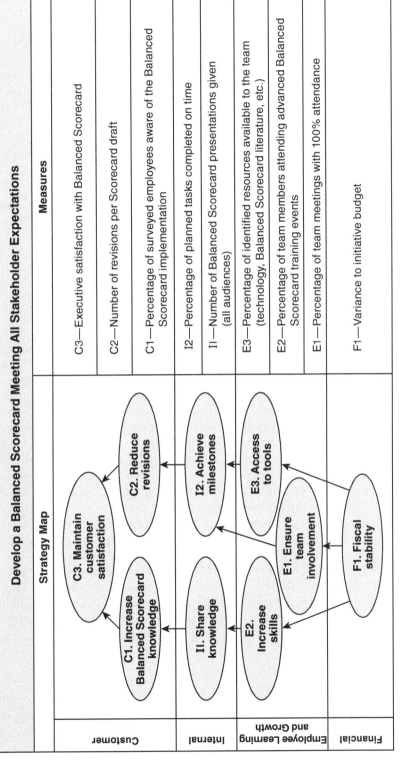

Develop a Balanced Scorecard Meeting All Stakeholder Expectations

Strategy Map	Measures
Customer	C3—Executive satisfaction with Balanced Scorecard
	C2—Number of revisions per Scorecard draft
	C1—Percentage of surveyed employees aware of the Balanced Scorecard implementation
Internal	I2—Percentage of planned tasks completed on time
	I1—Number of Balanced Scorecard presentations given (all audiences)
Employee Learning and Growth	E3—Percentage of identified resources available to the team (technology, Balanced Scorecard literature, etc.)
	E2—Percentage of team members attending advanced Balanced Scorecard training events
	E1—Percentage of team meetings with 100% attendance
Financial	F1—Variance to initiative budget

YOUR BALANCED SCORECARD DEVELOPMENT PLAN

From time to time my phone rings with a request to help turn around a troubled Balanced Scorecard implementation. As you know, challenges in executing change initiatives can stem from any number of sources, but in this large nonprofit the culprit was a distinct lack of planning. This agency was as unprepared from a planning standpoint as it was enthusiastic about the Scorecard. Unfortunately, the interest and exuberance they felt for the tool failed to compensate for their lack of organization. Virtually every meeting was slowed to a merciless crawl to discuss process questions. Team members and other stakeholders were naturally curious about the next steps in the process, but leaders of the Scorecard implementation had barely thought through the current meeting, let alone the entire implementation journey.[23] This lack of planning significantly slowed what could otherwise have been a very swift and successful implementation.

As with any major initiative, you'll require a carefully crafted development plan to guide the work of your Balanced Scorecard team. Every organization is different when it comes to planning and executing significant change efforts. Some feel a highly detailed plan that encompasses thousands of lines in Microsoft Project is the only way to capture all the necessary elements of the work. I recall arriving at the offices of one new client, barely completing introductions to the Scorecard team, and having a phone book–size plan thrust upon my lap. Others use less formal means, outlining only the most critical tasks and tracking them on MS Excel or Word documents. This section of the chapter outlines the key steps in developing your Balanced Scorecard based on experience and research. When creating your own plan, develop one that will be accepted by your team and sponsor based on the prevailing culture of your organization. Be sure to include all the important elements of the implementation. Whether you display them as big chunks or decompose them into 1,000 is up to you. One thing is certain: You'll be spending lots of time in meetings while developing your Balanced Scorecard. For some suggestions on maximizing this time see the box entitled "Meetings, Meetings, Meetings."

This entire book is a Balanced Scorecard development and implementation plan. After all, it is titled *Balanced Scorecard Step-by-Step*. The steps outlined next will present summary information of the task to help you prepare your campaign. The steps will be translated into the many tasks necessary for your success in subsequent chapters.

The Planning Phase

Before you begin the work of building a Balanced Scorecard, you must lay the groundwork for the implementation ahead. This chapter was written to help you do just that. To summarize, the planning phase includes these six steps, which we have discussed in this chapter:

Step 1   Develop a guiding rationale for your Balanced Scorecard.

Step 2   Determine the appropriate organizational unit.

Step 3   Secure executive sponsorship.

Step 4   Form and train your Balanced Scorecard team.

Step 5   Formulate your implementation plan.

Step 6   Develop a communication strategy and plan for your Balanced Scorecard implementation.

Clients sometimes tease us consultants because we tend to answer many questions with "It depends." But this response is often necessary since much of the work we perform is a function of many variables often beyond our control. It is with the caveat of "it depends" that I suggest timing for this and all phases of the implementation plan. If you have a full-time Balanced Scorecard champion leading the events just outlined, you should be able to accomplish them within four to six weeks. I urge you to take the necessary time to complete these actions successfully. Nothing is stopping you from developing a Balanced Scorecard without a communication plan or clear objectives for the implementation, but your efforts will be severely compromised without these stakes in the ground. The Employee Learning and Growth perspective of the Scorecard is the "enabler" of the other three perspectives. The planning phase of the initiative is similar in that it enables the development work to follow by clearly articulating what you plan to achieve, with whom, why, and how.

The Development Phase

Consider the steps presented next as a framework for your development of the Balanced Scorecard. As I noted earlier, every organization is unique and will want to emphasize different aspects of the Scorecard process. One of the many benefits of the Scorecard, one that has greatly contributed to its longevity and unabated growth, is its flexibility in adapting to the constraints of every organization. Take advantage of that flexibility when constructing your plan.

You will note that a number of executive workshops are built in throughout the process. The importance of executive consensus throughout the development phase cannot be overemphasized, hence the inclusion of these checkpoints. However, it may prove virtually impossible to convene your senior management team this frequently. If group meetings are not possible, ensure your team members are consistently reporting to their "home" executives with team progress and gathering feedback from the executive to use to guide the future direction of the team's work.

Step 1   Gather and distribute background material. The Balanced Scorecard is a tool that describes strategy. In order to fulfill this promise, your team must have ample access to background

Meetings, Meetings, Meetings

It seems we spend more time than ever in meetings, but is the time well spent? There's a tale about Will Rogers being invited to sit in on a committee meeting of an organization that ordinarily didn't permit the presence of outsiders. When the meeting was over Will remarked, *"I agreed to repeat nothing and I'll keep my promise. But I gotta admit, I heard nothing worth repeating."* You can't afford to have your Scorecard team members thinking, or worse yet, saying something similar after your meetings. And you will have meetings — recent studies suggest over 65% of Scorecard implementing organizations used work meetings to accomplish their tasks. Here are a few things you can do to maximize the effectiveness of your Balanced Scorecard meetings:

- *Determine your purpose:* Are you holding the meeting to share information, generate ideas, etc.?

- *Determine desired outcomes:* What do you want to accomplish during the session? Ensure everyone is aware of the desired outcomes when the meeting begins.

- *Evaluate attendance:* Nobody likes being invited to a meeting in which they have little to contribute. Determine who you need in attendance and simply distribute minutes to those who are not essential to achieving your outcomes.

- *Assign roles:* Determine in advance who will facilitate the meeting, who will act as the scribe, and who will fulfill the vital role of timekeeper.

- *Provide structured pre-work:* Provide attendees with relevant materials well in advance of the meeting and emphasize the importance of completing the pre-work.

- *Stay on time:* Get in the habit of starting and ending all meetings on time. Don't reward latecomers by reviewing what they've missed.

Several excellent articles and books have been written on the topic of effective meeting management. For a simple and pragmatic look at the subject I recommend Thomas Kayser's 1990 book, *Mining Group Gold* (Serif Publishing).

material on the organization's mission, vision, values, strategy, competitive position, and employee core competencies. Use internal resources such as your strategy and marketing groups to assist you with this effort. If you're publicly traded, many resources are at your disposal to garner information on past performance. Press releases, stories in the business media, analyst reports, and the like will all provide valuable information.

Step 2 *Provide Balanced Scorecard education.* At this point in the process, you have steeped your team in the fundamentals of the Balanced Scorecard but the tool still represents a black hole to much of your employee population, including the senior management team. Plug this gap early and effectively with a comprehensive Scorecard training session designed to outline the challenges that led you to select the Scorecard, fundamental principles of the model, success stories, and how you plan to guide the implementation. Invite as many people as you can comfortably fit into a venue for this first training session. This is no time to practice education snobbery; you need to win the hearts and minds of every employee, explaining to them what the Balanced Scorecard is all about.

Step 3 *Develop or confirm mission, values, vision, and strategy.* Based on the information gathered in Step 1, you should be able to generate a consensus of where your organization rests in terms of these critical items. If you do not have one or all of these Scorecard raw materials, you will have to work with your executive team to develop them. Chapter Three provides a detailed review of each of these elements of an effective Scorecard.

Step 4 *Conduct executive interviews.* We've previously stressed the importance of executive involvement in the Scorecard process, and it should come as no surprise that involving the entire executive team early in the process is an absolute must. During these interviews with senior management, the team will gather feedback on the organization's competitive position, key success factors for the future, and possible Scorecard objectives and measures. Chapter Four provides a guide for your executive interview process.

Step 5 *Develop your Strategy Map.* Armed with a solid working knowledge of the Balanced Scorecard's core principles, having reviewed copious amounts of background materials, and possessing years of combined industry knowledge and experience, your team is well prepared to construct the organization's Strategy Map of performance objectives. The simple one-page graphical representation of your strategy will describe and powerfully communicate to everyone in the company what is absolutely critical to your success in each of the four Balanced Scorecard perspectives. We'll immerse ourselves deeply in the development of Strategy Maps in Chapter Four.

Step 5a *Executive workshop.* Gain senior management consensus on the Strategy Map developed by the team. Capture and incorporate any recommendations from the executive group.

Step 5b *Gather employee feedback.* Ultimately, you expect your Balanced Scorecard to provide information that allows all employees to determine how their day-to-day actions link to the organization's strategic plan. Therefore, you need to poll your managers and employees to ensure that they feel you've captured in the Strategy Map the critical elements of value to your whole organization.

Step 6 *Develop performance measures.* Your team will translate each of the objectives on the Strategy Map into metrics you can track to provide insight into the execution of your strategy and establish accountability throughout the company. Chapter Five is devoted to the topic of performance measures.

Step 6a *Executive workshop.* The process begins to become real when actual hard-hitting metrics are laid on the table for executive review. It is vital that all members of the executive team commit themselves to the measures brought forward.

Step 6b *Gather employee feedback.* This is an optional step. While you desire employee feedback at every turn of the Scorecard wheel, ultimately the highest-level performance measures must be owned by the senior management and therefore you would expect their stickiness factor to be off the charts. Consider using this opportunity to explain to your staff precisely why the particular measures you plan to use were chosen.

Step 7 *Establish targets and prioritize initiatives.* Without a target for each of your measures, you'll have no way of knowing whether improvement efforts are yielding acceptable results. The data from your metrics provide you with only half the picture. A target gives meaning to measure results by, affording a point of comparison. However, setting targets may be among the most challenging aspects of your entire implementation. Many organizations have little actual practice in or techniques for establishing meaningful performance targets. Additionally, all measures should be accompanied by initiatives designed to bring the targets to fruition. Chapter Six explores these topics in greater depth, providing advice on setting targets and methods to prioritize competing initiatives.

Step 8 *Gather data for your first Balanced Scorecard report.* Dare to be bold and proclaim that within 60 days of developing your performance measures, you will be conducting your first management meeting with the Balanced Scorecard at the helm. To do this will, of course, require gathering the data necessary to supply that initial report. You may be thinking "We'll never have all the data!" and you are probably correct since most new Scorecard adopters will be missing at least a portion of the data for performance metrics as they ramp up their reporting efforts. However, don't let that stop you from the many significant benefits that can accrue from discussing the measures you do have: focus, alignment, and improved resource allocation decisions to name but a few.

Step 9 Those rockin' granddads the Rolling Stones, the elder statesmen of music royalty, recently made a stop on their world tour here in San Diego and I would love to have seen them in action but as the concert date loomed ever closer did I take any action? No, I just kept saying to myself, "I'd love to see them." Earth to Paul: buy a ticket! There was absolutely nothing in the way of me wailing my heart out to "Satisfaction" with the exception of that tiniest of details, but for some reason I let the opportunity slip. Some Scorecard implementing organizations make the same mistake by talking a great game about the alignment and focus they are going to derive from the tool but failing to achieve it because they simply refuse to place the Scorecard at the center of their management meeting and reporting agenda. Repeat after me: To execute strategy, we must discuss strategy. Getting to your first Balanced Scorecard report should be the number one priority in the initial stages of your implementation. Unlike me with the Stones, who, knowing them will probably be touring for another twenty years, you don't have the luxury of time so make reporting a high priority on your list.

Step 10 *Develop the ongoing Balanced Scorecard implementation plan.* The steps just outlined will get you from point zero to the development of a Balanced Scorecard measurement tool. I stress the word "measurement." The remainder of this book will focus on the evolution of that *measurement* tool to the cornerstone of your organization's *management system.* Later chapters provide you with the tools for linking the Balanced Scorecard to all key management processes within the firm. Cascading accountability for results to lower levels of the organization, linking budgeting and planning to strategic aims, and aligning reward systems are all vital operations that can be positively impacted by the presence of an effective Balanced Scorecard.

Getting from Step 1 in the planning phase to Step 10 in the development phase can take anywhere from 4 to 12 months—I've seen both. The amount of time your organization expends on the implementation will *depend* (there is that word again!) on a number of factors: commitment of the executive team, allocation of resources to the project, size and complexity of the organization for which a Scorecard is being built, and organizational readiness for a change of this magnitude. Exhibit 2.8 presents a possible timeline for both the planning and development phases, with special emphasis on the word "possible." As already discussed, your timing will be impacted by several factors and may not follow the linear approach suggested in the exhibit.

COMMUNICATING THE BALANCED SCORECARD

My wife says I am just plain nosy, always asking people questions about themselves, but I ascribe my inquisitive nature to my mother and her Scottish heritage. Whether it's nature or nurture, there is no denying the fact I like to ask questions, which comes in very handy when you make your living as a management consultant. One question that invariably comes up when I meet someone for the first time is "What do you do?" Not surprisingly, after filling me in on their profession, most people ask about my job. When I tell them consulting in the area of Balanced Scorecard is my vocational choice, I get as many quizzical looks and as I do nods of recognition. Not everyone is aware of the Balanced Scorecard, a fact that presents opportunities for me as a consultant and both opportunities and challenges for you in your efforts to drive acceptance of the tool.

At this point it's a safe assumption that many people in your organization may not have even heard of the Balanced Scorecard and your reading thus far in this book qualifies you as the leading authority of Scorecard knowledge. Even those who do profess some familiarity with the concept may be completely skeptical of its ability to effect any real change. And it's very important to remember that the Balanced Scorecard is a tool of change. Most change efforts struggle to succeed, with lack of communication being a chief cause of the potential failure. Professor and author John Kotter has said, *"Without credible communication, and a lot of it, employees' hearts and minds are never captured."*[24] Most organizations fail to heed this valuable advice, and their change efforts are the worse for it. These challenges must be met head on during your implementation efforts if you expect employees to begin using this tool to make real business decisions. A carefully constructed communication strategy and plan will prove to be a great ally in the struggle to enlighten all employees and win support throughout your Balanced Scorecard development process.

Exhibit 2.8 Balanced Scorecard Implementation Timeline

Week	1	2	3	4	5	6	7	8	9	10	11	12	13	14	15	16	17	18	19	20
Planning Phase																				
Step 1. Develop a guiding rationale for your Balanced Scorecard.	▮																			
Step 2. Determine the appropriate organizational unit.		▮	▮																	
Step 3. Secure executive sponsorship.	▮																			
Step 4. Form and train your Balanced Scorecard team.			▮	▮																
Step 5. Formulate your implementation plan.				▮																
Step 6. Develop a communication strategy and plan.					▮															
Development Phase																				
Step 1. Gather and distribute background material.						▮														
Step 2. Provide Balanced Scorecard education.							▮													
Step 3. Develop or confirm mission, values, vision, and strategy.							▮													
Step 4. Conduct executive interviews.								▮												
Step 5. Develop strategy map.									▮											
Step 5a. Executive workshop.										▮										
Step 5b. Gather employee feedback.											▮									
Step 6. Develop performance measures.											▮	▮								
Step 6a. Executive workshop.													▮							
Step 6b. Gather employee feedback.														▮						
Step 7. Establish targets and prioritize initiatives.														▮						
Step 8. Gather data for your first Balanced Scorecard report.																▮				
Step 9. Hold your first Balanced Scorecard meeting.																			▮	
Step 10. Develop an ongoing implementation plan.																				▮

63

As you read this you may be thinking: "Maybe I should skip on to the next section. After all, we really haven't done much on the Scorecard to this point, so what would we communicate? Nobody really needs to know anything yet; we'll wait until we have more to say." These are practically verbatim quotes from actual clients of mine. I can virtually guarantee that people are already aware of the Scorecard initiative, despite your lack of formal communication. For this awareness, you can blame—or thank, depending on your point of view—that most reliable of information sources, the grapevine. Every day and week that goes by with no information coming forth on the implementation is fostering mistrust among your employee base. You're about to invest tremendous effort into building a new management tool; don't let a lack of communication explaining the concept and the benefits it will produce derail that effort. Let's look at the elements of an effective communication plan you can use during your Balanced Scorecard implementation.

Objectives for Your Communication Plan

The starting point of your communication planning endeavors should be the consideration of a vision and objectives. Ask yourself why you are launching a communication plan and what you expect to achieve as a result. Is your primary focus on educating your key stakeholder groups or in winning the support of front-line employees? At Nova Scotia Power, a Canadian electrical utility, the Balanced Scorecard team used this vision to guide their communication efforts: *"To present the concepts of the Balanced Scorecard to the key constituents involved in both sponsoring and providing input to the implementation, and to provide all involved with regular updates regarding the team's progress during the implementation."* This simple statement provided the basis for all future communication efforts during the rollout. Your objectives should represent the unique attributes of your implementation and the culture of your organization, but in general most organizations include at least some of these ideas:

- Build awareness of the Balanced Scorecard at all levels of the organization.
- Provide education on key Balanced Scorecard concepts to all audiences.
- Generate the engagement and commitment of key stakeholders in the implementation.
- Encourage participation in the process.
- Generate enthusiasm for the Balanced Scorecard.
- Ensure team results are disseminated rapidly and effectively.

Establishing objectives for the communication plan will often lead you to the development of a theme or metaphor you can use to creatively "brand" your implementation. Some people like slogans and themes, others think they're hokey and convey little of value. Whatever your opinion, there is little doubt that themes are colorful and often memorable. And "memorability" is a huge weapon in the arsenal of communication. For Bridgeport Hospital, the communication theme was "Journey to Destination 2005," using the analogy of a bus trip to the future. Highways represented the hospital's five strategic imperatives, landmarks represented the objectives, and mile markers represented the performance measures.[25] Whatever phrase you choose should reflect your organization, your culture, and your aspirations.[26]

Elements of the Communication Plan

The simplest way to devise your plan is by utilizing the "W5" approach: who, what, when, where, and why. Each is discussed next in the context of communication planning.

- *Purpose/message (what/why).* This describes the information content defined in the plan. All communication plans will contain key messages that must accompany information deliveries. Your Balanced Scorecard initiative may have a number of key messages, including: how the Scorecard aligns with strategy implementation, the role of the Balanced Scorecard in relation to other change initiatives, or the new management philosophy represented by the Scorecard. Other content defined in the communication plan may include timelines, development status, issues, and education. Since the roles and responsibilities of your audience groups vary, the information messages should be tailored toward the target's role.

- *Audience (who).* This refers to the specific individuals or groups identified who will require messages during the implementation. Depending on the size and scope of your rollout, audiences will vary. However, plan to include your senior management team, steering committee if you're using one, middle management group, all employees, and your Balanced Scorecard team.

- *Frequency (when).* The information needs of your audience groups will dictate the amount of communication you provide, but I encourage you to do more than you think is necessary to ensure you penetrate the attention zone of an often-overwhelmed employee base. As authors Charan and Bossidy put it: *"It takes repetition, sometimes ad nauseam, to persuade everybody in an organization that the leader means what she's saying and that what she's saying needs to be taken seriously."*[27] Jack Welch, an executive who knows a thing or two about what it takes to make meaningful change take root inside a company, shares this graphic commentary on the frequency of communication: *"There were times I talked about the company's direction so many times in one day that I was completely sick of hearing it myself. But I realized the message was always new to someone. And so, you keep on repeating it."*[28] Simply put, do not risk losing the support and enthusiasm of any audience by limiting the amount of information they receive.

- *Delivery vehicle (where/how).* This describes the method chosen to broadcast the message and will depend on the needs of the audience. With today's technologies, choices of delivery vehicles are really just a function of the limits of your imagination. Consider any or all of these as possibilities: face-to-face meetings, group presentations, project plans, newsletters, workshops, brown bag lunches, video presentations, message kits, e-mails, news bulletins, raffles and contests, pay-stub messages, demonstrations, road shows, town hall meetings. Many organizations will create internal Web sites promoting the Scorecard and providing educational opportunities. The U.S. Army, which dubbed its Scorecard implementation the Strategic Readiness System (SRS), used such a tool; it was accessible around the world and contained a vast library of information resources. The army supplemented this online channel with print articles about the initiative, an annual conference on the topic, a newsletter, and periodic conference calls.[29]

- *Communicator (who).* This is the individual or group responsible for the content and distribution of the message. Again, the communicator will vary, based on the message and the needs of the audience. For example, more formal communications will normally emanate from the executive sponsor, while a member of the Scorecard team may write newsletter articles.

What you decide to communicate is ultimately up to you, but there is one thing you definitely should include in your communication plan: a glossary of terms. Virtually every organization I have worked for or with has used slightly different terminology to describe performance management terms. An "initiative" in one company might be known as an "objective" in another. "Critical success factors" in your shop may go by "key performance indicators" elsewhere. Semantics are important because in today's modern organization, many employees — knowledge workers — may have gone through a performance management initiative at another company using an entirely different vernacular. You want your Balanced Scorecard to foster teamwork, cooperation, and sharing of information. That will prove exceedingly difficult if your employees are speaking a different language from your implementation team. One organization I know of was nearing the end of a Balanced Scorecard initiative when it became clear that the Scorecard team was using terms that held very different meanings in the minds of the managers. At that late hour the team had to embark on an extensive campaign to educate the entire management group on the vocabulary of the rollout and ensure they shared common goals.

One final thought: Don't take the success of your communication efforts for granted. To ensure that communication activities are reaching targeted audiences, a communication effectiveness measurement effort is highly recommended. Survey target audiences regularly throughout the process, and assess your efforts on these criteria:

- *No contact.* The person has not heard of the Balanced Scorecard implementation.
- *Awareness.* The person has heard about the initiative but doesn't know what it is.
- *Conceptual understanding.* The person understands the Balanced Scorecard and any individual effects.
- *Tactical understanding.* The person understands both the personal and organizational effects of the Balanced Scorecard.
- *Acceptance.* The person will support the Balanced Scorecard and the changes it will bring.

A simplified communication plan is shown in Exhibit 2.9.

KEEP IN MIND

In his latest book, *The 8th Habit,* management scholar Stephen Covey tells the story of a certain species of Chinese bamboo. When you plant the bamboo, you see nothing for four years. Just a little shoot out of the ground and that's it. You weed, water, cultivate, nurture, and do everything you can to stimulate its growth, but you see nothing. In the fifth year, this particular species of Chinese bamboo grows to 80 feet. In its initial stages, all of the growth went underground in the root. Then, once it had its roots in place, all of the growth went aboveground and was visible.[30] The topics we covered in this chapter resemble the initial growth of the Chinese bamboo; we are nurturing the roots of your Balanced Scorecard implementation to ensure that, when it blossoms, it will have the strength to lead your organization for years to come. And the good news is you won't have to wait four years to see results. Keep these points in mind:

- The first question you must answer when developing a Balanced Scorecard is "Why?" A guiding rationale for your implementation ensures focus during the rollout and beyond, enhances communication efforts, and builds bridges between the work of alignment among the Scorecard and key management processes.
- Organizations embarking on a Balanced Scorecard project often assume the logical starting point for their efforts is a high-level corporate Scorecard. This may or may not be the case. We examined seven criteria for making the decision of where to begin your Scorecard effort: strategy, sponsorship, need, support of key managers, scope, data, and resources.
- If there is one undeniable fact of organizational life, it is that no initiative will prosper or even survive without executive sponsorship. The

Exhibit 2.9 Simplified Communication Plan for Your Balanced Scorecard Project

Audience	Purposes	Frequency	Delivery Vehicle	Communicator
Executive team	• Gain commitment • Remove obstacles • Report progress • Prevent surprises	Biweekly	Direct contact	Executive sponsor
Management	• Convey purpose • Explain concepts • Report progress • Gain commitment	Biweekly	• E-mail • Management meetings • Articles	Champion/team members
All employees	• Convey purpose • Introduce concepts • Eliminate misconceptions • Report progress	Monthly	• E-mail • Newsletters • Town hall meetings	Scorecard team members
Project team	• Track progress • Assign tasks • Review expectations	Weekly	• Team meeting • Status memos	Champion

Balanced Scorecard is no exception. You must find a willing and able senior executive who will act as an ambassador for your implementation. To secure executive sponsorship, you must find a senior manager whose values are consistent with those of the Balanced Scorecard ideology, demonstrate the results this tool can offer, and educate your senior team on the subtleties of the methodology.

- No single individual in your organization holds the necessary information to build an effective Balanced Scorecard. A group effort is required. Your team must include an executive sponsor, champion, work group members, and possibly an organizational change expert. For your team to construct an effective Scorecard, members must possess the requisite knowledge of this tool. Team training may consist of literature reviews, conferences, and case studies.

- A carefully conceived implementation plan consistent with your organization's culture and planning methods is a must for Balanced Scorecard success. Most Balanced Scorecard plans will encompass two distinct phases: planning and development.

- Because the Balanced Scorecard is primarily an agent of change, it is critical to craft a communication strategy and plan. Objectives of the plan may include: building awareness, providing education on key concepts, generating engagement and commitment, encouraging participation, generating enthusiasm, and providing results to interested parties. The "W5" approach of who, what, when, where, and why can be used to draft the elements of the plan.

Notes

1. Marcus Buckingham, *The One Thing You Need to Know* (New York: Free Press, 2005).
2. William Bridges, *Managing Transitions* (Cambridge, MA: Perseus Books, 2003), p. 63.
3. Jeanie Daniel Duck, *The Change Monster* (New York: Three Rivers Press, 2001), p. 51.
4. Paul R. Niven, *Balanced Scorecard Diagnostics: Maintaining Maximum Performance* (Hoboken, NJ: John Wiley & Sons, 2005), p. 30.
5. Ibid.
6. Lauren Keller Johnson, "Sharpening Strategic Focus at Canon U.S.A.," *Balanced Scorecard Report* (July–August 2005): 7.
7. Michael R. Vitale and Sarah C. Mavrinac, "How Effective Is Your Performance Measurement System?" *Management Accounting* (August 1995): 43.
8. Janice A. Klein, "Why Supervisors Resist Employee Involvement," *Harvard Business Review* (September–October 1984).
9. Robert S. Kaplan and David P. Norton, *The Strategy Focused Organization* (Boston: Harvard Business School Press, 2000).

10. Robert S. Kaplan and David P. Norton, "The Strategy-Focused Organization," *Harvard Business School Press* (Boston, MA, 2001).

11. Robert Simons and Antonio Davila, "How High Is Your Return on Management?" *Harvard Business Review* (January–February 1998): 70.

12. Ram Charan and Larry Bossidy, *Confronting Reality: Doing What Matters to Get Things Done* (New York: Crown Business, 2004), p. 195.

13. Rebecca Macfie, "Six of Our Top Chief Executive Officers Tell the *Independent* How They Stay at the Top," *Independent Business Weekly* (April 2001): 8.

14. Best Practices Benchmarking Report, *Developing the Balanced Scorecard* (Chapel Hill, NC: Best Practices, LLC, 1999).

15. Laura Downing, "Progress Report on the Balanced Scorecard: A Global Users Survey," *Balanced Scorecard Report* (November–December 2000): 7–9.

16. Harold L. Sirkin, Perry Keenan, and Alan Jackson, "The Hard Side of Change Management," *Harvard Business Review* (October 2005): 108–118.

17. Ibid.

18. Mark A. Huselid, Richard W. Beatty, and Brian E. Becker, "A Players or A Positions?" *Harvard Business Review* (December 2005): 110–117.

19. Bridges, *Managing Transitions,* p.19.

20. Best Practices Benchmarking Report, *Developing the Balanced Scorecard.*

21. David P. Norton and Randall H. Russell, "Mobilize Change through Executive Leadership," *Balanced Scorecard Report* (March–April 2005): 4.

22. Jim Billington, "The Three Essentials of an Effective Team," *Harvard Management Update,* 1997.

23. Paul R. Niven, *Balanced Scorecard Diagnostics: Maintaining Maximum Performance* (Hoboken, NJ: John Wiley & Sons, 2005), p. 58.

24. John P. Kotter, *Leading Change* (Boston: Harvard Business School Press, 1996).

25. Andra Gumbus, Bridget Lyons, and Dorothy E. Bellhouse, "Journey to Destination 2005," *Strategic Finance* (August 2002).

26. Paul R. Niven, *Balanced Scorecard Step-by-Step for Government and Nonprofit Agencies* (Hoboken, NJ: John Wiley & Sons, 2003), p. 93.

27. Charan and Bossidy, *Confronting Reality,* p. 236.

28. Jack Welch with Suzy Welch, *Winning* (New York: Harper Business, 2005), p. 68.

29. Robert S. Kaplan and David P. Norton, "The Office of Strategy Management," *Harvard Business Review* (October 2005): 73–80.

30. Stephen R. Covey, *The 8th Habit* (New York: Free Press, 2004), p. 327.

CHAPTER 3

Mission, Values, Vision, and Strategy

Roadmap for Chapter Three Anyone who has ever built a new house knows there are many things that must take place long before you ever cut a board or swing a hammer. First, in your mind's eye, you would conceive of the house you'd like to live in and work with an architect to devise the plans that bring your images to life. Once you have the blueprint in place, you can begin to assemble the materials you'll need to construct your house: lumber, nails, plaster, pipes, and wires, among a host of other items. Only then can you erect a sturdy house that will withstand the elements and provide you long-lasting comfort and enjoyment. Developing our Balanced Scorecard is not unlike this exercise. In the last chapter we described the importance of planning your efforts, setting objectives, gaining executive support, determining where to begin, developing your team, and communicating your implementation. Once you've completed those steps, you have a blueprint ready for your Scorecard. Like our hypothetical house, you're now ready to gather your raw materials and start building your Balanced Scorecard. This chapter describes the raw materials you'll need to construct a solid and sustainable Balanced Scorecard that will stand up to the volatile weather of the business environment.

The components of an effective Balanced Scorecard are your organization's mission, core values, vision, and strategy. In this chapter we'll examine each of these building blocks in detail and consider what they are, how to determine their effectiveness, review tips on developing them, and see their vital linkage to the Balanced Scorecard. As a Scorecard practitioner, you'll need to determine if the Balanced Scorecard you've developed is truly aligned with your mission, values, vision, and strategy (see Exhibit 3.1). This chapter equips you with the tools to make that critical determination.

MISSION STATEMENTS

I decided to write this book to offer my experience with the Balanced Scorecard. But, as is always the case in life, the more you give, the more

Exhibit 3. 1   The Balanced Scorecard Translates Mission, Values, Vision, and Strategy

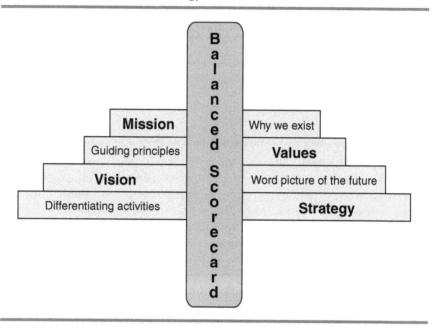

you get. Crafting these pages has provided me with endless learning opportunities, and this chapter is a great example. Words like "mission," "values," "vision," and "strategy" are business standards, widely accepted and (I thought) well understood. When I embarked on my research for this chapter, I was surprised to discover the many and varied definitions of these terms, particularly "mission" and "vision." Apparently I'm not the only one facing some confusion. In *The Dilbert Principle,* oft-quoted business sage Scott Adams has this to say about mission and vision: *"The first step in developing a vision statement is to lock the managers in a room and have them debate what is meant by a vision statement, and how exactly it differs from a mission statement. These are important questions, because one wrong move and the employees will start doing 'vision' things when they should be doing 'mission' things and before long it will be impossible to sort it all out."*[1] A former General Electric chief executive, perhaps after reading that, in a similar vein once said: *"Mission and values have got to be among the most abstract, overused, misunderstood words in business."*[2] Let's heed Scott's advice and sort this whole thing out before confusion reigns. What follows is my thinking on mission, values, vision, and strategy based on my experience and the work of many writers, theoreticians, and practitioners.

What Is a Mission Statement?

A mission statement defines the core purpose of the organization—why it exists. The mission examines the raison d'être for the organization beyond simply increasing shareholder wealth and reflects employees' motivations for engaging in the company's work. David Packard captured the essence of mission very well in a 1960 speech to Hewlett-Packard employees: *"A group of people get together and exist as an institution that we call a company so they are able to accomplish something collectively that they could not accomplish separately—they make a contribution to society, . . . do something which is of value."*[3] The mission attempts to capture the contribution and value that Packard so eloquently describes, illuminating the core purpose that draws us to our work and inspires our very best.

Unlike strategies and goals, which may be achieved over time, you never really fulfill your mission. It acts as a beacon for your work, constantly pursued but never quite reached. Consider your mission to be the compass by which you guide your organization. In today's hectic (to put it very euphemistically) business world, you need a star to steer by and your mission should provide just that.

Effective Mission Statements

Let's look at some characteristics of effective mission statements. These attributes should assist you if your organization does not currently use a mission statement. If you do have a mission, check it against these items to judge its effectiveness.

- *Inspire change.* While your mission doesn't change, it should inspire great change within your organization. Since the mission can never be fully realized, it should propel your organization forward, stimulating change and positive growth. Take, for example, the mission of 3M, which is *"To solve unsolved problems innovatively."* Such a simple and powerful mission is sure to lead 3M into many new and interesting fields as it attempts to solve the innumerable problems we face. Wal-Mart states its mission as *"Give ordinary folks the chance to buy the same things as rich people."* Retailing may look vastly different in 100 years than it does today, but you can bet that ordinary folks will still want the opportunity to acquire the same things as rich people!

- *Long term in nature.* Mission statements should be written to last 100 years or more. While strategies and plans will surely change during that time period, the mission should remain the bedrock of the organization, serving as the stake in the ground for all future decisions.

- *Easily understood and communicated.* Nobody would argue that our modern organizational world is awash in jargon. Buzzwords abound in offices around the world as we invent new and curious terms and phrases. While many people react negatively to buzzwords, some say they simply represent a sign of *"words in action and a culture on the move."*[4] Regardless of your opinion on the role of buzzwords in our modern life, they really have no place in a mission statement. Your mission should be written in plain language that is easily understood by all readers. A compelling and memorable mission is one that reaches people on a visceral level, speaks to them and motivates them to serve the organization's purpose. You can actually consider your mission a valuable recruiting aid in attracting like-minded individuals to take up your cause.

Developing Your Mission Statement

The first question to consider when writing your mission statement is: Who should be involved in the process? There are different schools of thought on this subject. Some argue the mission should be crafted by the CEO or some other executive, sent out for comments and revisions, and finalized without any meetings or committee involvement. Others believe the mission statement, with its inherent focus on capturing the hearts and minds of all employees, cannot possibly be drafted without employee involvement. Being the good fence-sitting consultant I am, I'll come down somewhere on the middle in this debate. In Chapter Two we discussed the importance of executive sponsorship for the Balanced Scorecard. We noted that executives were critical to the process of developing the Scorecard because most middle managers lack the overall perspective demanded in creating the document. Mission statements are similar in that you require the broad and high-level thinking of an executive to consider the spectrum of alternatives facing the organization. Charismatic leaders often possess the enviable ability of crystallizing the organization's place and future goals in compelling terms to be shared with all employees. Don't deny yourself the opportunity of gleaning your executives' wisdom and foresight. At the same time, you should also involve as many people as possible in reviewing the draft mission statement. Let employees at every level of the organization have the chance to kick the tires of this most important of documents. The mission must serve to galvanize everyone toward an exciting future, and without involvement in the process, commitment will be difficult if not impossible to acquire.

A very effective method for developing your mission is based on a concept known as the "5 Whys" developed by Collins and Porras.[5] Start with a descriptive statement, such as "We make X products or deliver Y services." Then ask: "Why is this important?" five times. A few "whys" into this exercise, and you'll begin to see your true mission emerging. This process works for virtually any product or service organization. A waste management company could easily move from "We pick up trash" to "We contribute to a stronger environment by creatively solving waste management issues" after just a couple of rounds. A market research organization might transition from "Provide the best market research data" to "Contribute to customers' success by helping them understand their markets." Notice that with each round of "why," you'll move closer and closer to your true reason for being as an organization, to the value or contribution you strive to create or make. This process is so powerful because it builds on the notion of abstraction. I define "abstraction" as moving to a different level, leaving characteristics out. We humans are great abstractors; just ask anyone about themselves and chances are the first thing you'll hear is "I'm an accountant" or "I work in high tech." We tend to let these descriptions or abstractions define us, and we perceive the world around us through that particular lens. Why not move down the abstraction ladder a bit and see yourself as a husband or wife, neighbor, amateur scientist, movie lover, and so on? Doing so opens up a world of possibility in our lives. Similarly, most organizations focus intently on the microdetails of their operations, failing to see the bigger issues that underlie their purpose. The "5 Whys" forces us to abstract to different levels, thereby leaving behind the myriad specific characteristics of our organizational being and discovering our true meaning. Exhibit 3.2 shares the mission statements of a number of organizations.

Why a Mission Is "Mission-Critical" to the Balanced Scorecard The Balanced Scorecard was not designed to act as an isolated management

Exhibit 3.2   Sample Mission Statements

Merck	To preserve and improve human life
American Institute of Certified Public Accountants	To provide members with the resources, information, and leadership that enable them to provide valuable services in the highest professional manner to benefit the public as well as employees and clients
3M	To solve unsolved problems innovatively
Wal-Mart	To give ordinary folk the chance to buy the same things as rich people
Walt Disney	To make people happy
Hewlett-Packard	To make technical contributions for the advancement and welfare of humanity
Marriott	To make people away from home feel that they are among friends and are really wanted
Sony	To experience the joy of advancing and applying technology for the benefit of the public
Mary Kay	To give unlimited opportunity to women
Cargill	To improve the standard of living around the world

tool; instead, it is part of an integrated approach to examining our business and providing us with a means to evaluate our overall success. Above all, the Scorecard is a tool designed to offer faithful translation. What does it translate? The Scorecard decodes our mission, values, vision, and strategy into performance objectives and measures in each of the four Scorecard perspectives. Translating this "DNA" of our organization with the Balanced Scorecard ensures all employees are aligned with, and working toward, the mission. This represents one of the great values of the Scorecard system. The mission is where we begin our translating efforts. A well-developed Balanced Scorecard ensures the measures we track are consistent with our ultimate aspirations and guides the hearts and minds of employees in making the right choices.

When developing objectives on the Strategy Map and performance measures, you must critically examine them in the context of the mission you've written for the organization to be certain they are consistent with that purpose. Would a measure of "market share of the richest 1 percent of Americans" make sense in light of Wal-Mart's mission? Probably not; in fact, it would reflect a fundamental shift in purpose. While Wal-Mart welcomes all shoppers, and I'm sure many price-conscious wealthy people shop there, it relies on a strategy of low prices to attract those who aren't "rich." 3M wants to "solve unsolved problems innovatively." If it develops a measure and target on its Scorecard to cut research, development, and training, would that be consistent with 3M's core purpose?

You can build and implement a Balanced Scorecard without a mission statement for your organization. It would still contain a mix of financial and nonfinancial measures linked together through a series of cause-and-effect relationships, but consider the tremendous value and alignment you create when developing a Scorecard that truly translates your mission. If you do have a mission, make certain the Balanced Scorecard you develop is true to the core essence reflected in the document. If you don't have a mission statement, I would strongly encourage you to develop one and see for yourself the focus and alignment you create when translating your mission into a Balanced Scorecard framework.

VALUES

What Are Values?

Competitive advantage can be derived from any number of sources in today's organizations. Superior strategies, innovative products, and exemplary customer service are just some of the many ways in which organizations seek to differentiate themselves from the pack. But for some organizations, the way they behave is what makes the difference and provides the source of their strength. We've all experienced situations that demonstrate this —

perhaps a hotel employee providing us with a missing essential from our travel bags or an amusement park worker who showed up to help at the exact moment before the combination of stress and joy (which only an amusement park can bring) became too much for us to bear. Chances are these acts didn't result from reading the latest management guru's book or from a desire to get a bigger bonus. No, they simply represent the way things get done at that organization: in other words, its values.

Values are the timeless principles that guide an organization. They represent the deeply held beliefs within the organization and are demonstrated through the day-to-day behaviors of all employees. An organization's values make an open proclamation about how it expects everyone to behave. In *Built to Last*, authors Collins and Porras suggest that visionary organizations decide for themselves what values to hold, independent of the current environment, competitive requirements, or management fads. They quote former Johnson & Johnson CEO Ralph Larsen on values: *"The core values embodied in our credo might be a competitive advantage, but that is not why we have them. We have them because they define for us what we stand for, and we would hold them even if they became a competitive disadvantage in certain situations."*[6] "What we stand for" is an important part of this quote. No universal set of right or wrong values exists; instead, each organization must determine or discover the core values that comprise its essence and hold importance to those within it. Organizations tend to have a small number of core values that truly reflect their very essence. A large number may indicate confusion between values and practices. While practices, processes, and strategies should change over time in answer to the many challenges that come our way, we expect values to remain the same, providing an enduring source of strength and wisdom.

In many organizations the core values represent the strong personal beliefs of the founder or CEO: for example, Walt Disney's belief in imagination and wholesomeness. Just as we would expect parents to exert great influence over the developing values of their children, it is the organization's leaders who set the tone for values within an organization. Therefore, leaders must constantly strive not only to develop appropriate values, but more important they must consistently mirror the values in their words and actions. As the Swiss Philosopher Henri Amiel once said, *"Every man's conduct is an unspoken sermon that is forever preaching to others."*[7]

Values-Driven Organizations

In reality, all organizations have a set of values. Author Richard Barrett recognizes this fact but suggests that the declaration of the underlying values is key: *"The critical issue is whether these values are conscious, shared, and lived, or remain unconscious, and undiscussed. When values are not defined, the culture of the organization is subject to the vagaries of the personality of the leader."*[8] Barrett goes on to suggest that if leaders are operating from self-interest, then the organization will do the same. However, if the personality of the leader is focused in higher levels of consciousness, then the organization will operate for the common good. We often associate positive values with the common good, holding certain beliefs and operating on them in the hope that our actions will result not only in economic profits but the improvement of society as well. Is there room in our modern economy, which often appears rather cutthroat, to say the least, for an organization to do well by doing good, living its values? Some organizations are proving that is in fact the case.

J. W. Marriott has noted, *"The concept of making employees feel really good about themselves seems to be missing from many companies' philosophies."*[9] He understands that if employees feel confident and content, generally happy with themselves and the job, this positive attitude will translate to better service for guests. Marriott has determined that being good to people is not only the right thing to do for employees but makes good business sense. For that reason, *"Take care of Marriott people and they will take care of Marriott guests"* is one of the Marriott hotel chain's core values.

Another great example of running a company with values at the helm comes from the East Coast of the United States: Tom's of Maine. Starting with a $5,000 loan from a friend, Tom and Kate Chappell began making products for home use that would not harm the environment. Beginning with the first nonphosphate liquid laundry detergent, they soon built a multimillion-dollar business supplying environmentally friendly personal care and wellness products. Founder Tom Chappell says, *"Your personal values can be integrated with managing for all the traditional goals of business—making money, expanded market share, increased profits, retained earnings, and sales growth. Not only can your personal beliefs be brought to work, they can work for you."*[10] The commitment to using natural ingredients in its products and serving customers and employees guides every decision made at the company. Tom's Statement of Beliefs, which serves as the company's core values, is shown in Exhibit 3.3.

A final example of values-driven organizations is provided by The Body Shop, an international skin and hair care retailer. The company was founded by Anita Roddick, who in 1976 began retailing homemade, naturally inspired products with minimal packaging. The organization rapidly evolved from one small shop in Brighton on the South Coast of England, to a worldwide network of shops, which now makes a sale every 0.4 seconds worldwide. The Body Shop has always believed that business is primarily about human relationships with its stakeholders: employees, franchisees, customers, communities, suppliers, and shareholders. The company continues to lead the way for businesses to use their voice for social and environmental change. Vocal against animal testing and the destruction of natural resources, The Body Shop also provides support to communities in need through sustained trading relationships, not exploitation. Not content to simply state its values, The Body Shop has put them to the test by

Exhibit 3.3   Tom's of Maine Statement of Beliefs

➤ WE BELIEVE that human beings and nature have inherent worth and deserve our respect.

➤ WE BELIEVE in products that are safe, effective, and made of natural ingredients.

➤ WE BELIEVE that our company and our products are unique and worthwhile, and that we can sustain these genuine qualities with an ongoing commitment to innovation and creativity.

➤ WE BELIEVE that we have a responsibility to cultivate the best relationships possible with our co-workers, customers, owners, agents, suppliers, and our community.

➤ WE BELIEVE in providing employees with a safe and fulfilling work environment, and an opportunity to grow and learn.

➤ WE BELIEVE that our company can be financially successful while behaving in a socially responsible and environmentally sensitive manner.

publishing a Values Report that details its performance on social, environmental, and animal protection issues. SustainAbility, which compared The Body Shop's entry against approximately 100 company reports as part of the United Nations Environmental Program, refers to the Values Report as "... *unusual in its efforts to integrate social and environmental reporting with considerable stakeholder engagement.*" The Body Shop continues to reap the rewards of living its values: It has been voted the second most trusted brand in the United Kingdom and it continues to grow worldwide.

Establishing Values

This section is titled "establishing values" but actually the question "Can we establish values?" might be appropriate. After all, each person and organization has a set of values that are demonstrated every day, a fact that was apparent even to Elvis Presley, who once said, "*Values are like fingerprints. Nobody's are the same, but you leave ' em all over everything you do.*"[11] Do the values reflect the true essence of the organization or simply the thinking of its current regime at the top? As previously noted, an organization's core values should not change but should act as the guiding principles for the organization as it reacts to the world around it. While this is the case, we must also recognize that, like virtually everything else, values within an organization will sometimes remain long after they cease to provide any benefit, and, in fact, they may become a hindrance to the ongoing success of the company. Some values may even prove unethical or unacceptable in the larger societal context. This doesn't suggest a wholesale change of values every few years to suit the current competitive landscape. It simply implies an honest evaluation of your organization and the recognition of which values truly represent its essence and are the keys to your enduring success.

The key to changing values and the underlying culture of an organization lies in open and honest identification of the current value systems that exist and are rewarded in the organization. One tool to help you in this endeavor was developed by Richard Barrett and is known as the corporate value audit instrument.[12] Individuals in the organization use three templates of values/behaviors to choose: the 10 values that best represent who they are (personal values), the 10 values that best describe how their organization/team operates (organizational values), and the 10 values they believe are most critical for a high-performance organization/team (ideal organizational values). This very illuminating exercise is used as a diagnostic tool to evaluate the strengths and weaknesses of existing values and culture. Organizations are able to assess the degree of alignment among personal, existing, and ideal organizational values, and identify the changes that are necessary to develop a successful and enduring value system. If you still need some assistance identifying values, author and consultant Jim Collins has developed a number of questions you can use to identify the core values in your organization:[13]

- What core values do you bring to work—values you hold to be so fundamental that you would hold them regardless of whether they were rewarded or not?

- How would you describe to your loved ones the core values you stand for in your work and that you hope they stand for in their working lives?

- If you awoke tomorrow morning with enough money to retire for the rest of your life, would you continue to hold on to these core values?

- Perhaps most important, can you envision these values being as valid 100 years from now as they are today?

- Would you want the organization to continue to hold these values, even if at some point one or more of them became a competitive disadvantage?

- If you were to start a new organization tomorrow in a different line of work, what core values would you build into the new organization regardless of its activities?

Establishing values for the organization, the principles to be relied on in good judgment to guide business decisions, cannot be considered a one-time event. Like a new garden that is brought to maturity by the warmth of the sun and the nourishment of fresh water, the values must be nurtured constantly to be embraced and lived. Consider the words of D & B chief executive Allan Loren: *"We made the values . . . part of the culture by constantly communicating them, so that everyone knew them, and by making sure that team members lived them. For some time, we opened every meeting by reading our values and guiding principle and discussing what we had learned by leveraging them.*

. . . We say clearly that if you don't live our values, it ultimately makes no difference what the results are."[14]

Values and the Balanced Scorecard

In the preceding section we discussed the possibility of changing the values of an organization and the mechanisms for achieving this result. The Balanced Scorecard represents the best solution for broadcasting your values, reviewing them over time, and creating alignment from top to bottom in the organization. The real key is alignment, having every employee see how day-to-day actions are consistent with the values of the company and how living those values contributes to overall success.

Chapter Seven discusses the concept of cascading the Balanced Scorecard, driving it down to lower levels of the organization while ensuring alignment throughout. When we cascade we allow employees at all levels to develop objectives and measures that represent how they influence corporate or business unit goals. The measures selected must be consistent with the values of the organization to ensure that everyone is headed in the same overall direction. Reviewing or "auditing" the measures on lower-level Scorecards provides a great opportunity to determine if the values you espouse are really those held by your employees up and down the corporate hierarchy. If you value innovation, for example, but your business units have no performance measures tracking innovation or development, then perhaps value innovation is not truly a guiding principle of their operations. Conversely, if all lower-level Scorecards contain measures relating to customer service but this value is not captured on the high-level corporate Scorecard, then perhaps you've missed a core value that is important to all of your employees.

Pragmatically, the Balanced Scorecard may also be used to track the extent to which your organization really lives its values. For organizations undergoing changes to values or suffering from turmoil, metrics that gauge adherence to stated values may be of great benefit. However, developing meaningful value-based metrics may prove challenging to even the most creative Scorecard builders. Possibilities include "mystery shopper" or casual observation techniques to determine if employees are behaving in accordance with your values. Calculating the percentage of employees who can recite your core values without prompting could also be used, but this would prove very difficult to track and may justifiably raise the ire of those being asked to list the company's values. Another possibility is identifying behaviors consistent with your values and basing at least part of the annual performance appraisal on the demonstration of these behaviors by employees.

A final thought on values in the organization comes from Tom Morris. Writing in his book *If Aristotle Ran General Motors,* Morris has this to say about the importance of values at work: *"People who are personally reassessing their lives in light of their deepest values will not find it easy to settle for less than a work environment that respects and encourages those values. They will certainly not be able to flourish, to be and do their best, in conditions that have not been wisely developed with sensitivity to what deeply moves people and what most fundamentally matters to us all.*[15] Exhibit 3.4 displays the values of some large organizations we're probably all familiar with.

VISION

What Is a Vision Statement?

Thus far in the chapter we've discussed the importance of a powerful mission to determine your core purpose as an organization and the values that you consider essential to achieving that purpose. Based on that mission and

Exhibit 3.4   Selected Statements of Values

General Electric
- Having a passion for excellence and hating bureaucracy
- Being open to ideas from anywhere and committed to working things out
- Living quality and driving cost and speed for competitive advantage
- Having the self-confidence to involve everyone and behaving in a boundary-less fashion
- Creating a clear, simple, reality-based vision and communicating it to all constituencies
- Having enormous energy and the ability to energize others
- Stretching, setting aggressive goals, and rewarding progress, yet understanding accountability and commitment
- Seeing changes as opportunity, not threat
- Having global brains and building diverse and global teams

Nordstrom
- Service to the customer above all else
- Hard work and individual productivity
- Never being satisfied
- Excellence in reputation; being part of something special

Walt Disney
- No cynicism
- Nurturing and promulgation of "wholesome American values"
- Creativity, dreams, and imagination
- Fanatical attention to consistency and detail
- Preservation and control of the Disney magic

those values, we now want to create a statement that defines where we want to go in the future. The vision statement does just that. The vision signifies the critical transition from the unwavering mission and core values to the spirited and dynamic world of strategy.

A vision statement provides a word picture of what the organization intends ultimately to become—which may be 5, 10, or 15 years in the future. This statement should not be abstract; it should contain as concrete a picture of the desired state as possible and also provide the basis for formulating strategies and objectives. A powerful vision provides everyone in the organization with a shared mental framework that helps give form to the often abstract future that lies before us. Vision always follows mission (purpose) and values. A vision without a mission is simply wishful thinking, not linked to anything enduring. Typical elements in a vision statement include the desired scope of business activities, how the corporation will be viewed by its stakeholders (customers, employees, suppliers, regulators, etc.), areas of leadership or distinctive competence, and strongly held values.

Do You Need a Vision Statement?

Virtually every organization in every industry has a vision statement. But despite its widespread use, it seems clear that the word "vision" is one of the most overused and possibly least understood words in business. One of the biggest problems is that a vision statement can mean different things to different people. Deeply held values, outstanding achievement, societal bonds, exhilarating goals, motivational forces, and raisons d'être are some of the many images conjured up by vision statements.[16]

In their book *Competing for the Future,* authors Hamel and Prahalad note that a wide variety of leaders from many walks of life have found themselves uneasy with the concept of "vision." They warn of vision statements that simply reflect an extension of the CEO's ego and the inherent danger in this approach to visioning. But they concede that every company needs a well-articulated view about tomorrow's opportunities and challenges. They choose the word "foresight" over "vision," saying: *"Vision connotes a dream or an apparition, but there is more to industry foresight than a single blinding flash of insight. Industry foresight is based on deep insights into the trends in technology, demographics, regulation, and lifestyles that can be harnessed to rewrite industry rules and create new competitive space."*[17] Others warn of the potential for a "dysfunctional" vision statement. For example, a vision statement could simply be wrong. Targeting the wrong opportunities or customers may create substantial corporate momentum toward the wrong future, momentum that could prove difficult to change. And the lack of reality reflected in a vision statement or a reliance on abstraction may create significant problems for the organization. Additionally, so many vision statements are simply repositories for the latest buzzwords that they appear empty and shallow. Employees will greet such statements with cynicism and question the competence of the executives who drafted the document.

Despite these cogent views, the vast majority of organizations have little doubt as to the value of a well-crafted vision statement. The power of a shared vision that is lived by all employees of the organization can provide a significant motivational force. John Kotter notes three important purposes served by a vision during a change process—and remember, the Balanced Scorecard is first and foremost an instrument of change:[18]

1. By clarifying the general direction for change, the vision simplifies hundreds or thousands of more detailed decisions.

2. The vision motivates people to take action in the right direction, even if the initial steps are personally painful.

3. Actions of different people throughout the organization are coordinated in a fast and efficient way based on the vision statement.

Regardless of the size of your organization, a skillfully created vision statement not only describes what you're attempting to accomplish but will serve to inspire all employees to join you in meeting the challenges that lie ahead. Ralph Norris of ASB Bank suggests: *"It's a lot easier to hold a steady course in a volatile and uncertain market if the company has a clear corporate vision. I think every organization should have a vision of where it's going— otherwise anywhere will do."*[19]

Effective Vision Statements

Everything discussed in this chapter is critical to your organization and your Balanced Scorecard implementation. However, the vision may represent the most critical component since it acts as a conduit between your reason for being as reflected in the mission, the values representative of your culture, and the strategy you'll put into execution to reach your desired future state. Without a clear and compelling vision to guide the actions of all employees, you may wind up with a workforce that lacks direction and thus is unable to profit from any strategy you put in place, no matter how well conceived. Let's look at some characteristics of effective vision statements:

- *Concise.* The very best vision statements are those that grab your attention and immediately draw you in without boring you with pages of mundane rhetoric. Often the simplest visions are the most powerful and compelling, like Starbucks' past refrain of "2,000 stores by 2000." If everyone in your organization is expected to act and make decisions based on the vision, the least you can do is create something that is simple and memorable. Consider it your organizational campaign slogan for the future.

- *Appeals to all stakeholders.* A vision statement that focuses on one group to the detriment of others will not win lasting support in the hearts and minds of all constituencies. The vision must appeal to everyone who has a stake in the success of the enterprise: employees, shareholders, customers, and communities, to name but a few.

- *Consistent with mission and values.* Your vision is a further translation of your mission (why you exist) and the values of underlying importance to your organization. If your mission suggests solving problems and one of your core values is constant innovation, we would expect to see a reference to innovation in your vision statement. In the vision you're painting a word picture of the desired future state that will lead to the achievement of your mission and ensure the two are aligned.

- *Verifiable.* Using the latest business jargon and buzzwords can make your vision statement very nebulous to even the most trained listener. Who within your organization will be able to determine exactly when you became "world class, leading edge, or top quality"? Write your vision statement so that you'll know when you've achieved it. While mission and values won't change, we would expect the vision to change since it is written for a finite period of time.

- *Feasible.* The vision shouldn't be the collective dreams of senior management; it must be grounded solidly in reality. To ensure this is the case, you must possess a clear understanding of your business, its markets, competitors, and emerging trends.

- *Inspirational.* Your vision represents a word picture of the desired future state of the organization. Don't miss the opportunity to inspire your team to make the emotional commitment necessary to reach this destination. The vision statement should not only guide but also arouse the collective passion of all employees. To be inspirational, the vision must first be understandable to every conceivable audience from the boardroom to the shop floor. Throw away the thesaurus for this exercise and focus instead on your deep knowledge of the business to compose a meaningful statement for all involved.

An inspirational vision statement is one of the greatest assets you can possess in your organization, and the rewards can be tremendous. Take the story of Albert Lai, a 19-year-old entrepreneur who, along with two other young business partners, sold his start-up mydesktop.com after just two years for over $1 million. Lai suggests that a clear vision and mission is critical for any entrepreneurs wanting to build their business: *"Having unified vision and mission statements for your organization allows you to have a benchmark and touchstone for when you have to make decisions for the future. This will help when there are no clear answers, or for critical decisions that will fundamentally impact your products and services."*[20]

Developing Your Vision Statement

The section on developing your mission statement began by suggesting the first order of business is determining who should actually be involved in the process. Should the mission represent a brilliant flash of insight from an omniscient CEO, or should the entire executive team share the arduous task? Penning your vision statement offers a similar challenge, with no simple answers. I'm going to describe two methods for developing your vision statement that represent a compromise on the either/or thinking of involvement of just the CEO or the entire executive team. The two methods are the interview method and the back-to-the-future technique.

As you might have guessed, executive interviews are the key component of the interview method for developing your vision. Each of the senior executives of your organization is interviewed separately to gather their feedback on the future direction of the organization. I suggest using an outside consultant or facilitator to run the interviews. A seasoned consultant will have been through many interviews of this nature and have the ability to put the executive at ease, ensuring that the necessary information flows freely in an environment of trust and objectivity. The interview should last about an hour and include both general and specific (industry and organization) questions, as well as a mix of queries oriented to the past, present, and future. Typical questions may include:

- Where and why have we been successful in the past?
- Where have we failed in the past?
- What makes us unique as an organization?
- Why should we be proud of our organization?
- What trends, innovations, and dynamics are currently changing our marketplace?
- What do our customers expect from us? Our shareholders? Our employees?
- What are our greatest attributes and competencies as an organization?
- Where do you see our organization in 3 years? 5 years? 10 years?
- How will our organization have changed during that time period?
- How do we sustain our success?

The interviewer summarizes the results of the interviews and presents them to the CEO. At this point the CEO will have the opportunity to draft the vision based on the collective knowledge gathered from the senior team. Once the draft is completed, the entire team convenes and debates the CEO's vision, ensuring it captures the essential elements they discussed during their interviews. You would not expect to have the first draft be accepted by everyone, and in fact that's the idea: You need to involve the whole team in the creation process. However, by giving the CEO the initial responsibility for declaring the vision, you ensure her commitment to the vision and have a working draft from which to begin the refinement process. Once the team has hammered out the vision statement, it should be reviewed and accepted by as many levels in the organization as logistically possible. With today's technology, that should include just about everyone.

I enjoy working with clients on the second technique, *back-to-the-future visioning*. The exercise can be administered either individually or with a group. I like using it with groups as the initial attempt to develop a draft vision statement, but it also works well in individual settings. In describing the method, I'll assume a group session. Distribute several 3- × 5-inch cards to each participant. To begin the session, ask the group to imagine they awake the next morning 5, 10, or 15 years in the future (your choice of time increment). In order to record their impressions, they've each been given a disposable camera to capture important images and changes they hoped might take place within their organization. At the end of each day's adventure, they must create a caption for the pictures they've taken during that day. Instruct the group to record their captions on the index cards. By the end of the trip they've cataloged the future in detail. Give the participants about 15 minutes to imagine their trip to the future and encourage them to visually capture as much as possible in their minds' eye. Ask the group: "What has happened with your organization—are you successful? What markets are you serving? What core competencies are separating you from your competitors? What goals have you achieved?" Once the 15 minutes are up, say: "Unfortunately, on the trip back to the present, the reentry was a little rough and the pictures were destroyed" (more animated and comedic facilitators can have a field day with this section) "but fortunately for you the captions remain." Record the captions from the index cards on a flip chart or laptop computer and use them as the raw materials for the initial draft of a vision statement. I enjoy this approach to vision statement development because it challenges the participants to engage all of their senses in the process, not simply their cognitive abilities.

These are just two of the methods I've found very useful in developing a vision statement. Fortunately for all of us, abundant literature and practice exists on this subject and you have many resources at your disposal. Other well-designed and -conceived techniques for drafting a vision statement may be found in *Built to Last* by Jim Collins and Jerry Porras[21] and *Transforming the Organization* by Francis Gouillart and James Kelly.[22] Once you've developed your vision, you'll be amazed at the power it provides, regardless of the industry in which you work. Michael Kaiser is president of the Kennedy Center for the Performing Arts in Washington, D.C. As you'll read, the power of vision is every bit as vital at this renowned performing arts center as it is at a manufacturing plant or high-tech laboratory. Kaiser explains: *"I think what leaders have to do is to provide a vision for the future. And what has been remarkable to me . . . is the power of a vision. If you can present [that vision] to people, either to people inside the organization who have been damaged or people outside the organization who have lost faith in what the organization can do, the power is remarkable."*[23]

Vision Statements and the Balanced Scorecard

When describing vision statements earlier in the chapter, I suggested they normally include the desired scope of business activities, how the corporation will be viewed by its stakeholders (customers, employees, suppliers, regulators, etc.), areas of leadership or distinctive competence, and strongly held values. When writing a vision for the organization we're attempting to move away from either/or thinking to embracing the power of "and." It's no longer a matter of satisfying one group using certain competencies at the expense of another. The vision has to balance the interests of all groups and portray a future that will lead to wins for everyone involved. The Balanced Scorecard is the mechanism we use to track our achievement of this lofty goal. The principle tenet of the Scorecard is balance, and more precisely using measurement to capture the correct balance of skills, processes, and customer requirements that lead to our desired financial future as reflected in the vision. It works equally as well if you're in the public or not-for-profit sector. The challenge of making your vision a reality remains critical, and the architecture of the Balanced Scorecard can be molded to help you do just that.

The Balanced Scorecard will provide a new, laserlike focus to your business, and the potential problems represented by a misguided vision are significant. We've all heard phrases like "What gets measured gets done," "Measure what matters," and many others. The Scorecard is essentially a device that translates vision into reality through the articulation of vision (and strategy). A well-developed Balanced Scorecard can be expected to stimulate behavioral changes within your organization. The question is: Are they the sort of changes you want? Be certain that the vision you've created for your organization is one that truly epitomizes your mission and values because the Scorecard will give you the means for traveling first class to that envisioned future.

STRATEGY

When I wrote the opening paragraph on strategy for the first edition of this book, my wife and I were preparing for a move to a new house. Fortunately, we were moving only about 12 miles, which greatly reduced the burden, but of course we still had to pack up our entire house room by room. Not a day went by during that move that I didn't hear at some point, *"When are you going to pack up your office?"* You see, I'm a packrat of sorts and have managed to hold on to virtually every article, book, and relevant (at least to me) scrap of paper that's come my way over the course of a lifetime. As part of my research efforts for this book, I've cataloged most of my archives and have discovered that a conservative estimate would reveal that about 90 percent of the documents have at least some reference to the concept of strategy. Where do I begin, and more important, if we ever move again, will I ever be able to pack it all? This plethora of materials really shouldn't come as a surprise since the field of strategy is undoubtedly the most chronicled subject in the world of business. What is amazing is that the disciplined study of business strategy really has been with us for only a few decades, but in that time it has spawned literally thousands of works. An additional challenge to discussing strategy is the fact that it has relevant connections with numerous other areas of study. Who among us doesn't know at least one person proudly displaying a copy of *The Art of War* in their office? Military strategy has been around for thousands of years. Historians, physicists, biologists, psychologists, and anthropologists to name but a few also contribute to the subject of strategy.

From the huge mountain of information that exists we must distill what is most critical to the discussion at hand. Developing a comprehensive strategy for your organization is beyond the scope of this book. Many well-written and cogent texts are available on the subject, and I will refer to some specifically. In this section I will focus on reviewing the common elements of strategy and, most important for us, will outline why strategy and the Balanced Scorecard must be woven together to get the maximum benefit from both.

What Is Strategy?

A prolific writer on the subject of strategy, Henry Mintzberg, provides this excellent synopsis of the subject to begin our discussion: *"My research and that of many others demonstrates that strategy making is an immensely complex process, which involves the most sophisticated, subtle, and, at times, subconscious elements of human thinking."*[24] As this quote illustrates, the difficulty with defining strategy is that it has different meanings for different people and organizations. Some feel strategy is represented by the high-level plans management devises to lead the organization into the future. Others would argue strategy rests on the specific and detailed actions you take to achieve your desired future. To others still, strategy is tantamount to best practices. Finally, some may consider strategy a pattern of consistency of action over time. Rather than focus on a stifling definition of this nebulous term, let's look at some of the key principles of strategy:

- *Different activities.* Strategy is about choosing a different set of activities from your rivals, the pursuit of which leads to a unique and valuable position in the market.[25] If everyone were to pursue the same activities, then differentiation would be based purely on operational effectiveness.

In the excellent book *Blue Ocean Strategy*, authors Kim and Mauborgne distill the essence of successful strategy to three elements: focus, divergence, and a compelling tagline.[26] I think it offers the freshest thinking on strategy to be produced in years: focus on key strengths, differentiate yourself from competitors on typical industry dimensions, and offer a memorable tagline.

- *Trade-offs.* Effective strategies demand trade-offs in competition. Strategy is more about the choice of *what not to do* than what to do. Organizations cannot compete effectively by attempting to be everything to everybody. The entire organization must be aligned around what you choose to do and create value from that strategic position.[27]

- *Fit.* The activities chosen must fit one another for sustainable success. Peter Drucker in his "Theory of the Business" suggests that our assumptions about the business must fit one another to produce a valid theory. Activities are the same; they must produce an integrated whole.[28]

- *Continuity.* While major structural changes in the industry could lead to a change in strategies, generally strategies should not be constantly reinvented. The strategy crystallizes your thinking on basic issues, such as how you will offer customer value and to what customers. This direction needs to be clear to both internal (employees) and external (customers) constituents.[29] Changes may bring about new opportunities that can be assimilated into the current strategy—new technologies, for example.

- *Various thought processes.* Strategy involves conceptual as well as analytical exercises.[30] As the Mintzberg quote at the beginning of this section reminds us, strategy involves not only the detailed analysis of complex data but also broad conceptual knowledge of the company, industry, market, and so on.

Using the elements just discussed as ingredients, an organization could cook up innumerable types of strategies, and over the years they have. In their book *Strategy Safari*, authors Ahlstrand, Lampel, and Mintzberg offer 10 schools of strategic thought that have emerged in the ongoing practice of management.[31] These 10 categories are presented for your review in Exhibit 3.5.

Strategy and the Balanced Scorecard: A Critical Link

I recently read an article discussing the execution of strategy in organizations. The article began this way: *"Take this quick quiz. Question #1: three frogs are sitting on a log. One decides to jump off. How many are left? You might think two, but the answer is three. One has decided to jump off. Question #2: three companies have poor earnings. One decides to revitalize key product lines, strengthen distribution channels, and become customer intimate. How many companies have poor earnings? You get the idea: deciding and doing are two different things."[32]

Exhibit 3.5   10 Schools of Strategic Thought

Design School: Proposes a model of strategy making that seeks to attain a fit between internal capabilities and external possibilities. Probably the most influential school of thought, and home of the SWOT (strengths, weaknesses, opportunities, and threats) technique.

Planning School: Formal procedure, formal training, formal analysis, and lots of numbers are the hallmark of this approach. The simple informal steps of the design school become an elaborated sequence of steps. Produce each component part as specified, assemble them according to the blueprint, and strategy will result.

Positioning School: Suggests that only a few key strategies (positions in the economic marketplace) are desirable. Much of Michael Porter's work can be mapped to this school.

Entrepreneurial School: Strategy formation results from the insights of a single leader, and stresses intuition, judgment, wisdom, experience, and insight. The "vision" of the leader supplies the guiding principles of the strategy.

Cognitive School: Strategy formation is a cognitive process that takes place in the mind of the strategist. Strategies emerge as the strategist filters the maps, concepts, and schemas shaping his or her thinking.

Learning School: Strategies emerge as people (acting individually or collectively) come to learn about a situation as well as their organization's ability to deal with it.

Power School: Stresses strategy formation as an overt process of influence, emphasizing the use of power and politics to negotiate strategies favorable to particular interests.

Cultural School: Social interaction, based on the beliefs and understandings shared by the members of an organization, lead to the development of strategy.

Environmental School: Presenting itself to the organization as a set of general forces, the environment is the central actor in the strategy-making process. The organization must respond to the factors or be "selected out."

Configuration School: Strategies arise from periods when an organization adopts a structure to match to a particular context that gives rise to certain behaviors.

Source: Adapted from Henry Mintzberg, Bruce Ahlstrand, and Joseph Lampel, *Strategy Safari* (New York: Free Press, 1998).

Although some organizations question the value of strategy in an era characterized by hyperchange, the vast majority consider strategy a mandatory component of success. The problem is not one of developing a strategy; numerous options are available for that task, as we saw in the previous section. The fundamental issue is one of implementation: translating the strategy into terms that everyone understands and thereby bringing focus to their day-to-day actions. Recall from Chapter One that 70 percent of CEO failures are not the result of poor strategy but of poor execution.

The Balanced Scorecard provides the framework for an organization to move from *deciding* to live its strategy to *doing* it. The Scorecard describes the strategy, breaking it down into its component parts through the objectives and measures chosen in each of the four perspectives. The Balanced Scorecard is ideally created through a shared understanding and translation of the organization's strategy into objectives, measures, targets, and initiatives in each of the four Scorecard perspectives. The translation of vision and strategy forces the executive team to determine specifically what is meant by sometimes imprecise terms contained in the strategy, such as "world class," "top-tier service" and "targeted customers." Through the process of developing the Scorecard, an executive group may determine "world class" translates to means zero manufacturing defects. All employees can now focus their energies and day-to-day activities toward the crystal-clear goal of zero defects rather than wondering about, and debating the definition of "world class." Using the Balanced Scorecard as a framework for translating the strategy, these organizations create a new language of measurement that serves to guide all employees' actions toward the achievement of the stated direction.

A key attribute of strategy formation is performing a different set of activities from your rivals. By choosing a distinct set of related activities, you have the opportunity to create unique value propositions for your customers and thus separate yourself from competitors. These activities must be reflected in the Balanced Scorecard, which should parallel the strategy. In other words, if you wish to distinguish yourself by engaging in a series of activities aimed at creating customer intimacy, then your Balanced Scorecard should reflect this strategic direction. We would expect to see linked measures through the four perspectives that, when taken together, will drive this strategy. Measures related to service of targeted customers should appear prominently in the Customer perspective, linked to relationship management metrics in the Internal Process perspective and perhaps selling skill measures in the Employee Learning and Growth perspective. This chain of linked measures that mirrors your chosen activities is hypothesized to drive revenue growth in the Financial perspective. Again, the Balanced Scorecard provides the means to describe and articulate the activities separating you from your competition.

It is possible to develop a Scorecard-like system without a clear and concise strategy, and many organizations do just that. However, this mix of financial and nonfinancial measures is better termed a key performance indicator scorecard or key stakeholder scorecard rather than a Balanced Scorecard. The problem with this approach is that you simply cannot harness the true power of the Balanced Scorecard without a strategy driving its construction. Key performance indicator (KPI) or constituent scorecards lack the ability to align an entire organization around a set of complementary themes that drive the organization toward its overall vision and mission. Instead they often reflect a number of good ideas that lack a coherent story or direction. The Balanced Scorecard and strategy truly go hand in hand. I believe Kaplan and Norton sum up this subject very well: *"The formulation of strategy is an art. The description of strategy, however, should not be an art. If we can describe strategy in a more disciplined way, we increase the likelihood of successful implementation. With a Balanced Scorecard that tells the story of the strategy, we now have a reliable foundation."*[33]

KEEP IN MIND

- A mission defines the core purpose of the organization—why it exists. The mission captures the contribution and value an organization wishes to deliver to humankind and provides a star to steer by in our turbulent world. An effective mission may be developed using the "5 Whys" technique and should inspire change, be easily understood and communicated, and be long-term in nature.

- The Balanced Scorecard allows an organization to translate its mission into concrete objectives that align all employees. To provide effective direction, the measures on a Balanced Scorecard must reflect the aspirations denoted in the mission statement.

- Values represent the deeply held beliefs within the organization and the timeless principles it uses to guide decision making. Values are often reflective of the personal beliefs emanating from a strong CEO or leader. We often associate positive values with the common good—doing good for others while achieving organizational goals. Several organizations, such as Disney, Marriott, and Tom's of Maine, have proven that profits and societal contributions are not in conflict and use their values to derive a competitive advantage.

- The Balanced Scorecard provides organizations with a means of evaluating the alignment of values throughout the organization. The Scorecard may also be used to track the extent to which an organization is living its stated values.

- The vision signifies our transition from the timeless mission and values to the dynamic and often messy world of strategy. The vision provides a word picture of what the organization ultimately intends to become. While the need for a vision statement has been questioned, most organizations agree it provides a critical enabler by clarifying direction, motivating action, and coordinating efforts.

- Effective visions appeal to all stakeholders, align with mission and values, and are concise, verifiable, feasible, and inspirational. Vision statements may be created through interviewing of senior executives or by leading group "visioning" exercises designed to enlist the full involvement of your team. The vision statement balances the interest of multiple stakeholders in describing how the organization will create future value. The role of the Scorecard is to capture the correct mix of competencies, processes, and customer value propositions that lead to your desired financial future.

- The study of business strategy has evolved rapidly over the past four decades, with numerous schools of thought emerging to proclaim the power of their insights. Effective strategy making involves combining a different set of activities from your rivals to produce value for customers.

- Using the Balanced Scorecard, organizations have a great opportunity to beat the odds of effective execution by translating their strategy into its component parts throughout the four perspectives. Strategy is then demystified as employees from across the organization are able to focus on the strategic elements they influence.

Notes

1. Scott Adams, *The Dilbert Principle* (New York: Harper Business, 1996).

2. Jack Welch and Suzy Welch, *Winning* (New York: Harper Business, 2005), p. 13.

3. James C. Collins and Jerry I. Porras, "Building Your Company's Vision," *Harvard Business Review* (September–October, 1996, pp. 65–77).

4. Julia Kirby and Diane L. Coutu, "The Beauty of Buzzwords," *Harvard Business Review* (May 2001, pp. 30–32).

5. Collins and Porras, "Building Your Company's Vision."

6. James C. Collins and Jerry I. Porras, *Built to Last* (New York: Harper Business, 1997).

7. Henri F. Amiel, *Amiel's Journey* (1852), Mrs. Humphry Ward (trans.) (Macmillan & Co, 1889).

8. Richard Barrett, *Liberating the Corporate Soul* (Boston: Butterworth Heinmann, 1998).

9. J. W. Marriott and Kathi Ann Brown, *The Spirit to Serve: Marriott's Way* (New York: Harper Business, 1997).

10. Tom Chappell, *The Soul of a Business* (New York: Bantam Books, 1993).

11. Quoted in Stephen R. Covey, *The 8th Habit* (New York: Free Press, 2004), p. 70.

12. Barrett, *Liberating the Corporate Soul.*

13. Jim Collins, *Leader to Leader* (San Francisco: Jossey-Bass, 1999).

14. Brian Hanessian and Carlos Sierra, "Leading a Turnaround: An Interview with the Chairman of D & B," *McKinsey Quarterly,* No. 2 (2005): 83–93.

15. Tom Morris, *If Aristotle Ran General Motors: The New Soul of Business* (New York: Henry Holt and Company, 1997).

16. Collins and Porras, "Building Your Company's Vision."

17. Gary Hamel and C. K. Prahalad, *Competing for the Future* (Boston: Harvard Business School Press, 1994).

18. John P. Kotter, *Leading Change* (Boston: Harvard Business School Press, 1996).

19. Rebecca Macfie, "Six of Our Top Chief Executive Officers Tell the *Independent* How They Stay at the Top," *Independent Business Weekly* (April 2001): 8.

20. Carly Foster, "Business Communications: 'Envision Your Business, Realize Your Goals,'" *Canadaone.com e-zine* (October 1999).

21. James C. Collins and Jerry I. Porras, *Built to Last* (New York: Harper Collins, 1994).

22. Francis J. Gouillart and James N. Kelly, *Transforming the Organization* (New York: McGraw-Hill, 1995).

23. Interview on National Public Radio's *Morning Edition*, March 26, 2001.

24. Henry Mintzberg, "The Fall and Rise of Strategic Planning," *Harvard Business Review* (January–February 1994).

25. Michael E. Porter, "What Is Strategy?" *Harvard Business Review* (November–December 1996).

26. W. Chan Kim and Renee Mauborgne, *Blue Ocean Strategy* (Boston: Harvard Business School Press, 2005), p. 39.

27. Ibid.

28. Peter Drucker, *Managing in a Time of Great Change* (New York: Truman Tilley/Dutton, 1995).

19. Keith H. Hammonds, "Michael Porter's Big Ideas," *Fast Company* (March 2001).

30. E. E. Chaffee, "Three Models of Strategy," *Academy of Management Review* (October 1985).

31. Henry Mintzberg, Bruce Ahlstrand, and Joseph Lampel, *Strategy Safari* (New York: Free Press, 1998).

32. Lawrence B. MacGregor Serven, "Can Your Company Actually Execute Its Strategy?" *Harvard Management Update* (May 1999).

33. Robert S. Kaplan and David P. Norton, *The Strategy Focused Organization* (Boston: Harvard Business School Press, 2001).

CHAPTER 4

Strategy Maps

Roadmap for Chapter Four   Since the execution of strategy is frequently a new and foreign destination for most organizations, the term "roadmap" seems only fitting to the discussion that will take place in this chapter as we closely examine the tool you will use to guide your path on the road to implementation: the Strategy Map. Our journey begins by considering exactly what a Strategy Map is, why it has burst upon the Balanced Scorecard scene proving to be as critical an innovation as the concept itself, and why you must develop one if you hope to overcome the discouraging odds of effective strategy execution.

Before you can draft a compelling Strategy Map, you must mine the many sources of potential information from which the Map will ultimately be constructed. We will review what to look for, where to find it, and how to conduct executive interviews that ensure senior leadership's stamp is clearly visible on your final product. From there our journey continues with a review of the four perspectives and how you can go about developing objectives for each. Objective statements—concise narratives that further articulate your objectives—will be carefully reviewed in the chapter along with extensive tips and tools for conducting Strategy Mapping workshops that are both effective and efficient. You may wonder how many objectives should appear on your Map; thus, the subject of quantity versus quality will be addressed to ensure your that your Strategy Map balances telling a cogent story with the brevity demanded by corporate audiences that frequently suffer from information overload. The chapter concludes with a brief foray into the creative realm, offering suggestions for customizing your Strategy Map, ensuring it is consistent with the culture and norms of your organization.

WHAT IS A STRATEGY MAP?

As I write this the days of 2005 have dwindled to a precious few, signaling the end of another year and heralding the arrival of that most time-honored tradition: the year-end list. This morning I opened the entertainment section of the newspaper to find not one critic's list of the "Top

Ten Movies of 2005," but a page full of recommendations from reviewers around the country. It seems these days, regardless of the field, critics and pundits abound, providing their insights on everything from technology trends to beautiful people.

While I doubt their musings will ever make the papers, the Balanced Scorecard, like any popular management tool, has its share of critics as well. In my experience two camps of discontent with the tool tend to emerge: Those who conceive of the Scorecard as a flash in the pan, flavor of the month, this too shall pass management panacea, and those occupying the other end of the spectrum who respect the tool's longevity but point to that very fact in an attempt to brand the system "stale." When confronted with the fad argument, I simply point to the undeniable fact that the Scorecard has been around for over 15 years and its popularity and the results garnered by organizations of all types and sizes around the globe continues unabated. The second contingent, complaining that the Scorecard has grown tired and offers precious few insights, is also misguided as the Scorecard has evolved nearly constantly since its appearance in 1990. First came the transition from measurement to strategic management system by forging links between the Scorecard and critical management endeavors such as budgeting, compensation, and performance reviews. Our knowledge of measurement has also expanded significantly over the life of the tool, with sophisticated metrics such as strategic job readiness appearing more frequently in well-informed Balanced Scorecards. Perhaps the most powerful breakthrough of the Scorecard, however, is its ability to communicate strategy clearly and succinctly to all stakeholders of an organization through the advent of Strategy Maps.

The earliest adopters of the Balanced Scorecard were attracted to the notion of supplementing financial measures with the drivers of future financial success, thereby bringing a healthy dose of balance to a measurement landscape long dominated by short-term, financially oriented metrics. Seductive in its simplicity and pleasing in results, the tool skyrocketed in popularity, but some organizations hit turbulence during their trajectory in the form of incorrect measures, those that demonstrated little insight into strategy execution. To overcome this vexing and potentially game-changing issue, Scorecard adopters began prefacing their discussion of measures with one of objectives: "What must we do well in each of the perspectives in order to execute the strategy?" Doing so created a context for the measurement challenge, making the selection of metrics, a task that always proves challenging, somewhat less complicated in the light of day provided by clearly articulated objectives.

As Balanced Scorecard teams began developing objectives from their strategies, they instinctively began linking them together, using arrows to depict patterns of cause and effect. For example, items such as quality and training were no longer disparate elements of a strategy, but were linked together through a bold line on a flipchart or whiteboard: "If we provide focused training to our employees that will allow us to produce high quality products with fewer defects." Drawing the relationships among objectives served several important purposes: It allowed Scorecard developers to quickly grasp important interdependencies, question assumptions, and simply create a better description of their unique strategies.[1] The Strategy Map was born, and as Kaplan and Norton observed, *"[It] has turned out to be as important an innovation as the original Balanced Scorecard itself."*[2]

We may define a Strategy Map as a one-page graphical representation of what you must do well in each of the four perspectives in order to successfully execute your strategy. "What you must do well" is answered in the form of objectives, concise statements typically beginning with a verb appearing in each of the perspectives. For example, in the Financial perspective you may have objectives such as "Increase return on investment" or "Improve asset utilization." The Employee Learning and Growth perspective may include objectives like "Leverage technology to execute strategy" and "Close skill gaps." As described, linking the objectives together in patterns of cause and effect from the enablers in the Employee Learning and Growth perspective through the performance drivers in the Internal Process and Customer perspectives up to the results of the Financial perspective allows you to tell your strategic story in a compelling way that is easily understood and embraced by all employees.

In the rest of the chapter we will examine how you can craft a Strategy Map that depicts your strategic story and sets the stage for powerful measures you can use to gauge your success. But first let's take a quick look at why a Strategy Map is a critical link in the performance management chain of any organization.

WHY YOU NEED A STRATEGY MAP

Think for a moment, and please make it just a moment since this may prove to be hazardous to your mental health, about the typical strategic plan produced in most organizations, maybe even your own. This is how an average plan was described recently by a pair of experts in the field:

> *The document normally kicks off with a lengthy description of current industry conditions and the competitive situation. Next is a discussion of how to increase market share, capture new segments, or cut costs, followed by an outline of numerous goals and initiatives. A full budget is almost invariably attached, as are lavish graphs and a surfeit of spreadsheets. The process usually culminates in the preparation of a large document culled from a mishmash of data provided by people from various parts of the organization who often have conflicting agendas and poor communication. In this process, managers spend the majority of strategic thinking time filling in boxes and running numbers instead of thinking outside the box and developing a clear picture of how to break from the competition . . . . Executives are paralyzed by the muddle. Few employees deep down in the company even know what the strategy is.*[3]

Exhibit 4.1 Strategy Map for a Fictitious Distribution Company

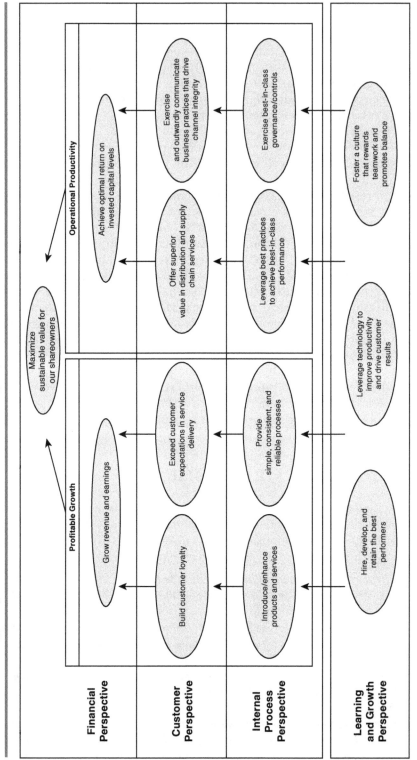

Given the menacing description above, it is little wonder fewer than 10 percent of organizations are able to execute their strategies, a fact elaborated on in Chapter One. The entire quote is alarming in its criticism of strategic plans, but what leaps off the page at me is the concluding sentence: "Few employees deep down in the company even know what the strategy is." How can something as vital as a strategy be acted on and effectively executed if the very people charged with the responsibility of carrying *it* out don't even understand *it* in the first place? Such is the case in the vast majority of companies groping in strategic darkness, imploring their teams to implement their unique strategy without taking the time or effort to explain exactly what the strategy represents.

Let's be charitable and suggest the typical strategic plan for any medium to large business runs between 50 and 100 pages of dizzying graphs, exhausting narratives, and mind-numbing bulleted lists. The challenge lies in extracting the core essence of the strategy, the nugget of clarity all employees are searching for, and sharing it with audiences at every level of the organization, enabling them to act on the knowledge, transforming it to value for the company. How can this monumental task be accomplished? You could turn your building's parking lot into a battlefield, holding strategy boot camp sessions during which corporate drill sergeants take your troops through their paces: "Johnson, what is our customer value proposition? . . . I'm waiting, Johnson . . . . . Johnson!! . . . Drop and give me fifty!" Probably not an effective technique in an era when employees of one large retailer are justifiably suing over lack of lunch breaks. If clarity is what is missing in most plans, Strategy Maps act as a powerful lens, transforming the obtuse world of strategic plans into dazzling focus by translating often nebulous and confusing verbiage into crystal-clear objectives that, if constructed properly, spell out in plain and simple language what must be done if the organization hopes to succeed and differentiate itself from competitors. Author John Gardner has suggested that *"[m]ost ailing organizations have developed a functional blindness to their own defects. They are not suffering because they cannot resolve their problems but because they cannot see their problems."*[4] In a very literal fashion, working in concert with the measures on a Balanced Scorecard, Strategy Maps bring problems and issues from darkness into light, allowing them to be combated and mitigated. The Map acts as an early warning system for the organization's strategy, signaling trouble when indicators suggest a problem with any element of the plan that has been designed to elevate the organization to prosperity.

DEVELOPING YOUR STRATEGY MAP

Outlined in the sections to follow are guidelines for developing a Strategy Map that acts as a faithful translation of your strategy and powerfully communicates it to all employees. We will begin by considering what must be done prior to creating the Map, including the question of whether the four perspectives are right for you, gathering background materials, and interviewing your executive team for their critical insights. At that point each of the four perspectives will be examined, with advice on how you can determine which objectives are right for you. Finally, tips and tools will be shared to ensure your Strategy Mapping workshop is run with maximum efficiency and effectiveness.

CHOOSING YOUR PERSPECTIVES

Are the Four Perspectives Right for You?

A critical question to consider when building a Strategy Map and Balanced Scorecard of measures is how many and which perspectives you will choose. Thus far, and for the remainder of the book, I speak exclusively of four perspectives: Financial, Customer, Internal Processes, and Employee Learning and Growth. But Kaplan and Norton themselves suggest the four perspectives *"should be considered a template, not a strait jacket."*[5] Many organizations have followed this guidance and developed additional perspectives for innovation, research and development, environment, suppliers, leadership, and the community.

The choice of perspectives for your Strategy Map and Scorecard should ultimately be based on what is necessary to tell the story of your strategy and create a competitive advantage for your organization. When you examine your strategy and attempt to translate it, who or what are the key constituents necessary to describe it? The four perspectives are broad enough to capture most constituents; however, if you feel your organization claims a competitive advantage as a result of relationships or processes based on another constituency, you may consider adding a separate perspective for this group. For example, a manufacturing firm may rely heavily on suppliers in order to manage its operations to the maximum of efficiency. Adding a perspective devoted to supplier relations could make good business sense for this organization. Of course, corporate governance is an area much in the news these past several years, thanks primarily to the spate of high-profile corporate failures brought on at least in part by poor or nonexistent governance practices. Signaling to all stakeholders your commitment to governance, you may feel it merits its own perspective on your Strategy Map and Balanced Scorecard.

Capturing the key stakeholders who contribute to your organization's success is critical to your Strategy Map. However, you should avoid simply including every possible contributor and designing a "Stakeholder Strategy Map." Maps and Scorecards of this nature identify the organization's major constituents and define goals for each. Sears' initial Scorecard, which was constructed around three related themes, illustrates a Stakeholder Balanced

Scorecard. The three themes were: "a compelling place to shop," "a compelling place to work," and "a compelling place to invest." Similarly, Citicorp used this architecture for its Scorecard: "a good place to work, to bank, and to invest."[6] These Scorecards focus on three key groups—employees, shareholders, and customers—but what is missing is the "how" of value creation that a truly Balanced Scorecard can provide. What value proposition will ensure that customers are satisfied and loyal? What processes must we excel at in order to drive this customer value proposition, and what competencies must our employees possess? These are the questions you must answer to develop a Map and Balanced Scorecard that tells the story of your strategy and demonstrates how you plan to execute that strategy. It should be noted that both Sears and Citicorp went on to develop strategic Balanced Scorecards that included insightful internal processes to complete the description of their strategies.

Let's not forget one of the many attractions of the original Balanced Scorecard system: its brevity. A well-constructed Strategy Map and Balanced Scorecard should tell the story of the organization's strategy through a relatively small number of objectives and measures woven together through the perspectives. As a communication tool, the Scorecard's ability to quickly and accurately transmit the organization's key drivers to a wide and broad audience is a fundamental benefit of the concept. So, choose the perspectives that allow you to capture the key stakeholders of the organization and describe how you will ultimately serve each and thereby successfully implement your strategy. The true test is whether you can easily intertwine your perspectives to tell a coherent story. Standalone perspectives that describe a constituent group but fail to link together with the other perspectives don't belong on a Strategy Map and Balanced Scorecard.

DOING YOUR HOMEWORK: REVIEWING BACKGROUND INFORMATION ON STRATEGY MAP RAW MATERIALS

Gathering and Reviewing Background Information

Each member of your Balanced Scorecard team will approach the implementation with certain preconceived notions regarding the nature of your business, its competitive position, future prospects, appropriate strategy, objectives, and measures. Level the playing field for your team by gathering and reviewing as much background material as you can find. You chose your team members based on their particular background and experience, but to build an effective Strategy Map and Scorecard, everyone must have access to the total pool of information that exists on your organization. Here are some of the sources of information you might consider:

- *Annual reports.* An invaluable source of information, your annual reports not only contain detailed financial information but also discuss your market position, key products, prospects for the future, and maybe even nonfinancial indicators of success.

- *Mission statement.* This may actually prove quite informative, and possibly entertaining. Ask each member of your team to recite the organization's mission statement. After all, most organizations do have one, and after reading Chapter Three, you definitely should have one.

- *Values.* Has your organization established its guiding principles?

- *Vision.* As with the mission, if you search hard enough, you should be able to find a vision statement for your organization. Or perhaps you've just developed one. Does it reflect the current organizational reality?

- *Strategic plan.* This is the mother lode of Map and Scorecard building information. If you are fortunate enough to have a coherent strategic plan that is based on your mission, values, and vision, you're off to a great start in the process. Most organizations aren't this fortunate and often their Scorecard rollout is delayed, or even derailed, as the organization struggles to produce a valid strategy.

- *Project plans.* If yours is like most companies, at any given time there will be dozens of initiatives swirling about, each vying for attention and resources. It's very important that you gauge which projects appear to be aligned with the strategy of the organization and have the support of influential executives. These initiatives may be candidates to remain as important action plans in achieving one or more Scorecard measures.

- *Consulting studies.* Consultants love to consume lots of paper and often leave behind treasure troves of valuable information. Regardless of what they've been studying at your organization, they most likely will have provided background information that will prove very helpful in your review process.

- *Performance reports.* You may not have a Balanced Scorecard, but every organization is run on some kind of management reporting system. Find and review at least a year's worth of these reports to determine what indicators of performance are currently deemed critical to the organization's success.

- *Competitor data.* Knowing what your competitors are doing, and, if possible, what they're tracking may help you determine some of your own key objectives and measures. But remember the essence of strategy: doing different things than your rivals to create value. Don't simply copy the objectives and metrics of your competitors. They may have mature processes that focus on different aspects of the value chain from your organization, and hence their objectives and measures may actually prove counterproductive to your efforts.

- *Organizational histories.* Has anyone chronicled the history of your organization? If so, it will likely provide a wealth of information on why the organization was started (mission), what the founders valued, key lessons learned over the years, and a picture of the future.

- *Analyst reports.* If you are publicly traded, analyst reports will provide an excellent glimpse into what the market values about your company. These documents often provide a wealth of statistical data as well.

- *Trade journals and news articles.* What is the business press saying about your organization? What you find here may have a strong impact on the objectives and measures you choose to influence public opinion.

- *Benchmarking reports.* Benchmarking is still quite popular, and many excellent studies are available on a wide variety of industries and functional specialties. While these documents provide good background and may stimulate discussion of potential measures, I caution against a reliance on them. Your Strategy Map and Balanced Scorecard should tell the story of your strategy. The objectives and measures you choose to represent that strategy may in some cases mirror those of other organizations, but it's the determination of the key *drivers* for *your particular* organization that will ultimately differentiate you from your rivals.

The sources just shown are not intended to provide an exhaustive list, and in fact you may uncover several more. In determining where to search for information, and to further reinforce Scorecard fundamentals within your team, consider using the Balanced Scorecard architecture to assist you in identifying sources of material. For example, under the financial perspective, you would ask yourself, "Where might we find information relating to the financial performance of the organization?" From that question, a number of candidates will likely spring to mind: annual reports, analyst reports, management reports, and so on. Exhibit 4.2 displays some of the sources you may discover under each element of the Balanced Scorecard.

What to Look for in Your Background Materials

The task of unearthing background material may appear somewhat daunting at first, but you will undoubtedly end up discovering more than you expected. While the information you collect will be informative, you should develop a plan to determine specifically what you hope to discern from your research. You'll also require a repository for the prodigious amount of material you're sure to generate now and during the rest of the implementation. On page 107 you will find a file structure you can use during your implementation.

One critical element to scrutinize is consistency. Are the documents providing a single view of the organization's mission, core values, vision, and strategies? Your Strategy Map and Balanced Scorecard development depends on a shared understanding of those vital elements throughout the organization. If you find conflicting information, document it carefully and make

Exhibit 4.2   Using the Balanced Scorecard to Find Background Information

Financial		Customer
• Annual report • Performance reports • Analyst reports • Trade journals • Benchmark reports		• Marketing department • Trade journals • Consulting studies • Project plans • Strategic plan • Performance reports • Benchmark reports
	Mission, Values, Vision, and Strategy • Mission statement • Values • Vision statement • Strategic plan • Organizational histories • Consulting studies • Project plans	
Internal Process • Operational reports • Manufacturing reports • Competitor data • Benchmark reports • Trade journals • Consulting studies • Project plans		**Employee Learning and Growth** • Human resources data • Trade journals • Core values • Benchmark reports • Consulting studies

the resolution of such discrepancies a goal of your executive interviews and workshop. Likewise you will want to record any findings that suggest a strong and unified view on the mission, values, vision, and strategy. During the executive interview process, you can confirm their ongoing validity.

Your review should also contribute several possible objectives and measures for each of the four Strategy Map and Balanced Scorecard perspectives. Specific objectives and metrics will no doubt be sprinkled throughout the documents you review, and while you may not always find exact references, the documents should lead you in the right direction. For example, operational plans will include details of some key processes employed at your company. These will help you determine objectives and measures in the

A Filing System for Your Balanced Scorecard Implementation

No matter how small or large your organization, any initiative of this magnitude is sure to generate a lot of information. Simplify your efforts by creating both paper and electronic filing methods to capture, store, and share the knowledge you develop. I suggest creating binders and electronic file directories that mirror the specific steps in your plan. For example, you may have a directory or binder titled "Background information." Tabs in your binder and subdirectories on your computer could be labeled, "Executive interviews," "Strategy information," etc.

The electronic filing is especially important since each member of your team will have preferred methods of naming and storing files. Develop a process everyone can agree on and insist that all relevant files be posted on a shared drive the whole team can access. Consider adding a date to every file created, or use another form of version control, to ensure you're always working with the most recent copy of your document.

For those of you with the resources, why not create a portal to capture all of your Balanced Scorecard information. That's exactly what the Information Technology Division of Worcester Polytechnic Institute did, creating a shared space that houses all Scorecard information including discussion groups and the latest announcements. A screen shot from their portal is provided in Exhibit 4.3.

This may seem like a small and logical step, but in my experience it is often overlooked until an abundance of documentation has been created, and nobody seems to know where anything is located. Developing a Balanced Scorecard is tough enough; don't make it even more difficult by hampering your efforts through poor data management.

Internal Process perspective. Similarly, your research may produce information regarding core competencies your organization hopes to leverage in the future. These competencies can help frame discussions of your Employee Learning and Growth perspective.

The concept of using the Balanced Scorecard as a Strategic Management System was introduced in Chapter One. Our goal in the evolution from a measurement system to a Strategic Management System is to make the Scorecard the cornerstone of management processes throughout the organization. Later chapters will detail the specific steps you'll need to take to

Exhibit 4.3   Screen Shot from "My WPI," the Scorecard Portal Created by the IT Division of Worcester Polytechnic Institute

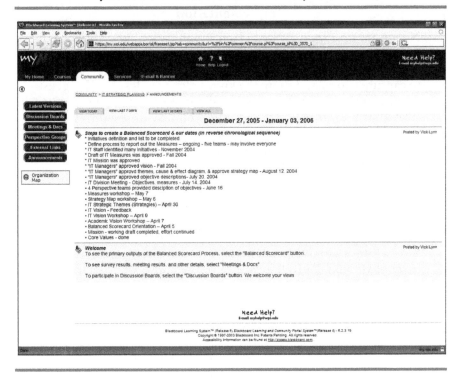

make this transition. For now, you should gather background material on your organization's key management processes, such as budgeting and business planning, compensation design and delivery, and management reporting. An in-depth understanding of these processes will be very beneficial when you begin linking them to your Balanced Scorecard.

Conducting Interviews to Gather Executive Input

Once you have gathered sufficient background information, you are ready to synthesize your findings and confirm them through a one-on-one interview process with each member of the executive team, galvanizing support for the Scorecard and gathering insights to be used throughout the implementation. Keep in mind that this is your first opportunity to work with the executive team on the Balanced Scorecard implementation. We all know how important first impressions are in business and in life. Ensure you're prepared to show your executive team the value of this concept and the ability of your team to deliver results. I would suggest this format for your interviews:

- *Review purpose.* Your executives should already be familiar with the Balanced Scorecard. However, you should take the necessary time to explain the importance of soliciting their feedback in building an effective Strategy Map and set of measures. Outline (briefly) what you will be covering during the meeting and the anticipated duration.

- *Strategy.* Begin the interview by collecting executive input on this critical element of the Balanced Scorecard. Unless asked specifically, don't share what you've learned from your research. You're attempting to determine how your executives view this item, and whether there is alignment among your senior team. You may use these questions:

  1. What makes your organization unique? (This is a comfortable question to begin with as it allows the executive to think broadly about the nature of the firm and its success.)

  2. What strategy or strategies are you pursuing to achieve success? (You may be required to provide a working definition of strategy since it connotes different things to different people. Try "game plan" or "blueprint.")

  If the executive you're interviewing provides little in the way of details, or doesn't feel the organization really has a strategy, you will need to redirect the questions. Take the opportunity to probe the executive on her views by asking: "Why do you feel we exist as an organization (mission)?" "What core values do we hold?" "Where do you see us in 5, 10, or 15 years (vision)?" "What must we do to reach that desired future (strategy)?"

- *Performance measurement.* Use this component of the interview to gather the executive's thoughts on what objectives and measures are critical to the organization's success. Ask:

  1. How will we achieve the strategies you just discussed?

  2. What data or measures do you currently use to gauge success of the organization?

  3. Do you have targets for the measures? If so, what are they?

  4. What data or reports are most useful, and why?

  Of this set, question 4 is particularly interesting. Most organizations are currently gathering an abundance of data, some of which is valuable and some of which is completely disregarded. In the future, the Balanced Scorecard should be the focal report of management reporting. Find out what executives are watching now, what they like, and what they don't like.

- *Implementation issues.* In the final phase of the interview you hope to determine how well the executive understands the Balanced Scorecard and what must be done if the implementation is to succeed. Ask:

  1. How would you rate your direct reports' knowledge of the Balanced Scorecard?

2. What would help enhance your team's understanding of this concept?
3. What are some of the barriers we may face in implementing the Balanced Scorecard, and how do we overcome them?

You'll notice from question 1 that I don't advocate simply asking your executives to rate themselves on Scorecard knowledge. What self-respecting executive in today's measurement-managed environment is likely to admit he's never heard of the concept? Instead, it is better to ask executives about their team. During the conversation you'll be able to gauge whether the executive appears to be knowledgeable of the subject himself. If he says, "Well, Joe's former company did a high-level Scorecard, cascaded it from top to bottom, and used it to drive strategic learning through the management review process," then you'll know this executive probably has a pretty good grasp on the concepts. Plus, you can now casually slip in something like "Sounds like you're pretty familiar with the Scorecard yourself. Have you experienced it before?" You'll now be able to glean from the executive any direct Scorecard experience. Knowing which members of the executive team possess significant Scorecard knowledge is a great asset. These members of the senior team can act as sounding boards for your team's efforts and should be the first to provide leadership and support for the initiative.

Schedule the interviews for one hour, and limit your questions to about 10. You want your executives to be able to fully share their feelings on these subjects and don't want to cut them off in the middle of a thought to move on to another question. I've seen executive interviews with as few as 2 or 3 questions to as many as 40 (no kidding!).

In addition to interviewing members of your executive team, consider meeting with other influential people in the organization who may be in a position to increase the odds of a successful implementation. At some point you'll be relying heavily on your Information Technology Department to collect and disseminate data so be sure and include them in the process. Finance, Human Resources, Marketing, and Operations will also be involved in the initiative. Don't use the same interview questions with these groups as you did with the executive team. The goal during those interviews is to inform the audiences of your plans and win their support and assistance. Executive interviews can be tricky. To help you through the process, several tips are presented in Exhibit 4.4.

DEVELOPING OBJECTIVES FOR EACH PERSPECTIVE

In this section each perspective of the Strategy Map will be explored. Based on my years of experience as a practitioner and consultant in this field, I provide suggestions for creating objectives. Don't feel, however, that you

Exhibit 4.4　Tips for Conducting an Effective Interview

Hold the interview in the executive's office. In order to receive candid feedback, it's critical that executives feel comfortable. People tend to be most comfortable on their own turf. Therefore, whenever possible, conduct your interviews in the executive's office. In addition to putting them at ease, by holding the interview in their office, you have the opportunity to learn more about them based on their furniture, pictures, desk decorations, etc. Something in their environment is sure to provide the spark for an ice-breaking conversation.

Don't interrupt. I've learned this the hard way. Some people are measured in their comments, taking time to formulate an appropriate response. Ensure that executives have completed their thought before jumping in or moving on to the next question. Derailing them, even if just for a second, may throw off the rhythm of the interview significantly.

Consider having a designated note taker. I have yet to have someone say yes to this question: "Do you mind if I take some notes while we speak?" However, some people feel distracted by the note-taking. Therefore, if possible, have one person ask the questions and a second person in the room solely to take notes. That way the interviewer can establish a comfortable rapport with the executives.

Be prepared to deviate from the script. It's crucial to have questions prepared in advance, but be ready to move from topic to topic as the conversation flows. You may pose a question about financial objectives to which an executive replies, "We have to focus on growing revenue, and we'll do that by educating our employees on the latest customer service skills." You have received not only a financial objective, but an employee learning and growth objective as well. Be sure you capture that information, and either follow up immediately or return to it when the time is right.

Be aware of body language (both yours and theirs). Establishing a comfortable rapport is critical in receiving open, honest feedback. Your body language can either facilitate or inhibit this. Be sure to show interest through appropriate eye contact and facial expressions. Also be on the lookout for potential clues emanating from their body language. Do they physically back up or cross their arms with certain questions? If so, you've stumbled onto an area that they either are not comfortable discussing with you or have strong feelings on. Either way, tread carefully here to ensure you maintain the level of safety and comfort you've worked hard to establish.

Source: Adapted from Paul R. Niven, *Balanced Scorecard Diagnostics: Maintaining Maximum Performance* (Hoboken, NJ: John Wiley & Sons, 2005).

must include in your Map every objective and topic outlined in the pages that follow. The suggestions are based on my review of hundreds of Strategy Maps and the common themes that emerge. While I would expect substantial overlap with the elements to be discussed, you must never lose sight of the fact that your Map is just that, yours. The objectives you choose should be directly translated from your distinctive strategy. Thus it will not be surprising to discover that you have created objectives or contemplated areas not specifically outlined in these pages.

Developing Objectives for the Financial Perspective

In Chapter One I introduced the Balanced Scorecard as a method organizations can turn to in order to overcome their almost exclusive reliance on financial measures of performance. A number of issues relating to financial indicators of success were discussed:

- They are not consistent with today's business environment, in which most value is created by intangible assets.
- Financial measures provide a great "rearview mirror" of the past but often lack predictive power.
- Consolidation of financial information tends to promote functional silos.
- Long-term value-creating activities may be compromised by short-term financial metrics from activities such as employee reductions.
- Most high-level financial measures provide little in the way of guidance to lower-level employees in their day-to-day actions.

Thus the question may be posed: "Should we include a Financial Perspective when developing our Strategy Map and Balanced Scorecard?" Despite their apparent shortcomings, the answer is yes. Well-constructed Strategy Maps and Balanced Scorecards are not complete without financial objectives and measures of performance. Scorecard practitioners recognize this fact, and most actually consider financial indicators to represent the most vital component of the process. One study indicated that 49 percent of organizations rate the Financial perspective as of higher importance than any other.[7] With the question of whether to include a Financial perspective answered in the affirmative, we may now progress to determining the specific objectives that will comprise this top level of our Strategy Map.

In my little corner of the world, the entrepreneurial spirit is alive and well. One neighbor sells cabinetry to home builders, another has been in the automotive repair business for decades, while a third applies her creativity by designing Web sites. While our businesses and business models vary rather dramatically, the common thread we share is the knowledge that despite the variety of our offerings, our fortunes will rise and fall based on two critical levers of success: the ability to sell more and spend less. As long as the profit imperative has been wedded with commercial undertakings, this tenet of business has applied: To produce an increasingly healthy bottom line, we must always attempt to sell more of our products and services while reducing the cost burden we incur. Thus when developing objectives for the Financial Perspective of the Strategy Map, virtually all profit-seeking enterprises will cast their net over the themes of revenue growth and productivity, both pursued in an effort to ultimately drive greater value for shareholders. Let's break each of these down a little further.

Revenue growth is customarily accomplished in one of two ways: selling entirely new products and services to the market or deepening relationships with existing customers, thereby enhancing the value offered and generating additional profitability. Many organizations will attempt to do both. In fact, that is a strategy pursued by the cable television network Home Box Office (HBO). Facing a ratings slump that prompted one critic to suggest a potential change in the network's once iconoclastic tagline from "It's not TV, it's HBO" to "It's not HBO, it's TV as usual," the network has responded by pulling the new products lever with a range of offerings, including DVD sales of existing hit programs and an assertive expansion into the theatrical movie business. Bolstered by such tactics, the network aims to become less reliant on subscriber fees. In fact, as of 2005 a full 20 percent of the network's approximately $3.45 billion revenue was derived from ancillary businesses.[8] Additionally, HBO has attempted to deepen relationships with existing customers by providing fee-paying audiences a broader range of channels, such as "HBO Comedy," "HBO Signature," and "HBO Family," each offering unique viewing experiences.

Enhancing productivity is similarly achieved using a two-pronged approach. The first option, one exercised by virtually every client I have ever worked with, is simply reducing current costs, be they personnel or administrative in nature. While this theme can often be recklessly pursued using a hacksaw approach, our second option under the productivity umbrella is improving asset utilization, and it typically requires the precision of a scalpel to be rendered effectively. For example, utilizing techniques such as just-in-time provides companies the opportunity to support greater sales with less inventory, and reducing machine downtime through sophisticated maintenance allows for greater throughput without commensurate investments in equipment.[9]

Although the choice of objectives for the Financial perspective appears relatively limited, this portion of the Strategy Map introduces a tension that must be managed should we hope to ultimately derive economic benefits from the execution of our strategy. The tension comes in the form of finding an appropriate balance between the two seemingly contradictory forces of revenue growth and productivity; just how much do we step on the pedal of growth without breaking the bank in the process? Conversely, if we focus almost exclusively on austerity as our model, do we risk alienating a marketplace hungry for innovative new products? Analyzing results over time will help you determine how to dynamically shift the focus between these two levers, but the point remains that in order to drive shareholder value (which, if yours is a for-profit endeavor, should sit atop your Strategy Map), you must include both revenue growth and productivity objectives.

Developing Objectives for the Customer Perspective

Friends of my wife's family, a wonderful couple her parents have known for decades, recently celebrated their fiftieth anniversary. Although Lois and I couldn't attend the celebrations in person, the least we could do was send along a card with our best wishes. As their big day approached we spent what seemed like hours at the card store meticulously eyeing each offering in an attempt to come across one with just the right feeling to match the momentous occasion. Finally we found what seemed to be the perfect card: sentimental without being gushy, offering a pleasant verse but allowing enough space for us to add our own congratulatory prose. So off to the car we went, pen in hand to add our two cents' worth to the card, and that, my friends, is when our simple task took a drastic turn for the worse. The inside of the card read:

> *An anniversary is laughter and good times to share, joy that increases year after year, and memories to treasure always. Congratulations on 50 Memorable Years Together.*

How difficult should it have been to add a few lines ourselves? Turns out it was akin to splitting the atom for us. After each putting forth suggestions and compromising every step of the way, this is what we came up with: "We're so happy to have shared many happy memories with you in our share of those 50 years." You don't have to be an editor to recognize this mess, it hits you like a pail of cold water on a winter's day; we used "share" and "happy" each twice in the course of only 18 words, and threw in "memories" despite the fact that it was already included twice in the main text of the card. Needless to say, this masterpiece was never mailed; in fact, I have it sitting on my desk as a tribute to what can happen when you try to write something by committee. The point I am trying to make is we are sometimes fooled into thinking a task will be relatively simple when it turns out to be quite challenging indeed, and that is precisely what can happen when developing objectives for the Customer perspective. Let me explain.

Just two little, seemingly innocent questions must be answered when developing objectives for the Customer perspective of your Strategy Map: (1) Who are our target customers? and (2) What is our value proposition in serving them? Much like our foray into card writing, these two queries can provide a more vexing challenge than first meets the eye. Let's begin with question 1, "Who are our target customers?" When appropriately prodded, every executive or manager would trot out an answer to this question, but often their behavior in the marketplace belies their response. Many organizations, while professing to dedicate themselves to a core customer segment, practice an "all things for all customers" mentality. In attempting to serve the needs of the broad landscape of potential consumers before them, in the process they tend to do little for anyone. Strategy, it should be noted, is as much about what *not* to do as what to do, and this advice applies readily to the choice of a customer segment: Not every potential customer group will fund your profitable growth or find your offerings valuable. Your challenge is determining which groups constitute the best market for your particular offerings, in light of your strategy, and focusing your Strategy Map objectives on that subset of customers.

Our second question to be pondered and answered when developing Customer objectives for our Strategy Map was: "What is our value proposition in serving our targeted customers?" The customer value proposition describes how you will differentiate yourself and, consequently, what markets you will serve. To develop a customer value proposition, many organizations will choose one of three "disciplines" articulated by Treacy and Wiersema in *The Discipline of Market Leaders*:[10]

- *Operational excellence.* Organizations pursuing an operational excellence discipline focus on low price, convenience, and often "no frills." Anyone who shops at Costco will recognize it as an operationally excellent company. Low prices and great selection bring us back.

- *Product leadership.* Product leaders push the envelope of their firm's products. Constantly innovating, they strive to offer simply the best product in the market. Sony Corporation with its focus on bringing new and innovative technology and home entertainment devices to market would be considered a product leader.

- *Customer intimacy.* Doing whatever it takes to provide solutions for customers' unique needs helps define the customer-intimate company. Such companies don't look for one-time transactions but instead focus on long-term relationship building through their deep knowledge of customer needs. In the retail industry Nordstrom is a great example of a customer-intimate organization; its tales of heroic customer service have reached mythic proportions.

The value proposition you select will greatly influence the objectives you choose since each will entail a different emphasis.

Objectives of Operational Excellence

Treacy and Wiersema sum up the operationally excellent organization in one word: formula. These companies make hard choices to stay ahead of the competition: *"less product variety, the courage not to please every customer, forging the whole company, not just manufacturing and distribution, into a single focused instrument."*[11] Let's examine the objectives these organizations may use to track their special combination of skills.

- *Price.* The core focus of most operationally excellent companies is a relentless pursuit of low prices. Wal-Mart, Costco, and Southwest Airlines all offer consistently low prices compared to their competition. As a result, we would expect such organizations to include objectives such as "Ensure lowest prices" or "Offer lower prices than competitors" or "Offer best value to the consumer" when completing the Customer perspective of their Strategy Map.

- *Selection.* Operationally excellent organizations realize their customers don't expect them to supply every product under the sun—that would be a direct contravention of their "formula" for success. However, it's crucial for them to ensure efficient inventory control so all products are available for customers. Therefore "Maximize inventory turns," "Ensure product availability," and "Minimize stockouts" may populate their Customer perspective.

- *Convenience.* Stripping away costs they perceive as not adding value for the customer is the stamp of truly operationally excellent companies. These costs may be tangible or intangible. Saturn provides a great example of an organization removing an intangible cost of doing business for its customers—the inevitable confrontation with the salesperson. Saturn's no-haggle pricing makes it easy for customers to quickly determine the total cost of buying a car. "Reduce customer complaints" relating to service or delivery represents a possible convenience objective.

- *Zero defects.* When doing business with an operationally excellent company, customers anticipate zero defects, whether they're buying a Big Mac at any one of McDonald's thousands of restaurants or expecting a package from FedEx. Streamlining operations and closely coordinating with suppliers paves the way for this lofty goal. "Reduce manufacturing defect rates" or "Eliminate service errors" will be prime candidates for inclusion on the Strategy Map.

- *Growth.* Value leadership is the mantra of operationally excellent companies. Raising prices for innovative products or providing heroic customer service would run counter to their efforts of providing seamless service and ultra-efficient operations. What they do want is growth in their chosen markets. These organizations have developed a winning formula and will expect to see "Growth in targeted segments" as the proof of their success.

Product Leadership Objectives

Product leaders aren't content with a "new and improved" strategy; instead they focus on creating an endless flow of innovative products that offer customers unmatched functionality. Producing products that customers continually recognize as superior is the driving force behind these companies. Here are some of the areas you might consider for objectives if you are a product leader:

- *Getting the word out is a must.* Product leaders will strive to promote strong brand images by supplying customers with products that offer enhanced functionality, save them time, and consistently outperform the competition. Since they are constantly innovating, product leaders may occasionally develop products for which the market is not quite ready. Treacy and Wiersema tell the story of the Remington Company, which developed typewriters in 1874. Mark Twain bought one immediately and even invested in the company, but it took a full 12 years before the product caught on in the mainstream. "Build brand awareness" could be used to ensure the market recognizes the many new products surfacing. Given their penchant for pushing the envelope of innovation, product leaders might include as an objective "Monitor help line calls per product" to determine the amount of interest, and possibly confusion, in their latest development.

- *Functionality.* We look to product leaders like Intel to offer consistently better functionality in all of their offerings. After all, it's not their price —which is most likely higher—or their threshold levels of customer service that bring us back. "Increase number of customer needs satisfied" may be included as an objective to ensure expectations are being satisfied.

Objectives for Customer Intimacy

Customer-intimate organizations recognize that their clients have needs beyond which their product alone can satisfy. They offer their customers a total solution that encompasses a unique range of superior services so that customers get the greatest benefit from the products offered. Here are some attributes of customer-intimate organizations and the objectives you might use should you follow the customer-intimate approach:

- *Customer knowledge.* To succeed, all customer-intimate companies require a deep and detailed knowledge of their customers. To gauge staff knowledge, they may develop an objective of "Increase training hours on products and services offered."

- *Solutions offered.* Customer-intimate firms also realize that customers are not turning to them for low cost or the latest product; it's the unmatched total solution they offer. Therefore, "Increase total number of solutions offered per client" may be included within the Customer perspective.

- *Penetration.* At the height of IBM's success, it was customer intimacy that assured its good fortune. The critical objective Thomas Watson put forth to his staff was customer penetration, or "Enhance share of targeted customer spending." The customer-intimate organization aims to provide complete solutions for its client base and needs to ensure these efforts are achieving success by deep penetration of accounts.

- *Customer data.* To offer the solutions only they can, these organizations also require abundant and rich data on their customers. "Increase percentage of employees with access to customer information" may be stated as an objective to ensure this key differentiator of success will be monitored.

- *Culture of driving client success.* Employees of customer-intimate organizations feel they've succeeded when the customer has attained success. This attitude is deeply rooted in their culture. Receiving an award from a cherished client as proof of their contribution would be the greatest prize a customer-intimate company can receive. "Increase number of customer awards received" is an objective they may develop to communicate this desire.

- *Relationships for the long term.* Customer-intimate organizations don't take a short view of any client relationships. Their goal is to build long-lasting unions during which they can increase their share of the clients' business by providing unparalleled levels of knowledge and solutions. The relationship doesn't end when the sale is made; in fact, it is just beginning. At Roadway Logistics customers are assigned "directors of logistics development" who stay close to the process and often move to client locations. "Provide staff at client locations" could be an objective speaking of the deep relationship these organizations maintain with their clients.

During client workshops I frequently share the value proposition theory and challenge the group to determine which of the three best describes their company. After pondering the request for a suitable length of time a number of possibilities will surface, but gradually the group will suggest that while they maintain a core strength in one of the value propositions in order to compete effectively, they must be "a little bit of all three." I am sure when you contemplate your own firm for a moment, you will come to the same conclusion. Perhaps you have competed traditionally by offering the best service in your class, but that certainly hasn't precluded you from offering new services as warranted by the market and generating profitability from efficient operations. Even Wal-Mart, which must be considered the very exemplar of an organization with a fixed value proposition of operational excellence, has recently demonstrated the desire to dip a toe in the pools of adjacent value propositions. Responding to a decline in same-store sales, a closely watched metric in the retail galaxy, CEO Lee Scott told reporters that while Wal-Mart's focus will always be on less affluent shoppers, "We need to widen our appeal to a broader range of customer." As a result, the giant retailer plans to improve the quality of its household goods and apparel and enhance its consumable offerings with organic and natural food, all of which sounds a lot like a step on the path toward the product leadership value proposition.[12] When it comes time for you to develop objectives for the Customer perspective of your Strategy Map, ensure you've given due consideration to each of the value propositions, which yet again demonstrates the importance of balance when engaging in this process.

Developing Objectives for the Internal Process Perspective

The journey of life is one of transitions. Of course, the most obvious comes in the form of aging, from the carefree days of childhood to adolescence, and eventually to adulthood with its many attendant responsibilities. For those of us who choose to wed, we transition from being on our own to sharing our life, love, and home with another. There are many points on our travels that mark a distinction, a change in the course. The Strategy Map shares this characteristic with us, and our discussion of the Internal Process perspective portrays just such a major transition. Thus far in our examination of the Map, we have focused exclusively on the "what" of value creation—what we are ultimately hoping to achieve through the execution of our strategy as represented by the objectives of revenue growth, sustained shareholder value, and customer loyalty, to name a few. Now we must transition our efforts from the "what" to the "how." How exactly will we fulfill our unique value proposition as displayed in the Customer perspective and ultimately achieve the lofty objectives set forth in the Financial perspective? The Internal Process perspective starts us down the road of that discovery.

Not surprisingly, the consideration of "how" can often entail a broader number of options than the higher-level "what" we discussed in the preceding sections. This is the case in virtually any undertaking. For example, let's say it is dinnertime, and you have decided you will satisfy your hunger by eating pizza—a craving I indulge frequently. The "what" has been declared—it's pizza for dinner—but let's ponder for a moment the how. You could: order a pizza and pick it up from your favorite purveyor, have a pizza delivered to your house, travel to the supermarket and pick up a frozen pizza, or (and this is an option rarely deliberated at my house) even concoct and bake your own cheesy culinary delight. Are you hungry yet? And to think we haven't even broached the subject of toppings! Let's get back to the subject at hand to get our minds off food. The Internal Process perspective, given its focus on the "how" of value creation, typically spawns the greatest number of objectives on the Strategy Map and correspondingly the largest volume of measures on the Balanced Scorecard. Your significant challenge here is limiting yourself to just those critical processes that truly drive value for your customers and allow you to reach the promised land of breakthrough financial results. My experience tells me this is the perspective in which you are most likely to struggle largely because of the broad universe of potential objectives from which to choose. The strongest advice I can give you, and forgive the colloquial nature of it, is keep it real. By that I am suggesting that you limit your focus on just those processes that are indeed vital to your success in executing your strategy; stick to your knitting here and you will produce a stronger product in the end. Oh, and for the record, I normally order pizza and pick it up. Speaking of which, if you ever find yourself in Ramona, California, I strongly recommend Ray's Giant New York Pizza.

Possessing a framework or lens to focus the discussion of Internal Process objectives can prove to be of immense value; here once again we are indebted to Scorecard architects Kaplan and Norton, who have developed just such a framework. In their extensive research on the topic, Kaplan and Norton have identified four clusters of processes that are applicable to virtually any business venture: Operations Management processes, Customer Management processes, Innovation processes, and Regulatory and Social Processes.[13] Let's use each of these to guide us through the labyrinth that is the Internal Process perspective.

Operations Management Processes   The most basic of the four clusters, Operations Management processes relate to the basic, day-to-day routine processes necessary first to produce and ultimately to deliver a product or service to the market. Of course, prior to actually creating a product or service, the materials necessary to bring it to life must be acquired. Thus sourcing- or purchasing-related objectives frequently find their way on to Strategy Maps. And little wonder, since competitive sourcing can reap tremendous bottom-line results for savvy companies. Take Ford Motors, for example; it is currently overhauling its $90 billion-a-year global purchasing process to offer larger, long-term contracts to a smaller group of suppliers, a switch managers believe could potentially save the company billions of dollars a year.[14]

In addition to sourcing, this cluster of processes may also include the actual manufacturing or production of the product or service, distribution, and risk management. Therefore, we may expect to see objectives such as "Increase throughput," "Maximize yield," "Attract channel partners," and "Minimize risk" appearing on the Internal Process perspective of the Strategy Map. The admonition stated earlier bears repeating here: Given the vast number of possible choices for this cluster alone, you must exercise steadfast discipline in focusing on just those processes that will allow you to execute your unique strategy. Throughout the 1990s many organizations dwelt almost exclusively in the Operations Management arena, relying on proven tools such as Total Quality Management and Reengineering to produce a competitive advantage. While this is undoubtedly a valuable pursuit, it may not represent a sustainable source of value. Reliable and efficient operations have become a de facto prerequisite for business success, hence the importance of creating objectives in each of the three remaining process clusters.

Customer Management Processes   Of all the quips uttered by Henry Ford in his lifetime, it is a virtual certainty that he will be best remembered for this famous dictum on customer choice as it related to the Model T: *"They can have any color they want as long as it's black."* Oh, how times have changed! Thanks to the flood of innovations ushered in during this the age of the Internet, the balance of power has swung dramatically from supplier to consumer. Recognizing this undeniable fact of postmodern business life, organizations have begun to pay increasing attention to customer management processes, and we would expect to see objectives on your Strategy Map relating to this critical enabler of success.

A number of subprocesses comprise this cluster, beginning with the acquisition of your target customer group. Acquiring customers is the purview of the marketing function, proactively communicating the company's value proposition in hopes of turning window shoppers into actual paying customers. "Proactively" is the key word in that sentence, as the story of Listerine reveals. You probably didn't know that Listerine was invented in the nineteenth century as a powerful surgical antiseptic. In later incarnations it served as a floor cleaner and a reported cure for gonorrhea. It didn't achieve tremendous success, however, until the 1920s, when it was pitched as a solution for "chronic halitosis," an arcane medical term for bad breath. The folks at Listerine aggressively marketed the tonic using ads featuring forlorn young men and women, eager for marriage but somewhat repulsed by their mate's rotten breath. Until this campaigning by Listerine, bad breath wasn't considered the debilitating social condition it has since become. In just seven years the company's revenues rose from $115,000 to more than $8 million.[15]

Before the good people at Listerine had the revelation that halitosis was a condition requiring absolute abolition, they would have carefully studied their potential customer base, determining user needs and targeting their solution accordingly. Understanding customers and customer behavior is a critical process that must be confronted should we hope to reap the rewards of our marketing efforts. As consumer products giant Kimberly-Clark CEO Thomas J. Falk simply states: *"If we understand our customer better than anybody else, I know we're going to win in the marketplace."*[16]

Once you have lassoed customers by understanding their requirements and pitching the perfect solution, you shift gears toward the remaining subprocesses in this cluster: retaining clients and deepening your relationship with them. Common objectives may include "Increase customer retention," "Cross-sell products to customers," and "Maximize share of customer spending." As we all know, defending the status quo in business is a recipe for mediocrity at best. The spoils go to those who can not only attract customers but retain them for the long term and have them constantly craving more, all of which leads us to our next cluster of Internal Process objectives: innovation.

Innovation Processes   Some days it seems as if there really is nothing new under the sun, a feeling I frequently get after watching the latest formulaic offering from Hollywood. But, in fact, virtually every field of endeavor known to man has been touched in some way by the guiding hand of innovation. Take Thoroughbred horse racing, for example, probably not a topic you would immediately associate with change, but even the sport of kings has benefited from a spark of innovation lit primarily by one brash American jockey.

For over two centuries riders had followed the ironclad tradition of sitting far back in the saddle, uprightly perpendicular to the horse using long stirrups and long reins, a method that provided a point of calm stability as the horse stretched its legs out ahead and behind. It had never occurred to anyone to consider an alternative until one day when a young jockey named Tod Sloan was galloping a horse that bolted, leaving Sloan suddenly struggling for control. Instinctually, Sloan climbed up out of the saddle and onto the horse's neck, regaining control of the runaway equine. While his fellow jockeys laughed, Sloan sensed he was on to something revolutionary. After experimenting with the new method for several weeks, he discovered that the horse's stride seemed to be freer and it was easier for him to work as one with the animal, a critical component for success in racing. While the grip of tradition tugged against the innovation, success won out and the "forward seat," as it was dubbed, soon wiped clear any memories of the upright style used for hundreds of years. And no wonder: It significantly reduced wind resistance, moved the rider's center of gravity forward, and afforded him a better look ahead.[17]

Maybe you don't spend afternoons with your elbows glued to the rails of a racetrack, but I would wager most of you either drive or at least have driven in an automobile. You talk about a hotbed of innovation. The first sentence of an article I recently perused on the subject sums it up best: "Buck Rogers Your Ride's Here!" Describing the wave of innovation surging over the auto industry, the authors note: *"Increasingly, cars will become electronic thinking machines—not just mechanical devices. Computer controlled systems will replace gears and cables for steering, braking and accelerating. Radar technology will allow a car to see nearby hazards and even initiate evasive maneuvers. Traditional gas engines are already losing their monopoly to gas-electric hybrids; in the works are engines that run on hydrogen or 'bio-diesel' made from inexpensive source material such as cooking oil."*[18] And it's not just the headline-grabbing global auto companies that are investing time, energy, and money in creating the automobile of the future. The United States Army, possibly in deference to the venerable adage "Necessity is the mother of invention," has also waged war on the status quo. The military calculates that a soldier in the desert needs about 20 gallons of water a day, 5 of which must be pure enough to drink, prepare food, and use for medical needs. Getting it to the troops is no simple task; in fact, moving water and other materials can often tie up 40 percent of troops deployed in the field. In a move right out of a MacGyver episode, the Army is currently experimenting with devices that transform vehicle exhaust into a drinking water supply by condensing and filtering emissions. Says one proponent: *"When you first hear about it you think the scientists have gone out of their minds . . . but once you taste the water you realize the potential."*[19]

So, are you fired up and ready to revolutionize your industry? Outlined next are a number of subprocesses, all of which may spawn objectives for your Strategy Map, residing under the broad umbrella of innovation. The first is *identification of opportunities*. Creative organizations must constantly be patrolling the shores of their own and other industries, engaging employees, working with lead customers, and applying technologies in an attempt to outwit the competition through innovation. Often the most fruitful ideas are taking shape in the corridors and cubicles of your company as employees ruminate on the challenges and opportunities you face. Recognizing this vast potential, some leading companies have formed "affinity groups"—associations of employees united by gender, race, ethnicity, or other traits—to create new strategies and products. For example, the Hispanic employee affinity group of Frito-Lay provided input for a line of guacamole-flavored potato chips that became a $100 million product.[20]

With appropriate opportunities identified, the next challenge is determining whether you will *fund internally, work with joint ventures, or outsource entirely*. Regardless of the choice, an objective may be required on your Map to ensure this vital link in the innovation chain is progressing as planned. At the heart of the innovation process is our next subprocess, *development* of the product or service, which may be marked with objectives relating to quality or yield. Innovation is frequently compared to a pipeline that is constantly flowing; thus at any given time you may be churning out a number of new products and services, possibly necessitating the inclusion of an objective or objectives relating to the *introduction* of new products to the market. Our final subprocess sees us actually *delivering* the product or service, which often results in objectives regarding distribution channel options and effectiveness.

Regulatory and Social Processes   Thus far our discussion of the Internal Process perspective has maintained a decided focus on what occurs within the four walls of the company. To conclude our look at this perspective, we must recognize that all organizations have important stakeholders and constituents beyond those four walls. Regulated industries must maintain positive relationships with regulators and other governmental officials and adhere to a number of environmental regulations. Additionally, all organizations must strive to be good corporate citizens in the communities in which they operate. Companies are beginning to realize that this is not only the right thing to do, but it makes good business sense. A study by the Conference Board of Canada found that 80 percent of Canadian managers feel their company's good reputation goes a long way in recruiting and keeping quality employees.

Those organizations required to follow guidelines regarding environmental or health and safety issues have a wonderful opportunity to use the Strategy Map and Balanced Scorecard as a tool for moving from strict compliance to leadership. Take, for example, the case of electric utilities, which must adhere to many environmental and health and safety guidelines enforced by various government agencies. When developing their Internal Process perspective of their Strategy Map, these organizations have the opportunity to move beyond simple compliance and establish themselves as leaders in the field. "Be recognized as an environmental leader" may serve as an inspiring objective for all employees, signaling the company's commitment to sustainable business practices.

With increasing frequency and intensity, many companies will use this section of their Strategy Map to demonstrate their allegiance to strong corporate governance practices, and little wonder when the rap sheets of many disgraced CEOs run longer than a politician's list of campaign promises. "Exercise best-in-class governance" is an objective repeated in many Strategy Maps, especially since the disastrous collapse of Enron and many other once high-flying, press-grabbing companies. As with every other objective appearing on the Strategy Map, this promise of strict governance must not be cloaked simply in appealing rhetoric but be backed with specific metrics and initiatives to ensure that it becomes a reality in a world that demands improved corporate citizenship.

To prove successful over time, a company both contributes to and relies heavily on the prosperity of the community. While the organization is not solely responsible for the welfare of the surrounding community, it is incumbent on the organization, and in its best interests, to monitor community success and ensure it is contributing to the area's ongoing prosperity. Bob Nelson expresses it effectively in his book, *1001 Ways to Energize Employees*. Bob says: *"These days the best organizations are involved in and contribute to their communities . . . . It all boils down to helping find ways to make their communities better places to live, work, and do business through the sharing of resources, the labor of their employees, or just plain old-fashioned cash."*[21] Bob chronicles a number of leading-edge organizations that have taken community involvement to a new level. One such company is Maryland spice manufacturer McCormick and Company. It opens its plant one Saturday each year for "Charity Day." Employees work their normal shifts, but all wages are directed to the charity of each employee's choice. In the spirit of community caring, McCormick donates twice the employee's daily wage to the charity. You could inspire community involvement by making a place for it on your Strategy Map with objectives such as "Become more involved in our community" or "Encourage community prosperity."

To close the discussion of Internal Processes objectives, let me repeat some advice I provided in Chapter One regarding cause-and-effect linkages among the four perspectives of the Strategy Map. In my opinion, the key linkages you should consider articulating on the Map (and in the Scorecard of measures) are between the Internal Process and Customer perspectives. In many ways the objectives appearing in the Employee Learning and Growth perspective, which will be discussed next, are the enablers of everything you're attempting to achieve, and thus they may not warrant one-to-one connections with other sections of the Map. However, the link between processes and customers is key, as it is here we signal two major transitions: from internal (employees, climate, processes) to external (customers) and from intangible (skills and knowledge, etc.) to tangible (customer outcomes and financial rewards). Customer outcomes signal the "what" of strategic execution, and Internal Processes supply the "how." Every organization should make an effort to document this equation explicitly, articulating specifically how it expects to transform its unique capabilities and infrastructure into revenue-producing results.

Developing Objectives for the Employee Learning and Growth Perspective

I once had a conversation with a consultant (from a firm that shall remain nameless) regarding one of his current client engagements. He described the project as one of developing a high-level performance management system and cascading it to lower levels of the organization. I naturally became quite excited about this since the topic is of great interest to me. "What have you put on your corporate Strategy Map?" I enthusiastically asked. He replied they had decided to focus on financial and operational objectives but weren't developing employee and learning objectives since "that stuff's going to happen anyway." *Wrong!* It's not going to just happen, you have to make a concerted effort to ensure it does. If you don't, you'll never really have a *Balanced* Scorecard or derive the benefits of the system. As we discussed in Chapter One, the value creation in today's organization is overwhelmingly dominated by the influence of human capital. People— their knowledge and means of sharing it—are what is driving value in our modern economy. Describing the activities that drive this value is the purview of the Employee Learning and Growth perspective.

The objectives appearing in this perspective of the Strategy Map are really the "enablers" of the other perspectives. Motivated employees with the right mix of skills and tools operating in an organizational climate designed for sustaining improvements are the key ingredients in driving process improvements, meeting customer expectations, and ultimately driving financial returns. Kaplan and Norton have noted that people often object to the placement of this perspective in Scorecard diagrams. Doesn't placing it at the bottom minimize its importance? Quite the contrary, the Scorecard architects say. It's at the bottom because it acts as the foundation for everything else above it. At a conference I attended some time ago, I had the good fortune to hear Bob Kaplan outline the Strategy Mapping process. When he came to the Employee Learning and Growth perspective, he described it as the roots of a powerful tree, which are the sources of support and nourishment leading to the blossoms of financial returns. His enthusiasm was tremendous throughout the talk, but I noticed a particular emphasis on this point as if to underscore its importance to sometimes incredulous audiences.

While most people would undoubtedly agree with everything stated thus far in the section—people are any organization's most crucial source of value, and thus developing objectives for the foundational Employee Learning and Growth perspective is critical—many will struggle when it comes time to actually take a marker to the flip chart and begin recording potential objectives. I can't say why this is with any degree of certainty, but the gravitational pull of traditional performance systems is an obvious culprit. Historically we've been taught to closely monitor financial returns, ensure efficiency of operations, and ensure happy and loyal customers—all things we can count with relative ease. Gauging the effectiveness of a workforce fully aligned with your strategy, however, can prove to be a significant challenge to even the most measurement-minded of firms. Some organizations will even delude themselves into thinking they do a top-notch job of reporting on people matters when simply tugging ever so slightly on the reins of reality displays an often shocking truth, as you will discover with this story. A client once told about meetings she was conducting with the senior Human Resources (HR) team at her organization during which they were receiving a brief on the many benefits of the Balanced Scorecard. During one session a very senior person proudly proclaimed they had "great HR reports that are tracked on a regular basis." My client was impressed but not a little confused and skeptical considering she, a veteran of more than 10 years with the company, had never seen a single one of those so-called great reports. A little sleuthing on her part revealed the startling fact that the reports had stopped being run a year and a half ago because nobody was doing anything with them. Senior management in HR, perhaps in the vein of "why let the truth ruin a good situation," thought the reports were still being run and making a major impact on executive decision making.

To ensure you avoid becoming a future victim of one of my anonymous stories, and to help you overcome the issues of creating Employee Learning and Growth objectives, we will once again rely on a helpful framework to provide scaffolding for our discussion. In the sections that follow, three distinct areas of "capital"—human, information, and organizational—will be reviewed. All of them should find a place on any well-constructed Strategy Map.

Human Capital—Aligning People with the Strategy The economist John Kenneth Galbraith once noted: *"People are the common denominator of progress. No improvement is possible with unimproved people."*[22] No improvement, and certainly no strategy execution, is even remotely possible without the right people, armed with the skills and knowledge required to make decisions and allocate resources in alignment with the company's chosen direction. Let's look at some possible objectives relating to human capital:

Closing skill gaps in strategic positions. As gasp-producing as this may be to career Human Resource staffers, not all jobs are created equally. While every individual within your company undoubtedly possesses unique and valuable talents, not all jobs being filled are critical to achieving your strategy. The first step in mobilizing the power of human capital is matching the best people with the most strategically critical jobs. To do this you must identify which positions within the organization are pivotal to ensuring the fulfillment of key processes as set forth in the Internal Process perspective and will ultimately drive your customer value proposition, thereby helping to ensure you achieve the financial objectives you've developed. Once the positions are chosen, competencies necessary for peak performance must be enumerated, enabling you to determine any gap that exists between incumbent employee talents and those desired to execute the strategy. Slamming the door shut on skill gaps is typically accomplished through a combination of training and retention of current staff, recruitment of new players, and succession planning to ensure the tap of knowledge runs freely.

Training for success. What management book, or any book for that matter, would be complete without a quote from the esteemed German novelist, playwright, and philosopher Johann Wolfgang von Goethe? In that spirit I offer this: *"Treat a man as he is and he will remain as he is; treat a man as he can and should be and he will become as he can and should be."*[23] To give people a leg up in becoming all they can be, many organizations will turn to training in specific areas to bolster skills and knowledge and ultimately improve the firm's fortunes. While objectives relating to training are wildly popular on Strategy Maps, a caveat on the subject of our next chapter, measurement, is in order. To prove effective, every objective appearing on the Map must be accompanied by a robust metric to provide a tracking mechanism, and this is especially the case with training. Simply counting the "number of training hours" is unlikely to lead to sustained corporate success. I once heard a consultant refer to such a measure as the "BIC" metric, with the acronym BIC standing for "butts in chairs." A change of behavior, not blisters on the backside, is what is required of this metric, a demonstration of the new skills or knowledge in action, leading to improved results. Therefore, when considering a training objective for your Strategy Map, look ahead to the next step of measurement and make an honest assessment of your ability to create a meaningful metric.

Recruitment, retention, and succession planning. Drawing on the classic What came first, the chicken or the egg? query, what should organizations begin with: creating a winning strategy and then populating their ranks with people to carry it out, or starting with the right people and then conjuring up a differentiating plan? In the study that inspired his book, Jim Collins, author of the wildly popular *Good to Great,* found evidence that winning companies have the proclivity to start with people and work from there. He notes: *"The executives who ignited the transformations from good to great did not first figure out where to drive the bus and then get people to take there. No, they first got the right people on the bus (and the wrong people off the bus) and then figured out where to drive it."*[24] I could probably fill a chapter with quotes denoting the unquestionable bond between people and corporate success. It is self-evident that no organization can succeed without the right people "on the bus," as Collins puts it. An objective related to recruitment and retention of associates qualifies as a must-have for Strategy Map development, but exercise caution in your wording. As General Electric's famous classification scheme of A, B, and C players gained momentum in the mainstream, I began to see more and more Strategy Maps including an objective such as "Recruit and Retain 'A' Level Employees" or "Recruit and Retain the Best and the Brightest." Far from elitist, the authors' intentions are good but the language inevitably stirs rancor within the rank and file who scratch their heads and wonder, "Just what does it take to be an 'A' level performer anyway?" Don't be careless with loaded language of this nature; if you plan to use such an objective, ensure you've carefully and clearly documented exactly what you mean by the associated terms.

You've attracted the right people for your team and have put in place mechanisms designed to keep them stimulated and satisfied for years to come, but what do you do as they inevitably begin to age and consider the lure of retirement? According to a new study by the Conference Board, more than 40 percent of the U.S. labor force will reach the traditional retirement age by the end of this decade, while the number of workers between ages 35 and 44 is expected to shrink by 7 percent.[25] This clash of demographic meteors leads to just one conclusion: Succession planning must be embraced by every organization concerned with capturing the knowledge of long-term workers and passing the torch to the next generation.

We all know that balanced diets and more exercise will enhance our health, but do we avail ourselves of tofu and treadmills? Not always, and such is the case with succession planning. Most organizations recognize at least intellectually that succession planning should drive leadership development, but many fail to take action. Why not? Here is what three experts on the subject suggest: *"Many people, from the CEO on down, consider the word 'succession' taboo. Planning your exit is like scheduling your own funeral; it evokes fears and emotions long hidden under layers of defense mechanisms and imperceptible habits. Perversely, the desire to avoid this issue is strongest in the most successful CEOs. Their standard operating procedure is to always look for the next mountain to climb, not to step down from the mountain and look for a replacement.*"[26] I currently have a client who slips this description on like a perfectly fitting suit; he is talented, motivated, inspiring, but bring up the word "succession" in his presence and the rockets begin to flare. Recognizing the trends, some forward-thinking organizations have begun formal programs to start the succession ball rolling. IBM, for example, encourages its 330,000 employees to post detailed descriptions of their job experiences in an online directory called the "Blue Pages," so that employees far from retirement can find knowledge before it walks out the door.[27]

Information Capital—Aligning Information with the Strategy   Research and analysis firm The Gartner Group estimates worldwide information technology (IT) spending during 2006 will reach an all time high of $2.6 trillion, yes, that is trillion, which is more than the gross domestic product of many countries or about the same amount Ben Affleck spent on the rock he gave Jennifer Lopez. Let's hope all those IT spenders get a better return on their investment than Ben managed.[28] If intellectual capital is fueling our modern economy, surely technology is the engine that keeps companies and entire industries chugging forward on the path of relentless progress.

Given the pervasive influence of technology, virtually every organization should consider an information capital objective when forming the Employee Learning and Growth perspective. In my experience working with a wide array of organizations, these objectives typically are phrased something like this: "Improve technology infrastructure," "Leverage technology," "Increase knowledge management and information sharing," "Gather, share, and use information effectively." The first example relates to the infrastructure component of information capital, ensuring you have the physical tools (mainframes, etc.) necessary to deliver information to users. The remaining examples center on the need of gathering stored information, sharing it widely, and having employees harness it in their day-to-day actions.[29] As with human capital, the critical dimension to consider when crafting an information capital objective is the linkage between technology and strategy. Your individual game plan for corporate success will undoubtedly require technology if you hope to outperform your rivals, and thus the choice of objectives should mirror the IT contribution you require to execute the strategy.

Organizational Capital—Sowing the Seeds of Sustainable Future Growth and Change   History provides many vivid portraits of men and women toiling against seemingly insurmountable odds and facing what appear to be overwhelming obstacles, only to turn sure defeat into stunning and glorious victory. Military sagas are replete with such tales of heroism and cunning, as is the field of exploration—it seems incomprehensible that Lewis and Clark, for example, could have led an expedition into virtually uncharted territory, spanning a vast continent and lasting two years with precious few supplies, to return with a treasure trove of scientific and cultural knowledge and suffer only one casualty! The human spirit is beautifully indomitable and can literally move mountains when inspired by a worthy cause. Within the organizational capital dimension we are seeking to draw on the infinite resources of human strength and capture both the hearts and minds of our employees, in an effort to make sustainable growth and prosperity a literal reality. Outlined next are two key elements you may consider when drafting objectives for this section of the Strategy Map: culture and alignment.

Let's begin our discussion of culture, this most elusive of topics, by attempting to define the term. One of the most useful explanations of culture I have come across is that offered by Stan Davis from the Columbia University Graduate School of Business, who suggests: *"Culture is a pattern of beliefs and expectations shared by an organization's members. These beliefs and expectations produce norms that can powerfully shape how people and groups behave."*[30] While this is a very helpful definition, to simplify the matter even further, we may think of culture as "the way we do things around here." If culture isn't the most "touchy-feely" of all management topics, the roll call in its class certainly would not take long to conduct. But how important is culture to an organization's success? Turns out it is a vital contributor. In their book, *Corporate Culture and Performance*, authors Heskett and Kotter discovered that over a 12-year period, firms with effective cultures achieved stock price growth of 901 percent compared to just 74 percent for those with ineffective cultures. Over that same span those with effective cultures saw revenue growth of over 680 percent while the ineffective group managed only 166 percent gains.[31]

As a consultant, I have the unique opportunity to peer through the window of culture at each of my clients, and believe me, the vistas provided are very enlightening indeed. For example, take this "Tale of Two Clients" I am currently working with. At the first, an organization priding itself on teamwork, positive feedback, and innovation, it is not uncommon for spontaneous rounds of applause to erupt during management meetings as executives note the accomplishments of others in helping the company reach its lofty targets. They openly cite their culture as a competitive advantage in their success. At the other end of the culture spectrum, the second client is characterized by a combative management and meeting style, an insular view of the world, and a CEO who is renowned for withholding information. Several insiders have confided in me that they believe this culture is holding them back and taking a severe toll on employees, many of whom appear to be actively disengaged. If you accept the proposition that people are your most critical resource, asset, whatever term you choose, then you owe it to yourself to gauge your current culture and determine whether it is aligned with your strategic direction.

The misalignment of culture and strategy is a volatile cocktail capable of disastrous results, as the story of Encyclopaedia Britannica illustrates.

For much of the firm's venerable history, its 32 volumes were considered the ultimate repository of knowledge from art to zoology. As the world transitioned from bound books to personal computers in the quest for information, Encyclopaedia Britannica was initially well positioned to make the transition. In 1989 the company introduced one of the earliest multimedia CD-ROM encyclopedias, *Compton's MultiMedia*. The culture of the company, however, stood in the way of maintaining the leadership position. That culture was dominated by a nationwide force of direct-to-home salespeople, the very force that had make Encyclopaedia Britannica a trusted household name. No one dared to tinker with the traditional sales format on which his or her livelihood depended. The sacredness of the direct sales force business model was the company's Achilles' heel. As a result, Encyclopaedia Britannica failed to develop a serious strategy for electronic products until it was too late. Annual unit sales collapsed from a high of 117,000 to about 20,000. It took the intervention of an outside investor and the abandonment of the direct sales approach to save what was left of the company.[32]

Shaping or manipulating a culture, which can take years of habitual and patterned behavior, is well beyond the scope of this book. However, I can offer a few concrete steps you can take to help manage and change your culture to ensure it exists in harmony with your strategy. The first is recruiting and selecting people you believe embody the culture you are attempting to either sustain or create. Who you choose to carry out your work and liaise with your team is completely within your sphere of control, so take the opportunity to select those individuals who will further your cultural aspirations. Second, manage your culture through intense socialization and training initiatives, demonstrating what you expect from employees. The means of accomplishing this are many, varied, and sometimes downright bizarre. As an example of the latter, consider the online brokerage and banking firm E*Trade. During their first meeting at this innovative company, new employees are required to stand on a chair and tell everyone in attendance something embarrassing about themselves. Doing so knocks down a lot of barriers and creates a bond between employees, allowing them to open up and feel comfortable asking questions of coworkers, since appearing to lack a little esoteric corporate information pales in comparison to the loss of face suffered from regaling deep dark secrets. Finally, you may advance culture using the formal reward systems of the organization. If you value teamwork, a customer-centric approach and attitude, and innovation, those traits should be tangibly rewarded in an effort to have that culture deeply entrenched.[33]

The problems of misalignment are frequently and colorfully reflected by parents of youngsters participating in soccer leagues.[34] If you've ever been to one of these "matches," you know what I'm referring to: a blur of frenzied activity around the ball with not a single player venturing more than a few feet from that maelstrom of action. There is no coordination of activities, just a mad scramble covering a few square yards of the pitch. Of course this is quite amusing if you're watching from the stands with your camcorder catching the moment for posterity; after all, the stakes are relatively minor. But for organizations, a lack of alignment can prove extremely hazardous to any hope of executing strategy. Employee actions must be aligned with mission, values, vision, and, most important, strategy, should you wish to fully exploit the advantages of intangible assets such as culture and knowledge. The first step on the road to an aligned organization is ensuring employee understanding of the building blocks of mission, values, vision, and strategy. Only through understanding will action follow. A simple and effective method of ensuring alignment is reviewing cascaded Balanced Scorecards from throughout your organization. While most Scorecards will rightly contain unique objectives and measures, they should be aligned toward a common strategy if you hope to have all oars rowing in a winning direction. We'll discuss the notion of alignment and cascading in greater depth in Chapter Seven.

DEVELOPING A SHARED UNDERSTANDING USING OBJECTIVE STATEMENTS

As shadows creep slowly across the floor the clock strikes five, flip charts cover virtually every square inch of wall space in the room, and all that remains of the afternoon snacks are a few stray chocolate chips and a solitary can of warm ginger ale. You're mentally drained but deep within you surges a drumbeat of satisfaction and accomplishment because you have just put the finishing touches on your first ever Strategy Map. Although it's doubtful that someone will now point a camera in your direction imploring you to yell "I'm going to Disney World," you are in line for a well-deserved break before moving on to the task of measures development. If you are like many of my clients, that break may comprise a week or two as the pressing calls of your "day job" relentlessly beckon. When, some time later, you do reconvene to brainstorm measures for each of the objectives on your Map, a strange sensation comes over you—you can't remember a thing about the objectives that grace the Map. Sure, broad themes are evident, but the specific nature and tone of each objective is a semantic mystery. The job of developing measures, a daunting one to begin with, has just been rendered significantly more difficult as a result of this cognitive lapse.

A simple method to avoid situations like this from blocking your progress, and severely testing your sanity, is the crafting of two- to three-sentence narratives for each objective soon after you have completed the Strategy Map. I refer to these notes as "objective statements" and feel they provide several benefits. Their primary function and advantage is clearly articulating specifically what is meant by each objective appearing on the Map. That alone can pay tremendous dividends, should your Map contain potentially cloudy objectives such as "Enhance productivity," which could be capably gauged by any number of metrics. Curious readers of your Strategy Map will also be grateful you took the time to pen objective statements as they serve to supplement what appears on the Map, filling in the blanks with crucial and explanatory information on why you have chosen the specific objectives they see before them. A well-written objective statement should be succinct (you're not writing a novel here; two or three sentences should suffice), clarify with precision what is meant by the objective and why it is important, outline how it links in your chain of cause and effect, and, finally, briefly outline how it will be accomplished. Here is an example of a well-composed objective statement from my client the Recreation Vehicle Dealers Association (RVDA):

Become the one stop resource for practical dealer information

RVDA staff should have so much knowledge about RV retail processes and information that anyone in the RV Industry with a question about RV retailing will come to RVDA first. This is important so that RVDA can help their members have an easy way to get information in one convenient place. We will accomplish this through more staff knowledge and increased communications with members, potential members, and the industry. To achieve this we must identify what information is required to support dealer operations and create standardized information systems that ensure the availability of needed data so that staff members can access and pass on information.

The most opportune time to craft objective statements is immediately following the workshop while the mental flame is still smoldering brightly and everything is crisp and fresh in your mind. To balance personal biases and perceptions that may emerge from individuals drafting the statements, have small teams of two or three people write them, ensuring what is created reflects the actual discussion of the day and the entire team's collective understanding of each objective.

CONDUCTING EFFECTIVE STRATEGY MAPPING WORKSHOPS

As with any important session, the Strategy Mapping workshop will require careful planning to produce successful results. Let's look at what should take place before, during, and after the event to ensure that your team generates a Strategy Map that depicts the story of your strategy in clear and compelling fashion.

Before the Meeting

Preparation is the key to success in any meeting situation. The first thing you must decide is who will facilitate the session. I suggest using an outside consultant or trained facilitator to manage the workshop. A skilled consultant or facilitator will be able to spark group thinking and apply proven techniques to ensure you achieve your goals for the session. Schedule the workshop for a full day, which, when you include breaks and time for a refueling lunch, will typically be eight hours. Here are some other items to consider before your session:

- *Distribute materials in advance.* The Strategy Map will translate your mission, values, vision, and strategy, so ensure the team has received the most recent versions of each of these documents. In addition, pass around the information you gathered from your executive interviews.

- *Determine where to hold the meeting.* I have no empirical evidence to back up this claim, but I firmly believe those Strategy Maps created at off-site locations, away from the hustle and bustle of the office, tend to be of a higher quality. The recipe for a powerful Strategy Map includes contemplation, careful analysis, and a healthy dose of creativity, all of which can be helped along by the right location. Too many people associate meeting rooms in their office buildings with long and boring speeches, useless information exchanges, and wasted time, so why not tip the scales in your favor by moving to a venue sure to stimulate creativity. You don't have to meet on a mountaintop in Utah, although I'm sure that would be inspirational; just get out of your building to a place with no negative associations for your team. I have been fortunate enough to lead Mapping workshops in quaint country inns, restored manors, rustic cabins, and of course lots of hotel conference rooms.

- *Prepare the room.* Regardless of where you stage your meeting, room preparation is a key. Post the mission, values, vision, and strategy on large banners or pages at prominent locations around the room. Everyone in attendance should be able to clearly see these documents for easy reference. Also post any particularly interesting or relevant quotes heard during your executive interviews. The senior management team must ultimately own this tool, and therefore you want to ensure their thinking is imprinted into everything you do. You must also have flip chart pages up and ready to capture input from the group. Have sheets prepared for each of the perspectives of the Strategy Map along with parking lot items, and other issues. Finally, we all know the old saying "The devil is in the details." Make sure you have an ample supply of flip chart paper, Post-it notes, pens, and tape to capture it all.

During the Meeting

Filmmaker Woody Allen is credited with saying "*Ninety percent of life is showing up.*" I've really enjoyed many of Woody's cinematic efforts, but I have to disagree with him on that point—at least as it relates to your Strategy Mapping workshop. Once your attendees "show up," then it's up to you to make sure everyone gets the most out of the session. You've done your

homework, distributed your materials, and have assurances of perfect attendance at your meeting. Now let's look at what must take place during the
session to guarantee a successful outcome.

- *Opening the meeting.* Your facilitator should thank everyone for attending,
  congratulate them on their efforts to this point, and clearly outline the
  challenging yet exciting work that lies ahead. She will also state her role
  in the session, that of objective facilitator. Goals for the meeting should
  also be presented, along with housekeeping items, such as timing and
  amenities (if you're offsite). Finally, the session's ground rules will be
  presented. While the session is meant to be casual, certain rules do apply.
  Specifically: active participation by all participants, no rejected ideas,
  and adherence to the time limits.

- *Capturing ideas.* If yours is a for-profit undertaking, you will typically
  begin the Map development by brainstorming objectives for the Financial perspective, followed respectively by Customer, Internal Process,
  and finally Employee Learning and Growth. I tend to shy away from
  pure group brainstorming despite its proven effectiveness and widespread use. Too often a few people tend to dominate the proceedings,
  leaving the less verbose mute in their chairs. Even if you have a relatively small team, start by breaking them up into groups to stimulate
  some good-natured rivalry and create stronger ideas. For example, let's
  say you have 10 people participating in the session; begin by splitting
  them into three groups: two consisting of 3 people and the third of 4.
  Each group will have 30 minutes to brainstorm as many objectives as
  they can muster, but they must be prepared to come to consensus on
  their top four before wrapping up. When the 30 minutes has expired,
  the deck is shuffled and participants are placed in two groups of 5.
  These groups, given approximately 40 minutes, spend a few minutes
  reviewing the various objectives generated in the smaller groups, then
  brainstorm themselves to come to consensus on what objectives they feel
  should comprise that perspective. Finally, the facilitator asks each group
  to volunteer its final objectives and leads a plenary discussion until the
  ultimate objectives are determined.

- *Keeping people engaged.* The first line of defense here is limiting distractions by asking people to surrender the ubiquitous accoutrements
  of modern business: cell phones, BlackBerries, and even iPods. Of course,
  surrendering them is probably not an option, as most people would
  consider that request tantamount to depriving them of oxygen. As a
  compromise ask that all such devices be turned off during the session
  to ensure that creative insights are not rudely interrupted by the William
  Tell Overture emerging from someone's bag. Standard facilitation advice
  applies to your Mapping workshop. You must ensure all voices are being
  heard, opinions and feelings honored, and thoughts captured. If ever
  a member of the team has become so disengaged as to actually begin

to doze off, I would recommend this intervention technique offered by a man who has probably never spent a day of his life in an office but knows a thing or two about human nature, Dave Barry: *"Have everybody leave the room, then collect a group of total strangers, from right off the street, and have them sit around the sleeping person and stare at him until he wakes up. Then, have one of them say to him, in a very somber voice, 'Bob, your plan is very, very risky, but you've given us no choice but to try it. I only hope, for your sake, that you know what the hell you're getting yourself into.' Then, they should file quietly from the room."*[35]

After the Workshop

Your team leader will hold the responsibility for taking the nuggets of raw material generated during the meeting and putting them into a draft Strategy Map form, which will then be distributed to the team for further review and refinement.

HOW MANY OBJECTIVES ON THE STRATEGY MAP?

To both inspire my clients and give them a mental leg up when developing Strategy Maps, I often share dozens of other Maps from clients and those in the public domain. As we're reviewing I ask the assembled group which Maps they like, which do not resonate with them, and why. Invariably, and I mean every single time, clients will state their unanimous preference for Maps with fewer objectives, citing the clarity, simplicity, and cogent nature of these renderings. And this is why I compare myself with Charlie Brown as he strides confidently toward the football ready to punt a mighty blow only to have Lucy yank it away at the last second. Why do I feel like poor old Charlie Brown? Because you would think he'd learn after all these years to anticipate Lucy's action, but he doesn't; instead, he's upended and lands with a thud on the turf every time. So it is with me; after hearing the rave reviews for compact Strategy Maps, I am certain every client will work diligently in our sessions to create something succinct, only to see the flip chart pages pile up like bills after Christmas and the number of objectives balloon into the 20s, 30s, and sometimes even 40s.

Of course a number of factors conspire to cause this rising tide of objectives. First of all, it is often simply easier to create a large number of potential and mediocre objectives than hone in with surgical precision on the critical objectives that truly translate your strategy and tell your story. The converse of this is a culprit as well: Given the important nature of the task at hand, many groups will leave no stone unturned in their quest to discover each and every relevant objective. Finally, since teams are customarily comprised of individuals representing various business units and groups, human nature seeps to the surface and has each person proposing objectives reflecting local interests.

Perhaps more than any single attribute, a well-constructed Strategy Map can provide clarity to a workforce hungry for insights into what is of truly strategic significance to the firm. It is difficult if not impossible to shine a light of clarity on your strategy if the Map you have chosen to faithfully represent that strategy contains 30 or 40 objectives, a situation bound to send people scrambling in every direction and potentially causing diffusion of responsibilities. The principal tenet of the entire Balanced Scorecard system is focus, a laserlike beam on what truly matters, keeping you riveted to the critical drivers of success and relegating the white noise to the periphery. Therefore, in my opinion, less truly is more when it comes to Strategy Map development. Despite the significant challenges in the task, you should devote your energies in drafting a Map that tells your story in the absolute minimum number of objectives. Of course I recognize that "absolute minimum" is a relative term open to interpretation; thus, as a rule of thumb, I would suggest you attempt to create your first Strategy Map with no more than 15 objectives. Doing so ensures your choices reflect only the vital few, eliminating the trivial many, and also assists you in limiting the number of performance measures you will ultimately track to monitor your ongoing success. For those of you gasping in horror at the thought of so few objectives, I give you this motivational quote from Robert Schiller, author of *Irrational Exuberance: "The ability to focus attention on important things is a defining characteristic of intelligence."*[36]

CUSTOMIZING YOUR STRATEGY MAP

My siblings and I often joke that our dad was born at least 20 years too early. One of the justifications we typically parade in support of that claim is the fact that Dad was a huge fan of Elvis Presley, this despite the fact that by the time Elvis really exploded in popularity, ushering in the era of rock 'n' roll, our father was already in his early 40s. We lost our dad last year, and for some reason I feel as if I need to carry on the Elvis torch in his honor, so while channel surfing on a recent evening I found *Jailhouse Rock*, a 1957 Elvis film, and had to watch. In the film, 22-year-old Elvis portrays Vince Everett, an ex-con looking to make a name for himself in the music business. From his first turn at the microphone it is obvious that Vince has talent, but he struggles to secure a recording contract, continually being told he sounds like everyone else. It's not until he begins to sing as he feels the song deep within himself that his true voice emerges, and when it does, when he discovers his authentic voice, the inevitable climb to stardom begins.

One of the chief criticisms I levy at the bulk of Strategy Maps sent my way for review by organizations that have already engaged in the process is they all tend to look alike, stuffed to the brim with the latest business jargon and predictable objectives. Remember, the Strategy Map is first and foremost a communication tool, signaling to everyone the key objectives required to execute your strategy. Therefore, it should reflect not only your strategy but also your unique culture, values, and even eccentricities. Most initial efforts remind me of Elvis's character Vince: They demonstrate talent but they don't represent the true voice of the organization. In the paragraphs that follow you will discover two organizations that broke the mold and developed out-of-the-ordinary but remarkably effective Strategy Maps.

Your first decision in personalizing the Strategy Map is choosing the structure of the document itself. If, for example, you're a for-profit enterprise, will you make the customary choice of placing the Financial perspective at the top of the map? Most organizations do so without really questioning whether that is indicative of their true beliefs and passion. Brother Industries (USA), Inc., is a fine example of a company that did take the time to ponder whether placing finances at the top of the Strategy Map was true to its strongest intentions. After careful consideration it decided customer satisfaction, a passionate belief held widely throughout the company, was most critical and thus the Customer perspective should be placed at the top of the Strategy Map hierarchy. Interestingly, that led to another question: "Does the hierarchical structure of the typical Strategy Map work for us?" Again, Brother chose the road less traveled and determined that the Map was primarily a communication tool and thus should be both interesting and original, corresponding to the culture of the organization. The resulting Strategy Map, one that has proven to be remarkably successful in communication and education efforts, is shown in Exhibit 4.5.[37]

Continuing with the theme of Strategy Map as communication tool, the more closely you can align the Map with other internal marketing campaign fundamentals, including colors, logos, and themes, the better. Eight point black font against a stark white background just isn't going to cut it for an employee base accustomed to slick graphics and vivid colors on everything from video games to cell phones. To drive acceptance from your employee base, Strategy Map aesthetics are almost as important as the very objectives comprising the Map. The Environmental Services Group of the Unified Port of San Diego understood the importance of creating a Map that told their strategic story but did so in a way that was sure to catch the attention of every associate. Shown in Exhibit 4.6 is the aquatic rendering the company engineered to display its very concise yet informative Strategy Map. Not only is this Map cleverly designed, but it captures the essence of the firm's operations in just eight objectives, ensuring focus on what truly matters.

KEEP IN MIND

- A Strategy Map is a one-page graphical representation of what you must do well in each of the four perspectives in order to effectively execute

Exhibit 4.5 Strategy Map of Brother Industries (U.S.A.) Inc.

Source: Reprinted with permission of the company.

your strategy. Strategy Maps are comprised of "objectives," concise statements typically beginning with verbs.

- Strategy Maps provide clarity and serve as powerful communication tools, outlining the critical objectives for success.

- The first question to consider when developing a Strategy Map is whether the four perspectives are right for you. The choice of perspectives should ultimately be based on what is necessary to tell the story of your strategy and create a competitive advantage for your organization.

- Numerous sources of information may provide insights into the objectives for your Strategy Map including: annual reports, mission and vision statements, strategic plans, and organizational histories.

Exhibit 4.6 Strategy Map of the Environmental Services Group of the Unified Port of San Diego

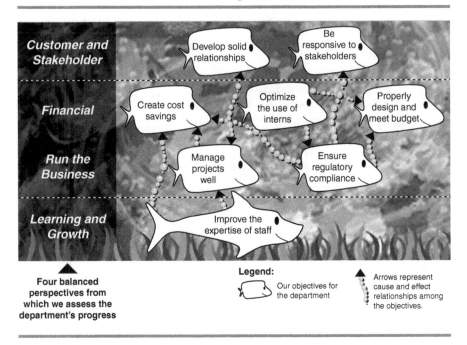

Legend:

Four balanced perspectives from which we assess the department's progress

⬛ Our objectives for the department

▲ Arrows represent cause and effect relationships among the objectives.

- Conducting executive interviews allows you to gather intelligence on potential objectives and galvanize senior leadership support for the implementation.
- Objectives for the Financial perspective of the Strategy Map will typically focus on shareholder value, revenue growth, and productivity.
- When developing the Customer perspective, three questions must be answered: Who are our target customers? What do they expect or demand from us? What is our value proposition in serving them? Most organizations will focus primarily on one of three value propositions—customer intimacy, product leadership, and operational excellence—while maintaining a baseline level of competence in the remaining two.
- Operations management, customer management, innovation, and regulatory and social represent the four clusters of processes most organizations will rely on to populate their Internal Process perspective.
- Often overlooked, the Employee Learning and Growth perspective acts as the enabler for the Internal Process, Customer, and Financial perspectives. Three distinct areas of capital—human, information, and organizational—will be relied on to help determine appropriate objectives for Employee Learning and Growth.

- An objective statement is a two- to three-sentence narrative that clarifies what is meant by each objective appearing on the Strategy Map, outlines why it is important, explains how it links in the chain of cause and effect, and briefly describes how it can be accomplished.
- Careful planning before, during, and after the Strategy Mapping workshop is required for a successful event. Holding the meeting offsite will often inspire greater creativity, resulting in more compelling Strategy Maps.
- While no magic number of objectives exists, the general rule of thumb suggests that "Less is more." In order to ensure focus on the vitally essential objectives, the total number should be limited to approximately 15 scattered across the four perspectives.
- Acceptance, understanding, and use of the Strategy Map are enhanced by customizing the product to your unique culture. Distinctive colors, logos, and themes will often result in a memorable effort that convincingly communicates your critical objectives.

Notes

1. Paul R. Niven, *Balanced Scorecard Diagnostics: Maintaining Maximum Performance* (Hoboken, NJ: John Wiley & Sons, 2005), p. 64.
2. Robert S. Kaplan and David P. Norton, *Strategy Maps* (Boston: Harvard Business School Press, 2004), p. xiii.
3. W. Chan Kim and Renee Mauborgne, *Blue Ocean Strategy* (Boston: Harvard Business School Press, 2005), pp. 81–82.
4. Stephen R. Covey, *The 8th Habit* (New York: Free Press, 2004), p. 271.
5. Robert S. Kaplan and David P. Norton, *The Balanced Scorecard* (Boston: Harvard Business School Press, 1996).
6. Robert S. Kaplan and David P. Norton, "Transforming the Balanced Scorecard from Performance Measurement to Strategic Management," *Accounting Horizons* (March 2001).
7. Ibid., p. 15.
8. Joe Flint, "As Critics Carp HBO Confronts Ratings Slump," *Wall Street Journal,* June 8, 2005.
9. Kaplan and Norton, *Strategy Maps,* p. 38.
10. Michael Treacy and Fred Wiersema, *The Discipline of Market Leaders* (Reading, MA: Perseus Books, 1995).
11. Ibid., p. 63.
12. James Covert, "Wal-Mart's Chief Says Retailer Needs to Widen Customer Appeal," *Wall Street Journal,* June 6, 2005.
13. Kaplan and Norton, *Strategy Maps,* p. 43.
14. Jeffrey McCracken, "Ford Seeks Big Savings by Overhauling Supply System," *Wall Street Journal,* September 29, 2005.

15. Steven D. Levitt and Stephen J. Dubner, *Freakonomics* (New York: William Morrow, 2005), p. 91.

16. Sarah Ellison, "Kimberly-Clark to Cut Staff by 10%, Shed 20 Plants," *Wall Street Journal*, July 25, 2005.

17. John Dizikes, *Yankee Doodle Dandy* (Lincoln: University of Nebraska Press, 2004), pp. 58–59.

18. Joseph B. White, "The Car of the Future," *Wall Street Journal*, July 25, 2005.

19. J. Lynn Lunsford, "Alchemy in the Desert," *Wall Street Journal*, October 4, 2005.

20. Frans Johansson, "Masters of the Multicultural," *Harvard Business Review*, October 2005.

21. Bob Nelson, *1001 Ways to Energize Employees* (New York: Workman, 1997).

22. Quoted in Gerald Nadler and William J. Chandon, *Smart Questions* (San Francisco: Jossey-Bass, 2004), p. 43.

23. Covey, *The 8th Habit*, p. 181.

24. Jim Collins, *Good to Great* (New York: Harper Business, 2001).

25. Kelly Greene, "Bye-Bye Boomers?" *Wall Street Journal*, September 20, 2005.

26. Jeffrey M. Cohen, Rakesh Khurana, and Laura Reeves, "Growing Talent as If Your Business Depended on It," *Harvard Business Review* (October 2005): 63–70.

27. Greene, "Bye-Bye Boomers?"

28. Quoted at www.dataquest.com/press_gartner/quickstats/ITSpending.html. August 2005.

29. Niven, *Balanced Scorecard Diagnostics*, p. 77.

30. Quote drawn from unpublished paper presented by BrassRing LLC, 2005.

31. John Kotter and James Heskett, *Corporate Culture and Performance* (New York: Free Press, 1992), p. 78.

32. Haig R. Nalbantian, Richard A. Guzzo, Dave Kieffer, and Jay Doherty, *Play to Your Strengths* (New York: McGraw-Hill, 2004).

33. Jennifer A. Chatman and Sandra E. Cha, "Leading by Leveraging Culture," *California Management Review* (Summer 2003).

34. This section is drawn from Niven, *Balanced Scorecard Diagnostics*, p. 80.

35. Quoted in *Motivational Manager* (September 2005): 14.

36. Robert J. Shiller, *Irrational Exuberance* (New York: Broadway Books, 2001).

37. Niven, *Balanced Scorecard Diagnostics*, p. 87.

CHAPTER 5

Creating Performance Measures

Roadmap for Chapter Five   In *Freakonomics,* a quirky and mostly irreverent glimpse into the world of economics, the authors strike a momentarily pragmatic chord when discussing the importance of measurement. They suggest: *"Knowing what to measure and how to measure it makes a complicated world much less so. If you learn how to look at the data in the right way you can explain riddles that otherwise might have seemed impossible. Because there is nothing like the sheer power of numbers to scrub away layers of confusion and contradiction."*[1]

We begin by examining exactly what a performance measure is and differentiating between performance-driving leading indicators and resultant lagging indicators. Next we review the four perspectives of the Balanced Scorecard and consider possible measures for each. A number of criteria are available to help you determine which measures should make up your Scorecard. We'll review each to ensure that you select the right measures for your organization. Once you've arrived at your performance measures, we'll consider whether you have an appropriate number to track the execution of your strategy adequately. Gathering data for your measures is a crucial and often challenging aspect of any Scorecard implementation. We share a performance measure data dictionary that will assist you in capturing all the essential elements of your performance metrics. Then we turn to the vital topic of effectively gathering feedback on your Scorecard from all employees. The chapter concludes by examining the future of your performance measures. Can we expect them to remain the same, or is change inevitable?

PERFORMANCE MEASURES: THE HEART OF THE BALANCED SCORECARD

What Are Performance Measures?

In the last chapter, I defined performance objectives as concise statements that describe the specific things we must perform well if we are to implement

143

our strategy successfully. But how do we know if we are in fact performing well on our objectives? We use performance measures use to determine whether we are meeting our objectives and moving toward the successful implementation of our strategy. Specifically, we may describe measures as quantifiable (normally, but not always) standards used to evaluate and communicate performance against expected results. However, no simple definition can truly capture the power that well-crafted and communicated performance measures can have on an organization. Measures communicate value creation in ways even the most charismatic CEO's speeches never can. They function as a tool to drive desired action, show all employees how they can help contribute to the organization's overall goals, and supply management with a tool to determine overall progress toward strategic goals. Thus measures are critically important to the Balanced Scorecard, but generating performance measures may not be as simple as you think. In a study by the American Institute of Certified Public Accountants, 27 percent of respondents stated that "the ability to define and agree upon measures" was the most frequent barrier to implementing or revising a performance measurement system.[2]

In this section we'll examine the powerful role of the performance measure in the Balanced Scorecard. The distinction between lagging and leading measures serves as our starting point, as differentiating between the two will prove essential in your measure development efforts. We'll then dissect each of the four perspectives of the Scorecard, review how to create specific measures for each, and examine different types of measures we might encounter. It is my hope that after reading this chapter, your organization won't feel that the ability to define and agree upon measures is the biggest barrier to developing your performance measurement system.

Looking Back and Looking Ahead: Lagging and Leading Measures of Performance

I gave a presentation at a software conference recently, and about halfway through the session, I thought: I'm getting lots of questions today, and everyone is really attentive—hardly a yawn to be seen! I bet I'll get good reviews from this group. My thought was based on the premise that I sought good reviews, and to get that positive feedback I believed had to hold the group's attention for the entire presentation period and encourage active participation. In effect, I hypothesized that a low number of yawns and a high number of questions would lead to positive reviews on my evaluation sheets. In other words, the "yawn" and "question" measures were the performance drivers (leading indicators) of my overall evaluation score (lagging indicator). That's the key distinction between the two: Lag indicators represent the consequences of actions previously taken, while lead indicators are the measures that lead to—or drive—the results achieved in the lagging indicators. For example, sales, market share, and lost-time accidents may all be considered lagging indicators. What drives each of these lagging indicators? Sales may be driven by hours spent with customers; market share may be driven by brand awareness; and lost-time accidents may be driven by the safety audit scores. Leading indicators should predict performance of lagging measures.

Your Balanced Scorecard should contain a mix of leading and lagging indicators. Without performance drivers, lagging indicators cannot inform us of how we hope to achieve our results. Conversely, leading indicators may signal key improvements throughout the organization, but on their own, they don't reveal whether these improvements are leading to improved customer and financial results. Coming up with the lagging measures probably won't pose much of a challenge, because measurement language is awash in such indicators: Sales, profits, satisfaction, and many others are common measures in use today. It's perfectly appropriate to feature a number of these lagging indicators on your Scorecard. While you may share such measures with many other organizations, your leading indicators set you apart by identifying the specific activities and processes you believe are critical to driving those lagging indicators of success. Lag and lead measures are contrasted in Exhibit 5.1.

Exhibit 5.1   Lag and Lead Performance Measures

	Lag	Lead
Definition	• Measures focusing on results at the end of a time period • Normally characterizes historical performance	• Measures that "drive" or lead to the performance of lag measures • Normally measures intermediate processes and activities
Examples	• Market share • Sales • Employee satisfaction	• Hours spent with customers • Proposals written • Absenteeism
Advantages	• Normally easy to identify and capture	• Predictive in nature, and allows the organization to make adjustments based on results
Issues	• Historical in nature • Does not reflect current activities • Lacks predictive power	• May prove difficult to identify and capture • Often new measures with no history at the organization

The Balanced Scorecard should contain a mix of lag and lead measures of performance.

MEASURES FOR THE FINANCIAL PERSPECTIVE

With each perspective of the Balanced Scorecard, the measures we choose should act as direct translations of the objectives we chose to comprise our Strategy Map, which themselves were faithfully translated from the organization's differentiating strategy. The measures provide insight into whether we are achieving our objectives and foster accountability for results, ensuring that we maintain the course of implementing our strategy. In Chapter Four, when discussing Financial objectives, I noted that most companies focus on revenue growth and productivity, both pursued in the goal of enhancing shareholder value. Therefore, we should extract our measures directly from those objectives.

Recall our discussion of the cable television operator HBO who, in an attempt to grow revenues, has begun selling many new products, such as DVDs of existing hit shows. Revenue from new products could prove to be an appropriate measure of HBO's success in such ventures. The company also decided to deepen its relationships with current customers by offering a broader range of channels; thus, tracking market share as a measure will provide HBO with the information needed to determine if it is making headway along this path.

Enhancing productivity, another vital financial mechanism, is also typically pursued by dual ends: reducing costs and improving the utilization of assets currently in place. Possible measures for these objectives include cost versus budget, expenses as a percentage of sales, and asset utilization. This last example brings to mind an important point: Never overcomplicate the measurement decision. I have been in workshops where "Improve utilization of assets" appears as an objective, obligating the team to craft a performance measure to use to gauge success over time. To me it seems fairly obvious that unless a brilliant flash of inspiration results in a never-before-pondered measure, wouldn't "Improve asset utilization" best be tracked by simply monitoring asset utilization? Don't spend hours looking for a measure that will not prove as effective as the obvious one. I am not suggesting that new and missing measures are not valuable; they are without a doubt, and you will have many opportunities to create such groundbreaking metrics. What I am suggesting is that, many times, the first measure that comes to mind regarding an objective—the obvious choice—is the most appropriate.

Although measures of growth and profitability are valuable, they cannot be relied on exclusively to tell the financial story of the enterprise. Take, for example, an organization that wants to grow earnings. Expanding operations and investing in a new plant will undoubtedly accomplish this objective, but at what cost? Shareholder value is enhanced only if the expansion is profitable and achieves a return greater than the cost of capital. It is possible for a company to increase earnings and still destroy shareholder value if the cost of capital associated with new investments is sufficiently high.[3] To determine whether financial investments are truly creating value, many organizations have turned to the calculation of economic value added (EVA). Simply put, EVA equals a firm's net operating profit after taxes less a capital charge. Using EVA as a yardstick, many organizations have a tool to evaluate the opportunity costs of various investment alternatives. For example, London-based Diageo PLC, which owns United Distillers & Vintners Limited, used EVA to gauge which of its liquor brands generated the best returns. The analysis determined that because of the time required for storage and care, aged Scotch didn't generate as much profit as vodka, which can be sold within weeks of being distilled. As a result of the EVA analysis, management at United Distillers began to emphasize vodka production and sales.[4]

Not every organization will choose financial measures relating to growth, productivity, or value. Others, especially those in the financial and insurance industries, may choose indicators of risk management to complement other financial measures. Westdeutsche Landesbank is a German wholesale bank represented in more than 35 countries worldwide. In developing financial measures at its New York City branch, West LB chose to augment its traditional financial measures of revenue growth and cost containment with measures of risk-adjusted return on capital. This addition reflected the importance of risk management in its portfolio.

Some organizations will venture beyond their accounting systems and look to Wall Street to supplement their financial perspective. Measures of share price and market valuation are often found on Balanced Scorecards. Those working in organizations that rely heavily on innovation and human capital (who isn't?) may desire a financial measure that captures the value of your intellectual assets. As with all Balanced Scorecard measures, the key is alignment to your strategy. The measures selected for the Financial perspective will help set your course in determining measures for the rest of the Scorecard, so ensure they accurately translate the objectives appearing on your Strategy Map. Your measures should tell your individual story, but to help get you started, Exhibit 5.2 provides a list of commonly used financial measures.

MEASURES FOR THE CUSTOMER PERSPECTIVE

When developing your Strategy Map objectives for the Customer perspective, I recommended using the three value propositions of operational excellence, product leadership, and customer intimacy as a framework for your deliberations. Let's return to those value propositions now and consider possible measures that may fall under each.

Measures of Operational Excellence

Operationally excellent organizations excel at wringing out every last drop of inefficiency and focus intently on their formula, in an uncompromising

Exhibit 5.2 Commonly Used Financial Measures

• Total assets	• Value added per employee
• Total assets/employee	• Compound growth rate
• Profits as a % of total assets	• Dividends
• Return on net assets	• Market value
• Return on total assets	• Share price
• Revenues/total assets	• Shareholder mix
• Gross margin	• Shareholder loyalty
• Net income	• Cash flow
• Profit as a % of sales	• Total costs
• Profit per employee	• Credit rating
• Revenue	• Debt
• Revenue from new products	• Debt to equity
• Revenue per employee	• Times interest earned
• Return on equity (ROE)	• Day sales in receivables
• Return on capital employed (ROCE)	• Accounts receivable turnover
• Return on investment (ROI)	• Days in payables
• Economic value added (EVA)	• Days in inventory
• Market value added (MVA)	• Inventory turnover ratio

desire to offer us great value. Outlined next are the attributes of operational excellence we discussed in Chapter Four. Let's revisit them using the lens of measurement.

- *Price.* More than any other determining factor, what brings us back to operationally excellent firms again and again is low prices. Therefore, we might expect to see measures such as "average price compared to key competitors" or "total cost of ownership" appearing on their Balanced Scorecard.

- *Selection.* This past holiday season during a trip to Costco I felt as if I were being stalked by a frenzied crew of their associates on a runaway forklift. Upon closer examination from a safe location, they were definitely frenzied alright but not in a desire to run me down. Instead their goal was to keep the shelves stocked for us desperate last-minute shoppers. Operationally excellent companies thrive on a rapid turnover of goods. Thus typical measures would include "inventory turns," "number of items out of stock," and "cash flow."

- *Convenience.* When you go to McDonald's for a Big Mac fix you're not expecting the pampering you'd receive at the Ritz Carlton or the choice awaiting you at a large buffet—you just want your burger and you want it now. McDonald's knows that and has designed the business infrastructure to make sure you experience the convenience of a hot meal served rapidly. Most operationally excellent companies include measures of convenience and accessibility as part of their Scorecards. Examples include "average wait times," "number of customer complaints," and "number of resolutions in first call" (for call centers).

- *Zero defects.* Mistakes or defects of any kind are anathema to operationally excellent companies. When uniformity is critical, variation must be removed from the system, and thus it is not surprising that many will invest in Six Sigma to stay on the path of zero defects. "Manufacturing yield" and "defect rates" may be closely monitored.

- *Growth.* Up, up, and up is the mantra of this high-flying set, and thus measures of growth will take a front-row seat. Examples include "revenue growth in targeted segments" and "number of new customers."

Product Leadership Measures

Product leaders succeed by providing their customers with new and innovative products that offer unique functionality not available in competitors' offerings. Of course every organization's wish list would probably include greater innovation and more breakthrough ideas, but one company that truly lives in the "innovation fast lane" is IDEO. A true innovation factory, IDEO has created thousands of products, services, environments, and digital experiences for hundreds of clients. If you've had your teeth whitened at BriteSmile, then you've been the beneficiary of IDEO innovation. If you visited "Workspheres," a collection of nine concepts that explore the theme of individuality in the context of corporate culture at the Museum of Modern Art in New York, you've benefited from IDEO innovation. Founder and chairman David Kelley typifies the IDEO culture when he says, *"Design is not a noun; it's a verb."*[5] Let's consider possible measures for product leading companies.

- *Getting the word out is a must.* Product leaders aggressively pursue the buzz that often accompanies a breakaway new product. Thus we might expect to see "brand image" or "brand awareness" gracing their Balanced Scorecard. Given their penchant for pushing the envelope of innovation, product leaders might also measure "help line calls per product" to determine the amount of interest, and possibly confusion, in their latest development.

- *Functionality.* You probably didn't know this but I am the proud curator of a cell phone museum housed, conveniently, in my house. Admittedly it's small, three phones, but that modest sampling spans some fourteen years, which represents about ten thousand years in tech time. I couldn't use the word "mobile" to describe my first cell phone, because unless you are blessed with the pipes of Arnold Schwarzenegger, you'd probably be too weak to port this toaster-sized device around for long periods of time. Comparing it to my current device is like contrasting the blunt rocks our ancestors used for mixing food with my shiny new Cuisinart. The advance in functionality is difficult for this mind to comprehend, but I do thank those responsible. Product leaders, those on the cutting edge of design, style, and functionality, must employ metrics that allow them to gauge their penetration of our needs. Expect to see measures such as "number of customer needs satisfied" and "number of new features offered" appearing within their Balanced Scorecards.

Measures for Customer Intimacy

By providing an unparalleled mix of superior services that offer a total solution, the customer-intimate organization is able to move beyond simply providing a product or service to cultivating a lasting relationship with their clientele. With measures in mind, let's reconsider a number of the attributes of customer intimacy we encountered in Chapter Four.

- *Customer knowledge.* "Access to key customer information" is a driving force in this endeavor. The more information the customer-intimate firm has about its customers, the better able it is to personalize, anticipate, and even predict customer patterns. A strong information foundation paves the way for this to occur. The information must provide users with a total view of the customer and must be integrated from all sources, meaningful and actionable, and user friendly.[6]

- *Solutions offered.* "Total number of solutions offered per client" or a derivative thereof is the obvious choice for tracking the solutions customers demand. You will undoubtedly invest significant time, effort, and resources in creating specialized offerings for your customers; therefore, it is important to balance a metric like "total number of solutions offered" with one reflecting customer profitability, sales volume, or margin improvement. You want to ensure that your investments in customized solutions are creating sufficient profitability to cover your costs.

- *Penetration.* With their credo of providing total solutions to customer needs never far from mind, we would anticipate customer-intimate organizations to track "share of wallet" or "market share."

- *Culture of driving client success.* Customers represent the ultimate arbiter of success for any organization, but it is the customer-intimate organization that labors most intensely to ensure positive experiences, and in so doing it relies heavily on a positive cultural foundation. "Reputation index," "number of customer awards received," and "number of referrals" will rank highly on the Scorecard of a customer-intimate enterprise.

- *Relationships for the long term.* Customer-intimate organizations are seeking the sort of relationship evident in the time-tested marriage of Paul

Newman and Joanne Woodward rather than the casual dalliances of, say, a Paris Hilton. In other words, they are in it for the long haul, working with you to provide solutions as your needs inevitably change. As a result, "customer turnover" and "customer retention" are likely measure candidates.

Although I have not mentioned the term specifically, it is a virtual certainty that "customer satisfaction" will be scrawled across a flip chart at some point during your measures development session. So popular is it that I have devoted an entire exhibit to this oft-cited metric. Please review Exhibit 5.3 to learn more about the perils and possibilities of customer satisfaction.

Other Sources of Customer Measures

Choosing your value proposition and identifying your target customer segments will greatly enhance your efforts in developing both objectives and measures for the customer perspective. However, they aren't your only options. Here are some other sources that can lead to measures you may wish to track.

- *Financial objectives and measures.* Don't forget that the Balanced Scorecard should tell the story of your strategy from financial targets through the customer, processes, and employee capabilities you'll need to achieve success. Once you've developed financial objectives and measures, ask yourself how they translate into customer requirements. For example, if you have a financial target of double-digit revenue growth, you may require greater customer loyalty or ambitious customer acquisition policies to achieve that goal.

- *The customer's voice.* The Internet is an incredibly powerful medium for spreading customer perceptions about your products and services, good or bad. Message boards and targeted sites across the vast universe of the Web likely contain a host of references to your company and its offerings. Take advantage of this opportunity by listening to what your customers have to say about you and then proactively defining yourself.

- *Moments of truth.* Any point at which a customer comes in contact with a business defines a moment of truth. The interaction can be either favorable or unfavorable and can have a great impact on future business. Mapping these moments of truth provides you with an opportunity to isolate the differentiating features you offer and design metrics to track your success.[7]

- *Look to your channels.* Today's organization may serve customers in a number of ways, each with unique processes. Take the example of a retailer. It may offer shopping over the Internet, in retail stores, and/or by catalog. Each of these channels has specific processes and will entail different

Exhibit 5.3   A Closer Look at Customer Satisfaction

Customer satisfaction may be the most popular measure in the Customer perspectives of Balanced Scorecards around the world. In one recent study, 70% of respondents noted it appeared on their Scorecard.[i] Popularity, however, is not always tantamount to effectiveness, and many pundits have begun to question the efficacy of this indicator. A chief complaint is the specious link between satisfaction and growth. As a glaring example of this possible deficiency, detractors point to K-Mart, which reported a significant increase in satisfaction scores on the American Customer Satisfaction Index (ACSI) while simultaneously experiencing sharp declines in sales and tumbling into bankruptcy.[ii] Others question the unrelenting drive exhibited by companies attempting to reach the pinnacle of 100% satisfaction. One recent study debunked the value of reaching 100% satisfaction, noting that customers who were only 80% satisfied spent as much as those who were reportedly 100% satisfied. It seems getting that extra 20% requires significant investments with little payback.[iii]

Despite these drawbacks, most companies will continue to include customer satisfaction on their Balanced Scorecards in attempt to discover the driving forces behind the purchase decision and how they can retain their customers for the long term. Most will turn to surveys as the primary means of data collection. A number of tips to keep in mind when developing and administering surveys follow.

1. **Survey a variety of customers.** Your current customers know you the best and are most likely to provide positive responses when asked about their experiences with your firm. To balance this bias, survey past customers, those you know have left, and competitors' customers to learn more about their buying habits.

2. **Ask about the specifics of their experience.** To know if customers are generally satisfied or not satisfied is directionally helpful, but to really ascertain what makes them tick, dig deeper to get their reaction to the many specific attributes of your products and services.

3. **Ask about competitors.** Henry Ford's dictum not withstanding, customers have plenty of choices. Satisfaction with your products is part of an overall spectrum of relative satisfaction based on their use of yours and competing products and services.

4. **Ensure the survey is administered by the head office or a third party.** A lot is riding on the results of these surveys, including financial incentives and resource perks. Unscrupulous employees may be tempted to deliberately manipulate results in their favor. Eliminate that possibility by using either head office staff or a third party to administer your survey.

5. **Keep it simple.** The longer and more complicated the survey is, the lower the response rate.

[i] Performance Measurement Survey by the American Institute of Certified Public Accountants and Lawrence S. Maisel, 2001.

[ii] Frederick F. Reicheld, "The One Number You Need to Grow," *Harvard Business Review* (December 2003): 49.

[iii] Christopher D. Ittner and David F. Larcker, "Coming Up Short on Nonfinancial Performance Measurement," *Harvard Business Review* (November 2003): 90.

Source: Paul R. Niven, *Balanced Scorecard Diagnostics: Maintaining Maximum Performance* (Hoboken, NJ: John Wiley & Sons, 2005) p. 103.

performance measures. For instance, when measuring checkout efficiency and speed in retail stores, error rates in keying items/prices into the register and the average length of a transaction might be monitored. Online, the same organization could monitor transaction ease by examining the number of fields into which the customer must enter information or the number of abandoned transactions. A catalog transaction would examine the number of rings it takes customer service representatives to answer calls and how long it takes to place the order.[8]

- *Work from the customer experience.* In *The Experience Economy* authors Joe Pine and Jim Gilmore suggest that the economy is undergoing a shift to experiences, in which every business is a stage and memorable events must be created for customers.[9] If you're like me, you may have started your day with a trip to your favorite coffee shop and shelled out anywhere from two to five dollars for one cup of coffee. The company that harvested the beans probably received the equivalent of about one or two cents, but we just paid about two hundred times that. Why? Because of the pleasurable experience the coffee shop provided to us. Look at the experience you're designing for your customers and you'll be sure to unearth a number of critical measures of success for the customer and all other perspectives of the Scorecard.

It is very important to include both lag and lead indicators in your customer perspective and in the entire Scorecard for that matter. However, I have seen many Balanced Scorecard teams get way off track by endlessly debating what is a "lag" measure and what represents "leading" performance. Some team members will undoubtedly suggest that every measure is in effect "lagging" because it is historical in nature. We could argue the semantics of this topic forever, but in the end it comes down to choosing measures and asking yourself, "What drives this measure?" Whenever you choose one measure and can hypothesize a relationship with a related metric you feel drives the performance of the first measure, you've determined a lag and lead relationship.

Use the just-listed techniques to help you generate measures for your own customer perspective. To get the creative juices flowing, Exhibit 5.4 presents a sample of customer measures.

MEASURES FOR THE INTERNAL PROCESS PERSPECTIVE

All of the measures appearing on your Balanced Scorecard will be directly translated from the objectives appearing on your Strategy Map via the question "How will we know if we are successful in achieving this objective?" Answering that query will help produce the performance measure(s) necessary to gauge success. With that question firmly planted in your mind, let's examine the framework for Internal Processes we explored in Chapter

Exhibit 5.4   Sample Customer Measures

- Customer satisfaction
- Customer loyalty
- Market share
- Customer complaints
- Complaints resolved on first contact
- Return rates
- Response time per customer request
- Direct price
- Price relative to competition
- Total cost to customer
- Average duration of customer relationship
- Customers lost
- Customer retention
- Customer acquisition rates
- Percent of revenue from new customers
- Number of customers
- Annual sales per customer

- Win rate (sales closed/sales contacts)
- Customer visits to the company
- Hours spent with customers
- Marketing cost as a percentage of sales
- Number of ads placed
- Number of proposals made
- Brand recognition
- Response rate
- Number of trade shows attended
- Sales volume
- Share of target customer spending
- Sales per channel
- Average customer size
- Customers per employee
- Customer service expense per customer
- Customer profitability
- Frequency (number of sales transactions)

Four and use it to help us determine possible measures you can include in your Balanced Scorecard.

Operations Management Measures

You will recall that operations management refers to the basic, routine, and day-to-day processes necessary to keep the engines of commerce humming at your company. A metaview of this cluster reveals subprocesses of sourcing, manufacturing, distribution, and risk management. The measures you choose will, naturally, be organization specific. For example, if yours is a mortgage lending company, you don't produce a physical product. Nevertheless, that does not preclude you from including operations management metrics. "Cycle time from application to funding" or "number of loans closed per employee" may appear on your Scorecard. Manufacturers, meanwhile, may focus rightly on "yield" or "throughput" for this perspective. Again, you must be disciplined as you complete this perspective. Faced with innumerable options for measurement, you must focus precisely on just those options that are critical to tracking your execution of key processes that drive value for customers and financial stakeholders.

Customer Management Measures

Five critical subprocesses comprise customer management: (1) selecting target customers, (2) acquiring them by proactively communicating our value proposition, (3) understanding their needs, (4) retaining customers, and (5) deepening our relationship with them. A simple yet powerful measure may accompany each subprocess on the Balanced Scorecard. For example, selection of customers may be tracked by "customer segmentation" or classification. Acquisition is often monitored by metrics of marketing effectiveness, demonstrating whether our investments in communicating what we have to offer are reaching our target audience. "Number of customer profiles" may act as a suitable proxy for understanding customer needs as we attempt to ferret out the eccentricities and peculiarities of our buyers. Retention should not be complicated; just measure retention! Finally, deepening relationships with our customers may be analyzed by using a measure of cross-selling, an attempt to open our target base up to a broader range of company offerings.

Innovation Measures

Joseph Tucci, CEO of information storage and management giant EMC, has been quoted as saying: *"Companies that are afraid to disrupt themselves constantly end up being disrupted."*[10] Disruption may take any number of forms, including corporate change and strategic shifts, but in this context we can apply the term to innovation—creating and supplying captivating new products and services to distance yourself from your competition. Among the myriad performance measures that may fit the bill under the heading of innovation are "dollars spent on research and development," "employee hours on research and development," "number of employee affinity groups," "number of new product joint ventures," "number of new products or services in the pipeline," "number of new products or services introduced," "new product or service cycle time" (length of time from conception to introduction), "revenue from new products or services," and "new product sales by channel."

Regulatory and Social Measures

Chief executives, especially those at the helm of large publicly traded companies, must feel as if they have an enormous bull's-eye stitched into the backs of their tailored Italian suits. Watchdog groups apply intense scrutiny to every facet of the executive world, from governance, to employee relations, to executive compensation. These days it's not enough to simply *be* a good corporate citizen; companies must make preemptive strikes, demonstrating in crystal-clear fashion their pledge to strong governance, adherence to regulatory and environmental standards, and commitment to social causes. Prominent measures on a Balanced Scorecard, especially if it is ultimately shared with external stakeholders, can help allay the diatribes of rabid critics by clearly displaying the metrics being monitored and actions taken in support of these vital issues. Among the measures that may be pursued in this arena are "compliance with environmental regulations," "number of audit findings," and "employee volunteer hours."

Exhibit 5.5 contains additional Internal Process measures for your consideration. The indicators shown are quite generic. Your challenge is to identify the unique processes that drive the customer value proposition in your organization and define specific measures that tell your particular story. While all perspectives of the Scorecard will reveal some very individual measures depending on the organization, it's the Internal Process perspective that normally contains the most one-of-a-kind indicators. You'll also discover that unlike traditional performance management systems, which focus on the incremental improvement of existing processes, the Balanced Scorecard and corresponding measures in your Financial and Customer perspectives may lead you to entirely new processes necessary to achieve your strategic aims. Uncovering these "missing measurements," as Kaplan and Norton call them, is often one of the most gratifying aspects of the Scorecard development process.

MEASURES FOR THE EMPLOYEE LEARNING AND GROWTH PERSPECTIVE

Continuing the trend established with the previous three perspectives, we will conduct our investigation of measures for the Employee Learning and

Exhibit 5.5   Internal Process Measures

• Average cost per transaction	• Breakeven time
• On-time delivery	• Cycle time improvement
• Average lead time	• Continuous improvement
• Inventory turnover	• Warranty claims
• Environmental emissions	• Lead user identification
• Research and development expense	• Products and services in the pipeline
• Community involvement	• Internal rate of return on new projects
• Patents pending	• Waste reduction
• Average age of patents	• Space utilization
• Ratio of new products to total offerings	• Frequency of returned purchases
• Stock-outs	• Downtime
• Labor utilization rates	• Planning accuracy
• Response time to customer requests	• Time to market of new products/services
• Defect percentage	• New products introduced
• Rework	• Number of positive media stories
• Customer database availability	

Growth perspective using the three distinct areas of capital described in Chapter Four: human, information, and organizational.

In case you are thinking of skimming this section, reasoning that Employee Learning and Growth is just "soft stuff," not worthy of getting your intellectual hands dirty, think again. It may indeed be soft, but the results these measures drive are as solid as a slab of granite. Need some evidence? David Maister has chronicled the link between satisfied employees and financial returns in his book *Practice What You Preach*.[11] He was convinced that happy employees really do drive financial success and set about to find the actual proof. In 1999 he surveyed 5,500 employees of a large advertising and media conglomerate who were dispersed among 139 offices in 15 countries. His study found that a company could boost its financial performance by as much as 42 percent by raising employee satisfaction by 20 percent.

Human Capital Measures

The late Peter Drucker suggested that any business can be as good as any other business. The only distinction is how it develops its people. Here are some suggestions for developing your most precious resource.

- *Using core competencies to measure skill development.* The term "core competence" was coined by Gary Hamel and C. K. Prahalad in their immensely successful book, *Competing for the Future*. Over time the phrase has evolved, and now "core competence" can be described as *"an attribute or behavior that individual managers and employees must demonstrate to succeed at their particular company."*[12] The first step in the core competence process is identifying the differentiating competencies you need to achieve your strategy. Experts agree that the best way of doing this is to involve as many people as possible from all levels of the organization. Focus groups and interviews can be used to assess company needs and competence gaps. If you haven't gone through this "competence inventory" process, it could represent a good first-year metric for your Scorecard. After all, you can't evaluate your current staff against desired skills until you've cataloged those skills you deem as necessary to create a competitive advantage. Once you do have an inventory of the skills your staff possesses and those required to execute your strategy, you can begin to attack the delta between the two. "Strategic job coverage ratio" is a possible metric for analyzing that gap over time.
- *Using personal development planning to boost competence holders.* Many organizations have introduced the idea of personal development planning (PDP) to assist employees in generating goals. This is certainly an admirable effort, but certain criteria must be stressed if PDPs are to prove beneficial to the employee or the organization. The principal issue is alignment to organizational strategic goals. The majority of personal goals in the plan should help the employee influence the achievement

of the company's strategy. Goals in the plan should also be measurable and include specific action steps. Once you've identified the core competencies you need to be a leader in your industry and your employees have developed plans that signal their contribution to your goals, you're ready to begin measuring. Track the percentage of employees who meet their PDP goals. Don't make it an annual measure. To motivate action on this important task, ask employees for quarterly or even monthly progress updates.

- *Measuring employee training.* Virtually every company will have at least one performance measure relating to employee training initiatives. And why not, since through training the organization gets better-skilled workers who are more versatile, while employees learn new skills and gain new ways of seeing their work and how it affects overall success. As we discussed earlier, the mistake most organizations make with training metrics is that they simply look at the raw amount of training offered: number of training hours per employee, for example. For training to prove effective, it must be linked to organizational goals and objectives, and companies should measure results of the training (i.e., the demonstration of new behaviors or skills), not just attendance. You should also encourage trained employees to share their newfound knowledge with their peers and networks in the company. Stephen Covey calls this "third-person teaching" and suggests that it offers many benefits to both the student and the teacher. For example, knowing you'll have to share what you're learning will motivate most people to pay greater attention and capture more of the information they're receiving. For those of you who are skeptical about the financial benefits of training, this example from Allstate Insurance may change your mind. After the Northbrook, Illinois–based insurance provider's education department designed and implemented an online Individual Retirement Account (IRA) products curriculum for agents and support staff, the company discovered a significant correlation between IRA accounts created and online training accessed. In the first half of 2003, on average, agents who accessed an online course called "Understanding IRAs" sold 55 percent more policies—a 29 percent increase in production—than agents who had not accessed the course.[13]

- *Employee productivity.* Investing in competency development and personal development planning should yield results in the form of greater productivity, and many organizations will measure just that. The problem with this measure, at least in its traditional form, is that it divides firm revenue by the number of employees. It's fairly easy to manipulate this ratio by reducing the number of employees, outsourcing entire functions, or increasing revenue in possibly unprofitable segments. As with the financial metric of economic value added, you should attempt to determine the value added per employee by deducting externally purchased materials from your numerator.

Information Capital Measures

Capabilities are a must for success in the new economy, but to achieve your goals, employees must have access to certain physical and intangible tools to get their jobs done. Let's consider some of these tools and how we might measure their impact on results.

- *The instruments of business.* A client I worked with recently was implementing a technology solution for her Balanced Scorecard program. Everything was going well until we found that a number of employees in remote offsite locations didn't all have computers on their desks; in fact, some didn't even have voice mail on their phones. They were still relying on those little pink "While you were out" forms to receive messages. We could have developed Scorecards for them, but many benefits of the program, such as real-time reporting and decision support, would be very limited, given their technology-deprived state. This may sound like an oversimplified performance measure, but you have to ensure your employees have up-to-date and modern equipment if you hope to compete in today's economy.

- *Access to information.* For those associates fortunate enough to have the necessary equipment, you need to make certain they can also retrieve the right information. What percentage of customer-facing staff have the ability to access detailed customer information within 30 seconds of a customer interaction? You should determine what information is critical to employee decision making and develop a performance measure that tracks the percentage of employees who have this information available to them.

- *Information capital readiness.* As with human capital, to prove effective, information and technology must be aligned with the organization's strategy to produce benefits. Therefore, monitoring "information capital readiness," an assessment of information technology (IT) capabilities versus needs, will provide us with insights into where we must invest in order to leverage technology as a competitive advantage.

Organizational Capital Measures

According to recent data gathered by the Gallup organization, less than 30 percent of American workers are fully engaged at work, while some 55 percent *are not* engaged. Another 19 percent are actively disengaged, meaning not just that they are unhappy at work but that they regularly share those feelings with colleagues.[14] All the training and sharing of information in the world will accomplish little if employees aren't motivated to perform their best or aligned with organizational goals. Here are some considerations when measuring culture, motivation, and alignment.

- *Employee satisfaction.* Perhaps the most common Employee Learning and Growth measure is the employee satisfaction rating. The vast majority of organizations attempt to take the pulse of their organizations through annual surveys and use the findings to design better ways to do things. At least that's how it's supposed to work. Unfortunately, many employees feel the annual survey is a sham and waste of money with the results gathering dust on a shelf and never acted on. Satisfaction is a very valuable metric, so ensure you use the data appropriately by swiftly acknowledging areas requiring improvement and developing action steps to improve them. You should also consider using the many technological tools at your disposal to gauge the mood of your employees more frequently. Corporate intranets and e-mail systems can be used to gather feedback from employees semiannually or quarterly. Given the pace of change in today's environment, you need the most up-to-date information from the front line if you expect to react quickly. Since surveys are the typical tool of choice for rendering satisfaction information, Exhibit 5.6 provides some helpful hints on design.

- *Alignment.* Your Scorecard should capture your strategy through the objectives and measures that make up your individual story. Chapter Seven describes how you can drive your high-level performance measures throughout the entire organization using the process of cascading. In the early stages of your Balanced Scorecard implementation, a good alignment measure is simply the number of Scorecards produced within the organization. Once the performance management discipline becomes more mature, you can refine the measure by analyzing individual Scorecards and assessing their "degree of alignment" (i.e., the percentage of measures directly relating to your strategic goals). Obviously the target should be 100 percent. This is a great way to perform a diagnostic check on your cascaded Scorecards.

- *Encourage healthy lifestyles.* Experts suggest that over 50 percent of all mortality is related to lifestyle choices. Many organizations will include occupational health and safety measures in the Employee Learning and Growth perspective, such as lost time accidents, workers' compensation claims, and injury frequency rates. However, enlightened companies are moving beyond these lagging indicators and attempting to offer employees an environment that facilitates and encourages them to adopt better lifestyles. Organizations pursuing this "health promotion" philosophy are attempting to create a win-win environment in which employees take responsibility for their own well-being and employers reap the benefits of lower lifestyle-related costs. And the bottom-line results can be significant. The Coors Brewing Company found that it got as much as a $6.15 return for every $1 invested in a corporate fitness program. Companies including Equitable Life Assurance, General Mills, and Motorola have all reported at least a $3 return for every dollar invested.[15] You can measure your health-promotion initiatives by tracking the number of employees who take advantage of the program or

Exhibit 5.6   Creating Effective Surveys

Keep these points in mind when creating employee surveys:

- Ask questions related to observable behavior, not thoughts or motives. (This allows respondents to draw on firsthand experience and not inference.)
- Measure only those behaviors that are linked to your organization's performance. (Awareness of your new cafeteria hours may be interesting, but is it relevant to your results?)
- About one-third of questions should lead to a negative response. (This avoids people's natural tendency to agree to things.)
- Avoid questions that require rankings. (We tend to remember the first and last things in a list, which may bias our answer to the question.)
- Make sure the survey can be completed within 20 minutes. (Everyone is busy. Spending an hour to complete a 100-question survey may elicit a negative response that shows up in the respondent's answers.)

Source: Adapted from Palmer Morrel-Samuels, "Getting the Truth into Workplace Surveys," *Harvard Business Review* (February 2002): 111–118.

gauging employee attitudes regarding lifestyle choices. These measures may also be considered leading indicators of other popular Employee Learning and Growth measures such as absenteeism, morale, and productivity per employee.

Exhibit 5.7 provides some additional Employee Learning and Growth measures you may consider for your Balanced Scorecard.

FINALIZING YOUR BALANCED SCORECARD MEASURES

At this point in your implementation, you will have developed a multitude of potential measures in each of the Scorecard perspectives. Every one of those metrics will have a fan in at least one member of your team. Your challenge now is to cull the herd of possible measures down to the select few that accurately and faithfully translated the objectives appearing on your Strategy Map and capture the essence of your strategy. Let's begin our work by examining a number of criteria you can use to select the most well-suited measures for your organization. We'll then discuss how many measures should appear on your Scorecard and ways to gain feedback from both executives and employees.

Criteria for Selecting Performance Measures

One of the many benefits of the Balanced Scorecard is that it forces organizations to make difficult choices among a variety of alternatives. Choices

Exhibit 5.7   Employee Learning and Growth Measures

- Employee participation in professional or trade associations
- Training investment per customer
- Average years of service
- Percentage of employees with advanced degrees
- Number of cross-trained employees
- Absenteeism
- Turnover rate
- Employee suggestions
- Employee satisfaction
- Participation in stock ownership plans
- Lost-time accidents
- Value added per employee
- Motivation index
- Outstanding number of applications for employment
- Diversity rates
- Empowerment index (number of managers)

- Quality of work environment
- Internal communication rating
- Employee productivity
- Number of Scorecards produced
- Health promotion
- Training hours
- Competency coverage ratio
- Personal goal achievement
- Timely completion of performance appraisals
- Leadership development
- Communication planning
- Reportable accidents
- Percentage of employees with computers
- Strategic information ratio
- Cross-functional assignments
- Knowledge management
- Ethics violations

regarding objectives, targets, and initiatives to achieve our targets must all be deliberated on in developing a Scorecard that serves as the cornerstone of our management system. Nowhere is the process of making hard choices more evident than in the selection of performance measures. These measures are really the centerpiece of the Scorecard system and will provide the point of reference and focus for the entire organization. Here are several criteria that experience and research have proven to be effective in helping you evaluate and pick your measures.

- *Linked to strategy.* This one gets the vote for most obvious, but its importance cannot be overstated. The Scorecard is a tool for translating strategy into action through the objectives and measures that tell the story of your strategy. Choosing performance measures that don't have an impact on your strategy can lead to confusion and lack of clarity as employees devote precious resources to the pursuit of measures that don't influence the firm's overall goals. Having said that, you might have difficulty finding a direct link from every measure to your strategy. Most businesses will have a number of "diagnostic" performance measures that are important to the day-to-day efficient functioning of the business but don't seem to correspond directly to a strategy. We need to monitor these factors to ensure that the organization remains in control and is able to respond quickly to items that require immediate attention. While these indicators are important, they are not necessarily strategic. Recall our discussion of value propositions. An organization pursuing a customer-intimate strategy will devote the majority of its efforts to providing total solutions to customer needs through deep knowledge. This is the firm's focus, but it can't ignore logistics issues (operational excellence) or product functionality (product leadership). Maintaining threshold standards of performance in these areas may require the inclusion of performance measures on the Scorecard.

- *Quantitative.* Scorecard practitioners often are tempted to include measures that rely on subjective evaluations of performance, such as rating suppliers' performances as "good," "fair," or "average." Of course, the principal issue with this approach is that 10 people rating the same supplier may come up with completely different approaches and responses. However, if the same supplier was evaluated on a percentage of on-time deliveries, the results are objective and convey the same meaning to all involved. Everyone knows what 10 percent connotes, but your definition of "average" and mine could vary significantly. If you're creative, virtually all performance measures can be calculated mathematically. I once worked with a medical services unit at a government agency. A key performance metric was the distribution of trauma reports in a timely fashion. The unit's original measure was "reports issued." In other words, a simple yes or no would suffice as the indication of performance. With a little tweaking we improved the measure by restating it as "the percentage of trauma report recipients receiving the document on time."

- *Accessibility.* Kaplan and Norton often discuss the merits of "missing measures"— the performance measures you didn't capture in the past that came to light only as a result of the Balanced Scorecard development process. Undoubtedly, new and innovative measures are a wonderful benefit of the Scorecard; in fact, missing measures may signal that entire value-creating processes are not currently being managed. However, I caution you to avoid selecting "wish list" performance measures, the type that require significant investments in IT infrastructure to collect. You'll learn fairly quickly that you must be pragmatic when selecting performance measures. One group I worked with recently developed a Scorecard for their business unit that was considered by the group executive as the pride of the entire organization. But when it came time to actually report the information, the data were completely uncollectable without significant investments in technology. I'm not suggesting you avoid new and innovative measures; just be sure to calculate the costs and benefits of their collection. Data requirements are discussed later in this chapter.

- *Easily understood.* Your ultimate goal should be to create a Scorecard that motivates action. It's difficult to do so when your audience doesn't grasp the significance of the measures you've selected. At a glance, Scorecard readers should be able to explain both the operational and strategic significance of every measure. The desired direction of movement of the measure should also be obvious. If your employees don't know whether a high value for the measure is good or bad, then you probably need to rethink the measure.

- *Counterbalanced.* Let's say you own a fast food restaurant and are interested in improving your customer satisfaction scores. As we all know, these restaurants can become pretty crowded during peak hours, so you decide to increase staff and lower prices. The increased staff should be able to handle current and future demand created by your lower prices and will drive increased satisfaction. However, what effect will lowering prices and increasing staff have on your profitability? Unless the volume spikes dramatically, chances are profitability will plummet since you've increased your cost base and lowered your revenue. Some call this effect "suboptimization" (i.e., the improvement of one or more measures at the expense of others). While your Scorecard will require that you make trade-offs and decisions regarding where to allocate resources, you don't want to create a situation in which focusing on certain measures actually hinders your ability to compete. In the case of our fast food establishment, we would want to counterbalance our satisfaction rating with a measure of "revenue per employee." We need to ensure that despite our lower price structure, the resulting volume and efficiencies from increased staff are allowing us to maintain revenue targets.

- *Relevant.* The measures appearing on your Scorecard should accurately depict the process or objective you're attempting to evaluate. A good test is whether measure results are actionable or not. If some aspect of performance failed, you should be able to recognize the significance of the problem and be able to fix it. This issue is demonstrated through the use of performance indices, which many organizations use on their Scorecards. An index is a combination of several individual measures combined in some way to result in a single overall indicator of performance. Employee satisfaction may appear on your Scorecard as an index of the weighted average performance of turnover, absenteeism, complaints, and survey results. Indices are a great way to quickly depict a number of performance variables in a single indicator, but they have some inherent weaknesses. First of all, they may obscure results and limit action. If turnover at your organization was at an all-time high but was given a low weight in your employee satisfaction index, you may never know there are problems, because the overall index could appear to be on target. If key staff members are among those leaving the firm and you haven't mounted a response, you may soon pay a heavy price in other areas of performance as reflected on the Scorecard. Indices also frequently fail to pass the "easily understood" criterion. A "logistics" index appearing in the Internal Process perspective may contain valuable information but be baffling to those outside of the supply chain side of the organization.

- *Common definition.* Your Scorecard will likely contain a number of esoteric performance measures, and that's perfectly appropriate since it's your strategic story you're telling. However, problems occur when you place measures on the Scorecard that are loosely defined or not defined at all. On-time delivery may be a crucial metric, but what does "on-time" mean? You must specify the precise meaning of your performance measures and ensure you have agreement from your entire team. "Customer satisfaction" could have a very different meaning for a team member from Marketing than it does for someone from Finance. The process of agreeing on measure definitions is yet another example of how the Scorecard building process brings seemingly disparate functions together as they work to ensure the measures capture a meaning that allows all to contribute meaningfully to success.

Exhibit 5.8 provides a worksheet you can use to choose among the performance measures you've gathered. List the measures under the appropriate perspective and rate each according to the criteria supplied. I would suggest you rate each measure out of a possible 10 points on each of the individual criteria. For example, if you were to measure economic value added on your financial perspective, it may score a 10 for "accessibility," given the purely financial nature of the information. However, it could warrant a 5 or under on "ease of understanding" since most employees will probably not be familiar with the metric.

How Many Measures on Your Balanced Scorecard?

Clients often ask me how many measures to include on a Balanced Scorecard. As discussed with Strategy Maps, the interesting thing is that many organizations are very concerned with creating too many measures but then go ahead and do just that. Since I've been working in the performance management arena I've witnessed a steady rise in the average number of measures appearing on organizational Scorecards. Technology is a major contributor to the volume of performance measures. Several years ago, when organizations had few reporting choices, they were more or less forced to minimize the number of measures they tracked. With the advent of functionality-rich Scorecard software, companies now have the ability to track literally hundreds or even thousands of measures throughout the organization. The question is: How many is too many? While no optimal or magic number of measures exists, there are guidelines you should follow to ensure that you have an appropriate number of measures for your organization.

Exhibit 5.8   Worksheet to Select Balanced Scorecard Measures

Measures	Linkage to Strategy	Ability to Quantify	Accessibility	Ease of Understanding	Counter-balanced	Relevance	Common Definition	Total Points	Comments
FINANCIAL									
Measure 1									
Measure 2									
Measure 3									
CUSTOMER									
Measure 1									
Measure 2									
Measure 3									
INTERNAL PROCESS									
Measure 1									
Measure 2									
Measure 3									
EMPLOYEE LEARNING AND GROWTH									
Measure 1									
Measure 2									
Measure 3									
Overall Assessment of Current Measures:									

Most Scorecard practitioners and consultants have settled on a figure of 20 to 25 measures as being appropriate for your highest-level Balanced Scorecard. Benchmarking studies of Scorecard implementations across a variety of industries have returned similar findings. Don't be constrained by these numbers, however. If you require 30 measures to describe your strategy adequately, use that number. Similarly, if you can tell your story in 15 measures, don't add measures that do little more than pad the Scorecard. The other frequently asked question is whether the measures should be equally dispersed across the four perspectives. Again, what matters most is ensuring that the measures faithfully translate your objectives and describe your strategy in a way that is transparent to anyone reading the Scorecard.

Creating a Performance Measure Data Dictionary

You have now evaluated all your measures and have selected a set you're ready to share with your executive team and later your fellow employees throughout the organization. But before you do that you need to catalog them in a measure "data dictionary." According to the dictionary definition of the word "dictionary," it is a "book that lists . . . . the topics of a subject." That is precisely what you're crafting in this step of the process— a document that provides all users with a detailed examination of your Balanced Scorecard measures, including a thorough list of measure characteristics. Creating the measure data dictionary isn't a very glamorous task, but it is an important one. When you present your Balanced Scorecard to executives and employees, they will undoubtedly quiz you on the background of each and every measure: "Why did you choose this measure?" "Is it strategically significant?" "How do you calculate the measure?" "Who is responsible for results?" The data dictionary provides the background you need to quickly defend your measure choices and answer any questions your audience has. Additionally, chronicling your measures in the data dictionary provides your team with one last opportunity to ensure a common understanding of measure details.

Exhibit 5.9 presents a template you can use to create your own measure dictionary. You must complete four basic sections of the template:

1. Essential background material on the measure
2. Specific measure characteristics
3. Calculation and data specifications
4. Performance information relating to the measure

Let's examine each of these sections in some detail, using the example provided in the exhibit.

Measure Background   At a glance, readers should be able to determine what this measure is all about and why it's important for the organization to track.

Exhibit 5.9 Balanced Scorecard Measure Dictionary

Perspective: Customer	Measure Number/Name: C01/Customer Loyalty Rating	Owner: G. Garfinkel, VP Marketing
Strategy: Revenue growth	Objective: Increase customer loyalty	

Description: The customer loyalty rating measures the percentage of surveyed customers stating they prefer our products to competitor offerings and will purchase our products again. Our research indicates that loyal customers make more frequent purchases and tend to recommend our brands to others. Therefore, we believe increasing customer loyalty will help us achieve our strategy of revenue growth.

Lag/Lead: Lag	Frequency: Quarterly	Unit Type: Percentage	Polarity: High values are **good.**

Formula: Number of quarterly survey respondents answering yes to survey questions #5: "Do you prefer our products compared to competitor offerings?" **and** #6: "Will you purchase our products again?" **divided** by the total number of surveys received.

Data Source: Data for this measure are provided by our survey company, SST. Each quarter it performs a random survey of our customers and provides the results electronically to our marketing department. Data are contained in MS Excel spreadsheets (MKT SURVEY.xls, lines 14 and 15). Data are available the 10th business day following the end of each quarter.

Data Quality: High—received automatically from third-party vendor	Data Collector: Sierra Burdette, Marketing Analyst

Baseline: Our most recent data received from SST indicates a customer loyalty percentage of 59%.	Target: Q1 2001: 65% Q2 2001: 68% Q3 2001: 72% Q4 2001: 75%

Target Rationale: Achieving customer loyalty is critical to our revenue growth strategy. The quarterly increases we're targeting are higher than in past years but reflect our increased focus on loyalty.

Initiatives:

1. Seasonal promotions
2. Customer relationship management project
3. Customer service training

- *Perspective.* Displays the perspective the measure falls under.
- *Measure Number/Name.* All performance measures should have a number and name. The number is important should you later choose an automated reporting system. Many such systems require completely unique names for each measure, and since you may track the same measures at various locations or business units, you should supply a specific identifier. The measure name should be brief but descriptive. Software may limit the number of characters you can use in the name field.
- *Owner.* The Balanced Scorecard transmits your key strategies for success to the entire organization and also creates a climate of accountability for results. Central to the idea of accountability is the establishment of owners for each and every measure. Simply put, the owner is the individual responsible for results. Should the indicator's performance begin to decline, it's the owner we look to for answers and a plan to bring results back in line with expectations. Exhibit 5.9 lists a specific individual as the owner of the measure. However, some organizations feel more comfortable assigning ownership to a function, not a person. They rationalize that while people may come and go, functions tend to remain, and assigning the ownership to a function ensures the responsibilities inherent in the task are not lost when a new person comes on board. This argument has merits, but I recommend you use actual names rather than functions. Seeing your name associated with the performance of a key organizational measure tends to promote more action and accountability than does seeing a job function.
- *Strategy.* Displays the specific strategy you believe the measure will positively influence.
- *Objective.* Every measure was created as a translation of a specific objective. Use this space to identify the relevant objective.
- *Description.* After reading the measure name, most people will immediately jump to the measure description, and it is therefore possibly the most important piece of information in the entire dictionary. Your challenge is to draft a description that concisely and accurately captures the essence of the measure so that anyone reading it will be able to grasp why the measure is critical to the organization. In our example we rapidly learn that customer loyalty is based on a percentage, what that percentage is derived from (survey questions), and why we believe the measure will help us achieve our strategy of revenue growth (loyal customers buy more and recommend our products).

Measure Characteristics   This section captures the meat-and-potatoes aspects of the measure you'll need when you begin reporting results.
- *Lag/Lead.* Outline whether the measure is a core outcome indicator or a performance driver. Remember that your Scorecard represents a hypothesis of your strategy implementation. When you begin analyzing your

results over time, you'll want to test the relationships you believe exist between your lag and lead measures.

- *Frequency.* How often do you plan to report performance on this measure? Most organizations have measures that report performance on a daily, weekly, monthly, quarterly, semiannual, or annual basis. However, I have seen other time frames, such as "school-year" for one government agency. Attempt to limit the number of semiannual and annual measures you use on your Scorecard. A measure that is only updated once a year is of limited value when you use the Scorecard as a management tool to make adjustments based on performance results.

- *Unit Type.* This characteristic identifies how the measure will be expressed. Commonly used unit types include numbers, dollars, and percentages.

- *Polarity.* When assessing the performance of a measure, you need to know whether high values reflect good or bad performance. In most cases this is straightforward. We all know that higher income and customer loyalty is good, while a high value for complaints reflects performance that requires improvement. However, in some cases the polarity issue can prove quite challenging. Take the example of a public health organization. If it chooses to measure caseloads of social workers, will high values be good or bad? A high number of cases per social worker may suggest great efficiency and effectiveness on the part of individual workers. Conversely, it could mean the social workers are juggling far too many clients and providing mediocre service in an attempt to inflate their caseload numbers. In cases like this you may want to institute a dual polarity. For example, up to 25 cases per social worker may be considered good, but anything over 25 would be a cause for concern and necessitate action.

Calculation and Data Specifications   Information contained in this section of the dictionary may be the most important yet most difficult to gather. To begin reporting your measures, you need precise formulas, and you must clearly identify sources of data.

- *Formula.* In the formula box, you should provide the specific elements of the calculation for the performance measure.

- *Data Source.* Every measure must be derived from somewhere, as from an existing management report, third-party vendor-supplied information, customer databases, the general ledger, and the like. In this section you should rigorously attempt to supply as detailed information as possible. If the information is sourced from a current report, what is the report titled, and on what line number does the specific information reside? Also, when can you access the data? If it's based on your financial close process, what day of the month can you expect final numbers? This information is important to your Scorecard reporting cycle since you'll be relying on the schedules of others when producing your Scorecard. The more information you provide here, the easier it will be to begin actually producing Balanced Scorecard reports with real data. However, if you provide vague data sources or no information at all, you will find it exceedingly difficult to report on the measure later. A warning: Spend the time you need to thoroughly complete this section. I have seen a number of Scorecards proceed swiftly through the development stage only to stall at the moment of reporting because the actual data could not be identified or easily collected.

- *Data Quality.* Use this area of the template to comment on the condition of the data you expect to use when reporting Scorecard results. If the data are produced automatically from a source system and can be accessed easily, they can be considered "high." If, however, you rely on an analyst's Word document that is in turn based on some other colleague's Access database numbers that emanate from an old legacy system, you may consider the quality "low." Assessing data quality is important for a couple of reasons. Pragmatically, you need to know which performance measures may present an issue when you begin reporting your results. Knowing in advance what to expect will help you develop strategies to ensure the data you need are produced in a timely and accurate fashion. Data quality issues may also help direct resource questions at your organization. As we discussed earlier, one of the benefits of the Scorecard is in the "missing measures" it often helps you unearth. If the information is truly critical to strategic success, then perhaps the organization should invest in systems to mine the data more effectively.

- *Data Collector.* In the first section of the template, we identified the owner of the measure as that individual who is accountable for results. Often this is not the person we would expect to provide the actual performance data. In our example, G. Garfinkel the VP of Marketing, is accountable for the performance of the measure, but Marketing Analyst Sierra Burdette serves as the actual data contact.

Performance Information   In the final section of the template we note our current level of performance, suggest targets for the future, and outline specific initiatives we'll use to achieve those targets.

- *Baseline.* Users of the Balanced Scorecard will be very interested in the current level of performance for all measures. The baseline is critical to the work of those tasked with developing targets.

- *Target.* Some of you may be saying right now, "At this point in the process we haven't set targets. That's the next chapter. So what do we do here?" Very true, we'll cover targets in Chapter Six. However, some of your measures may already have targets. Perhaps a goal of 15 percent return on equity is clearly outlined in your latest analyst reports. Or lowering emission levels at your plants by 5 percent is legislated by your state government. Wherever targets exist, use them now. For those measures that don't currently have targets, you can leave this section blank and complete it once the targets have been finalized. List whatever targets you have based on the frequency of the measure. In this example, I've shown quarterly customer loyalty targets. Some organizations may find it difficult to establish monthly or quarterly targets and instead opt for an annual target, but track performance toward that end on a monthly or quarterly basis.

- *Target Rationale.* As with the last measure, this will apply only to those measures for which you currently have a performance target. The rationale provides users with background on how you arrived at the particular target(s). Did it come from an executive planning retreat? Is it an incremental improvement based on historical results? Was it based on a government mandate? For people to galvanize around the achievement of a target, they need to know how it was developed and that, while it may represent a stretch, it isn't merely wishful thinking on the part of overzealous executives.

- *Initiatives.* At any given time, most organizations will have dozens of initiatives or projects swirling about. Often only those closest to the project know anything about it, and possible synergies between initiatives are never realized. The Scorecard provides you with a wonderful opportunity to evaluate your initiatives in the context of their strategic significance. If an initiative or project cannot be linked to the successful accomplishment of your strategy, why is it being funded and pursued? Use this section of the template to map current or anticipated initiatives to specific performance measures. Chapter Six will return to the subject of initiatives.

Gathering Employee Feedback on the Balanced Scorecard

Ultimately, you expect your Balanced Scorecard to provide information that allows all employees to determine how their day-to-day actions link to the organization's strategic plan. Most experts will tell you that the executive of your organization must own the Balanced Scorecard if it is to be effective in generating results. I don't disagree but would add that while executives may own the Scorecard, it's the employees who must accept the tool and be willing to use it if you hope to achieve any of the breakthroughs this concept can bring. Your battle of Scorecard success will be fought and won or lost on a day-to-day, decision-by-decision basis at the front lines of commerce. I've mentioned the rise of human capital frequently throughout this book. If you truly believe that employee knowledge makes the difference in achieving organizational victory, do yourself an immense favor and find out what employees think about your Scorecard before you ask them to use it as a management tool.

Here are three methods you can employ to capture what your employees think about your Balanced Scorecard.

1. *Conduct a Balanced Scorecard open house.* The County of San Diego, California, has instituted a wide-ranging performance management program to better serve the citizens of this sixth most populated county in the United States. It began by developing Balanced Scorecards for the Health and Human Services agency (HHSA). With a budget of over $1 billion and 5,000 employees, HHSA is larger than many corporations. Given the diverse nature of services offered throughout the agency, HHSA asked each of its program areas to develop Balanced Scorecards that demonstrated how each successfully serves its customers. A Balanced Scorecard implementation team made up of county personnel and consultants worked with each program to develop Scorecards over a four-month span. Once preliminary Scorecards were built, the team looked for a way to share what had been developed with all employees and gather their feedback. They decided to hold what they termed "validation sessions." Four sessions were held—two in the morning and two in the afternoon. Upon entering the conference room, participants were greeted by Scorecard implementation staff and given a folder to hold the information they would gather during the event. Each session was kicked off with a short presentation from the team leader, who provided an overview of the initiative, benefits to be derived from performance management, and the work that lay ahead. Once the presentation concluded, participants were free to visit several booths manned by Scorecard team members. Each booth featured a number of different Scorecards that the participants could review and discuss with the team. A kiosk was also set up to give employees the opportunity to take a test drive of the Scorecard software that would be used to report results. Feedback forms were distributed and participants were encouraged to provide their input. The event was a great success since employees from across the agency had the chance to participate in the evolution of performance measures and see how other groups within HHSA were measuring their outcomes.

2. *Use your intranet.* Take advantage of the technology that currently exists within your organization by broadcasting Scorecard updates over your intranet. Establish a page on your internal Web that contains information updates on Scorecard progress, performance management presentations, quotes from executives on the value of the Balanced Scorecard, and frequently asked questions. Once you have a draft Scorecard, post it on the intranet and ask employees to send their comments via e-mail to the Scorecard team. Or create a chat room or blog and post all comments received on the Balanced Scorecard. It's always important to foster as much conversation about the Scorecard

as you can since these informal exchanges may lead to breakthroughs in knowledge. The intranet is a very efficient way of gathering feedback from a large number of people in a short period of time.

3. *Hold management meetings or town halls.* If you hold regular meetings that bring together your entire management team, use that venue to share the draft Scorecard. Devote time to providing Scorecard background, the methodology employed in building the Scorecard, and what has been developed thus far. You should also prepare the audience for the challenges awaiting them, for example, developing their own Balanced Scorecards and using the system to run their businesses. Breakout sessions by business group are a good way to have managers start thinking about the benefits the Balanced Scorecard will bring to their group. During breakouts, specific business groups and departments will be able to assess how well the current Scorecard measures capture their concerns and competitive advantages. Town hall meetings can also be a great way to share what you've developed with a large number of employees. You'll undoubtedly have to schedule a number of these sessions to ensure that everyone has the chance to participate. The key to these sessions is to share information and gather feedback, so ensure the dialog is not one-way but instead fosters communication between employees and the Scorecard team. Whether you conduct management meetings or town halls, attempt to have an executive open the meeting. This shows senior management support for the concept and may help convince incredulous staffers that the Scorecard is in fact here to stay.

DO PERFORMANCE MEASURES REMAIN THE SAME?

Before we end our discussion of performance measures, we must consider the question of their longevity within the Balanced Scorecard. "Will we have the chance to change our measures?" and "Should measures change?" are two of the most frequent questions I hear once an organization has launched a Balanced Scorecard program. Some people fear that once they commit to measuring a certain element of performance, they're obligated to keep that measure as long as the Scorecard is in existence. That definitely is not the case.

The Balanced Scorecard is designed to be a dynamic tool, flexible and capable of change as conditions warrant. Over time you can expect a number of changes to take place within your measures. In the most extreme case you may abandon a strategy you've pursued based on Scorecard results that prove that much of your hypothesis was invalid. In that case you would likely develop a new strategy for your organization and select new and corresponding objectives and measures that act as direct translations of the new strategy. Even if you don't completely renounce a current strategy, you should review your performance measures at least annually in conjunction with your planning events (strategic planning, business planning, budgeting, etc.). Evaluate measures to ensure that they are still valid in light of current and anticipated business conditions and that they can remain key chapters in your strategic story.

Many organizations tend to make subtle changes to measures as they gain experience with the Balanced Scorecard system. The method of calculation may change to better capture the true essence of the event under investigation, or the measure's description may be enhanced to improve employee understanding of its operational and strategic significance. You may also change the frequency with which you collect performance data. For example, you may have attempted to track employee satisfaction monthly, but the logistics of gathering the data simply proved too challenging. In that case you wouldn't forsake this important indicator; rather you would simply change the reporting period to something more amenable to measurement. Changing your performance measures is yet another way to tap into the collective knowledge of your organization. Be sure to advertise the fact that you're about to consider measure changes for the coming fiscal year, and give the entire employee base the opportunity to provide feedback regarding beneficial adjustments.

The caveat regarding such changes is this: Don't alter your measures simply because you don't like the current crop or the results aren't what you expected. The Balanced Scorecard is about learning: learning about your strategy, learning about the assumptions you've made to win in your marketplace, and learning about the value proposition you've put forth. Sometimes you won't enjoy what your measures are telling you, but don't simply treat these alterations from plan as defects. Instead use them to question and learn about your business.

KEEP IN MIND

- Measures are quantifiable (normally, but not always) standards used to evaluate and communicate performance against expected results.
- The Balanced Scorecard should contain a mix of lagging and leading indicators of performance. Lagging indicators represent the consequences of actions previously taken, while leading indicators drive, or lead to, the results achieved in lagging indicators. As an example, absenteeism may be considered a leading indicator of employee satisfaction.
- Strategy Maps are comprised of objectives, concise statements of what we must do well in each perspective to execute the strategy. But how do we know if we are achieving the objectives that appear on the Strategy Map? Performance measures provide the answer by allowing us to gauge our progress. The measures we choose should be directly translated from

the objectives that make up our map, which in turn were directly translated from our strategy.

- Creating a Balanced Scorecard of performance measures requires making difficult choices among a vast number of possible metrics. Fortunately, there are a number of criteria you can employ to assist you in making your decision. Scorecard measures should be linked to your strategy, quantitative, accessible, easily understood, counterbalanced, relevant, and based on a definition shared by all involved. Each potential measure should be evaluated in the context of all criteria to determine which will be included in your Scorecard.

- As the Balanced Scorecard methodology continues to gain prominence, the number of measures tracked by most organizations has increased steadily. The advent of functionality-laden software, which facilitates the tracking of thousands of measures, has contributed greatly to the proliferation in the number of measures. The key in determining the appropriate number of measures for your Scorecard lies in their ability to coherently and completely capture your strategic story. Some organizations may require as few as 12 measures, while others will require 25 or more. Research of Scorecard practitioners across a variety of organizations has revealed most use between 20 and 25 measures for their highest-level organizational Scorecards.

- Performance measure data dictionaries chronicle all relevant aspects of your indicators, allowing everyone to learn, at a glance, the nature and specifics of your measures. Create a dictionary that includes, for each measure: background, characteristics, calculation and data elements, and performance information.

- If the Balanced Scorecard is to gain traction at your organization, your entire group of employees must understand the tool and be involved in its development if they are to be expected to use it as a management tool. Open houses, your intranet, and town hall meetings are all methods you can use to gather Balanced Scorecard input from your employees.

- Measures on the Balanced Scorecard will evolve and change over time. Change may come in the form of entirely new strategic directions that require corresponding measures, or could be more subtle. Organizations will often adjust measure descriptions, methods of calculation, or frequency of collection as the performance management system advances in maturity.

Notes

1. Steven D. Levitt and Stephen J. Dubner, *Freakonomics* (New York: William Morrow, 2005), p. 14.
2. Performance Measurement Survey by the American Institute of Certified Public Accountants and Lawrence S. Maisel, 2001.

3. Robert E. Quinn, Regina M. O'Neill, and Lynda St. Clair, *Pressing Problems in Modern Organizations (That Keep Us Up At Night)* (Amacom, 2000).

4. Dawne Shand, "Economic Value Added," *Computerworld* (October 2000).

5. Quote taken from IDEO's Web site, www.ideo.com.

6. Dennis Sparacino and Cindy O'Reilly, "Leveraging Customer Metrics for Strategic Decision Making," *Telemarketing and Call Center Solutions* (October 2000).

7. See Jan Carlzon, *Moments of Truth* (Cambridge, MA: Ballinger, 1987).

8. Terrence L. Foran and Arvin Jawa, "Golden Opportunity," *Catalog Age* (March 2001).

9. B. Joseph Pine and James H. Gilmore, *The Experience Economy* (Boston: Harvard Business School Press, 1999).

10. Ram Charan and Larry Bossidy, *Confronting Reality* (New York: Crown Business, 2004).

11. David Maister, *Practice What You Preach: What Managers Must Do to Create a High- Achievement Culture* (New York: The Free Press, 2001).

12. Marie Gendron, "Competencies and What They Mean to You," *Harvard Management Update* (September 1996).

13. Tommy Galvin, "The 2004 Top 100," *Training Mag.com* (January 6, 2006).

14. Jim Loehr and Tony Schwartz, *The Power of Full Engagement* (New York: Free Press, 2003), p. 5.

15. Ibid., p. 65.

CHAPTER 6

Setting Targets and Prioritizing Initiatives

Roadmap for Chapter Six When we began our Balanced Scorecard journey, I described this tool as three things: measurement system, strategic management system, and communication tool. This chapter provides the final pieces you require to create your Balanced Scorecard measurement system and communication tool: setting targets and prioritizing initiatives. It also lays the foundation for our next challenge: instituting the Balanced Scorecard as the cornerstone of your managerial processes.

The strong human desire to meet a predetermined goal has been with us from time immemorial. Many centuries ago Seneca said, *"If a man knows not what harbor he seeks, any wind is the right wind."* Oliver Wendell Holmes weighed in on the subject with this piece of wisdom: *"The great thing in this world is not so much where we are, but in what direction we are moving."* Seneca and Holmes were erudite gentlemen, but their advice can't compete with this pearl from that wisest of all sages, Yogi Berra: *"If you don't know where you are going, you might wind up someplace else."* Although these quotes represent vastly different times, places, and perspectives, what they have in common is the focus on a future destination, in other words, a target. Balanced Scorecards need performance targets to fully tell your strategic story. Without a corresponding target, your performance data lack the feedback necessary for analysis and decision making.

This chapter examines the critical role of targets in the Balanced Scorecard. Organizations may pursue different types of targets associated with specific time frames. We will look at three possible target time frames you may use with your Balanced Scorecard, as well as supporting organizational elements to ensure they motivate the right performance. Because setting targets can prove to be a challenging endeavor, we provide several sources of target information to help you complete this task. As with performance measures, your targets should be subject to a formal review process. We also consider some techniques you can employ to ensure that your targets receive appropriate feedback.

Initiatives describe specifically how a performance target will be met: the action steps, processes, projects, and plans that will bring the targets to life. At any given time, most organizations will be pursuing a multitude of different initiatives. The vital consideration is whether the initiatives are helping you meet your strategic goals or not. We'll examine organizational initiatives in the context of the Balanced Scorecard, and I'll describe a four-step process for ensuring that you have the right initiatives in place to support the achievement of your strategy.

EVERY BALANCED SCORECARD NEEDS TARGETS

Like many people I enjoy playing golf. The game cast its spell on me when I was sixteen and I've been a hopelessly optimistic hacker ever since. Mark Twain called golf, "a good walk spoiled" but I can't get enough of it. When I started thinking about how to begin this chapter my mind wandered to the golf course—I'm not sure if that was a flash of brilliance or a futile attempt at distraction! Either way it produced an insight. Imagine playing a round of golf without flags and holes. At what would you aim? How far would you try and hit the ball, and in what direction? I suppose you could step up to the first tee box, place your ball on a tee and wail away. Wherever the ball landed would be good enough and you could go on to the next hole—maybe even with a smile on your face. But how do you know if your game is getting any better, what is the standard? Flags, and the holes in which they're placed, provide us with something to aim at, something on which we can place our attention and unwavering focus. By aiming at the flag and counting the strokes to put the ball in the hole we have a means of judging our performance against a predetermined standard, called par. And we love the challenge of attempting to "make par." Of course we humans have always had a desire to meet our goals and succeed. Cultures around the globe, including ancient Peruvians and Egyptians, believed that writing out a goal in advance would help ensure a positive outcome. On the walls of caves they painted pictures representing their goals.

We've come a long way from drawing on cave walls, but our desire to succeed by meeting a challenge has remained the same. Like a golf course without flags or holes, the Balanced Scorecard is incomplete without a set of targets to motivate and inspire breakthrough performance. Targets make the results derived from measurement meaningful and tell us whether we're doing a good job. An on-time delivery percentage of 65 percent really doesn't tell us much unless we consider that performance in the light of our desired results. Only by combining our actual performance with a target does this feedback become meaningful. Our on-time delivery rate of 65 percent takes on a lot more relevance when we learn that the industry standard is 80 percent and our chief competitors all have percentages hovering in the high 70s. Armed with this knowledge, we see that our rate requires improvement if we are to compete effectively in the marketplace. We might now set an aggressive target of 85 percent on-time delivery for the coming year. As performance data accumulate, they are now imbued with meaning in the context of the target, and we can evaluate trends and make decisions regarding how to make certain we meet or exceed that target. Predicting future results is also facilitated by monitoring our results as compared to the target. And finally, accountability is fostered by assigning ownership for results to an individual responsible for achieving the target.

Using performance targets is a standard and accepted procedure among Balanced Scorecard practitioners. One study found that 93 percent of respondents *"employed quantitative goals that have been directly aligned with Scorecard measures."*[1] In case you're wondering why it wasn't 100 percent, some organizations will use targets of a subjective nature, ratings such as "fair" or "average," for example. As we discussed in Chapter Five, this practice should be avoided whenever possible; it is always preferable to apply a quantitative standard in order to maximize objectivity.

Different Types of Targets

A target can be defined as a quantitative representation of the performance measure at some point in the future, that is, as our desired future level of performance. The word "future" is key to the notion of targets. When developing targets. we can choose to evaluate performance against a goal just for this month, quarter, or year, or we could develop a longer-term aspiration requiring additional effort and performance. In this section we'll examine three types of targets, each associated with a different time frame.

Long-term Targets: Big Hairy Audacious Goals (BHAGs)

On May 25, 1961, President Kennedy made this bold proclamation: *"This nation should commit itself to achieving the goal, before this decade is out, of landing a man on the moon and returning him safely to earth."*[2] This statement represents the best essence of a big hairy audacious goal, or BHAG. *Built to Last* authors Jim Collins and Jerry Porras coined this term to describe the seemingly outrageous goals that organizations establish as powerful mechanisms to stimulate progress.[3]

The idea behind a BHAG is that it will dramatically shake up an organization by throwing at it a monumental challenge that cannot be achieved through business-as-usual operations, but will instead require tremendous effort. BHAGs, as evidenced by their dramatic challenges, are necessarily long-term goals with a clear and compelling finish line toward which all energies can be focused. Most BHAGs take between 10 and 30 years to accomplish. The long time frame serves two purposes. First, a worthy BHAG is unlikely to be met in a year or two. The extreme challenge it represents will take many years to conquer. Second, an extended time horizon ensures executives do not sacrifice long-term results for the sake of achieving a short-term goal.

With increasing frequency, public sector and nonprofit organizations are turning to BHAGs in an effort to stimulate progress on long-standing societal ills. For example, the American Heart Association recently announced its "impact" goal of reducing coronary heart disease, stroke, and key risk factors by 25 percent by the year 2010. Making the challenge all the more formidable is the fact that this goal covers the entire U.S. population, not a small control group. CEO M. Cass Wheeler suggests the goal will be achieved in part by holding the organization's feet to the fire with a set of strong performance measures, such as the rates of coronary heart disease, stroke, uncontrolled high blood pressure, obesity growth, diabetes growth, the prevalence of tobacco use, high cholesterol, and physical activity.[4] In Canada, the federal government recently announced a wide range of long-term targets aligned with closing the gap in the quality of life between native Canadians and the rest of the population. Among the goals to which the government has held itself accountable are reducing infant mortality, youth suicide, childhood obesity, and diabetes by 50 percent in 10 years and closing the educational gap so that by 2016, the high school graduation rate for aboriginal students will equal that of other Canadian students.[5]

Midrange Targets: Stretch Goals

Whereas BHAGs reach out and grab the entire organization, serving as a unifying focal point for one immense goal, stretch targets normally apply to a wider variety of activities. Essentially, we're taking the BHAG and breaking it down into its component parts. Stretch targets are set three to five years in the future. Although they are not quite as dramatic or outrageous as BHAGs, they do represent discontinuous operations. Moving customer loyalty from 40 percent to 75 percent over a three-year period would constitute a stretch target, as would doubling stock price or inventory turnover.

Consider the story of Honeywell. In the mid-1990s when Michael Bonsignore assumed the role of CEO, he faced a very difficult situation. *Business Week* magazine warned that investors were becoming impatient and the board was upping pressure to show results. Lackluster financial numbers put major demands on the new CEO to right the ship. One of Bonsignore's first acts was to establish a powerful stretch target of achieving $10 billion in annual revenue by the year 2000, a remarkable goal for a company that hadn't produced much more than $6 billion in over a decade. Bonsignore later recalled, *"I wanted to send a very strong signal to the organization. We were gonna do something different or die trying."*[6] Despite initial resistance by Honeywell executives, the organization eventually rallied around the target and set about to achieve it. By 1999 Honeywell had achieved sales of $9.9 billion. The establishment of a powerful stretch target helped orchestrate this impressive turnaround.

One of the best pieces of self-help advice I have ever received was this: *"Whatever you focus on expands."* Think about that for a moment, recalling times in your life when you had a single-minded determination to achieve something. Better yet, start living it today, focusing intently and sending positive energy toward what you want in your life. The principle is similar within organizations: The goals we set reflect our energy and our focus. Business guru Michael Hammer suggests, *"Your reach should exceed your grasp. If you set modest goals, you'll never do anything but perform modestly."*[7] As we all know, in this age of hypercompetition, modest performance is a sure ticket to being steamrolled by our competitors.

Short Term: Incremental Targets

We all know that a journey of 1,000 miles begins with a single step. So it is with the incremental performance target. For each of the measures on the Balanced Scorecard, these goals are normally established on an annual basis. They provide a quantitative goal for our measures and allow us to gauge our progress toward stretch goals and ultimately BHAGs. Incremental targets act as an early warning system, providing timely feedback relating to the achievement of our desired future state as represented in stretch targets and BHAGs. Most organizations use annual targets; however, greater benefits can be derived by aligning targets with the reporting frequency of performance measures. For example, you may wish to measure "market share" on a quarterly basis. Your target for the year is 50 percent, but you may be able to break that down to 40 percent for the first quarter, 44 percent in the second, 48 percent in the third, and, finally, 50 percent at year-end. Having targets for each of the quarters endows actual results with more meaning for decision making since you can now make valid comparisons between actual and targeted results.

Are All Three Target Types Necessary?

Based on our discussion in the last section, we see that the three classes of targets can work together in shaping an organization's future. BHAGs set the desired long-range future vision, which is then decomposed into a number of stretch goals. Feedback on the attainment of stretch goals is received by analyzing performance results in the short term. Ideally, you should construct targets relating to each time period. However, in practice, this is infrequently done, at least during the early stages of a Scorecard implementation. Just establishing incremental performance targets often proves to be a significant challenge, especially considering the fact that a number of performance measures may be brand new with little in the way of baseline data to support a logical target. Here are some items to consider when establishing each type of target.

- *BHAGs need organizational support systems.* Achieving a BHAG will take many, many years, possibly even decades. One sure-fire way to derail a BHAG is to put in place management systems that not only don't support the achievement of the BHAG but actively work against it. Compensating executives on short-term profit while simultaneously pursuing a BHAG of revolutionary long-term growth is a contradiction that will ensure the latter goal is never reached. To help organizations reach the lofty realms of their BHAGs, author Jim Collins describes "catalytic mechanisms" as the link between performance and objectives. Catalytic mechanisms *"transform lofty aspirations into concrete reality. They make big, hairy, audacious goals reachable."*[8] Collins uses the example of 3M, which urged its scientists to spend 15 percent of their time experimenting and inventing in the area of their own choice. This mechanism was designed to ensure that innovation and creativity remain the hallmark of 3M.

- *Make stretch targets realistic.* While seemingly outlandish claims and goals that seek to galvanize an organization are the domain of the BHAG, stretch targets must be firmly rooted in reality to be accepted. Imagine hiring a personal trainer to help you achieve your fitness goals. After one workout together your brawny teacher notes, "Someday you could compete in the Olympics." You feel pretty good about that until the teacher then says: "So tomorrow we're going to get you ready by lifting 400 pounds over your head 10 times." Unless you're a trained weightlifter, that goal clearly isn't rooted in reality. Rather than motivating you, it may deter you from even showing up at the next session. Unfortunately, many organizational stretch targets seem to be chosen with as little rigor as our hypothetical example. Achieving zero manufacturing defects in one month or doubling net earnings in six months is equally unrealistic. Even if employees are somehow motivated to achieve such goals, they are often ill-equipped to do so since they lack the knowledge, tools, and means necessary to produce. For stretch targets to prove effective, they must motivate employees while at the same time being grounded in reality. Additionally, as with BHAGs, you must put in place management systems that complement the achievement of your stretch targets.

- *Let the games begin — incremental performance targets.* Increment means "added amount." When organizations create targets of this nature that is very often what they do: add (or subtract) a small amount to the previous year's number: Increase sales by 5 percent, lower supplies expense by 10 percent. The question is: What is an appropriate number to add or deduct? Some managers become very adept at developing targets they camouflage as stretch when in fact they know very well they can achieve them with a minimum of effort. This can be very dangerous; it may appear from inside that the organization is attempting to improve continuously, when in fact it's merely a charade and competitors are improving at a much quicker rate. All targets on the Balanced Scorecard should be subject to a rigorous review process to ensure that the numbers suggested are in fact meaningful targets which represent significant effort to achieve. Rather than accepting targets at face value, managers and executives must quiz the target setter, questioning her assumptions, generating alternatives, and generally determining that the target is the result of careful analysis, not meticulous game playing.

Not every measure on your Scorecard will have an associated big hairy audacious goal. That would prove nearly impossible to manage and could lead to a diffusion of priorities throughout the organization. However, you should attempt to develop stretch targets for each of your measures. These stretch targets will play an important role when you link the Balanced Scorecard to your organization's budgeting process (discussed in Chapter Eight). Of course, incremental targets should also form a part of your Scorecard. For every measure, you must form a picture of where you want to be in three to five years and the incremental steps you'll take to get there.

Sources of Target Information

Many organizations have serious difficulty in developing targets for their measures. In certain cases managers appear hesitant to commit themselves to an actual target they will be bound to honor and judged against. With coaching, positive feedback, and the passage of time, this reluctance may be overcome. Often, however, it is not managerial apathy that precludes the development of targets but simply the fact that because the measure is brand new, there is no baseline to work from; or a lack of potential sources of target information might hold people back. You can find information that will help you create targets for your particular measures in a number of places.

- *Employees.* You should never forget that those closest to the action are in the best position to provide information on what it takes to exceed stakeholder expectations. No matter what type of business you're in, your employees have a unique glimpse into the customer experiences and internal processes that drive value throughout the organization. Involving employees in target setting will also help increase buy-in and support for the Balanced Scorecard as a management tool.

- *Trends and baselines.* A trend analysis or other statistical technique will help you establish a baseline projection if past data exist. You can use these baseline data to help you predict future levels of performance under conditions similar to those experienced in the past. That's a key point. If your organization or industry is subject to increasing levels of volatility, incremental improvement from previous baselines may not be enough to sustain profitable performance. Trends work best when you're in a period of relative stability.

- *Executive interviews.* When you met with your executives earlier in the process, they may have shared what they felt was a required level of performance to achieve success. Similarly, your executive workshops, conducted throughout the process of developing a Scorecard, will likely yield potential Scorecard targets.

- *Internal/external assessments.* If you've recently gone through any kind of strategic planning process, you've undoubtedly conducted an assessment of strengths, weaknesses, opportunities, and threats (SWOT). Information from these assessments will help you determine appropriate targets to maximize opportunities and minimize threats.

- *Feedback from customers and other stakeholders.* Expectations from these important groups may yield information you can use when establishing performance targets. Customers may have explicit or implicit standards to which they expect all vendors to adhere. Involving stakeholders in the target-setting process also demonstrates your commitment to working with everyone involved with your enterprise to produce mutually beneficial results. Recall our earlier discussion of customers rating your performance on the Internet. Don't miss this opportunity to engage your customers in a dialog about what constitutes great performance in their minds.

- *Industry averages.* A number of credible agencies monitor the performance of virtually all industries. J. D. Power and Associates comes to mind for the automobile industry. Your organization is most likely affiliated with some industry or trade association that may have valuable information regarding performance across your industry on selected metrics. Be careful to ensure any data you use are consistent with your methodology for measurement. Many organizations follow vastly different methods of calculating even the most common performance measures.

- *Benchmarking.* Examining best-in-class organizations and attempting to emulate their results is effective—to a point. It's very important to try to achieve the same level of success as the star performers in your industry, but benchmarking has a downside as well. First of all, most organizations will simply focus on one element of operations when conducting a benchmarking study: perhaps innovation processes, month-end closing processes, or call center operations. The problem with this approach is that the best-in-class company you're studying probably has a number of different activities it combines to drive a unique mix of value for customers (the essence of strategy, as espoused by Michael Porter). Copying just one element of this formula may lead to isolated improvements but fail to bring about breakthrough financial performance. Additionally, the organizations you review may have different customers, processes, and resources. Perhaps they allocate significant human and financial resources to the process under the microscope, and that's what accounts for their success.

Gaining Approval for Your Targets

Your executive team should own the responsibility for approving the targets appearing on your highest-level Balanced Scorecard. Ultimately, it's the executives who own this tool, and they must feel that the goals on the Scorecard represent exceptional performance, which will require great effort and collaboration to successfully accomplish. Approving targets is yet another opportunity for your senior team to break out of functional silos and demonstrate how their particular role in the organization contributes to overall success. The team must ensure the targets displayed on the Scorecard will combine to produce the breakthrough financial results they anticipate. If the VP of Manufacturing commits to tremendous gains in supply-chain activities and the VP of Sales extends a willingness to produce unheard-of sales increases, you would expect a correspondingly high target from the chief financial officer. Again, each part of the Scorecard and each member of the senior management team is part of the larger system, the greater whole that is made stronger through the power of relationships.

Chapter Five noted the importance of gathering employee feedback on your performance measures. While employees don't have approval on highest-level Scorecard targets, they must have the opportunity to review them and provide feedback. The last thing you want is for employees to perceive your targets as edicts issued from on high with no regard to the toll they will exact on those who have to do the actual work. Employee concerns regarding targets, their viability, and likelihood of success should be captured and fed back to senior management. Even if executive team members decide that a controversial target must remain in the Scorecard to produce desired results, they can use the opportunity to communicate their decision to staff and explain why the inclusion of this particular target is critical. To win at this Balanced Scorecard game, you must take advantage of every single opportunity to educate, communicate, and motivate your staff.

PRIORITIZING ORGANIZATIONAL INITIATIVES

By this point you have developed a Strategy Map of objectives and a Balanced Scorecard of measures telling the story of your strategy, and you have populated the model with targets that will lead you to unparalleled success. But you're not finished yet. The last piece in the puzzle of using the Balanced Scorecard as a measurement system is the development and prioritization of initiatives that will help you achieve your targets. Initiatives are the specific programs, activities, projects, or actions you'll embark on to help ensure you meet or exceed your performance targets. The target is your "end in mind" for the performance measure, and to get there, you need to determine what investments you must make in initiatives to guarantee a positive outcome.

If yours is like most organizations, there will be no shortage of initiatives under way at any given time. Employee engagement, customer relationship management, facilities upgrades, growth initiatives, and infrastructure modernization are all examples of the myriad projects that could be swirling about your organization right now. The interesting thing about most organizational initiatives is the broad spectrum of disciplines and processes they intend to influence. Besides their wide variety of focal points, they're probably each sponsored by a different manager or executive and executed with independent human and financial resources. The question of interest to us is this: Are they strategic in nature? Every initiative at your organization will undoubtedly drive local improvements in the area it is focused on improving. If not, chances are that it would not have been sponsored. But are the improvements you'll derive actually leading to the fulfillment of your Balanced Scorecard targets and hence your strategy? A critical examination of your current initiatives may yield interesting insights. You may find that you simultaneously have many initiatives and too few![9] An abundant number of projects gaining support may not be geared toward any specific element of your strategy, while concurrently the actions you need to take in order to achieve your Scorecard targets may not be represented with a single initiative.

When developing your Balanced Scorecard, you undoubtedly developed many performance measures that had never been considered before at your organization. This is particularly the case with the leading indicators of success, the drivers of future financial performance. Your performance-driving lead measures are the unique ingredients of your recipe for success and are not easily duplicated by competitors. If the measures themselves are new, then it's a sound bet that no initiatives are currently under consideration to ensure their success. Every original metric you uncover could mean you have a corresponding strategic process not being managed or not being managed effectively. A value proposition of customer intimacy, for example, necessitates processes ensuring deep customer knowledge housed within the Internal Process perspective of the Scorecard. If, upon examination, you have developed innovative new measures for capturing customer knowledge but not the associated activities or processes to support them, you really have no way to meet your targeted expectations. Doing so will require launching explicit initiatives that support the new managerial processes and measurements. Let's look at a method you can use to ensure that you have the right initiatives in place to support your Scorecard measures.

Ensuring the Right Initiatives Are in Place

In case you need a little incentive to complete your trek through this arduous terrain of initiative prioritization, here's a metaphorical carrot. Establishing the initiatives that truly provide support in your pursuit of strategic goals is one of the best and easiest ways to gain a quick economic payback from a Balanced Scorecard implementation. Think about it: You've probably got dozens of initiatives competing for scarce human resources, even more scarce financial resources, and the ultimate in scarce resources, the time and attention of senior management. Projects that aren't helping you achieve your strategy are not only counterproductive; the excess use of human and financial capital could be causing you to lose ground to your competitors. Eliminating nonstrategic initiatives by using the laser-like lens of the Balanced Scorecard will quickly free up valuable resources that can be funneled into projects that create real value and lead to competitive advantage.

Four steps will lead us to the promised land of prioritized strategic initiatives:

1. Perform an inventory of all current initiatives taking place within the organization right now.
2. Map those initiatives to the objectives of our Strategy Map.
3. Seriously consider eliminating nonstrategic initiatives, and develop missing initiatives.
4. Prioritize the remaining initiatives.

Let's consider each of these steps in more detail.

Developing an Inventory of Current Initiatives

To make an informed decision regarding which initiatives are strategic and which aren't, you must first gather information on all projects currently under way throughout the organization. This will mean searching under a lot of rocks, because you may find initiatives in every corner of the organization. Your executive team should be able to provide excellent input on current initiatives, since each project most likely has an executive sponsor. Managers and specific department heads will also be aware of current initiatives that affect them. Your strategic planning department may keep a detailed listing of all projects taking place at any given time, and such a document will prove invaluable to you. Finally, the finance staff will most likely be keeping tabs on project-related costs and be able to provide you with a roster of current initiatives. To aid in the decision-making process that will follow, ensure that you have the initiative's name, the objective to be achieved from the project, projected costs, any discounted cash flow analysis performed, anticipated timeline, and names of people involved.

Mapping Initiatives to Your Strategic Objectives

Armed with an exhaustive accounting of the initiatives currently under way, you're now ready to map those projects to the objectives you've identified in each of the four perspectives of your Strategy Map. It sounds easy enough: Take an initiative and look at it in the context of each objective. If it contributes to the achievement of an objective you mark it as such. If it doesn't you, leave that grid empty. However, simply evaluating the initiative based on its name may be problematic. Perhaps the title doesn't reflect the true nature of the tasks being undertaken, or perhaps ancillary activities do in fact support strategic objectives. Perform an appropriate amount of due diligence when completing this step. The first thing to do is determine specifically what you classify as "strategic." Every organization should have a definition of this term. Carefully review the information you gathered during your inventory step to ensure you have an adequate understanding of the true goals of each and every initiative. Speak to the sponsors, project team members, and those affected by the initiative to ensure that you've determined its full scope of activities and potential results. Each initiative should include supporting documentation to assist you in making this important decision. Those initiatives that are not fortified with critical information such as linkage to strategy, resource requirements, and net present value analysis are prime candidates for elimination in our next step. It will be very difficult to avoid having a little subjectivity creep into your analysis, but as we've discussed, strategy is messy business and often considered as much an art as a science. Exhibit 6.1 displays a template that will assist you in identifying which initiatives map to specific objectives. List your strategic objectives as they appear on your Strategy Map on the left side of the document. The upper portion of the template provides space to record your initiatives. In our example only one initiative, 'facilities beautification' cannot be directly linked to a strategic objective on the Strategy Map.

Eliminating Nonstrategic Initiatives and Developing Missing Initiatives

After thoughtfully judging the strategic value of each initiative, you must give serious consideration to canceling or reducing in scope those that do not contribute to the achievement of your strategy. Again, this is easier said than done. Every initiative will have a number of ardent supporters throughout the company who will most likely resist any attempts to destroy what they've built. Not only are resources on the line here, but relationships and perceived power are as well. The diplomatic skills of your Balanced Scorecard executive sponsor will be called into action during this step. Before simply abandoning those initiatives that don't appear to add strategic value, dig a little deeper and investigate the possibility of consolidating projects that, taken individually, don't lead to the fulfillment of strategy but, when combined with others, have synergistic possibilities that could translate to strategic breakthroughs. Should you require new

Exhibit 6.1   Mapping Initiatives to Objectives

Perspective	Objectives	Benchmarking	Maintenance Overhaul	ISO 9002	Frequent Purchase Program	IT Tools and Training	360 Feedback	Global Communication	Partner Program	Just-in-Time Mfg.	Decision Training	Facility Beautification	New Pricing Programs
Financial	Grow revenue	●											●
	Increase asset utilization									●			
Customer	Increase partnering								●				
	Build loyalty				●								
	Grow market share				●								
Internal Process	Develop customer information					●							
	Reduce downtime		●	●									
Employee Learning and Growth	Develop core competencies							●					
	Increase empowerment						●				●		

191

initiatives to fill the void created by new performance measures, develop them on a solid foundation. Ensure that there is: an executive willing to sponsor the new initiative, clearly defined plans and project scope, a legitimate budget, and the commitment of resources necessary to successfully complete the initiative. Exhibit 6.2 provides a template outlining the attributes and fields you should consider when documenting any new initiatives.

Prioritize Strategic Initiatives

Now that you have a definite number of initiatives you consider strategic, you must rank them in order to make resource allocation decisions (assuming you don't have unlimited financial and human resources). Chapter Eight discusses the role of initiatives in the budgeting process in greater detail, but for now let's consider how you can make a rational decision among competing alternatives. The key is basing the decision on a common set of criteria that will determine the most appropriate initiatives given your unique priorities. Obviously, the initiative's impact on driving strategy is the chief concern, but you can't ignore investment fundamentals like cost, net present value, and projected time to complete. Essentially, every initiative should have a valid business case to support its claim as being necessary to achieve your strategy. Once you've drafted business cases for each of the initiatives, you can use a template similar to the one shown in Exhibit 6.3 to assist in making the prioritization decision. Each criterion you choose is assigned a weight depending on its importance within your company. The assignments are subjective, but strategic importance should always carry the greatest weight in the decision. Next, each initiative must be scored on the specific criteria listed in the chart. You may use ratings of between 0 and 10, or if you prefer a wider scale, use 0 to 100. I've used 0 to 10 in my example. Before assigning points to each, you must develop an appropriate scale. For example, a net present value (NPV) of greater than $2 million may translate to 10 points. NPV of $1.75 million yields 9 points, and so on. Involving more than one executive on a full-time basis may translate to a score of 2 points in the "resource requirements" section since such involvement could impose a heavy burden on the organization. Develop scales that work for you. However, to ensure mathematical integrity, always have a high value represent preferred performance. Those initiatives generating the highest scores should be approved and provided budgets to ensure their timely completion. In our example, initiative #1 generates a higher total score than initiative #2, despite the latter's impressive scores on five of the six criteria. The reason for the discrepancy is the critical variable of strategic linkage. Initiative #1 demonstrates a strong linkage to strategy while #2 is missing that connection. We'll return to the topic of initiatives and budgets in Chapter Eight.

Exhibit 6.2   Strategic Initiative Template

Date: [　　　　　　　　]

This template is intended as an enterprise-wide tool to enable the Executive to quantify, assess, and prioritize proposed strategic initiatives based on their impact on strategic objectives.

Please limit input and commentary to the space provided and use minimum 10-point font.

Line of Business/Business Unit: [　　　　　　　　　　　　　　]

Strategic Initiative Name: [　　　　　　　　　　　　　　　]

Executive Owner: [　　　　　　　]   Initiative Leader: [　　　　　]

Anticipated Start Date: [　　　　　　]   Anticipated End Date: [　　　　　]

Initiative Description/Scope:

[　　　　　　　　　　　　　　　　　　　　　　　　　　　　]

Strategic Impact	**Strategic Impact (H, M, L)**
Describe Strategic Impact:	
Financial	
Customer	
Internal Process	
Employee Learning and Growth	

Resource Allocation Requirements

Capital & Operating Budget ($000)	2002	2003	2004	2005
Capital Spending Profile	$0	$0	$0	$0
Operating Budget Spending	$0	$0	$0	$0

Economic Fit

NPV: Net Present Value	
IRR%: Internal Rate of Return	
Payback Period	

Investment Summary ($000)	2002	2003	2004	2005
Revenue (incremental)	$0	$0	$0	$0
Revenue (retained)	$0	$0	$0	$0
Expense Savings	$0	$0	$0	$0

Net FTE Impact (+/− FTE's)				

(continues)

Exhibit 6.2   Strategic Initiative Template *(Continued)*

Key Dependencies

Key Risks to Successful Implementation and Mitigation Activities

Describe Internal Impact (employees/processes) of this Initiative

Describe External Impact (customers/suppliers/shareholders) of this Initiative

Milestones, Deliverables, and Corresponding Due Dates

Key Milestone	Deliverables	Due Date

Key Initiative Resources (Top 5 Involvement)

Name	Time Allocation (%)	Explanation of Time Allocation

Exhibit 6.3 Prioritizing Balanced Scorecard Initiatives

Criteria	Weight	Description	Initiative #1		#2		#3		#4	
			Points	Score	Points	Score	Points	Score	Points	Score
Linkage to strategy	45%	Ability of the initiative to positively impact a strategic objective	7	3.2	1	.45				
Net present value	15%	Present value of initiative benefits discounted 5 years	5	.75	10	1.5				
Total cost	10%	Total dollar cost including labor and materials	5	.50	10	1.0				
Resource requirements (key personnel)	10%	Key personnel needed for the initiative including time requirements	8	.80	10	1.0				
Time to complete	10%	Total anticipated time to complete the initiative	8	.80	10	1.0				
Dependencies	10%	Impact of other initiatives on the successful outcomes anticipated with this initiative	3	.30	10	1.0				
				6.35		5.95				

THE REWARDS ARE WORTH THE EFFORT

Developing and prioritizing initiatives to support your Balanced Score-card can be one of the most difficult aspects of the implementation. As discussed earlier, making these decisions can affect long-standing relationships among different functional areas and result in negative perceptions of organizational power wielding. However, this important task can also provide you with the first of many opportunities to show the economic value of the Balanced Scorecard by highlighting those initiatives that do in fact lead to the fulfillment of your strategy and those that merely soak up precious resources. Aligning initiatives with strategy also greatly facilitates the use of the Balanced Scorecard as a strategic management system by providing a method of linking the budgeting process with strategy and strategic planning. Finally, clarifying and prioritizing is yet another opportunity to utilize the Scorecard to increase accountability. Every initiative will have an executive sponsor who feels passionate about the project and strongly believes it will yield tremendous results. Using the Balanced Scorecard to validate your investments allows you to confirm or deny those beliefs.

Many organizations are already beginning to harness the value of aligning initiatives with strategy by using the Balanced Scorecard. When Crown Castle International, a leading provider of leased towers, antenna space, and broadcast transmission services, engaged in the exercise of rationalizing, it was able to pare its overall list of initiatives from 180 down to 12! CEO John Kelly even suggested the process wasn't overly difficult: *"Actually, it was pretty easy to cut our list down from 180 to 12 because people had a very clear understanding of what our strategic priorities were. We racked and stacked all initiatives, and looked at which ones were most important relative to the four elements of our strategy."*[10]

Chapter Five discussed the fact that a good Balanced Scorecard contains a mix of leading and lagging indicators of performance. Without performance drivers, lagging indicators cannot inform us of how we hope to achieve our results. Conversely, leading indicators may signal key improvements throughout the organization, but on their own they don't reveal whether these enhancements are leading to improved customer and financial results. Targets and initiatives are similar in that one without the other simply won't lead us to the results we desire. A target without supporting initiatives is missing the "how" of meeting our performance goals. And initiatives without targets don't signal whether the results we've achieved are what we expected or commensurate with any predetermined standards. Developing targets and initiatives can prove challenging. The tools and techniques outlined in this chapter will enable you to develop challenging targets and associated supporting initiatives that will ensure your Balanced Scorecard tells your story—complete with how you'll ensure a happy ending!

KEEP IN MIND

- Developing performance targets and supporting initiatives completes the work of building a Balanced Scorecard that tells the story of your strategy and acts as a powerful measurement system and communication tool.

- Targets make the results derived from measurement meaningful and tell us whether we're doing a good job. Performance data without associated targets has no meaning or context that can be used to evaluate performance and make decisions.

- Many organizations use a combination of three distinct yet related target types, each with a corresponding time frame. Big hairy audacious goals, or BHAGs, are long-term targets that act as compelling mechanisms used to guide organizations toward tremendous breakthroughs. Given their often seemingly outrageous nature, BHAGs normally take 10 to 30 years to complete. To really galvanize employees in the pursuit of a BHAG, organizations will require supporting organizational systems. Catalytic mechanisms are one such system. They represent specific processes geared toward stimulating the achievement of a BHAG.

- Stretch targets also promote discontinuous operations but are based on a shorter time frame, normally three to five years. Many organizations will develop a stretch target for each of the performance measures appearing on their Balanced Scorecards. To prove effective, the stretch target must represent a great challenge but must also be rooted in reality.

- Incremental targets are the (normally) annual targets that, if achieved, will lead to the fulfillment of stretch targets. They serve as the guideposts to the larger goals represented by stretch targets. Managers sometimes attempt to game the system by developing targets that appear to represent a huge challenge but in reality are easily achievable.

- A variety of information sources are available for establishing performance targets. Employees, trend analyses, executive interviews, assessments, stakeholder feedback, industry averages, and benchmarking are all possible origins of potential targets. Once targets have been set, they should be reviewed by employees but approved by your executive team.

- Targets may supply much-needed motivation, but achieving your goals requires the activation of specific initiatives. Initiatives represent the projects, processes, action steps, and activities you engage in to ensure successful measure outcomes. Most companies suffer from an abundance of initiatives that bear little relation to the organization's strategy. Paradoxically, the Balanced Scorecard may lead to the development of additional initiatives. However, these new initiatives will prove necessary to achieve the strategic goals of the organization.

- Four steps are necessary to ensure that you have the right initiatives in place at your organization:

  1. Develop an inventory of all initiatives currently under way. Gather information on project costs, expected benefits, linkage to strategy, key players, and timelines.

  2. Map those initiatives to the objectives appearing on your Strategy Map. Be sure to work closely with initiative supporters to be certain you know the specifics of each project before deciding on its strategic relevance.

  3. Eliminate, consolidate, or reduce in scope those initiatives that are not contributing to your strategy, and consider developing initiatives to support the new objectives and measures never before used at your organization.

  4. Prioritize your strategic initiatives. Each one should have a corresponding business case that will provide an objective basis for making the decisions.

- Prioritizing your Scorecard initiatives is a difficult but important task. One of the key benefits emerging from the process is the identification of projects that truly drive strategic results and those that simply drain resources. Highlighting this potentially expensive difference by using the Scorecard as a lens demonstrates the economic value to be derived from the Balanced Scorecard.

Notes

1. Best Practices Benchmarking Report, *Developing the Balanced Scorecard* (Chapel Hill, NC: Best Practices, LLC, 1999).

2. Daniel J. Boorstin, *The Americans: The Democratic Experience* (New York: Vintage Books, 1974).

3. James C. Collins and Jerry I. Porras, *Built to Last* (New York: Harper Business, 1997).

4. Bill Birchard, "Nonprofits by the Numbers," *CFO Magazine*, July 1, 2005.

5. Beth Duff-Brown, "Canada Pledges $4.3B for Native People," Associated Press release reported in *North County Times* (November 26, 2005).

6. Martin Puris, *Comeback* (New York: Times Business, 1999).

7. Ellen M. Heffes, "Measure Like You Mean It: Q & A with Michael Hammer," *FEI.com* (March 2002).

8. Jim Collins, "Turning Goals into Results: The Power of Catalytic Mechanisms," *Harvard Business Review* (July–August 1999), pp. 70–84.

9. Robert S. Kaplan and David P. Norton, *The Strategy Focused Organization* (Boston: Harvard Business School Press, 2001).

10. Janice Koch, "The Challenges of Strategic Alignment: Crown Castle's CEO Shares His Perspectives," *Balanced Scorecard Report* (July–August 2004): 11.

CHAPTER 7

Cascading the Balanced Scorecard to Build Organizational Alignment

Roadmap for Chapter Seven   Now that you have built a Balanced Score-card eloquently describing your strategy, it's time to take it to the streets! Okay, maybe not the streets, but at least to the corridors and cubicles of your company. The next task in our Scorecard journey is to use the high-level Scorecard you've created as a template for the creation of aligned Scorecards from top to bottom within your organization. This chapter will describe how you can do just that and along the way ensure that all employees are pursuing goals that are consistent with, and lead to, the achievement of your strategy.

Most of us today are knowledge workers and as such we look for meaning and contribution to form an integral part of our working lives. Cascading the Balanced Scorecard allows employees to develop objectives and measures linked to overall organizational goals. For successful cascading, everyone in the organization must possess a deep understanding of the objectives and measures that make up the highest-level Scorecard. We'll examine what it takes to ensure your organization has that all-important understanding. From that point forward it's a matter of influence. How do lower-level units and groups influence those high-level Scorecard indicators? We'll look at how to develop aligned Scorecards and explore examples from organizations that have traveled the path themselves.

The entire organization stands to benefit from cascading the Balanced Scorecard. To that end we'll investigate how you can develop Scorecards for your shared service units and even drive the Scorecard down to the individual employee level.

Every Scorecard you develop, regardless of what level of the organization it represents, must link back to overall objectives if you're to derive value from this process. The chapter concludes with a review of how you can effectively review and evaluate the Scorecards produced from every corner of your company.

WHAT DOES "CASCADING" THE BALANCED SCORECARD MEAN?

Before describing the techniques and processes necessary to properly cascade your Balanced Scorecard, I should describe what is meant by the term. "Cascading" refers to the process of developing Balanced Scorecards at each and every level of your organization. These Scorecards align with your company's highest-level Scorecard by identifying the strategic objectives and measures that lower-level departments and groups will use to track their progress in contributing to overall goals. While some of the objectives and measures used may be the same throughout the entire organization, in most cases lower-level Scorecards include items reflecting the specific opportunities and challenges faced at those levels. Many successful practitioners have made their highest-level Scorecard just the first piece in a program that links all employees from the shop floor to the executive boardroom through a series of cascading Balanced Scorecards.

Cascading the Balanced Scorecard Links All Employees to Your Strategy

In his book *Simplicity,* author Bill Jensen suggests that a leading cause of work complexity is unclear goals and objectives.[1] You're probably thinking you've got that problem licked since you've taken the initiative and developed a Balanced Scorecard with very clear objectives and measures that work together to tell your unique strategic story. Not so fast. Jensen goes on to note that another major contributor of work complexity is lack of alignment of goals.[2] Does your organization have clear alignment of goals from top to bottom? Do the people answering the phones at your company know how their day-to-day actions are contributing to the achievement of the company's strategy? What about a midlevel manager in sales; would she know? Does anyone below the executive ranks have a clear idea of how they support the organization's overall goals? In a large number of organizations, the answer is no. In a recent Harris Interactive poll of 23,000 U.S. residents employed full-time, only 37 percent said they have a clear understanding of what their organization is trying to achieve and why. The same study discovered that only 9 percent believed their work teams had clear measurable goals.[3]

Even in those organizations that have developed Balanced Scorecards, severe alignment issues may hamper their desire to outperform rivals. Some people subscribe to the notion that a Balanced Scorecard is the exclusive domain of the senior management team. Lower-level employees are welcome to look at the measures on the Scorecard, maybe even learn from them, but their performance can be monitored by other systems, such as the performance review process. Organizations that believe this are betting on the superiority of awareness over alignment, but unfortunately for them, that is simply not the case. Will mere awareness of corporate strategy, objectives, and measures lead to improved decision making on the front lines of the organization? Probably not. How does awareness of a customer intimacy strategy help a customer service representative deal with an irate customer who demands immediate satisfaction? It doesn't.

All employees need the opportunity to demonstrate how their specific actions are making a difference and helping the company fulfill its strategic objectives. The best way to do this is by cascading the Balanced Scorecard to every far-reaching level of the organization. When we cascade the Scorecard—driving it down to lower levels in the company—we provide a way for all employees to see how their day-to-day actions relate to the lofty aims espoused in the strategic plan. For employees, strategy is no longer some poorly understood treatise formulated by senior management but is transformed into specific objectives and measures they need to achieve in order to make a meaningful contribution to success. And that is precisely what every single employee in your organization wants more than anything else: to make a contribution. This is the era of the knowledge worker. These highly skilled purveyors of talent differ from their organizational ancestors in one key respect. Unlike earlier workers who depended on the organization to supply machines and other modes of production, these workers carry the means of production—their knowledge—with them. Peter Drucker suggested that in this era of the knowledge worker, employees should be considered volunteers. A volunteer doesn't provide her valuable knowledge, skills, and experience for the hope of tremendous monetary reward or personal advancement. Very often volunteers crave that which eludes them in their nine-to-five world: meaning and contribution. A lack of alignment between personal objectives and corporate strategy obscures the hope of finding true meaning and contribution in work. Cascading the Balanced Scorecard helps restore this possibility by providing all employees, regardless of function or level, with the opportunity to demonstrate that what they're doing is indeed critical to the overall efforts of the organization.

Not only does the cascading process align employee actions with strategy, it is consistently cited as a key factor in the success of Balanced Scorecard programs. In fact, Kaplan and Norton have discovered that the greatest gap between Balanced Scorecard Hall of Fame organizations and all others occurs in aligning the organization to the strategy: *"This demonstrates that effective organizational alignment, while difficult to achieve, has probably the biggest payoff of any management practice."*[4] This is not surprising, really, when you consider that through alignment, you're harnessing the greatest resource known to humankind: the minds and hearts of your employees. Successful Scorecard implementers know that those on the front line must embrace and use this tool if it is to reach its maximum effectiveness. Cascading the Scorecard allows you to reach your entire organization and supply them with the means of answering the critical question: How do I add value and make a meaningful contribution to our success? The answer lies in the objectives and measures embedded in Balanced Scorecards throughout your organization.

THE CASCADING PROCESS

Exhibit 7.1 displays the cascading process typically followed by most organizations. The highest-level Balanced Scorecard, often the one that is used to gauge the effectiveness of the organization as a whole, is the starting point for cascading efforts. The objectives and measures contained in that Strategy Map and Scorecard are then driven down to the next level in the organization, which will often comprise individual business units. At the third level of cascading, specific departments and groups develop Balanced Scorecards based on the Scorecards "in front" of theirs, in this case the business unit Scorecard. The final level shown is that of team and personal Balanced Scorecards. Organizations cascading to this level will gain the maximum value from the Balanced Scorecard by ensuring that all employees, regardless of function or level, have developed objectives and measures that align with overall organizational objectives.

The process outlined in Exhibit 7.1 should be considered *descriptive*, not *prescriptive*. If you've begun your Balanced Scorecard efforts within a specific business unit, that Scorecard would comprise your highest-level card and you would cascade based on the objectives and measures it contains. Similarly, you may work in a public sector or nonprofit organization and use different terminology to describe the various levels of your organization. Again, focus on the theory of cascading rather than the specific terminology contained in the diagram. The process works equally well whether you work in a Fortune 1000 company, a local community group, or a state government agency. Sections that follow examine the specific steps of the cascading process in further detail.

Understanding Is Key to the Highest-Level Balanced Scorecard

The cascading process begins at the top with your highest-level Balanced Scorecard. The first six chapters of this book have outlined how you should go about creating the Strategy Map of objectives and Scorecard of measures, so the specifics of those processes will not be examined here. What will be emphasized in this section is the importance of employee knowledge and understanding of the objectives and measures that make up the high-level Scorecard ("Scorecard" in this context refers to the map and measures).

Your highest-level Balanced Scorecard identifies the key objectives and measures of success that weave together in a series of cause-and-effect relationships to tell the story of your strategy. It is absolutely imperative that everyone in the organization understand the strategic significance of these

Exhibit 7.1   The Cascading Process

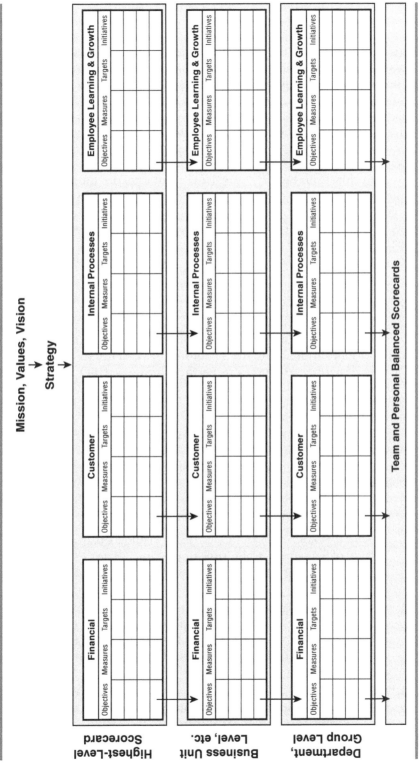

core elements before they begin creating their own Balanced Scorecards. This is particularly true for those individuals who carry the responsibility of leading the development of Scorecards at lower levels of the organization. If these individuals don't possess a deep knowledge of the high-level objectives and measures, it will be very difficult for them to construct Scorecards that are truly aligned to the organization's high-level goals.

Flawed assumptions occasionally cause companies to inadvertently sabotage their own efforts when they reach this step in the Scorecard process. Some organizations believe lower-level employees are incapable of understanding critical value-creating activities and processes that ultimately drive success. Executives in these firms maintain that topics ranging from economic value added to customer segmentation to supply chain best practices are the sole domain of the executive boardroom and employees are merely the actors hired to play out the drama they've masterfully orchestrated. Nothing could be further from the truth. In fact, successful organizations question this assumption and spend the necessary time and money to educate employees on these concepts with outstanding results. Consider as an example the innovative Brazilian firm Semco. Employees in this company, often cited for its creativity and innovation, participate in virtually every facet of organizational life, from choosing real estate, to designing manufacturing facilities, to determining their own pay. CEO Ricardo Semler strongly believes the driving force of productivity is motivation and genuine interest, and that is spawned from trusting employees to perform their jobs in ways that make sense to them.[5]

To ensure that the employees of your organization understand the objectives and measures appearing on your high-level Balanced Scorecard, you should embark on a significant communication and education program. In Chapter Five, I discussed three possible ways of gaining employee feedback on your Balanced Scorecard. You also can use these methods to prepare your teams for the cascading process to follow. The three methods are:

1. *Conduct a Balanced Scorecard "open house."* Follow the example set by the County of San Diego, California, during its Balanced Scorecard implementation. Invite employees to attend an open house during which the Balanced Scorecard is shared, discussed, reviewed, and critiqued.

2. *Use your intranet.* Post your new Balanced Scorecard on the intranet and include background on the strategic and operational significance of the measures, quotes from executives on the value of the Balanced Scorecard, and future plans for cascading your measures throughout the entire company.

3. *Hold management meetings or town halls.* If you hold regular meetings that bring together your entire management team, use that venue to educate your team on the Scorecard you've created. Town hall meetings can also be a great way to share what you've developed with a large number of employees.

Creative Scorecard practitioners will undoubtedly find many other methods of educating staff on the Balanced Scorecard. Brochures, videos, and inserts accompanying pay stubs are just a few of the many ways in which you can take the opportunity to explain the inner workings of your Scorecard to all employees.

Focus on "Influence" at the First Level of Cascading

Once you feel comfortable that employees have gained a sufficient understanding of your high-level Scorecard, you can begin the process of having them develop Balanced Scorecards that outline their own contributions to the organization's success. The key to creating aligned Scorecards is the concept of "influence."

A dictionary might define the word "influence" as the ability to produce an effect, and that is exactly what we have in mind when cascading the Balanced Scorecard. All employees should have the chance to produce an effect on the organization's outcomes. Their forum for doing so is the Balanced Scorecard. When developing Scorecards at this first level of cascading, the relevant question to guide the proceedings is: What can we do at our level to help the organization achieve its goals? The Scorecards you create here will align with the high-level Scorecard but won't necessarily contain the same measures. That's a key point warranting some attention. Many people consider cascading a simple exercise of chopping up high-level objectives into bite-size pieces scattered throughout the organization. That approach might work for certain financial metrics, such as revenue or costs, but how do you reasonably allocate customer loyalty or new product development? An effectively cascaded Balanced Scorecard is not one that simply contains bits and pieces of the highest-level Scorecard. High-level organizational measures could be completely meaningless to the people at lower rungs of the organizational ladder. A better approach is to carefully examine the high-level Scorecard and determine which of the objectives and measures you can *influence* at this level of the organization.

Nova Scotia Power Inc., the Canadian electric utility discussed previously, started its Balanced Scorecard program by first creating a high-level Corporate Scorecard that told the story of the strategy as it prepared for deregulation in the Canadian utility industry. To ensure that all employees had the opportunity to participate in the fulfillment of the strategy, the company subsequently cascaded the Balanced Scorecard to all levels of the organization. Over 100 Scorecards were created, spanning the executive team at corporate headquarters to the shop floors of power plants. Exhibit 7.2 shows an example of this cascading effort. In the example we see how a business unit selected objectives and measures based on the corporate Balanced Scorecard. Targets shown are for illustrative purposes only.

Take a look at the middle portion of the exhibit, the Customer Service and Marketing Balanced Scorecard. This level of the organization represents the

Exhibit 7.2　Cascading the Balanced Scorecard at Nova Scotia Power

Corporate Scorecard			
Perspective	Objective	Measure	Target
Customer	**Increase Customer Loyalty:** Move beyond "satisfied" to "loyal" customers	**Customer Loyalty Rating:** A composite index of earned customer loyalty	75%

Customer Service and Marketing Scorecard			
Perspective	Objective	Measure	Target
Internal Processes	**Increase Customer Loyalty:** Move beyond "satisfied" to "loyal" customers	**Redesigned Customer Processes:** Number of redesigned customer processes and services	5

CS&M Information Technology Scorecard			
Perspective	Objective	Measure	Target
Internal Processes	**Effective Desktop Support:** Provide effective desktop support for CS&M employees	**Service Requests:** Number of desktop service requests completed	500

first level of cascading at Nova Scotia Power. To build an effective Scorecard, the Customer Service and Marketing business unit carefully reviewed the corporate Balanced Scorecard and determined which of the objectives and measures on that Scorecard it could influence. One measure appearing on the corporate Balanced Scorecard was "customer loyalty rating." The Customer Service and Marketing business unit was obviously interested in this critical indicator and felt it could positively influence its outcome. Therefore, this business unit chose to develop a performance measure on its Balanced Scorecard that would indicate how it felt it could increase customer loyalty. But take a close look at the measure it developed. First of all, although the corporate objective and measure appeared in the Customer perspective, the measure developed by Customer Service and Marketing was better suited to the Internal Process perspective of the Scorecard. The objective this business unit chose mirrored the corporate objective, but the new measure better captured how it could *influence* the corporate indicator of "customer loyalty rating." The business unit knew from research that a number of key customer processes contained specific bottlenecks and issues that were consistent sources of customer dissatisfaction. It felt that by redesigning the most troublesome of those processes, it would be able to positively influence "customer loyalty rating" at the corporate level. Following the technique of determining which corporate objectives and measures it could influence allowed the Customer Service and Marketing business unit to create a Balanced Scorecard that demonstrated to the entire company how the unit would contribute to Nova Scotia Power's success.

When developing Balanced Scorecards for this (or any subsequent) level of the organization, you should not expect each group to influence every objective and measure appearing on the high-level Scorecard. Organizations derive value by combining the disparate skills of all employees within every function, and each group will rightly focus on the objectives and measures over which it may exert an influence. Having said that, a major benefit of the cascading process is watching creativity bloom throughout the organization as groups begin to contemplate how they might contribute to an organizational goal once considered well outside their sphere of influence.

The Importance of Influence Continues with Lower-Level Scorecards Depending on your organizational architecture, the next level of cascading you engage in could be to the department, group, or team level. As discussed earlier, you may use different terminology to describe the various levels that exist within your organization. However, regardless of the name, the principle of influence remains the same. At this level within the organization, Scorecards should be based on those to whom these groups report. We would not expect an individual marketing department, for example, to develop a Balanced Scorecard based on the corporate Scorecard. More likely, the Marketing group's indicators would be derived from the Sales and Marketing business unit's Balanced Scorecard. To illustrate this point, let's continue with the example outlined in Exhibit 7.2. The Customer Service and Marketing (CS&M) business unit of Nova Scotia Power has developed a Balanced Scorecard based on the objectives and measures it can influence on the corporate Scorecard. CS&M is comprised of a number of smaller groups, one of which is Customer Service and Marketing Information Technology (IT). When developing its Scorecard, the employees of CS&M IT looked to the business unit's Scorecard to determine which objectives and measures they could impact. They saw that CS&M was measuring "redesigned customer processes." The IT group will not be directly involved in redesigning customer processes, but it believes it can positively influence this objective. For the CS&M team to redesign a number of key customer processes, members will rely heavily on desktop support functions as they experiment with new and innovative ideas. The IT group recognizes this and hypothesizes that by quickly and accurately completing service requests, it will enable the CS&M business unit to achieve its goal of redesigning troubled customer processes.

The measures in each of the three Scorecard excerpts on Exhibit 7.2 are not identical, but they are *aligned*. Employees of the IT group within CS&M know that by efficiently completing service requests, they are not only assisting the business unit in achieving its goals but are also making a key contribution to the corporate objective of improving customer loyalty. Similarly, senior management within Nova Scotia Power can rest assured that employees at the front lines now have goals that are consistent with the corporation's objectives.

In addition to different performance measures, lower-level Balanced Scorecards may contain a greater number of measures. The measures that describe your strategy in the corporate Balanced Scorecard are often very high-level abstractions—customer loyalty, employee satisfaction, and so on—with many details omitted. As you move to lower levels of the organization, the specifics necessary to achieve success on the corporate measures are filled in as part of the business unit, department, and team Scorecards. Filling these gaps may require more than a one-to-one measure relationship. In our Nova Scotia Power example, the CS&M IT group may require two or even three measures to ensure that it assists the business unit to meet its goal of redesigning customer processes. The challenge, of course, is finding an appropriate number of measures; the last thing you or anyone in your organization wants is the classic paralysis by analysis syndrome brought on by a boatload of performance measures that leaves you swimming in a sea of data. Use the criteria presented in Chapter Five to help you finalize the measures appearing in all cascaded Scorecards.

Assisting in the Development of Aligned Balanced Scorecards

In every organization there are those people who have a natural affinity to the Balanced Scorecard and the method of management it entails and those who view it as yet another panacea being forced down their throat by an overzealous senior management team. Regardless of where the majority of your employees fall, one thing is certain: They will require assistance in developing their Balanced Scorecards. Here are a some tips that will help you ease the cascading process.

- *Consider cascading principles.* Before you begin your cascading efforts, you must consider a number of questions that will inevitably surface from groups charged with creating lower-level Scorecards. The first question to ponder is: Will all groups be required to use the four perspectives? Some may wish to change the labels, customizing the Scorecard to reflect their group's unique culture and norms. There are pros and cons to personalizing; doing so generates greater buy-in from staff, but it may confuse overall efforts of comparing results across the organization. A second question is: Are there certain objectives and measures all groups must use? If your organization is pursuing a cost containment initiative, for example, you may insist that all business units, departments, and teams include an objective of "reduce costs" and an associated measure of "budget variance." While such edicts greatly assist in aggregating results, you must balance that win with the potential drawback of reducing creativity in objective and measure development at lower levels. A final question to consider is: Will we limit the number of objectives and measures appearing on cascaded Balanced Scorecards? Recall from our discussion that cascaded Scorecards generate significant volumes of objectives and measures, sometimes far too many. Your goal in introducing the Balanced Scorecard is to focus on the critical few enablers of success, and that vision may be blurred significantly should lower-level groups find themselves awash in data.

- *Provide clear accountabilities, guidelines, and personal assistance.* You may think that the Balanced Scorecard is the most elegantly simple and logical tool ever to be developed, but those managers and employees who have never built a Scorecard may be feeling a good deal of trepidation. It's important to develop some devices up front to help them through the process. Discuss the Scorecard whenever possible, distribute it to all employees, share articles and books that provide useful information, and, most important, develop templates they can use to guide them through the process of developing their own Balanced Scorecard. Help also comes in the form of clear accountabilities and timelines so that people know exactly what is expected of them and when. But the single most critical thing you must do is provide personal assistance. Share the expertise that resides on your Balanced Scorecard team across your organization. Your team can lead training sessions on Scorecard concepts and then act as facilitators during the development of Balanced Scorecards. The Scorecard and functional knowledge they possess will prove an unbeatable combination.

- *Use business plans.* The highest-level Balanced Scorecard at your organization was the product of a careful translation of your unique strategy. As you cascade the Scorecard to successively lower levels of the organization, you may not find specific strategies, missions, and visions. Most groups will have a business plan, since the practice of developing annual plans is well established in most organizations. These business plans can be an invaluable source of information to help business units, departments, and teams develop their Scorecards. Most plans will contain information on key processes, objectives, initiatives, and costs. Once the Balanced Scorecard becomes embedded in the management system of your organization, it may replace business plans.

Shared Service Balanced Scorecards

Shared service groups are what we sometimes call corporate resources or corporate staff. Human Resources (HR), Accounting and Finance, and

Information Technology are all examples of shared service units found in virtually all organizations. These departments provide specialized services to the business units and corporate entity they serve, and should do so at a cost and level of quality superior to external vendors. Few would question the importance of services rendered by these groups, but all too often they appear to be islands unto themselves, miles away from the strategy being directed by the organization's leaders. Scorecard architects Kaplan and Norton discovered that the strategies of 67 percent of HR and IT organizations are not aligned with business unit and corporate strategies, nor do HR and IT departmental plans support corporate or business unit strategic initiatives.[6] A Balanced Scorecard takes these groups to task and monitors their performance to ensure that the services they provide are aligned with business unit and corporate strategic objectives.

Since many shared service units will not have a specific strategy, but instead focus on meeting the needs of their internal customers, these units sometimes find it difficult to begin the Scorecard development process. Lacking a specific strategy, they wonder what should form the basis of their Balanced Scorecard. For that reason organizations often negotiate service-level agreements (SLAs) between business units and shared service groups. These documents spell out in detail the level of service required by the business unit on specific processes and products supplied by the shared service unit. Costs, objectives, and key indicators of desired performance are also included. The SLA now forms the basis of Scorecard development for the shared service unit. Not all organizations will be large enough to require formal SLAs between business units and shared service groups. Lacking a formal SLA, shared service units may follow the advice outlined earlier in this chapter. By reviewing the corporate Scorecard, the shared service group can determine which objectives and measures it can influence most directly and develop its own performance measures based on those indicators. For example, should a goal of improving employee turnover appear on the corporate Scorecard, we would expect the HR group to develop cascaded performance measures to make this a reality.

Given the flurry of outsourcing activity under way in most large organizations, the Balanced Scorecard is an ideal method for shared service units to demonstrate the unique value they contribute to the organization. Producing positive results on Scorecard measures exhibits a rationale for their continued existence. Beyond this very pragmatic reason for cascading the Scorecard to shared services there lies a deeper and more compelling justification. Employees of these groups often feel very little connection to the overall strategy of the organization. While those in manufacturing may see the actual product being developed, and marketers work diligently to create demand, those in shared service groups often have little insight into the products and services that drive the organization. Cascading the Balanced Scorecard provides this much-needed line of sight, allowing employees within shared services to see the connection between their work and the overall strategy of the organization.

Personal Balanced Scorecards

Very few organizations excel at the task of developing meaningful goals and objectives for individual employees. In fact, the annual performance appraisal process is one fraught with issues for both management and employees alike. Companies will expend significant energy in promoting a formal appraisal process, issuing memos, providing templates with information on the competencies and behaviors they desire to see, and training employees on how to develop an effective plan. However, there is often little follow-up beyond this initial splash of activity. CEO icon turned corporate curmudgeon Jack Welch blames it on the paper chase, suggesting that *"if your evaluation system involves more than two pages of paperwork per person, something is wrong!"*[7] When I discuss the performance appraisal process with new clients, I'm often greeted with rolling eyes and shaking heads. Even those organizations that do follow up on the appraisal process and hold review sessions with employees are invariably behind schedule. It is amazing how this critical activity involving the most precious of resources tends to get pushed to the back burner. But when we critically examine the process at most organizations, there is little wonder why this sorry state of affairs exists. Very often the performance ratings are completely subjective and based purely on a manager or supervisor's limited view of employee performance. This does little to engender trust on the part of employees; instead they are suspicious of the process. Throughout the performance period there is little feedback to employees, and even if feedback is offered, it typically concerns outcomes and results, not behaviors. But the most egregious omission is the lack of alignment between personal and organizational goals. Employees have little or no idea how success on their performance review will positively impact the company's success.

Cascading the Balanced Scorecard to the individual employee level can mitigate if not entirely eliminate many of the issues we find with the normal performance appraisal process. Here are some of the many benefits to be derived from having employees develop their own personal Balanced Scorecards.

- *Builds awareness of the Balanced Scorecard.* Developing Scorecards at the individual level provides yet another opportunity to share with all employees the principles and techniques inherent in the Balanced Scorecard system.
- *Generates commitment to the Scorecard.* There is little doubt that increased involvement in virtually any activity will tend to increase commitment to that cause. So it goes with the Balanced Scorecard. Having employees

learn about the Scorecard and develop their own series of linked objectives and measures will certainly boost support from this critical audience.

- *Increases comprehension of aligned Scorecards.* In order to craft their individual Scorecards, employees must first understand the objectives and measures appearing in all cascaded Scorecards, from the high-level organizational Scorecard to the business unit Scorecard, to their team or department's Scorecard. Thus, cascading supplies an outstanding training opportunity.

- *Offers a clear line of sight from employee goals to organizational strategy.* Developing personal Balanced Scorecards that align to team or department Scorecards allows every employee to demonstrate how specific actions are making a difference and leading to improved overall results.

- *Builds support for the goal-setting process.* Using the Balanced Scorecard can breathe new life into often tired and irrelevant employee goal-setting processes.

The format you follow for personal Balanced Scorecards is limited only by your imagination. Exhibit 7.3 provides one possible version of a template your employees can utilize to develop personal Balanced Scorecards. This template is based on the cascading efforts of an electric utility organization. In the document I have merged three key areas—cascaded Scorecards, incentive compensation, and personal development plans. To maximize educational and practical value, the document it is split into two pages. Page 1 outlines mission, vision, and strategies and establishes a line of sight for the employee. It illustrates the cascading Scorecards that are relevant to that individual and summarizes the organizational, business unit, and departmental Balanced Scorecards. Displaying this "individualized cascading" demonstrates the path that has led to this point and greatly facilitates the completion of the Personal Balanced Scorecard on page 2.

While we might consider page 1 a learning opportunity, page 2 has a more specific purpose: It allows the individual employee to define the specific objectives and measures he will pursue to help his department reach its objectives, supply potential incentive awards, and outline the action steps he'll take to achieve success. We'll return to the discussion of linking the Balanced Scorecard to compensation in Chapter Nine. Here are the three specific steps that must be taken to complete page 2 of the template.

1. The individual must develop the objectives, measures, and targets that comprise her individual Scorecard. By displaying all linked Scorecards on page 1, with discussion and coaching the development of personal goals should flow quite smoothly.

2. The individual must then select the appropriate weights for each measure when determining their incentive possibilities. The manager or

supervisor will have final approval on the weights and associated targets, ensuring that they are challenging but attainable. The perspectives are also weighted to denote the areas in which the employee is able to exert the most influence. In this example perspective weights are equal. We will return to the discussion of employee targets during our review of the Balanced Scorecard's role in compensation in Chapter Nine.

3. Finally, the employee may begin to construct a personal development plan (PDP) based on the goals established on her Scorecard. This document may or may not replace the need for a formal PDP, but it will certainly facilitate the development of that document by identifying the individual's key areas of focus.

The creation of personal Balanced Scorecards completes the chain of linked Scorecards from the boardroom to the back room, and in so doing can also incorporate the key elements of incentive compensation and competency attainment.

This section focused almost exclusively on the benefits employees can derive from developing personal Balanced Scorecards: knowledge of the Scorecard system, understanding of organizational objectives and measures, and alignment with overall goals. However, senior managers also have much to gain from this process. Cascading to this level allows managers to gain a high level of visibility into the specific actions contributing to, or detracting from, overall organizational results. Take the case of one travel agency I worked with. Senior managers at this organization monitor a productivity index that tracks the number of tickets issued per hour by individual agents. The measure appears on the corporate Balanced Scorecard but is also cascaded down to the individual agent level. When actual results began to lag expectations, senior managers looked to their cascading Balanced Scorecards for an answer. Examining regional performance (the first level of cascading) on the productivity index provided little information since most areas were producing similar results. However, when managers examined specific site Scorecards, they found some very interesting deviations that were driving the high-level corporate outcome. It turns out that agents who catered to professional service firms (attorneys, accountants, consultants) were producing consistently lower results than other groups. When questioned, these agents noted that clients from these firms frequently changed plans, which made it difficult to actually issue a ticket. Without the questions spawned by the Balanced Scorecard, senior management could have made the faulty and dangerous assumption that these sites were simply poor performers and taken inappropriate action. Armed with the knowledge gleaned from cascaded Balanced Scorecards, managers were able to adjust the targets to more accurately reflect the nature of clients served by different sites.

Exhibit 7.3 Personal Balanced Scorecard Template, Page 1

Name: _____   Department: _____   Date Covered: _____

Mission: Provide low-cost energy to help our communities prosper   **Vision:** Be the #1 energy supplier by 2010
Utilize state-of-the-art technology and human capital principles to drive profitable growth

Perspective	Corporate Scorecard Measures	Business Unit Measures	Department Measures
Financial	F1. Return on equity F2. Lower service agreement costs	F1. Manageable cost reduction F2. Rationalize capital spending F3. Increase miscellaneous revenue	F1. Lower administrative spending
Customer	C1. Customer loyalty rating C2. Sales volume	C1. Customer loyalty rating C2. Outage performance index C3. Meter reading C4. Call center performance C5. Reliability index	C1. Customer loyalty rating C2. Meeting commitments
Internal Process	IP1. Environmental performance IP2. Number of new products and services	IP1. Environmental performance IP2. Service quality programs in place IP3. Service quality programs	IP1. System maintenance IP2. Inspections
Employee Learning and Growth	E1. Safety rating E2. Employee commitment rating E3. Employee development	E1. Number of accidents E2. Employee commitment rating E3. Employee development E4. Employee development	E1. Number of personal accidents E2. Number of vehicle accidents E3. Employee commitment rating

Exhibit 7.3   Personal Balanced Scorecard Template, Page 2

Perspective	Objective	Measure	Weight	Threshold	Midpoint	Stretch	Related PDP Goals
Customer 25%	Increase customer loyalty	Presentations to local trade groups	40%	10	15	20	• Develop 5 new professional contacts this year • Join 2 trade associations
	Ensure outage reliability	Plant visits	60%	20	30	50	
Employee Learning and Growth 25%	Promote safety	Departmental injuries	60%	2	1	0	• Attend safety training course
	Develop skill sets	% employees completing business education	15%	80%	90%	100%	• Complete facilitator training
	Develop skill sets	Complete personal development plan	10%				• Complete PDP by midyear
	Enhance employee commitment	Departmental commitment rating	15%	75	80	85	• Support employee volunteer efforts
Internal Process 25%	Provide meter reading and meter changes	% on-time readings	50%	90%	95%	100%	
	Enhance system maintenance	Conduct plant audits	50%	25	40	45	
Financial 25%	Minimize administrative spending	Local costs	55%	Budget	Budget less 1%	Budget less 2%	• Complete 2 courses in finance
	Grow revenue	Increase departmental miscellaneous revenue	45%	5% increase	10% increase	25% increase	• Lead department brainstorming sessions on revenue enhancement

REVIEWING AND EVALUATING CASCADED BALANCED SCORECARDS

Depending on the size of your organization, you may develop dozens of cascaded Balanced Scorecards at all levels of the company. The benefits of alignment and increased knowledge cannot be overstated, but danger may lurk if you don't carefully monitor the Scorecards being created. Unrealistic targets, missing measures, and departments working against each other may all result if you don't put a review and evaluation process in place to ensure truly aligned Balanced Scorecards. A two-phased approach ensures your Scorecards are telling a consistent story throughout the company.

Your Balanced Scorecard team should hold the initial responsibility of personally reviewing the cascaded Scorecards created within their specific business units. Based on their experience, team members have the knowledge to effectively critique objectives and measures, ensuring consistency in form and approach across the organization. Once business units and departments have distributed their Scorecards, the Balanced Scorecard team can review them and later hold sessions with the submitting departments to discuss refinements and improvements.

Once groups across the company have had the chance to make adjustments to their Scorecards based on your team's input, you're ready to open them up to the real test—their peers. The open house approach used by the County of San Diego is an excellent means of gathering the feedback of a significant number of people in a fun and organized fashion (see Chapter Five. Invite employees to review the Scorecards of their peers and offer their suggestions for clarification and improvement. The first point in that sentence—clarification—is significant. Despite their best efforts to make Scorecards clear and concise, it's difficult for individual groups not to use esoteric words and phrases in their Scorecards. Employees from other areas of the company will be quick to assess the "readability" of colleagues' Scorecards and open up the possibility of rewording or changing specific items to make them more understandable to a wide audience. Another exciting outcome of these Scorecard sharing sessions is the learning that often occurs. Within the modern business enterprise, interdependencies between groups serve to propel the company forward. Some are explicit and widely known; others are implicit. Sharing objectives and measures on Balanced Scorecards often motivates business units and departments to critically examine their relationships and challenge other groups to provide measures that impact their working relationship. For example, there may be internal customer-supplier relationships that need to be documented on Balanced Scorecards. Sharing Scorecards also inspires creativity as groups will build on the measures shown in others' Scorecards to modify and improve their own efforts.

Here are some things to look for when reviewing the cascaded Balanced Scorecards at your organization:

- *Linkage to related Scorecards.* Don't forget the key principle here is cascading—driving the Scorecard to lower levels in the organization. Each Scorecard should contain objectives and measures that influence the next Scorecard in the chain.

- *Linkage to strategy.* The Balanced Scorecard is a tool for translating strategy. The measures appearing on cascaded Scorecards should demonstrate a linkage to the organization's overarching strategy.

- *Appropriate targets.* Target setting can be a difficult exercise requiring significant professional judgment. Ensure cascaded targets will lead to the fulfillment of higher-level targets throughout the chain of linked Balanced Scorecards.

- *Coverage of key objectives.* The chief tenet of cascading is that of influence: What can we do at our level to influence our business unit/organizational/ and so on Scorecard. Not every group will influence every high-level objective, but across the company the complete population of highest-level objectives should receive adequate coverage.

- *Lag and lead indicators.* Cascaded Scorecards should contain an appropriate mix of lagging and leading indicators of performance.

Cascading—Final Thoughts

No matter how you employ the Balanced Scorecard system—as a measurement system, a strategic management system, a communication tool—it can produce tremendous benefits. But cascading, if implemented effectively, may pay the biggest dividends of all. Driving the Scorecard to every level of the company signals to each employee what the key drivers of success are at your company and provides everyone with the opportunity to define how he or she contributes to that success. You also create a consistent language in the company—the lexicon of measurement that guides action and can lead to breakthrough results. Leading Scorecard practitioners are recognizing the value of cascading. A recent study found that over 60 percent of participating organizations were driving the Scorecard to lower levels.[8] Allowing every employee to participate in setting meaningful objectives and measures can generate a flourishing spirit of involvement and partnership that leads to amazing results for everyone involved.

KEEP IN MIND

- This chapter described how you can involve your entire workforce in the Balanced Scorecard process by using the highest-level Scorecard as a template for producing aligned Scorecards throughout the company.

- "Cascading" refers to this process of developing Scorecards at all levels of your firm. These Scorecards align with your organization's highest-level Scorecard by identifying the strategic objectives and measures lower-level departments and groups will use to track their progress in contributing to overall company goals.

- Developing a high-level organizational Scorecard is a great way to gauge your success in meeting strategic objectives and to generate awareness of strategy on the part of your employees. But will mere awareness of organizational strategies lead to change at all levels of the company? To maximize the effectiveness of the Scorecard, every group should have the opportunity to develop linked Scorecards that demonstrate how they're contributing to the company's goals.

- To cascade the Balanced Scorecard successfully, everyone in the organization must understand the operational and strategic significance of the objectives and measures appearing on the highest-level Scorecard. Organizations may use a combination of communication and education efforts to ensure this understanding is present before attempting to cascade the Scorecard.

- The essence of cascading the Scorecard to lower levels of the organization is captured in the word "influence"—the ability to produce an effect. Strategic business units should examine the highest-level organizational Scorecard and ask, What can we do at our level to help the organization achieve its goals? Which objectives and measures are we in the best position to influence? Departments and groups within business units must ask a similar question: What can we do at our level to help the business unit achieve its goals? Which of their objectives and measures can we influence?

- To ensure successful cascading, a number of questions must be answered, including: Will all groups be required to use the four perspectives? Are there certain objectives and measures that must appear on all cascaded Balanced Scorecards? Will we limit the number of objectives and measures appearing on lower-level Scorecards?

- Shared service units (HR, IT, Finance, etc.) should also be encouraged to develop Balanced Scorecards. To assist these groups in building Scorecards, many organizations will encourage business units and shared service units to enter into service-level agreements. These agreements specify the outcomes expected by the business unit (the customer) and form the basis for the development of shared service unit Scorecards. Lacking formal service-level agreements, shared service units may build Scorecards by examining how they influence high-level organizational outcomes.

- Personal Balanced Scorecards represent the final frontier of cascading. Driving the Scorecard to the individual level allows employees to craft the goals they will track to spell their contribution to overall success. Both the employee and the organization stand to benefit from developing Scorecards at the employee level. Employees gain a greater insight into overall strategy and their role in its fulfillment, while the organization receives a rich abundance of potential data from which to glean new insights.

- Cascading may create dozens of Balanced Scorecards within your company. Their value is enormous, provided they align with overall goals and tell a consistent story. To ensure this is the case, you should launch a rigorous review and evaluation process in conjunction with your cascading efforts. Once again, your Balanced Scorecard team will be called on as the first line of defense, reviewing Scorecards and working with groups across the company to refine, modify, and improve their offerings. Inviting feedback from your employee base is also an excellent way to engender cooperation, information sharing, and commitment to the Balanced Scorecard.

Notes

1. Bill Jensen, *Simplicity: The New Competitive Advantage* (Cambridge, MA: Perseus Publishing, 2000).
2. Ibid., p. 26.
3. Stephen R. Covey, *The 8th Habit* (New York: Free Press, 2004), p. 2.
4. David P. Norton and Randall H. Russell, "Best Practices in Managing the Execution of Strategy," *Balanced Scorecard Report* (July–August 2004): 3.
5. Ricardo Semler, *Maverick* (New York: Warner Books, 1993).
6. Robert S. Kaplan and David P. Norton, "The Office of Strategy Management," *Harvard Business Review* (October 2005): 73–80.
7. Jack Welch with Suzy Welch, *Winning* (New York: Harper Business, 2005), p. 104.
8. Best Practices Benchmarking Report, *Developing the Balanced Scorecard* (Chapel Hill, NC: Best Practices, LLC, 1999).

CHAPTER 8

Using the Balanced Scorecard to Strategically Allocate Resources

Roadmap for Chapter Eight   Very few people have much good to say about budgets and the budgeting process employed at most organizations. Former Secretary of Defense Frank C. Carlucci once said, *"The budget evolved from a management tool into an obstacle to management."* Jack Welch weighed in on the subject by suggesting that *"the budgeting process at most companies has to be the most ineffective practice in management."*[1] There is little doubt that the traditional budget process, which was designed about 80 years ago and has remained virtually the same ever since, is due for transformation. In this chapter we'll explore the budgeting process, examining specific issues and offering possible methods to improve this most long-standing of organizational traditions.

The chapter begins with a look at some of the issues plaguing the budget process as it currently stands. A chief concern here is the very disturbing fact that few organizations make an attempt to link budgets with their strategy. In the past they may not have possessed the tools to forge this link; however, the Balanced Scorecard provides the means of making this critical connection. Given the budget process's many problems, it is not surprising that organizations have begun to tinker with and, in some cases, totally abandon the practice. We'll look at some of the current trends in "new budgeting."

The bulk of our work in this chapter is devoted to the examination of how the Balanced Scorecard can be used to effectively drive the budgeting process. We begin this analysis with an overview of the roles of cascading and initiative setting and present a five-step process of linking budgets to strategy through the careful use of the Balanced Scorecard. The chapter concludes by considering some of the many benefits to be derived by using the Balanced Scorecard to lead the budgeting process.

BEMOANING THE BUDGET

We are all well aware of the dizzying pace of change in the modern organizations we populate. Everything seems to be going at warp speed with all indications that it's only going to get faster and more chaotic in the years ahead. But, when I wrote the first edition of this text it was summer, and even for the most harried of modern employees that cherished season will often trigger a slightly slower pace and relaxed attitude. Some companies still even practice that seemingly ancient rite of four-day workweeks during the "lazy" days of summer. So perhaps you too slip into a comfortable summer groove and are able to enjoy the long days (even if they are spent at the office), but beware, it is probably right around the corner. What is this potentially horrific *it* to which I am referring? The much dreaded annual plan and budget document, that's what. If your company is like most, and assuming you have a December 31 fiscal year-end, you'll probably receive a forty- or fifty-page manual designed to kick-start the annual budgeting process some time around mid-August. Several months of paper pushing, mind-numbing analysis, and endless game playing later you just might have something worthy of presenting to your Board of Directors. And if you're really lucky they might provide their approval before you're sipping champagne to ring in the New Year. If you think I'm exaggerating, think again. A Hackett Benchmarking study conducted in the late 1990s found the average organization invests more than 25,000 person days per billion dollars of revenue in the planning process, and the average time to develop a financial plan is four and a half months.[2] Ford Motor Company is reported to have determined its total planning and performance measurement cost amounts to a staggering $1.2 billion per year.[3]

The often loathsome budgeting process most companies follow today is not significantly different from the original technique developed about 80 years ago to assist the early industrial giants like DuPont and General Motors control their costs. Back in those days, companies operated in a vastly different environment from that to which you and I have become accustomed. Customer choice was virtually unheard of. Additionally, globalization certainly wasn't an issue, since businesses operated almost exclusively in their local area, and fiscal environments were relatively stable. The consistent thread running through the business processes of the day was control. Senior management developed plans, and employees were expected to carry them out with complete adherence to routine, repetitive steps. Control reports depicting deviations from the carefully crafted plans were fed back up the chain of command, and new orders were issued to treat these defects.

The world of business we inhabit today is vastly removed from that of our organizational ancestors. Globalization and the rise of powerful economies in countries such as China and India mean intense competition in all industries, where customers have virtually unlimited choice and access to information. Fiscal environments are less stable, and the rate of change is frenetic to say the least. We are also attempting to evolve from the age of control to one of empowerment. In this environment the once-vaunted budget is often out of date almost immediately after it is produced. But like so many relics of a bygone era, the traditional budget remains. Not only does the current budgeting process stand in direct opposition to many of the forces driving the modern enterprise, but its execution is often seriously flawed. Consider:

- 66 percent of surveyed *CFO Magazine* readers believe their planning process is influenced more by politics than by strategy.[4]
- In a *CFO* survey 88 percent of respondents stated they were dissatisfied with budgeting.[5]
- For many companies, planning processes are not yet fully utilized as decision-making functions and are hampered by excessive levels of detail, extended cycle times, and a focus on the wrong information.[6]
- 60 percent of organizations don't link budgets to strategy.[7]

Politics and gaming the system seem to go hand in hand with the budgeting process at many companies. At one firm I worked, everyone in our department had a strange sense of pride stemming from the fact that our boss's budget negotiation skills were highly regarded throughout the company. He knew his way around the ins and outs of the game, that's for sure. "Promise less and ask for more" was his mantra, and it seemed to work since our targets always seemed comfortably achievable. Looking back, I recognize the many problems he was creating. His incessant game-playing inevitably lengthened an already interminably long budgeting process, virtually guaranteeing that nothing would be established before the start of the following year. Was he really protecting us? No, his weak targets merely served to limit our need to exercise creativity and search for breakthrough solutions. No doubt there are those in your organization who are masters of the budgeting game too.

Perhaps the most frightening shortcoming of the current budget process is reflected in the fourth bullet point above: 60 percent of organizations don't link budgets to strategy. Think about that for a minute. The budget spells out in painstaking detail what the organization expects to receive and what it will spend in the months ahead. In effect, this allocation is a strong signal of what the organization truly values. If spending is not aligned with the strategy, then just what does that demonstrate about priorities, and how does the budget bring the organization any closer to achieving its strategic goals? As disturbing as the 60 percent statistic is, it really should not come as a surprise to us. Most organizations have separate processes for business planning and budgeting and strategic planning. The strategic planners are busy crafting the plan that will elevate the firm above its competitors while independently another group is developing the operating and capital budgets for the coming year. The problem with this approach is that human and financial resources are linked to short-term financial targets as espoused in the budget and not to the goals of the strategy. I spent most of Chapter Seven discussing the merits of alignment. As troubling as a lack of staff goal alignment is, unfocused spending is equally problematic. Fortunately, by utilizing a cascaded series of Balanced Scorecards, your organization can overcome many of the problems presented by today's budget process. A little later in the chapter I'll describe techniques for using the Balanced Scorecard to drive the budgeting process, but now let's take a look at some other thoughts on revising the budgeting process.

BANISHING THE BUDGET

The topic of budgeting has been the subject of considerable study and debate. Perhaps the greatest depth of knowledge and experience comes from a group known as the Beyond Budgeting Round Table (BBRT). Formed as a result of a partnership with the Consortium for Advanced Manufacturing International (CAM-I), the BBRT seeks to develop management processes appropriate for the modern enterprise. Not surprisingly, the BBRT sees budgets as a major bane to the effective operation of all companies. Since its inception in 1998, the BBRT has grown from a primarily European membership to establishing roots in countries around the globe.

The BBRT's research focuses on answering a fundamental question: How are leading companies that have abandoned, radically changed, or significantly deemphasized their centralized planning and budgeting processes now fulfilling their well-established purposes?[8] The answer, as supported by the BBRT's research findings, is that leading organizations have developed new performance and management processes that do not rely on budgets but instead focus on creating adaptive organizations based on empowerment and accountability. The BBRT's poster child for corporate success without budgets is the Swedish bank Svenska Handelsbanken. This 510-branch bank, founded in 1871, has consistently delivered leading financial performance despite changing economic tides. BBRT white paper authors Jeremy Hope and Robin Fraser believe former Handelsbanken president Dr. Jan Wallander has been key to the bank's enduring success, saying that he *"is a real visionary who could see that the way large organizations were being managed was fundamentally flawed."*[9] And the key to his success? According to Dr. Wallander himself, it was radical devolution supported by the dismantling of the budget model. During his tenure, Wallander powerfully transformed the Handelsbanken world by changing the culture, attacking bureaucracy and top-down controls, and freeing individual managers to make decisions concerning their businesses. Continuous improvement at the bank is now driven by pressure to outperform competitors and peers on key measures of performance. Annual budgets and plans are nowhere to be found. The results have been impressive: Costs are lowest in the industry, employee turnover is practically nonexistent, and a rate of 25 percent compound total shareholder return has been achieved over the past 18 years. Other organizations following the BBRT's methodology have also fared well with *"early indications from over 200 companies showing that there is a statistically significant correlation between the BBRT model and competitive success."*[10]

Rather than dismantling the budget process entirely, many organizations have turned to rolling forecasts to strike a compromise between the need for planning and the desire for flexibility. Rolling forecasts generally extend six quarters into the future and allow a stronger integration of planning and budgeting than the typical calendar-year budget. Each quarter the plan is reviewed, and executives are able to change directions or fund strategic projects based on current business conditions. Managers are likely to support rolling forecasts since they provide them with much-needed flexibility in taking advantage of new opportunities as they arise. That's one of the key advantages of the rolling forecast. Often an organization will spot an opportunity in midyear but the set-in-stone budget, which has already allocated every penny of discretionary spending, won't allow for the funding of what could turn out to be a competitive advantage for the firm. Of course the converse is true as well: Utilizing rolling forecasts provides companies with enhanced flexibility in heading off unforeseen challenges. The San Diego Zoo learned this firsthand when exotic Newcastle disease, one of the most infectious bird diseases in the world, reached Southern California two years ago. The zoo, which houses perhaps the most valuable collection of birds anywhere, quickly mobilized into action to protect its animals by shutting down public exhibits, changing and cleaning staff uniforms daily, and even sanitizing the tires of arriving delivery trucks. In all the Zoological Society spent over $500,000 on quarantine measures alone, an item that had not appeared in the annual budget. The expense was well justified, however, as not a single case of the disease reached the zoo's cages. CFO Paula Brock credits the organization's reforecasting process with saving the day by allowing managers to redirect resources to combat the deadly disease.[11] Despite the advantages of rolling forecasts, critics do exist. They contend that rolling forecasts are time-consuming to prepare and may not completely eliminate the politicking and in-fighting that so often characterizes the budgeting process.

Some organizations have actually decided to embark on a Balanced Scorecard implementation in order to retool, or even replace, the budgeting process. SKF, a leading manufacturer of rolling bearings with manufacturing sites in over 100 countries, is one such company. Back in 1995 with dissatisfaction for the budget process growing ever stronger, SKF turned to the Balanced Scorecard in order to *"replace the budget, which was perceived as having largely negative effects, while still retaining the positive features of a budget, e.g. setting targets and discipline in meeting commitments."*[12]

Even if you are not quite ready to completely banish the budgeting process from your managerial landscape, you would likely benefit from tinkering with or reengineering parts of the process. Let's now turn our attention to how you can use the Balanced Scorecard to align the allocation of resources with your strategy.

STRATEGIC RESOURCE ALLOCATION WITH THE BALANCED SCORECARD

Exhibit 8.1 provides an overview of the steps necessary to link the Balanced Scorecard to the budgeting process. Most of this will look very familiar since the preceding seven chapters covered most of these items in detail.

Based on the organization's mission, values, vision, and strategy, a high-level organizational Scorecard is built. That Scorecard contains a series of linked objectives (which appear on the strategy map) and measures that use cause-and-effect relationships to tell the story of the organization's strategy. Focusing on the high-level Scorecard, business units, departments, shared service units, and perhaps even individual employees develop their own aligned Balanced Scorecards documenting how they will influence the

Exhibit 8.1   Linking the Balanced Scorecard to Budgeting

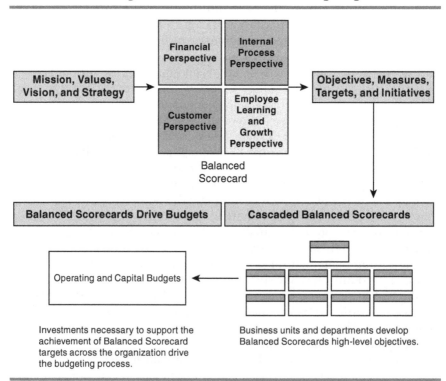

achievement of corporate goals. Each of these cascaded Scorecards will not only contain objectives, measures, and targets in each of the four perspectives; they should also include the initiatives each group will pursue in order to successfully meet their targets. These initiatives will entail the allocation of resources, which are quantified and used to form the basis of budget submissions. Sounds simple enough, right? Let's break down these steps beginning with the crucial topic of cascading.

Cascading Balanced Scorecards Sets the Stage for Strategic Resource Allocation

Recall the worrisome statistic that 60 percent of organizations do not link budgets to strategy. Just for a moment let's give those organizations the benefit of the doubt. There is a good chance they didn't have the means necessary to link their budgets to strategy. Being the typical top-down, command-and-control organizations, they issued directives from senior management and asked business units and departments to develop budgets supporting those plans. So that's what they did—using the same old politics and game-playing that saw them through previous budget seasons. Without Balanced Scorecards, the business units and departments had little ways to show how they could impact an overall strategy. With a Balanced Scorecard, however, the story changes significantly. Now units and departments from across the firm develop meaningful objectives and measures that are a direct translation of Scorecards from higher levels.

A hallmark of the cascading process is the inclusive nature of the task. No Scorecard can be built effectively in isolation. It is only through the involvement of all those with a stake in the outcomes that valuable Balanced Scorecards emerge. The same principle readily applies to budgeting. With a Balanced Scorecard as the guide, managers are wise to solicit feedback and involvement of every employee when developing budgets. Some have done just that. For example, at Supertel Hospitality, a Norfolk, Nebraska, hotel franchiser with 63 properties, everyone participates in creating yearly budgets. Housekeepers are even asked to project how much linen and other supplies they'll need and make a budget for those items. An executive at the firm believes that the process contributes to lower turnover and higher profits.[13] At the Canadian telecommunications company TELUS, employees in the operator services division are being assigned budget responsibility in an effort to reduce the unit cost of operator-assisted calls. Managers say the response has been "unbelievable," with more than 10 percent being cut off the cost structure: *"Just engaging people in making decisions is rewarding in itself."*[14]

The cascaded Balanced Scorecards emerging from every facet of the organization allow all employees to understand the firm's direction and participate in ensuring a successful outcome. Employees now possess an all-important line of sight between what they do every day and how those actions affect organizational outcomes. The logical next step is determining what initiatives must be undertaken to meet Scorecard targets. It is the Scorecard initiatives that forge the powerful link among budgets, Scorecards, and, ultimately, strategy.

Balanced Scorecard Initiatives: The Glue That Binds Budgets to Strategy

Chapter Six defined initiatives as the specific programs, activities, projects, or actions you will embark on to help ensure you meet or exceed your performance targets. Initiatives are designed to close the gap between current performance and that embodied in the stretch targets established. The target is your end in mind for the performance measure, and to get there, you need to determine what investments in initiatives are necessary to guarantee a positive outcome. Investments may be the key word in that sentence; after all, what is a budget if not an exercise in determining appropriate investments—in people, processes, technology, and so on? The key is to ensure that the initiatives you decide to fund are strategic in nature and will help you achieve the goals you have set to propel the organization forward. Funding nonstrategic initiatives is not only a waste of valuable financial resources but will undoubtedly consume another precious resource: the time and attention of already busy managers.

STEPS IN LINKING BALANCED SCORECARDS TO BUDGETS

The remainder of the chapter will outline the specific steps you can follow to ensure that the budget you establish reflects your strategy. But first a word on timing. Even if the budget process at your organization is crying out for reengineering, and you are very eager for the Balanced Scorecard to come to the rescue, it may not be feasible during year 1 of your implementation. If you are introducing the Scorecard for the first time, that alone will supply a major challenge to the status quo of operations at your company. As previously discussed, the Scorecard introduces an entirely new framework for management, one that places strategy, not financial controls, at the center of the organizational universe. Gaining the support and commitment of your entire workforce will take some time, and attempting to forge a link between budgets and Balanced Scorecards, no matter how great the potential rewards, may be a bit much for the typical company bandwidth to absorb. Most organizations I've worked with have waited until the Scorecard management process is more mature and accepted as part of the overall management strategy of the organization. Of course, the time necessary to achieve this will vary with every organization. As a general rule, you need a high-level Scorecard and a series of cascaded Balanced Scorecards to effectively execute the budget/Balanced Scorecard link.

Often this can be accomplished during year 2 of your implementation. Having said all that, if you have developed Scorecards throughout the organization during year 1 of the implementation and feel your company is ready for more positive change, by all means take advantage of your momentum and make the hugely beneficial link of Balanced Scorecards to budgets.

Step 1. Plan Ahead

You probably already have a well-established budget process that includes a very thick document distributed to all budget preparers throughout the company. Use that device plus a variety of other communication forums to get the word out about the "new" budgeting process that is driven by the Balanced Scorecard. Audiences around the company must be prepared for what lies ahead: the new processes and methods you will use to generate budgets that align spending with your strategy. As with every other aspect of the Balanced Scorecard we have reviewed, it is imperative that you provide ample assistance to those responsible for developing budgets. Once again, your Balanced Scorecard team should form the first line of assistance, providing training, guidance, and support.

Step 2. Develop or Refine the High-Level Organizational Balanced Scorecard

The organizational Balanced Scorecard sets priorities for the company as a whole, describing to everyone the key objectives and measures that signal success. All subsequently cascaded Scorecards will align with the measures appearing on this Balanced Scorecard.

Step 3. Build Cascaded Balanced Scorecards

Business units, departments, teams, and individuals develop Scorecards that demonstrate how they can influence higher-level objectives and outline the specific indicators they will track. The Scorecards must include both targets necessary for breakthrough performance and the specific initiatives that require funding to make certain those targets are met. Ideally, the budget should support year 1 targets in a series aimed at achieving the stretch goals you developed for each performance measure (see Chapter Six for a review of target setting).

Each initiative appearing on the Scorecard should provide clearly stated resource requirements: that is, the operating and capital dollars needed to fully support them. This leads to a question: Will the Balanced Scorecard for a specific business unit or department contain all the resource requirements necessary to operate the group? In other words, should typical budget line items, such as salaries, benefits, supplies, travel, and the like, be split up among the initiatives appearing on the Balanced Scorecard? There are different schools of thought on this subject. Kaplan and Norton suggest that organizations should follow a method of "dynamic budgeting," which represents the combination of operational and strategic budgeting.[15] The operational budget is used to support the allocation of resources necessary for recurring operations, while the strategic budget directs spending on the key initiatives designed to close the gap between current and desired performance on critical strategic drivers. Kaplan and Norton contend that most of an organization's spending will be determined by the operational budget as a result of the large base of products and services currently existing within the firm. Others suggest that only one budget should be used and that it should contain the entire mix of operational and strategic elements necessary to reflect a true picture of the organization. Following this route forces the organization to critically examine current operations in light of budget requests and to determine how operational expenses are linked to strategic requests. This is obviously easier said than done, but there are tools to assist in the calculation. Activity-based management techniques are one way to examine current operations and determine which activities actually drive costs within the organization. Using an activity view of organizational expenses may facilitate the allocation of current operations to strategic initiatives.

Proponents of the one-budget school would also suggest that simply thinking in terms of the linkage between current expenses and strategy will foster important conversations within the organization and motivate managers to contemplate how their day-to-day actions are contributing to strategic results. Your choice of budgets will depend on the ability to accurately assign ongoing costs to strategic initiatives, past attempts at changing the budget process, and how senior executives feel about the subject. The process described here works equally well for a strategic budget or one budget encompassing both operational and strategic elements.

Related to this discussion is the issue of how you can ensure that senior management will fund initiatives aimed at improving the leading indicators of performance, the often "softer" measures, such as employee retention and customer satisfaction. Every initiative should be supported by a valid business case that includes how the initiative impacts a strategic goal as well as the cost, timing, resources, and dependencies involved. Applying these criteria to a nonfinancial indicator of performance might be challenging, but it is certainly not impossible. Take the case of Fidelity Investments. It has developed a number of innovative measures, such as management depth, employee retention, and work climate, all aimed at improving employee performance. To support requests for funding, the team demonstrates what is "broken" at the organization, how the new measures would fix it, what it would cost, and the expected savings from making the repairs. In effect, they outline the return on investment (ROI) for each measure.[16] Your initiatives, whether they relate to hard or soft measures, should be accompanied by supporting documents that provide a justification for funding. To level the playing field, everyone should use the same basis of evaluation when rationalizing initiatives. Whether it is discounted cash flow analysis, internal rate of return, payback period, total costs, or a host of other potential yardsticks, the key is to apply them uniformly across the organization. See Chapter Six for more help in prioritizing initiatives.

Step 4. Compile Results

The budget process generates a lot of paper, no doubt about it. Even in this so-called era of the paperless organization, the annual budgeting season exacts a heavy toll on the tree population. Hundreds of spreadsheets producing reams of analysis and countless iterations of budget submissions serve to keep printers and photocopiers humming from August to December. In virtually every section of this book I've described problems and then suggested how the Balanced Scorecard can step in and save the day. Not this time. At least during the first year, using the Scorecard to drive the budget process will definitely require some paper. Budget preparers must be provided with templates they can complete to make the ultimate job of compiling all spending requests a little easier. You can attempt to do this electronically, but unless you are very advanced in the ways of paper conservation, you will be receiving most of your submissions on good old-fashioned paper. The light at the end of the tunnel starts to appear in year 2 as the process matures. Those preparing budgets should become increasingly comfortable with methods of filing Scorecard-related budget submissions electronically. Also, software providers are creating new and exciting programs aimed at expediting this process. Exhibit 8.2 presents a simplified template that groups may use to record their budget submission.

In this example the Mortgage Lending department of a bank has outlined three initiatives it believes are crucial in achieving a 75 percent

Exhibit 8.2   Simplified Budget Submission Form

Business Unit/Department: Mortgage Lending				
			Resource Requirements	
Measure	Target	Initiatives	Operating	Capital
Customer Loyalty Rating	75%	Account officer training program	$250,000	$175,000
		Affiliate marketing	$125,000	$350,000
		Customer information system	$150,000	$750,000

customer loyalty rating. (Keep in mind that this illustration shows just one measure from the group's Scorecard. It will have many more.) Everything in the exhibit must have backup documentation for support, including the detailed Balanced Scorecard for Mortgage Lending, a breakdown of the specific elements comprising the initiative, and the related costs. These details are necessary for executives to make an informed decision regarding which initiatives to fund and which to defer.

Once all groups have submitted their proposals, budget requests may be summarized according to specific Balanced Scorecard strategies or objectives. Exhibit 8.3 provides a form designed for that purpose. Here we see that one of our fictional bank's strategies is to become customer focused. To do that it has developed three objectives on the Balanced Scorecard: increase customer loyalty, increase customer confidence, and increase flexible solutions. The next column shows the bank's current performance on each of those objectives. Customer loyalty is green, which signals acceptable performance; customer confidence is yellow, which raises a flag of caution; and flexible solutions is red, meaning it is performing below target. The last two columns provide a rollup of budget requests from around the organization related to the objectives.

Executives can use this simple form to determine where the majority of spending requests are being directed and to take action to ensure there is an appropriate balance in the allocation of resources. As customer loyalty in the example is green, it is performing at a satisfactory level. Executives must determine how much they are willing to spend to sustain this performance. Similarly, they must determine how much to commit to flexible solutions, which is currently performing below expectations. Customer confidence is currently displaying yellow or cautionary performance. How much should be spent to bring it in line with targeted expectations?

Exhibit 8.3   Budget Requests by Balanced Scorecard Strategy

Customer Strategy: Become Customer Focused			
Objective	Current Scorecard Status	Budget Request Operating $000s	Budget Request Capital $000s
Increase customer loyalty	Green	$XXM	$XXM
Increase customer confidence	Yellow	$XXM	$XXM
Increase flexible solutions	Red	$XXM	$XXM
Percentage of total spending		44%	38%

Step 5. Finalize the Budget

Once you have tallied the budget requests that have been generated from groups around the organization, you will undoubtedly encounter a gap — or perhaps a chasm: the difference between what you know you can afford to spend, still meeting reasonable return on equity estimates, and the total of requests submitted by budget-hungry business units and departments. This is when things get interesting and the real value of using the Balanced Scorecard to drive budgets comes to the fore.

To finalize the budget, each business unit leader should make a formal presentation to fellow executives outlining the budget submissions from her group; what they encompass, why they are strategically significant, and how they will positively impact Scorecard targets. Everyone in attendance during these presentations will be aware of the gap that exists between desired and possible spending, and this sharing of information will be critical in helping the executive team process information, engage in productive dialog, and decide which initiatives are truly strategic and necessary. At this point the process becomes iterative with executives reviewing and questioning the proposals, attempting to determine which are worthy of inclusion in the budget. To ease the decision-making process somewhat, you may wish to develop an internal ranking system for the initiatives you propose. You can devise a simplified rating system to represent the potential impact of removing a specific initiative on the Balanced Scorecard. For example, a "1" might indicate an initiative that could be eliminated and have minimal impact on the group's ability to achieve its target. A "2" might translate to an initiative that could be cut, but with a definite effect on the group's ability to meet targeted expectations. Finally, initiatives assigned a "3" could represent those that are deemed crucial to the successful achievement of Scorecard targets. The ratings will be necessarily subjective, but they will serve as a powerful impetus for conversations centered on establishing spending priorities.

Benefits of Using the Balanced Scorecard to Drive the Budgeting Process

The methods and techniques described in this chapter may appear very simple; in fact, you may consider them too simplistic to work in your organization. I am intentionally advocating a rudimentary approach here. We often benefit from questioning our exceedingly complex processes and getting back to the core purposes represented by our actions. What is the fundamental purpose of a budget? To allocate scarce resources among a variety of possible alternatives. What better way to do that than to use the Balanced Scorecard, which is a direct and faithful translation of our strategy? Only those initiatives that meaningfully contribute to the fulfillment of strategic objectives should be undertaken. Many organizations are beginning to embrace the possibility of simplicity in organizational life and are questioning the core purposes of all corporate actions. For a number of years Nova Scotia Power has conducted its annual budgeting process on a model similar to that which I describe here. Rather than missing the complexity, most of those involved welcome the elegant ease of linking the Scorecards to budgets. One senior director says: *"This is the best budget process we've ever had. I simply develop a Scorecard, show what investments I need to fulfill my targets, and submit that for approval."* Here are some other benefits accruing to those who choose to let the Scorecard lead the way for developing budgets.

- *Reinforces your key strategies.* Rather than taking last year's budget and adding or deducting a certain percentage, the Balanced Scorecard puts strategy at the center of the budget cycle. Making strategy synonymous with budget dollars is a great way to get a lot of people to stand up and take notice. Your organization is a double winner. In order to prepare effective budgets, managers and employees must firmly grasp the essence of the strategy, which increases organizational knowledge and learning. Second, and equally important, the budgets submitted demonstrate how individual groups plan to have a real impact on the strategy.

- *Reduces game-playing.* Instituting a system like the Balanced Scorecard, which features strategy as the key principle, reduces the likelihood of the typical game-playing that characterizes traditional budgeting efforts. Forcing everyone to demonstrate a direct link between their spending plans and the strategy puts all the cards on the table, so to speak. Asking for a little more and promising a little less just won't cut it in this environment sparked by producing commitments that display real strategic value.

- *Leads to cooperation.* For any retooling of the budgeting process to work, managers must switch their mind-set away from trying to hit their own personal budget numbers and toward a team approach focused on meeting the organization's strategic objectives. The Scorecard facilitates this switch in direction by encouraging an open dialog among all involved on what represents the optimal mix of spending that will achieve broad corporate goals. In fact, increased cooperation and sharing of information is one of the key benefits to be derived from this process. Prior to using a Scorecard-led approach, managers may be unwilling to share spending plans, fearing any inappropriate disclosure could lead to a reduction in funds. With the Scorecard in place, managers are encouraged to explore synergies among groups and look for ways that everyone can achieve individual goals, which, when aggregated, will translate to a win at the organizational level as well.

- *Facilitates learning.* Organizations should carefully review the results achieved from budget decisions. A postaudit review should be conducted to determine if a certain initiative did in fact produce the expected benefit. Like the Scorecard itself, which is based on management's hypothesis of the relationship among performance objectives and measures, funded initiatives represent a hypothesis. They must be subjected to the same rigorous testing as Scorecard objectives and measures to ensure that the theory behind them is valid and producing results.

- *Saves time.* According to one recent study, the median number of days to prepare the annual budget is lower for organizations that align their plan with strategy (63 days) than for those that do not (80 days).[17] We all know that the protracted nature of the budgeting process is a huge drain on organizational resources; any reduction in the overall span of time is a major step forward.

KEEP IN MIND

- The budgeting process that exists in most modern enterprises is strikingly similar to the techniques originally developed over 80 years ago. At that time markets were stable, customer choice was nonexistent, and companies competed in local areas only. Given these circumstances, budgets served very well in their primary function as control tools for the early industrial pioneers.

- Today, as we move from control to empowerment as the central guiding force of organizations, many are questioning our reliance on this seemingly antiquated tool. Today's budgeting and planning process is burdened by time-consuming details, game-playing, and general dissatisfaction on the part of executives, managers, and employees alike. However, the most troubling aspect of this process is the lack of alignment between spending as outlined in the budget and organizational goals as demonstrated in the strategic plan.

- As organizations have grown over the past decades, separate functions have emerged to control what should be two interdependent processes. Strategic planners focus on developing plans to lead the organization into the future, while business planners and budgeters independently develop operating and capital plans.

- Budgets have increasingly come under the microscope in recent years, and some organizations have taken radical action to improve their processes. The Beyond Budgeting Round Table (BBRT) suggests new performance and management processes that eradicate a reliance on budgets and instead focus on creating adaptive organizations based on empowerment and accountability.

- Rolling forecasts have been hailed by proponents as a vast improvement over the typical budgeting process. These (generally) six-quarter forecasts provide flexibility to executives eager to take advantage of emerging opportunities. While an improvement, rolling forecasts are not a panacea for the budgeting process. They are time-consuming and may not eliminate game-playing and turf protection typical during budget time.

- Organizations can use the Balanced Scorecard to develop budgets that place strategy at the center of the process. Spending is dictated by the ability to influence strategic goals rather than a simple recalculation of the previous year's submission.

- Five steps are necessary to use the Balanced Scorecard to drive the budgeting process. During step 1 organizations must plan their attack and widely communicate their intention of having the Scorecard lead the budgeting process. Balanced Scorecard team members must be active in the education and communication efforts which follow. In step 2 a high-level organizational Scorecard should be developed (or updated) to begin the actual process. This document provides the necessary means for the development of cascaded Scorecards throughout the firm, which forms the basis of step 3. These Balanced Scorecards include not only objectives and measures, but also the targets and initiatives necessary to achieve success on Scorecard indicators. The investments needed to support the initiatives are used in making budget submissions that directly impact strategy. During step 4 results are compiled from across the organization. Executives can use simple tools to ensure that spending is appropriately balanced on the critical success factors imperative to driving the strategy. The budget is finalized during an iterative process of analysis and dialog in step 5. Executives advance their spending requirements and engage other senior managers in discussions regarding the strategic impact of their requests.

- Placing the Balanced Scorecard at the forefront of budget development offers many benefits. Key strategies are reinforced as a result of the knowledge and analysis necessary to draft budgets that link spending to organizational objectives. Game-playing is significantly reduced since budget preparers must demonstrate a clear connection between spending appeals and strategy. Not only are politics mitigated, but cooperation is fostered. Business units and departments seek synergies to ensure their funding is approved. Learning is accelerated as organizations use actual Scorecard results to begin questioning the assumptions surrounding initiatives in the budget. Finally, linking budgets to strategy reduces the amount of time necessary to produce an annual plan.

Notes

1. Jack Welch with Suzy Welch, *Winning* (New York: Harper Business, 2005), p. 189.
2. Hackett Benchmarking Solutions. www.thgi.com.
3. Jeremy Hope and Robin Fraser, "Who Needs Budgets?" *Harvard Business Review*, February 2003. p. 111.

4. Cathy Lazere, "All Together Now," *CFO Magazine,* February 1998.

5. Russ Banham, "Revolution in Planning," *CFO Magazine,* August 1999.

6. Hackett Benchmarking Solutions, www.thgi.com (June 14, 2001).

7. Robert S. Kaplan and David P. Norton, *The Strategy Focused Organization* (Boston: Harvard Business School Press, 2001).

8. Jeremy Hope and Robin Fraser, "Beyond Budgeting White Paper," CAM-I Beyond Budgeting Round Table (May 2001).

9. Ibid., p. 12.

10. Ibid., p. 3.

11. Tim Reason, "Budgeting in the Real World," *CFO* (July 2005): 44.

12. Nils-Goran Olve, Jan Roy, and Magnus Wetter, *Performance Drivers* (New York: John Wiley & Sons, 1999).

13. "High Performance Budgeting," *Harvard Management Update* (January 1999).

14. Ibid., p. 3.

15. Kaplan and Norton, *The Strategy Focused Organization.*

16. Tad Leahy, "Budgeting on the Softer Side," *Business Finance* (April 2001).

17. Reason, "Budgeting in the Real World."

CHAPTER 9

Additional Balanced Scorecard Linkages: Compensation and Corporate Governance

Roadmap for Chapter Nine   An anonymous sage once noted: *"Money is the root of all evil."* To which George Bernard Shaw wittily retorted, *"Lack of money is the root of all evil."* I think we can probably all point to evidence of both. Regardless of where you stand on this issue, one thing is clear: Organizations have in the past and will continue in the future to reward excellence with the allocation of monetary rewards. This chapter will investigate how the Balanced Scorecard can be profitably linked to your incentive compensation system.

We begin by tackling an age-old question: What motivates people in the workplace? Is it the fulfillment resulting from a job well done that drives satisfaction, or does the promise of a regular paycheck bring us back day after day? We'll see that the increasing use of incentive compensation plans can pay dividends for your Balanced Scorecard program by providing additional education and support opportunities.

More than any other aspect of the Balanced Scorecard, the linkage to compensation is extremely variable and customizable. A seemingly endless stream of possible programs will greet every organization making the decision to tie rewards with performance. This chapter includes an overview of the critical planning and design elements you must consider when constructing your own Balanced Scorecard link to compensation. The choice of design is ultimately yours; however, the chapter also provides you with a number of alternatives currently in use at leading Scorecard organizations.

Since the passage of the Sarbanes-Oxley Act in 2002, following a spate of high-profile business scandals, organizations have spent billions of dollars and millions of man-hours complying with the new regulations. Has the administrative burden forced on the backs of corporations led to improved governance and safer waters for investors? At this point, the results are mixed. Many pundits suggest the answer to reform lies partially in providing boards with greater insights into corporate activities and value-creating processes; if so, the twenty-first-century board would be well served using a Balanced

Scorecard approach. In this chapter we will examine the cries for change heard round the world and consider a template that boards can use to construct their own Strategy Map of performance objectives.

A QUESTION OF MOTIVATION

I have a friend who loves to work on old cars. Nothing makes him happier than getting up at the crack of dawn on a Saturday morning, taking a hot cup of coffee out to the garage, and settling in under the hood of his latest project. He gets lost in the challenge of rusty old parts that lie before him, and before he knows it the sun is setting. Nobody is paying him to spend his time in the garage toiling over cars that will never produce a dime of payback for him. He does it purely for the joy it brings to him. In other words, he is intrinsically motivated to perform the work. To get me out there is another matter entirely. Someone would have to offer a very large inducement for me to spend my Saturdays cooped up in a garage surrounded by dilapidated auto parts. I would require extrinsic motivation to perform the same work.

The debate over intrinsic versus extrinsic rewards and motivation has been raging for decades. Intrinsic rewards may produce fulfillment and a sense of pride, while extrinsic rewards hold the possibility of sharpening our focus on what must be done in order to succeed. Interestingly, a significant body of evidence suggests that extrinsic rewards can impede intrinsic motivation. For example, researchers Mark R. Lepper and David R. Green watched school-age children at play to assess what they most enjoyed doing. Soon after they began giving each child a reward every time he or she engaged in the preferred activity. In every instance, the child's interest rapidly decreased when an award was involved. In a second study, the researchers provided a prize to adults who successfully completed a puzzle. Once again, interest in the activity plunged when an award was present.[1] On a broader stage, it appears that more money in our lives does not increase happiness. Between 1957 and 1990 per-person income in the United States doubled, taking inflation into account. During that same period rates of depression rose nearly tenfold and the incidence of alcoholism, suicide, and divorce all grew dramatically while reported levels of happiness failed to increase.[2]

Applying the intrinsic versus extrinsic motivation debate to the organizational world means reducing it to a fundamental question: Why do people work? Is it rewards, money, and other forms of compensation that provide the impetus for our daily trek to the workplace? Or do we perform our duties out of a sense of self-fulfillment and pride? According to most pundits, the latter is the prevailing rationale for engaging in work. They suggest that while extrinsic motivators may work in the short term, their long-term viability is very limited since they fail to satisfy basic human needs, such as fulfillment and meaning. I have mixed feelings on this topic. On one hand, I know from personal experience that working on an interesting and meaningful project with dedicated and talented people who share common goals is extremely rewarding. As Robert Louis Stevenson said in 1882, *"When a man loves the labor of his trade beyond any question of success or fame, the gods have called him."* On the other hand, I have a mortgage payment that comes due every 30 days, and "meaning and fulfillment" don't mean a thing at the bank. The discussions and arguments over this topic will most likely continue for decades to come.

You may or may not subscribe to the merits of extrinsic motivators, but the fact is that more and more companies are turning to reward systems as they look to gain an advantage over competitors. Hewitt Associates discovered in 2001 that 78 percent of surveyed businesses have at least one type of variable pay plan in place, up from 70 percent in 1999 and 47 percent in 1990.[3] In a consistent finding, the Society for Human Resource Management (SHRM) discovered that 69 percent of companies offer some type of incentive compensation.[4] In the years ahead we can expect to see those numbers creep ever higher if the results of one recent study reported in *CFO IT* magazine are any indication. The authors asked these questions of respondents: "What are the top three drivers of your employees' effectiveness/performance?" The number-one response, offered by 66 percent of those surveyed, was compensation and other rewards. The second question was: "If you wanted to increase the value your company derives from its workforce, where would you focus?" Again, compensation was the most popular answer with 61 percent of respondents stating a link between compensation and metrics as the driving force to generating greater value.[5]

This increase in incentive pay plans could have a positive impact on the acceptance of the Balanced Scorecard at your organization. In a recent study of leading Balanced Scorecard–adopting companies, the author found: *"Surveyed companies . . . have been most successful in securing high levels of awareness and acceptance of the Balanced Scorecard at the executive level. Awareness and acceptance among business unit leadership was also shown to be high, but at the management, professional and operational/support levels, greater difficulty was clearly being experienced in reaching satisfactory levels of acceptance."*[6] Cascading the Balanced Scorecard will obviously alleviate this deficiency of awareness, but linking the Scorecard to compensation is another powerful means of substantially boosting employee knowledge and support of the Scorecard.

Thirteen of the 15 companies included in the study have linked pay to their Balanced Scorecard system. While each used different processes and specific programs, they all share a common belief that aligning employee rewards with the achievement of Balanced Scorecard measures is a powerful mechanism for generating focus on what is important to the organization. This is especially the case in lower levels of the company, where clear lines of sight between daily employee actions and overall goals are sometimes blurry at best. Linking the Balanced Scorecard to your compensation system makes crystal clear what is valued and what outcomes are necessary to achieve performance rewards.

Some will argue that aligning rewards to Balanced Scorecard targets provides merely extrinsic motivation and could possibly hamper innovation, creativity, and fulfillment. A more optimistic, and pragmatic, view illuminates another possibility. Linking the Scorecard to compensation is simply an added bonus (pun intended) that completes a true win/win arrangement. Simply developing the Balanced Scorecard and sharing it with employees across the organization holds the strong prospect of increasing intrinsic motivation. Employees, possibly for the first time, now have the opportunity to gain an in-depth knowledge of the company's strategy and define the role they will play in its achievement. Developing the Strategy Map, brainstorming performance measures, and questioning the hypothesis that underlies the Scorecard are all intellectual tasks that serve to stretch the cognitive and organizational abilities of every employee participating in any level of Scorecard development. There is little doubt that knowledge and involvement are powerful levers in enhancing intrinsic motivation. The Balanced Scorecard offers the possibility of both. Providing extrinsic rewards should not lead to the erosion of motivation produced by developing the Balanced Scorecard. Rather it acts as a laser, focusing the attention of all employees on the critical drivers of organizational success. The two motivational factors work together in this scenario. Involving all employees in the development of Balanced Scorecards increases intrinsic motivation, which is used to develop breakthrough solutions in the achievement of Scorecard targets. Exceeding the targets then translates into performance rewards to be shared by all those who made the valuable contributions necessary for success.

DESIGN ATTRIBUTES TO CONSIDER

No two Balanced Scorecard implementations will be completely alike. Each and every organization choosing to use the Scorecard system will manipulate the tool to fit individual culture, current managerial processes, and the state of organizational readiness for such a major change initiative. Linking the Scorecard to compensation will result in even greater individual differences. Historical pay preferences, possible presence of union contracts, and the variety of job classes are but a few of the many factors affecting the incentive pay decision. Let your creativity soar here and you will be rewarded with a program that cements focus and alignment toward your overall goals. When the going gets tough, think of those traveling the Scorecard path before you, 86 percent of whom agreed or strongly agreed that the Scorecard should be linked to compensation in order to help support appropriate behavior.[7]

To assist you in designing a customized system, here are some issues to consider. Note that all references to compensation refer to "variable" or "incentive" compensation. Base salary is normally not affected by the Balanced Scorecard.

Planning the Compensation Link

- *Purpose.* What is the overall purpose of your linkage of compensation to the Balanced Scorecard? What specific behaviors are you attempting to encourage or discourage? How will the new pay plan affect the culture of the organization? Having an overarching purpose in mind will help guide your efforts in a direction that best suits your individual needs.

- *Communication.* Steven Covey has referred to employee compensation as rice bowl issues. Messing with someone's rice bowl, whether in a positive or negative vein, is bound to stir up a lot of interest. There tends to be an air of controversy surrounding even the most well-intentioned compensation schemes, so it's in your best interests to communicate the specifics of the plan to your entire employee audience as soon as the plan is developed. Actually, the plan should be reviewed and discussed with employee focus groups even before it is developed. You must ensure that employees believe the plan is fair and equitable. Communication efforts not only enlighten everyone as to the compensation plan but may also be used to demonstrate the value and benefits to be derived from using the Balanced Scorecard as a key component of your overall management system.

- *Development.* Who will be involved in the development of the new program? As with all other aspects of the Balanced Scorecard, you should attempt to involve a variety of participants in the design of your new pay program. The different perspectives and functions represented will help ensure the new process is perceived as fair and equitable throughout the company. Perceived fairness is an issue that should not be taken lightly. Research of pay programs at a variety of companies has demonstrated that employees are more concerned with the equality and fairness represented by the program than they are with the actual amount of monetary rewards available.

- *System review.* There is a lot at stake with your compensation plan, and once up and running it is certain to be closely watched by all employees. Make it clear from the outset that you plan to review the entire program within 12 months of its initial launch. Stating this forthrightly from the beginning will send a strong signal that you are committed to making any adjustments to ensure that the plan functions as anticipated in a manner that has everyone's best interests at heart. This way if modifications must be made, they will not be perceived as changing the rules in midstream or altering the program to stack the deck in management's favor.

Design Elements

- *Timing.* You may be eager to link rewards to performance and consider establishing the bond in the first year of your implementation. However, you must consider a number of issues prior to launching the program. The primary concern relates to the measures you have selected for your initial Balanced Scorecards. As we have discussed, the performance measures represent a hypothesis, or your best guess, as to what it will take to execute your strategy. Most organizations I work with make changes to their original Scorecard objectives and measures as their implementation progresses along the path to maturity. Linking pay to measures that may or may not stand the test of time is a dangerous proposition. Employees will be motivated to achieve the targets you establish, and as we've all heard, "You get what you measure." Can you afford to pay for results that don't necessarily assist you in fulfilling your strategic objectives? Another issue is data collection. The Scorecard often results in the development of brand-new performance measures for which no reliable data source is available. Obviously you do not want to link rewards to measures you cannot accurately report. In addition to the possibility of inaccurate data, you may not have the requisite systems to manage the pay program. Variable compensation is among the least automated items on a typical profit and loss statement, but given the potentially volatile swings of payouts, you need ways to track your compensation liability accurately.

- *Involvement.* Will every employee be eligible for participation in the new pay program, or is involvement limited to certain categories of your staff? Many organizations will pilot the linkage of compensation to the Balanced Scorecard with their executives. This approach certainly has merit since the senior team was most likely involved in the development of the Scorecard and has a vested interest in the outcomes of all performance measures. However, it is often the lower levels of the organization who lack awareness and knowledge of the Balanced Scorecard. Extending the pay program to all employees greatly enhances the likelihood of increasing knowledge and advocacy of the Balanced Scorecard. Related to the issue of involvement is the question of whether incentive pay should be awarded to individuals or groups. Awarding individuals recognizes outstanding achievement and can motivate excellent performance in the future. However, most organizations today rely heavily on interdependence and the sharing of information across the enterprise. In such an environment, rewarding individuals could potentially impede the knowledge sharing and collaboration necessary to generate innovative solutions. Practitioners are mixed on this point. Some provide only group rewards in an effort to stimulate teamwork and collective accountability; others provide a mix of individual and team rewards.

- *Number of performance measures included.* Psychologists suggest that we humans have difficulty concentrating on more than seven items at any given time. Have you ever noticed how many things seem to involve the magical number seven? Consider the Seven Habits of Highly Effective People and the seven deadly sins. Does this mean we should limit to less than seven the number of performance measures linked to compensation? Some would say yes, and suggest that a lesser number of measures is yet another way to sharpen focus on the critical drivers of success. No magic number exists, but when initially creating the Scorecard-to-compensation link, most practitioners will limit the number of measures impacting pay, often choosing one measure from each of the four perspectives. Some even restrict the bond to one key metric. In the mid-1990s, Continental Airlines determined that the key to its turnaround was on-time departures and paid a $65 cash bonus to all nonmanagement employees in any month in which the company was in the top five of U.S. carriers on the measure.

- *Perspectives of measures.* Not only is the number of measures linked to compensation an element for consideration, but the type of measure must also be contemplated. Will you attach rewards to the achievement of only the most verifiable and objective indicators, normally represented by financial measures, or will meeting targets of measures in other perspectives also lead to rewards? In one study focusing on the linkage of compensation to the Balanced Scorecard, it was discovered that leading Scorecard organizations are aligning rewards with measures from all four perspectives. However, the weights assigned to each perspective were not always equal. Most respondents applied a heavier weight to Financial measures, which averaged about 40 percent of the potential reward. Customer, Internal Process, and Employee Learning and Growth perspectives were weighted approximately 20 percent each.[8] Deciding to include nonfinancial measures in your calculation can heighten the challenges associated with the process. While you would like your nonfinancial indicators to focus on outcomes, a key benefit of the Scorecard is the articulation of leading indicators of performance that are not always outcome based. For example, you may hypothesize that "hours spent with customers" is a leading indicator of "repeat purchases." However, aligning compensation with "hours spent with customers" could lead salespeople to spend unnecessary time with nonpurchasing customers simply to boost the chance of receiving an incentive award. Incentives should be balanced so that both leading and lagging indicators of performance are appropriately represented and lead to the outcomes you desire.

- *Measure timing.* Another measure-related consideration is whether rewards should be linked to short-term or long-term performance. Some argue that the Balanced Scorecard is a tool for sustaining success over the long term (an assessment with which I obviously agree), and thus a true indication of success is best measured by examining enduring accomplishment. Additionally, by linking rewards to long-term success, there is no incentive to sacrifice long-term benefits for the sake of achieving a short-term gain. Others point to the motivational benefit of providing more frequent rewards along the path to long-term prosperity. Proponents of this camp suggest that generating positive Scorecard results and sharing the rewards with employees on an annual or even more frequent basis serves to strengthen the commitment of all participants to the achievement of strategic goals.

- *Performance thresholds.* Some believe that paying incentives on individual measure results when overall organizational objectives have not been met obscures the focus needed from all employees. For that reason some organizations will not distribute any rewards unless a predetermined standard or cap is met. Normally this hurdle is represented by a high-level financial metric, such as return on equity. This approach ensures that all employees know very well what the key driver of success is for the organization and helps them align their efforts in exceeding it. However, the problem with this course of action is that employees may feel bitter or resentful if for reasons beyond their control a high-level financial objective has fallen short while other performance goals are met.

- *Funding.* Don't forget this very pragmatic element of any compensation plan—from where does the money flow? Will the potential payouts associated with exceeding Scorecard targets be funded from the firm's budget, or do you expect savings generated from the Scorecard to self-fund the incentives? And just how much do you plan to offer in incentives? Involving both your executive team and the professionals in your Human Resources department will help you develop solutions to these issues.

METHODS OF LINKING THE BALANCED SCORECARD TO COMPENSATION

As noted earlier in the chapter, you have virtually unlimited choices when making a link from the Balanced Scorecard to compensation. The many permutations and combinations of award triggers, measures, and potential outcomes are staggering. Organizations pursuing this link will undoubtedly travel many different routes but all arrive at the same conclusion: Aligning rewards with Scorecard results leads to increased attention on the critical drivers of the organization. Let's examine some of the methods used to combine Scorecard measures and compensation.

Basing Rewards on Overall Results

The simplest method of tying Balanced Scorecard performance to rewards is using the highest-level organizational Scorecard as the barometer of success and arbiter of bonuses. Under this scenario a certain percentage of incentive compensation is available to employees, should the organization achieve some or all of its goals. Each measure on the high-level Scorecard is assigned a weight, with total weights across the four perspectives summing to 100 percent. Financial targets often receive a higher weight, reflecting the value management continues to place on achieving fiscal success. As results are tracked, percentage payouts are calculated and distributed. Depending on the level of program sophistication, this allocation of rewards may take place monthly, quarterly, semiannually, or annually. Here is an example of how the program might work. Let's say an organization is willing to extend a 10 percent annual bonus (of base salary) to employees based on Scorecard results. The company tracks a total of eight measures across the four perspectives, as shown in Exhibit 9.1.

Final results are reported at year-end, and the employee bonus is calculated as shown in Exhibit 9.2.

The organization achieved its return on equity target. Since that target makes up 30 percent of the total weight of all measures, employees will receive 3.0 percent of their base salary based on that result. Based on the positive Scorecard results achieved, the total award adds up to 7.5 percent of base salary. In this example the payout is conducted annually. However, to ensure that employees remain locked in on overall goals, the organization would be wise to provide regular (perhaps monthly) feedback on Scorecard results.

The simplicity of this method makes it very transparent and ideal for communication to the entire workforce. Because Scorecard results are monitored throughout the year, they form the basis for strategic conversations from top to bottom within the firm. Issues associated with this technique

Exhibit 9.1   Sample Targets

Perspective	Measure	Target	Weight
Financial	Return on equity	15%	30%
	Revenue growth	25%	10%
Customer	Customer satisfaction	75%	15%
	Repeat purchase percentage	80%	5%
Internal Processes	On-time delivery	90%	10%
	Manufacturing efficiency	85%	10%
Employee Learning and Growth	Competency attainment—percentage of employees gaining 3 new competencies	70%	12%
	Employee turnover	5%	8%

Exhibit 9.2   Sample Payment

Perspective	Measure	Target	Weight	Actual	Payout
Financial	Return on equity	15%	30%	16.5%	3.0%
	Revenue growth	25%	10%	20%	0
Customer	Customer satisfaction	75%	15%	77%	1.5%
	Repeat purchase percentage	80%	5%	75%	0
Internal Processes	On-time delivery	90%	10%	85%	0
	Manufacturing efficiency	85%	10%	85%	1.0%
Employee Learning and Growth	Competency attainment— percentage of employees gaining 3 new competencies	70%	12%	75%	1.2%
	Employee turnover	5%	8%	4%	0.8%
	Total Payout				7.5%

include the degree of stretch involved in the targets and the lack of any thresholds that must be achieved before bonuses are awarded. Using this method of incentive compensation, it is conceivable that employees will receive a bonus whether the firm achieves its overall financial objectives or not. This could send a message inconsistent with the theory of the Balanced Scorecard, which asserts that positive results on measures in the lower perspectives will drive improved financial performance.

Driving the Link to All Levels of the Organization

Many Scorecard-adopting organizations put tremendous energy into establishing the all-important line of sight from individual action to overall goals. This process of cascading not only informs employees how they can influence results, but also serves as a powerful mechanism for using the Balanced Scorecard as a true strategic management system. In Chapter Eight we reviewed how a series of cascaded Balanced Scorecards may be used to launch the strategic allocation of resources that ensures that budget requests align with strategy. In this section we discuss the use of cascaded Scorecards as the springboard for making a connection between the Scorecard and compensation. In contrast to the approach discussed earlier, which relied on overall corporate results to dictate bonus allotments, using the cascading technique aligns awards with results that hit closer to home for employees. Cascading displays how individual employees are able to influence higher-level goals, and the associated compensation link demonstrates the rewards that await outstanding performance at the business unit, department, or individual level.

Nova Scotia Power Inc. is one organization that used the cascading method of linking the Balanced Scorecard to compensation. The utility's Scorecard implementation had proven very successful even from the earliest stage of development. However, managers continually noted that until the new system was linked to paychecks, it would never become "real" in the minds of most employees. Senior management took this advice to heart and developed a system of incentive compensation that aligned rewards with the successful achievement of Balanced Scorecard targets.

The first level of compensation cascading at Nova Scotia Power took place when each member of the executive team developed a personal Balanced Scorecard based on the corporate Scorecard. The weights assigned to each perspective and associated measures were relatively balanced; however, each executive overweighted those areas in which he or she was best able to contribute. For example, the vice president and chief financial officer developed a Scorecard with representative measures in each of the four perspectives, but the Financial perspective and related measures were assigned the greatest weight, given the nature of the CFO's work and its impact on these critical indicators. Similarly, the vice president of Sales and Marketing overweighted the Customer perspective. Scorecards developed at the executive level contained a mix of measures, some pulled directly from the corporate Balanced Scorecard and others describing how the executive would influence the corporate indicators. Rather than using one target for each measure, three were developed, with each indicating increasing degrees of stretch. Percentages of base salary were linked to each measure, representing its degree of difficulty. A threshold target stood for minimum acceptable performance on the measure. No incentive compensation would be paid on a measure for which the threshold was not achieved. Midpoint targets represented better-than-average performance and therefore warranted increased rewards. Finally, stretch targets were considered best in class and required significant effort to be met. Therefore, additional incentives awaited their achievement.

Balanced Scorecards were then developed at the business unit, department, and individual level of the organization. As with the executive Scorecards, every group or individual assigned weights to each perspective and measure and developed corresponding threshold, midpoint, and stretch targets. All Scorecard measures and targets were reviewed and approved by management to ensure adequate coverage of corporate strategic themes and achievable yet challenging targets. Nova Scotia Power wanted to leave no doubt in employees' minds that meeting their return on equity target was critical for the ongoing success of the organization. Therefore, they decreed that no incentive awards would be paid unless the corporation met this financial target. This message served to galvanize employees around meeting their own Scorecard targets, which they knew from cascading experience would help drive the overall corporate results.

Competency-Based Pay

Compensation firm Towers Perrin has reported that while only 8 percent of surveyed organizations currently use competency-based pay systems, a whopping 78 percent plan to implement such a system in the near future.[9] As the world of work continues to evolve from machines to knowledge, the focus on competencies appears to make sense. Organizations have squeezed practically every last drop out of process improvement and reengineering. What is left but the greatest source of productivity enhancements of all: human knowledge. Competency-based systems, with their painstaking attention to the attributes and behaviors necessary to compete effectively in today's environment, can drive the changes organizations need to succeed. Basing pay on competencies is a dramatic shift from the old world of seniority-dependent pay.

As we saw when discussing the Employee Learning and Growth perspective earlier in the book, all employees can use the Balanced Scorecard to track the addition of key competencies. As a logical extension, incentive compensation may be directed toward the acquisition of competencies. Employees who can demonstrate that they have been able to add new competencies to their repertoire are allotted an incentive award. One potential drawback is the concern that an exclusive focus on competencies may lead to lesser concentration on actual performance results. Therefore, a caveat when considering this approach is that pay for competencies must be balanced with results, especially in the short term. Other measures on the Balanced Scorecard can be used to provide a balance between new skills and attributes and the results they collectively produce.

Gainsharing

Gainsharing is an improvement system that relies on employee actions to enhance organizational results. Key measures of performance are developed and targets for improvements or cost savings are agreed on. Any savings generated from the improved results are shared with employees through incentive bonuses. Gainsharing experts suggest that organizations engaging in this technique *"must be willing to engage in at least some form of employee involvement that shares business information, educates employees in the economics of business, and encourages suggestions. Without moving information, knowledge, and power downward, it is unlikely that a significant line of sight will develop and that the plan will be successful."*[10] Sounds to me like they are saying that a Balanced Scorecard is needed to make gainsharing work. The Scorecard involves employees in its design, provides unlimited educational opportunities, encourages suggestions through the questioning of assumptions, and creates a powerful line of sight.

Performance measures developed for the Balanced Scorecard can serve as the guiding force behind a gainsharing program. Each of the four perspectives may contain measures that have an economic element and can be used to drive cost savings throughout the organization. As Scorecard results are tracked over time, any savings can be distributed to employees in the form of incentive compensation.

Nonmonetary Rewards

A recent study conducted by Mercer Human Resource Consulting discovered that 70 percent of companies now use some type of nonmonetary recognition for incentive rewards.[11] As powerful as the lure of a pocketful of greenbacks can be, sometimes it helps to have a tangible reward in front of us to focus our attention on something we can see, feel, and grasp. That's what Goodyear found a few years back when it sponsored a campaign to improve tire sales. Two large employee groups were monitored; one was offered monetary rewards, the other was offered merchandise. The group receiving tangible rewards outperformed the cash awards group by nearly 50 percent.[12] Programs of this nature appeal to a basic desire of people to want what we don't have. While a cash bonus is nice, chances are the prudent voice in our head will scream that paying down some debts with the windfall or starting a child's college fund is the only thing to do. But when management dangles a flat-screen TV in front of us, it's difficult not to picture ourselves curled up on the sofa channel-surfing to our heart's content. For some people, that physical product creates more desire and attention than the ephemeral joy of cash and makes nonmonetary rewards a worthwhile supplement to cash bonuses.

For some companies the idea of a cash-based incentive program makes great sense, but union contracts prohibit the use of such tools. In these circumstances creative teams have developed innovative ways of recognizing employee and organizational success without distributing the usual monetary award. Kaplan and Norton describe the case of Texaco Refinery and Marketing Inc. (TRMI).[13] Constrained by their union agreements, this organization turned to a points program to reward success. Points, each with a par value of $1, were awarded based on plant-wide, work-group, team, and individual results. The accumulated points could be redeemed for merchandise, travel, and retail awards. Results were swift and dramatic. In the very first year of the plan, two plants set records for utilization, expense reduction, and safety.

THE BALANCED SCORECARD AND
CORPORATE GOVERNANCE

A Wake-up Call for Change[14]

I can add little to the flood of articles, editorials, television shows, books, and even movies portraying the devastation wrought by the collapse of once-revered corporate high-flyers like Enron and WorldCom. While management malfeasance was promoted to an elevated art form at these companies, it is clear that their boards were not functioning at the required level to safeguard investors or employees. At Enron the failing took place principally within the board's audit committee, while at WorldCom the willingness of directors to approve lavish loans and compensation proved to be the weak link that would result in the company's undoing. Bankruptcy proceedings typically follow these ignominious lapses, and while such events are demoralizing at any company, regardless of their size and scope of operations, when you're talking hundreds of billions of dollars and the loss of thousands of jobs, the results can be cataclysmic.

What Boards of Directors Really Need

In the wake of the debilitating scandals plaguing the corporate world, the U.S. government has enacted some of the toughest securities and governance legislation to hit business since the 1930s. The headliner of this wave of government intervention is the much-discussed and debated Sarbanes-Oxley Act of 2002. Undoubtedly the act has our best interests at heart, but as the law of unintended consequences is ever-present, it has also spawned many significant challenges for organizations attempting to comply with its prodigious sections and subsections. The primary challenge is simply finding the time and resources to complete the tasks mandated by Sarbanes-Oxley; some organizations have suggested that thousands of hours must be dedicated to the task on an annual basis. AMR Research says that companies will spend $6.1 billion overall in 2005 to meet Sarbanes-Oxley requirements.[15]

It is still too early to tell whether these reforms are leading to a reduction in corporate malfeasance, but at the very least it would be comforting to learn that perceptions were changing. Sadly, that is not necessarily the case. In conjunction with the Directorship Search Group and the Institutional Investors Institute, consulting giant McKinsey surveyed 150 U.S. corporate directors serving as members of boards of more than 300 public companies across all economic sectors and 44 U.S.-based fund managers with a total of $3 trillion in assets under management on the topic of board governance. Asking "To what extent have recent reforms improved Board governance?" 63 percent of the directors and 83 percent of the fund managers replied "a little or moderately."[16] And most directors simply aren't happy about the law; 72 percent of U.S. directors say it has made their boards "more cautious" rather than "better."[17] Considering the thousands of person-hours and billions of dollars dedicated to compliance with these new standards, these findings are discouraging to say the least.

Perhaps the heavy hand of the law is not all that is required in implementing the massive changes necessary to restore trust and confidence in corporate governance. A root cause analysis of the shortcomings affecting boards of directors may reveal a more fundamental issue—the lack of in-depth knowledge of their business's strategy and operations. Recent studies have suggested that upward of 40 percent of directors don't sufficiently understand their firm's value-creation process.[18] Not surprising when you consider that the average board member spends just 90 hours per year on board business, much of which is spent sitting in meetings for which the preparation amounts to a cursory glance at a thick binder handed to unsuspecting board members as they walk through the door.

To fulfill their significant, and now highly regulated, responsibilities, board members need information that goes beyond high-level graphs and abstractions and provides a penetrating view inside the organization's strategy and value-creating mechanisms. Going a step further, management professor and governance catalyst Edward Lawler has suggested that boards need a Balanced Scorecard to illuminate corporate performance: *"Boards need indicators of how customers and employees feel they are being treated . . . how the company operates . . . about the culture of the organization."*[19] In retrospect, it seems plain that the Balanced Scorecard should be utilized to advantage by time- and information-starved board members. After all, it reflects the organization's strategy, providing a complete map of landmarks on the journey to strategic success and a concise tale of how the seemingly disparate elements that comprise the tool weave together to create the firm's competitive advantage. It's all there: financial yardsticks craved by public markets, the customer value proposition feeding the economic engine, the key internal processes that resolutely chug along in creating value day in and day out, and finally, the human, information, and organizational capital awaiting transformation into tangible results. This is the information of substance that boards can use as raw materials for meaningful dialog and debate on strategy and operations as they work to fulfill their sacrosanct obligations.

The Next Frontier: Board of Directors Balanced Scorecards

The corporate Balanced Scorecard significantly enhances the board's oversight capacity by providing a revealing glimpse into the strategy execution efforts of the company, but today's directors, facing unprecedented pressure to adhere to leading-edge governance standards, require a tool to assess their own performance as well. Enter the board Balanced Scorecard, a tool in the arsenal of pioneering boards that wish to maximize their contribution to corporate performance and sustain the ability to add value in the years to come through the identification and evaluation of key performance measures utilizing the proven Scorecard framework. As a first step in the board Scorecard process, a Strategy Map of objectives, such as the generic example in Exhibit 9.3, should be constructed.[20] Let's work through the four perspectives of this map, outlining the considerations that must be made when selecting objectives.

There is an assumption that, if the board capably performs its required tasks, those efforts will contribute to the corporation's ability to achieve financial success. Therefore, the Financial objectives comprising the board Strategy Map should be drawn directly from the organization's corporate Strategy Map. As discussed in Chapter Four, these objectives normally include an overarching objective relating to shareholder value as well as ones that outline how the organization will achieve the dual objectives of increasing productivity (through cost reductions and improved asset utilization) and growing revenue (from selling new products or deepening relationships with existing customers).

For this map, the Customer perspective has been renamed Stakeholder, in recognition of the many groups that have a stake in the performance of the board. Thus, the initial task in crafting objectives for this perspective is determining the stakeholder groups that must be satisfied as the board works to fulfill its obligations. From the objectives appearing in Exhibit 9.3, we might infer that this board has chosen shareholders and employees as the critical stakeholder groups. "Ensure compliance and accountability" will allow stockholders to sleep a little easier, secure in the knowledge that the board has their best interests at heart. While not explicitly stated, society at large will also benefit from this objective, avoiding the high costs of litigation, productivity declines, and unemployment that frequently result from corporate shenanigans. Shareholders will also be pleased to see that the board will "[a]pprove strategy and monitor corporate performance." Finally, all employees will benefit from the board[s] that "[c]ounsel[s] CEO and monitor[s] executive performance."

The Internal Processes objectives articulate how the outcomes in the Stakeholder perspective will be achieved through efficient and effective board processes. In order to achieve compliance and accountability as shown in the Stakeholder perspective, this board must ensure compliance with all laws and regulations, make certain the company has effective internal controls, and diligently work to improve disclosure practices, improving transparency and visibility into the firm's operations. Stakeholders also demand that the board approve strategy and monitor corporate performance; thus internal processes must be developed to achieve this significant undertaking. In this example, the board will monitor performance using the company's corporate Balanced Scorecard, approve funding for and monitor strategic initiatives to ensure that spending is aligned with

Exhibit 9.3 Board of Directors Strategy Map

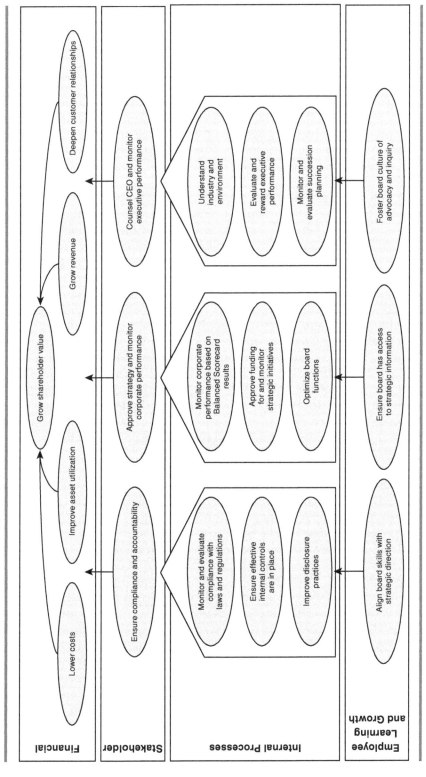

strategy, and, finally, optimize its own functions, such as board structure and procedures in an effort to ensure they function as efficiently as possible. A major endeavor of any board is counseling the CEO and monitoring executive performance. This board will attempt to achieve that objective by first ensuring it has a firm grasp on the company's industry and underlying economic and political environment. Evaluating and rewarding executive performance and monitoring succession planning ensure that successful executives are rewarded for a job well done and a pipeline of future leaders is waiting in the wings.

A well-constructed Learning and Growth perspective must contain objectives focused on three separate but integrated dimensions of capital: human, information, and organizational. Under the mantle of human capital, the board represented in Exhibit 9.3 will work to ensure skills align with the firm's strategic direction. Board members must possess the requisite financial literacy and business acumen to contribute meaningfully in their capacity. Regarding information capital, the board must press the company to provide access to strategic information, so members can provide insight and effectively monitor corporate performance. Finally, it is vital for the board to approach work with a spirit of advocacy and inquiry. Some governance experts have suggested that board members don't behave effectively in meetings if they are unwilling to raise important issues and challenge the CEO on the firm's current performance and strategic direction. Boards must rise to this challenge by balancing the seemingly competing demands of advocating on behalf of the firm, acting as its tireless champion, while also serving the needs and preserving the trust and confidence of stakeholders by encouraging robust dialog on challenging and potentially controversial issues.

The Strategy Map paints a compelling picture of the board's endeavors, but to track performance day in and day out, the board must translate the objectives into performance measures and targets. Strategic initiatives—the projects relied on to achieve targets—must also be brainstormed, funded, and monitored for effective performance. And what are the payoffs awaiting boards proactive enough to make this leap of faith into the Balanced Scorecard world? For starters, board operations will become much more effective and efficient as board members glean new insights into their core activities and gain the ingredients they need to divert attention from the perfunctory reviews of the past toward the dialog that will ignite the opportunities of the future. Stakeholders will undoubtedly applaud this intrepid move as well, since the board's Balanced Scorecard will highlight members' public commitments to safeguard stakeholder investments. This transparency and enhanced visibility not only ensures improved board functioning, but may have positive financial ramifications for the company; according to one study, more than 75 percent of institutional investors surveyed were prepared to pay a premium for well-governed companies.[21]

KEEP IN MIND

- On the meaning of success, prolific inventor Thomas Edison once said, *"One might think that the money value of an invention constitutes its reward to the man who loves his work. But speaking for myself, I can honestly say this is not so . . . . I continue to find my greatest pleasure, and so my reward, in the work that precedes what the world calls success."* This is an eloquent description of what we now refer to as intrinsic motivation, the derivation of meaning and satisfaction from the joy of the task at hand. At the other end of the motivation spectrum is extrinsic motivation. Performing a task for the promise of a reward is characteristic of the extrinsically motivated individual. Despite Edison's inspiring words, the fact remains that an increasing number of organizations are offering monetary incentives to reward outstanding performance. If these rewards are extended to all levels of an organization, they can support the Balanced Scorecard by providing another way to focus employee attention on the select drivers of success.

- The Balanced Scorecard often provides intrinsic motivation since it clearly outlines how employees can influence and contribute to high-level strategy. Extrinsic rewards can supplement this knowledge by supplying incentives to achieve stated objectives.

- Pay is a sticky subject at many organizations, and significant attention is paid to the compensation scale. As a result, most companies will devise a linkage between the Balanced Scorecard and their compensation system that is customized to meet unique challenges and needs.

- Several planning and design components must be considered before attempting to link the Scorecard to compensation. Planning aspects include the purpose of making the bond between your Scorecard and compensation systems, how you'll communicate the program, who designs it, and how it will be reviewed and judged.

- When designing the system, several other considerations must be made. Timing is an important decision. Will the Scorecard be linked to compensation in your first year of implementation, or will you wait until the program is more stable and mature? Since many organizations will adjust their initial Scorecard measures, it may be prudent to forge a bond between the Scorecard and compensation in your second year. When selecting performance measures that will be tied to compensation, you must consider the number, perspective, and timing. The establishment of thresholds that must be met before any rewards are paid is another possibility to be discussed. Finally, you must determine how you will fund your incentive plan. Awards may be part of your budget or self-funded through savings generated from Scorecard results.

- The most convenient method of linking the Scorecard to compensation is basing payouts on the results achieved with your high-level organizational Scorecard. This approach is ideal for communicating the Balanced Scorecard and elevating the importance of organizational indicators. However, it does little to reward outstanding performance at the business unit, department, or individual level. To alleviate this shortcoming, organizations may develop lower-level Scorecards and use them as the basis for a link to compensation. This way all employees have the chance to show how their actions are leading to improved results and are rewarded for their local efforts. The Balanced Scorecard can also be used for incentives relating to competency-based pay systems and gainsharing methodologies. In both cases performance measures from the Balanced Scorecard provide the potential means for the allocation of rewards. For those organizations unwilling or unable to offer monetary rewards, the option exists of distributing nonmonetary rewards to employees based on Scorecard results.

- Despite the billions of dollars spent on compliance-related activities, most boards are not confident that the changes have improved governance practices.

- To fulfill their significant, and now highly regulated, responsibilities, board members need information that goes beyond high-level graphs and abstractions and provides a penetrating view inside the organization's strategy and value-creating mechanisms.

- In order to penetrate the value-creating processes of their companies and fulfill their highly legislated responsibilities, some boards have developed Strategy Maps and Balanced Scorecards.

Notes

1. Jim Loehr and Tony Schwartz, *The Power of Full Engagement* (New York: Free Press 2003), p. 138.
2. Ibid., p. 137.
3. Jennifer Kaplan, "Sun Uses Incentive Compensation to Boost Supply-Chain Performance," *CFO.com* (March 26, 2001).
4. Reported in *Synygy Magazine* (Fall 2005).
5. Reported in *CFO IT* (Fall 2005).
6. Todd Manas, "Making the Balanced Scorecard Approach Pay Off," *ACA Journal* (Second Quarter 1999).
7. Raef A. Lawson, William G. Stratton, and Toby Hatch, "Scorecarding in North America: Moving Toward a Best Practices Framework, Part I," *Cost Management* (July–August 2005): 25–34.
8. Manas, Making the Balanced Scorecard Approach Pay Off."
9. Marie Gendron, "Competencies and What They Mean to You," *Harvard Management Update* (September 1996).

10. Edward E. Lawler III, *Rewarding Excellence* (San Francisco: Jossey-Bass, 2000).

11. Alix Nyberg, "Motivating the Middle," *CFO* (October 2005): 63–70.

12. Adrian Gostick and Chester Elton, *Managing with Carrots* (Salt Lake City, UT: Gibbs-Smith, 2001).

13. Robert S. Kaplan and David P. Norton, *The Strategy Focused Organization* (Boston: Harvard Business School Press, 2001).

14. Note: The sections on corporate governance are drawn from Paul R. Niven, *Balanced Scorecard Diagnostics: Maintaining Maximum Performance* (Hoboken, NJ: John Wiley & Sons, 2005). I have provided updated statistics in some areas.

15. William M. Bulkeley and Charles Forelle, "How Corporate Scandals Gave Tech Firms a New Business Line," *Wall Street Journal* (December 9, 2005).

16. Robert F. Felton, "What Directors and Investors Want from Governance Reform," *McKinsey Quarterly*, No. 2 (2004).

17. From "Surveying the Field," *Wall Street Journal* (January 30, 2006).

18. R. Felton and M. Watson, "The Need for Informed Change in the Boardroom," *McKinsey Quarterly*, No. 4 (2002).

19. "Board Governance and Accountability," an interview with Edward E. Lawler III, *Balanced Scorecard Report* (January–February 2003): 12.

20. In preparing this generic map, I have drawn on the work performed in this area by Michael Nagel of the Balanced Scorecard Collaborative, as presented in a Balanced Scorecard Collaborative Net Conference on May 27, 2004.

21. McKinsey and Company, "Global Investor Opinion Survey: Key Findings" (2002).

CHAPTER 10

Reporting Balanced Scorecard Results

Roadmap for Chapter Ten   Despite best efforts and intentions, the development of a Balanced Scorecard doesn't guarantee its use in guiding day-to-day decision making. Frequent reporting of results, however, can bring the Scorecard to the organizational forefront drawing the attention of all employees. But how to report the Scorecard? Do you rely on paper-based reports, or venture into the ever-expanding world of performance management software to find the solution? This chapter will explore the critical choice of how to report Scorecard results.

The earliest Scorecard users counted on good old-fashioned paper reports to supply information. Despite this very low-tech solution, many early adopters achieved great success. However, as the use of the Scorecard has grown and expanded from a measurement system to a strategic management system and communication tool, many users have turned to technology.

Prolific science fiction author Arthur C. Clarke once noted, *"Any sufficiently advanced technology is indistinguishable from magic."* One look at the impressive array of Scorecard software tools on the market today and you'll probably agree. With the many bells and whistles available, making an informed decision can be a great challenge. We'll examine a number of criteria to help you wade through the choices. Technological solutions aren't for everyone. Some organizations will feel more comfortable pursuing other forms of reporting, while some may simply not wish to commit the extensive financial and human resources necessary when investing in a software solution. We'll look at other options and discuss what some organizations have done in lieu of technology.

Been to any good management meetings lately? Most experts on the topic don't think so, citing a lack of conflict, no structure, and very little discussion of what truly matters as prime explanations for why most of us try to avoid these often time-wasting diversions. Many Balanced Scorecard adopters have been able to breathe new life into the management review process by using Scorecard results as the agenda for strategy-centered discussions. This chapter will explore the management review process and guide you on how to stage a meeting that focuses on strategy and moves organizational white noise into the periphery.

AUTOMATING THE BALANCED SCORECARD

When the Balanced Scorecard was developed and began to gain favor in the early 1990s, less than a handful of software vendors offered ways to automate this revolutionary management tool. Still, many organizations took advantage of the Balanced Scorecard's elegantly simple methodology and achieved tremendous results. These pioneers blazed the Scorecard trail using nothing more than spreadsheet-based paper reports with some color graphs mixed in to spice things up a bit. They proved you don't need sophisticated tools and a big budget to benefit from the Balanced Scorecard. But then again, the Scorecard methodology had not matured and entered its period of greatest sophistication at that point. Most practitioners relied on the Scorecard as a new and improved measurement system but had yet to tap its huge potential as a strategic management system and communication tool.

By the mid- to late 1990s the Balanced Scorecard landscape had changed dramatically. Strategy maps were on the horizon; organizations began to cascade the Scorecard from top to bottom, attempting to align all employees with overall goals; and linkages from the Scorecard to budgets and compensation were more frequently reported. The old paper-based reporting systems that had been established with the first Scorecards simply could not meet the challenges represented by these innovative extensions. As is always the case, creative and adaptive organizations recognized this opportunity and were quick to supply automated Scorecard software solutions to fill the void. Scorecard practitioners of all sizes welcomed the options, functions, and add-ons provided with open arms. And why not, since the new software facilitates even greater focus and attention on the many benefits to be derived from using the Scorecard system. Recent studies suggest that organizations are rapidly embracing the magic of technology; one survey found that 70 percent of respondents were using some type of software in their implementation.[1]

Automating your Balanced Scorecard provides a number of benefits and maximizes its use as a measurement system, strategic management system, and communication tool. The advanced analytics and decision support provided by even the simplest Scorecard software allow organizations to perform intricate evaluations of performance and critically examine the relationships among their performance measures. Automation also supports true organization-wide deployment of the tool. Cascading the Scorecard across the enterprise often leads to the development of dozens or more Scorecards. Without the use of an automated solution, managing the process and ensuring alignment can prove difficult. Communication and feedback may also be dramatically improved with Scorecard software. Commentaries used to elaborate on a specific measure's performance may spawn a company-wide discussion and lead to creative breakthroughs based on collaborative problem solving made possible only through the wide dissemination of Scorecard results. Information sharing and knowledge are also enhanced by the software's ability to provide relevant links to interested users. A hyperlinked measure may be just the beginning in the user's journey to a variety of knowledge-enhancing sites including the mission statement, the latest comments from a valued customer, or the results of a much-anticipated benchmarking study.

Choosing Balanced Scorecard Software

As discussed, in the past few years the number of companies providing Balanced Scorecard software has increased substantially. The market has become increasingly competitive with large enterprise resource planning (ERP) vendors, midsize software enterprises, and small niche players vying for a share of this ever-enlarging market. The choice of which vendor will supply your software is one of the most difficult and important decisions you'll be forced to make during your Scorecard implementation. There is a lot on the line here: not only the effective reporting and analysis of your Scorecard measures but, equally vital, the acceptance of the tool by your workforce. Adding to the challenge is the fact that software selection can be a very esoteric business, and most of us probably don't count this skill among our core competencies. Obviously, you'll rely heavily on your Information Technology (IT) colleagues to help guide you through the dizzying maze of choices you're about to encounter. To supplement their assistance, we present a host of criteria to consider when making your decision.

Design Issues: Configuration of the Software   This section examines a number of the Scorecard software setup and design elements.

- *Time to implement.* Software programs for the Balanced Scorecard can run the gamut from simple reporting tools to sophisticated enterprise-wide management solutions. Therefore, major differences exist in the time and resources necessary to implement the system. You must determine what your thresholds are in terms of timing and resource requirements necessary to have the system up and running.
- *Various Scorecard designs.* This book focuses exclusively on the methodology of the Balanced Scorecard. However, at some point you may wish to track other popular measurement alternatives, such as the Baldrige criteria, total quality management (TQM) metrics, or any number of different methodologies. The software should be flexible enough to permit various performance management techniques.

- *User interface/display.* Most Balanced Scorecard software features a predominant display metaphor. It may use gauges similar to those you would see in the dashboard of a plane or automobile, boxes that are reminiscent of organizational charts, or color-coded dials. Some of these simply look better (i.e., more realistic and legitimate) than others. That may sound insignificant, but remember, you're counting on your workforce to use this software faithfully; if they find the instrumentation unrealistic or, worse, unattractive, that could significantly impact their initial reaction and ongoing commitment.

- *Number of measures.* Most Scorecard practitioners are (on average) increasing the number of measures they track, partly because the new software tools allow unlimited measures to be entered. Too many measures can distort an organization's focus and blur what is truly important. However, your software must be flexible enough to handle enough measures to accommodate tracking results from across the organization.

- *Strategy maps.* The software you choose should be capable of effectively and faithfully depicting your organization's Strategy Map, allowing for drill down by each objective.

- *Measures, targets, and initiatives.* Measures, targets, and initiatives are the backbone of the Scorecard system. You should be able to easily enter all of these elements in the software.

- *Cause-and-effect relationships.* Your Scorecard software should provide a means of demonstrating the cause-and-effect linkages that describe your strategy. Capturing your story with compelling and easy-to-understand graphics is critical if you hope to benefit from the information sharing and collective learning the Balanced Scorecard offers.

- *Multiple locations.* The software should accommodate the addition of performance measures from a variety of physical and nonphysical locations.

- *Descriptions and definitions.* Simply entering names and numbers into the software is not sufficient for communication and eventual analysis. Every field in which you enter information must be capable of accepting textual descriptions. Upon launching the software, the first thing most users do when looking at a specific performance indicator is examine its description and definition.

- *Assignment of owners.* The Scorecard can be used to enhance accountability only if your software permits each performance indicator to be assigned a specific owner. Since other people may assist the owner and/or enter data, it is beneficial if the software provides the ability to identify these functions as well.

- *Various unit types.* Your performance indicators are likely to come in all shapes, sizes, and descriptors from raw numbers, to dollars, to percentages. The tool you choose must permit all measure types.

- *Frequency of reporting.* Not all performance indicators will be tracked with the same degree of frequency. Sales, for example, could be tracked annually, quarterly, monthly, weekly, or even daily, while employee surveys are most likely conducted and reported only once or twice a year. However, you may wish to view past performance in different time increments than originally reported: You may wish to view on-time delivery (reported monthly) annualized for the past two years. Your software should provide this flexibility.

- *Relative weights.* All measures on the Balanced Scorecard are important links in the description of your strategy. However, most organizations will place greater emphasis on certain indicators. Perhaps financial measures are vital at the outset of your implementation. A good Scorecard tool should permit you to weight the measures according to their relative importance.

- *Aggregate disparate elements.* This phrase simply means that your program should be able to combine performance measures with different unit types. This can best be accomplished with the use of weighting (see above). Measures are accorded a weight that drives the aggregation of results regardless of the specific unit type of each indicator.

- *Multiple comparatives.* Most organizations track performance relative to a predefined target, for example, the budget. However, it may be useful to examine performance in light of last year's performance, relative to your competitor, or against a best-in-class benchmarking number. The software should allow a number of comparatives.

- *Graphic status indicators.* Users should be able to ascertain at a glance the performance of measures based on an easy-to-understand status indicator. Many programs take advantage of our familiarity with red (stop), yellow (caution), and green (go) metaphors.

- *Dual polarity.* For the software to produce a color indicating measure performance, it must recognize whether high values for actual results represent good or bad performance. Up to a certain point results might be considered good, but beyond a certain threshold they may be a cause for concern. For example, it may be perfectly appropriate for a call center representative to answer 15 calls an hour, but responding to 30 may indicate the representative is rushing through the calls and sacrificing quality for the sake of expediency. The software solution should be able to flag such issues of dual polarity.

- *Cascading Scorecards.* Users should be able to review Balanced Scorecards from across the company in one program. Ensure your software allows you to display aligned Scorecards emanating from throughout the organization.

- *Personal preferences.* "My" has become a popular prefix in the Internet world, with "My Yahoo," "My Home Page," and so on. The information age has heralded a time of mass customization. And so it should be with your Balanced Scorecard software. If desired, users should be able to easily customize the system to open with a page displaying indicators of importance to them. Having relevant information immediately available will greatly facilitate the program's use.

- *Intuitive menus.* Menus should be logical, easy to understand, and relatively simple to navigate.

- *Helpful help screens.* Some help screens seem to hinder users' efforts as often as they help them. Check the help screens to ensure they offer relevant, easy-to-follow information.

- *Levels of detail.* Your software should allow users to quickly and easily switch from a summary view of performance to a detailed view comprising a single indicator. Navigating from data tables to summary reports, then back to individual measures should all be easily accommodated. Users will demand this functionality as they begin actively using the tool to analyze performance results.

Reporting and Analysis   Any software solution you consider must contain robust and flexible reporting and analysis tools. This section explores a number of reporting and analysis factors to be considered during your selection process.

- *Drill-down capabilities.* A crucial item. The tool must allow users to drill down on objectives comprising the Strategy Map and measures appearing on the Scorecard to increasingly lower levels of detail.

- *Statistical analysis.* Your software should allow you to perform statistical analysis, for example, trends, on the performance measures making up your Balanced Scorecard. Additionally, the statistics should be multidimensional in nature, combining disparate performance elements to display a total picture of actual results. Simply viewing bar charts is not analysis. Users require the opportunity of slicing and dicing the data to fit their analysis and decision-making needs.

- *Alerts.* You will want to be notified automatically when a critical measure is not performing within acceptable ranges. Alerts must be built into the system to provide this notification.

- *Commentaries.* Whether a measure is performing at, above, or below targeted expectations, users (especially management) need to quickly determine the root cause of the performance and be aware of the associated steps necessary for sustaining or improving results. Commentary fields are essential to any Scorecard software program.

- *Flexible report options.* "What kind of reports does it have?" is invariably one of the first questions you'll hear when discussing Scorecard software with your user community. Ours is a report-based and -dependent culture, so this shouldn't come as a surprise. What may be surprising is the wide

range of report capabilities featured in today's Scorecard software packages. Test this requirement closely, because some are much better than
others. An especially important area to examine is print options. We
purchase software to reduce our dependency on paper, but as we all know
it doesn't necessarily work that way. Ensure the reports will print effectively, displaying the information clearly and concisely.

- *Automatic consolidation.* You may wish to see your data presented as a sum,
  average, or year-to-date amount. The system should be flexible enough
  to provide this choice.

- *Flag missing data.* At the outset of their implementation, most organizations will be missing at least a portion of the data for Balanced Scorecard measures. This often results from the fact that the Scorecard has
  illuminated entirely new measures never before contemplated. The software program should alert users to those measures that are missing data,
  whether it is for a single period or a totally empty measure.

- *Forecasting and what-if analysis.* Robust programs are able to use current
  results to forecast future performance. It's also very useful to have the
  ability to plug in different values in various measures and examine the effect
  on related indicators. This what-if analysis provides another opportunity to critically examine the assumptions made when constructing the
  Strategy Map.

- *Linked documents.* At a mouse click users should be able to put measure
  results into a larger context by accessing important documents and links.
  Annual reports, CEO videos, analyst reports, discussion forums, blogs,
  and a variety of other potential links can serve to strengthen the bond
  between actual results and the larger context of organizational objectives.

- *Automatic e-mail.* To harness the power of the Balanced Scorecard as a
  communication tool, users must be able to launch an e-mail application
  and send messages regarding specific performance results.

Technical Considerations   This section examines hardware and software
technical dimensions associated with your software selection.

- *Compatibility.* Any software you consider must be able to exist in your current technical environment.

- *Integration with existing systems.* Data for your Balanced Scorecard will
  probably reside in a number of different places: financial data from your
  general ledger, customer information from your customer relationship
  management (CRM) system, and other measures from an ERP system.
  Your software should be able to extract data from these systems automatically, thereby eliminating any rekeying of data. Users who seem reluctant to use the Scorecard software often point to redundant data entry
  as a key detraction of the system. Therefore, the ability to automatically
  extricate information with no effort on the part of users is a big plus.

- *Accept various data forms.* In addition to internal sources of data, you may collect performance information from third-party providers. The software should be able to accept data from spreadsheets and ASCII files.

- *Data export.* Sometimes getting information out is as important as getting it in. The data contained in the Balanced Scorecard may serve as the source for other management reports to boards, regulators, or the general public. A robust data export tool is an important component of any Scorecard software.

- *Web publishing.* Users should have the option of accessing and saving Scorecard information using a standard browser. Publishing to both an internal intranet and the Internet is preferable.

- *Trigger external applications.* Users will require the capability of launching desktop programs from within the Balanced Scorecard software.

- *Cut and paste to applications.* Users may wish to include a graph or chart in another application. Many programs enable users to copy and paste with ease.

- *Application service provider option.* An application service provider (ASP) is a company that offers organizations access to applications and related services over the Internet that would otherwise have to be located in their own computers. As IT outsourcing grows in prominence, so does the role of ASPs. Many Scorecard software vendors offer this service, which gives anyone direct access to the Balanced Scorecard, for a monthly (normally) fee based on the number of users.

- *Scalability.* This term describes the ability of an application to function well and take advantage of changes in size or volume in order to meet a user need. Rescaling can encompass a change in the product itself (storage, random access memory [RAM], etc.) or the movement to a new operating system. Your software should be scalable to meet the future demands you may place on it as your user community and sophistication grow.

Maintenance and Security   Ensuring appropriate access rights and on-going maintenance are also important criteria in your software decision. Elements to consider include:

- *System administrator access.* Your software should allow for individuals to be designated as system administrators. Depending on security a number of these users may have access to the entire system.

- *Ease of modification.* You should be able to alter your views of performance easily with little advanced technical knowledge required.

- *Control of access to the system.* I prefer open book management with complete sharing of information across the enterprise. Organizations practicing this participative form of management give it glowing reviews for the innovation and creativity it sparks among employees. The Scorecard facilitates open sharing of information through both the development of a high-level organizational Scorecard and the series of cascading Scorecards that allow all employees to describe their contribution to overall results. However, many companies wish to limit access to the system. Therefore, a software program should allow you to limit access to Strategy Maps and measures by user and develop user groups to simplify the measure publishing process.

• *Control of changes, data, and commentary entry.* Likewise, not all users will necessarily be required to make changes, enter data, or provide result commentaries. Only system administrators should have the power to change measures, and only assigned users should have access to entering data and commentaries.

Evaluating the Vendor   Chances are you will be presented with a wide array of software choices from both industry veterans and upstarts you have never heard of. Either way, performing a little due diligence on the vendor is always a good idea.

• *Pricing.* As with any investment of this magnitude, pricing is a critical component of the overall decision. To make an informed decision, remember to include all dimensions of the total cost to purchase and maintain the software. This includes the per user license fees, any maintenance fees, costs related to new releases, training costs, as well as salaries and benefits of system administrators.

• *Viability of the vendor.* Is this provider in for the long term, or will any vicissitudes of the economy spell their demise? After reading this book you all know that financial information is like looking in the rearview mirror, but nonetheless you should ask to see vendors' audited financial statements to assess their financial position and growth potential. Since they're in the business of providing Scorecard software, you would expect them to steer their own course using the Balanced Scorecard. Ask them to review Scorecard results with you. For reasons of confidentiality, they may have to disguise some of the actual numbers, but you should still glean lots of valuable information on the organization's future prospects.

• *References and experience.* By examining the profiles of past clients, you can determine the breadth and depth of experience the vendor has accumulated. While no two implementations are identical, it will be reassuring to know the software company has completed an installation in an organization with some similarity to yours, whether it's the same industry or an organization of a comparable size. References are especially important. When discussing the vendor with other organizations that have been through the process, quiz them on the vendor's technical skills, consulting and training competence, and ability to complete the work on time and on budget.

- *Postsale service.* You'll inevitably have many bumps in the road as you implement your new reporting software. Bugs hidden deep in the program will be detected, patches will be required, and thus a lifeline to the vendor is crucial. How much support are they willing to offer, and at what cost? Do you have a dedicated representative for your organization, or are you at the mercy of a call center? These are just a couple of questions to ask. Never forget that software companies owe a lot to us, the users. New functions and features are very often the product of intense lobbying on behalf of function-starved users who sometimes end up knowing more about the product than the vendor. So don't be shy with your requests!

While evaluating and ultimately choosing a software provider can prove to be an arduous task, the rewards, in the form of enhanced momentum, greater analytical tools, and streamlined cascading, often pay tremendous benefits. Exhibit 10.1 provides a screen shot from one Balanced Scorecard software program.

Technology Caveats

It has been reported that 5 percent of Scorecard users select a technology solution before designing their Balanced Scorecard and about 29 percent design the Scorecard and choose technology at the same time.[2] There are serious dangers associated with these approaches. When technology is chosen before or concurrently with the design of the Scorecard, it can *become* the Balanced Scorecard in the minds of the user community. The term "Balanced Scorecard" is relegated to generic status and is considered a task performed by the latest software acquisition. Of course, it's actually the other way around: The software is just an enabler or facilitator of the enhanced use of the Scorecard. If you choose software prior to developing the Scorecard, a distinct possibility that valuable training resources will be diverted from Scorecard education to the acquisition of software skills arises. I have seen organizations that go through very rote Scorecard education sessions, discussing only the four perspectives and the system's departure from traditional financial-based measurement systems. Very little training is conducted on the art of developing Strategy Maps and selecting strategic measures; instead the focus is shifted to developing proficiency in using the new software. These organizations pay a heavy price when attempting to mold the Scorecard into their management processes. They have devoted so little time and attention to the fundamentals of the Balanced Scorecard and how to create and use it effectively that often they have to start all over again when users demonstrate that they simply don't understand how this new system works.

Many software packages are now offering libraries of performance measures that users may choose from to rapidly develop and begin reporting

Exhibit 10.1   Screen Shot from a Balanced Scorecard Software System

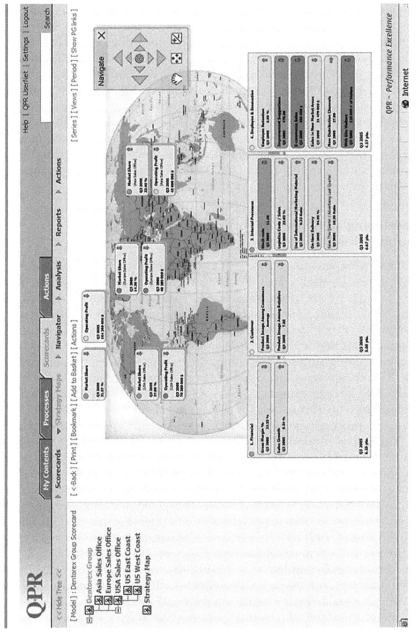

a Balanced Scorecard. The trade-off of speed for careful reflection frightens me. A great deal of the value offered by the Balanced Scorecard is derived from the often difficult but always rewarding process of thoughtfully and faithfully translating a strategy into the objectives and measures necessary to see it implemented successfully. Further, strategy is about differences, doing different things, and combining different activities to drive a unique mix of value. The measures you choose must represent your organization's individuality. Sure, there may be some measures you share with many other companies, but the real differentiators are the new measures that you hypothesize as driving future results. Will a predefined library contain exactly the measures that describe who you are as an organization? Probably not.

Developing Your Own Reporting System: Building Rather than Buying

Automated Scorecard solutions offer a great many benefits and are becoming more sophisticated all the time, but they don't always come cheap. Deploying a system across the entire organization is often just the beginning. Add the inevitable consulting, training, maintenance, and new release fees, and you could soon be looking at a staggeringly large bill. For smaller organizations and for larger companies attempting to control their spending, purchasing software may simply be cost prohibitive. As noted earlier, the original Scorecard practitioners relied heavily on paper-based reports with some later graduating to intranet applications, and they achieved great results. So, fortunately for the vast number of smaller enterprises out there, the procurement of Scorecard software is not a prerequisite of success.

With today's desktop publishing tools, even the humblest paper-based Scorecard report can resemble a glossy business publication. Text, graphics, and numbers can all be formatted to artistically represent the organization's business while also delivering valuable Scorecard results. Additionally, publishing Balanced Scorecard results on the organization's intranet offers a viable option for sharing results with minimal investment. One client of mine, known for his creativity and often quirky solutions, devised a unique approach to the reporting question. He created a three-sided board, about six feet tall, and complete with wheels for ease of transport. Results were posted each month on each side of the board: corporate measure updates on one, key strategic initiatives on a second side, and probably the most viewed of the three, the monthly incentive compensation calculator. The wheels turned out to be the greatest innovation, however, transforming the device from a wacky conversation piece to a roaming meeting agenda. The CEO insisted his managers roll the board into conference rooms when conducting meetings and use the posted results to stimulate discussions on corporate and business unit progress. When not roaming the hallways the board was posted in common areas such as the company's foyer—

where it caused more than one unsuspecting visitor to cast a quizzical double take—and the cafeteria where, coffee stains notwithstanding, the board served as grist for many a lunch-time conversation. The total cost of this investment was minimal but the payback in the form of enthusiasm and frank discussion has been substantial.

Before you decide to completely forgo investing in Scorecard software, remember that building your own solution is not without some significant issues. Perhaps the biggest barrier is data entry. The vast majority of automated tools will connect to current organizational systems, automatically drawing measure data and performing necessary calculations. Homegrown systems require manual data feeding to churn out Scorecard reports. Should you cascade your Scorecard across the company, this data entry could go from a minor task to a major burden requiring hundreds of hours to complete. Plus you'll have to design a system to gather the data and will undoubtedly encounter resistance from those unwilling or seemingly unable to supply the data for their measures. Finally, manual data entry brings with it the attendant risk of inaccurate data being entered into the system. Quality control will consume additional time and energy.

Ultimately the decision to automate or not will depend on a number of factors. Your organization's readiness to implement and administer the system, the amount of resources you're willing to commit, the sophistication of your Scorecard, and of course the cost are all elements of the decision.

THE STRATEGY-CENTERED MANAGEMENT MEETING

Problems with Most Management Meetings

What do these activities, seemingly disparate at first glance, have in common: mowing your lawn, researching insurance rates, and reading the phone book? While these chores may seem not to share many characteristics, the thread that unites them is the fact that, when asked, most people say they would rather engage in any of these than attend a management meeting at their company.[3] Nothing seems to engender as much eye rolling and frustration as the traditional management powwow that, nine times out of ten, produces more yawns and heartburn than breakthrough "aha" moments. Just why are we plagued with such poor meetings, sessions during which, by one study's findings, over 80 percent of the time is spent on items creating less than 20 percent of the organization's value?[4] Let's examine two possible explanations for our less than stellar performance in this time-honored management tradition: lack of conflict and the paucity of contextual structure.

To say most management meetings are boring is akin to suggesting Vice President Dick Cheney's shooting of his hunting buddy was a minor news item—both massive understatements. A major contributor to the boredom quotient in most work sessions is a lack of constructive conflict, the sandpaperlike dialog necessary to rough up the usual optimistic and idealistic drivel being spoon fed to most audiences. If this sounds harsh, think of your own experiences in recent meetings. Unless yours is one of the tiniest of minorities, you probably know what I'm referring to: meetings that are characterized by a once-around-the-room update from everyone in attendance during which sunny reviews are shared, Power Point slides are reviewed by glossy-eyed attendees, and only the politest of questions are raised. One pair of researchers has suggested that deeply ingrained rules of etiquette cause people to silence themselves to avoid embarrassment, confrontation, and other perceived dangers.[5] That statement has a major ring of truth to it.

Simply put, it's time to take the gilded edge off silence and acquiescence in management meetings and toss in equal measures of tough questions and constructive conflict. Author and management consultant Patrick Lencioni, scribe of the aptly titled *Death by Meeting*, suggests that leaders must look for legitimate reasons to provoke and uncover relevant, constructive ideological conflict and jolt participants a little within the first 10 minutes of a meeting, so that they understand and appreciate what is at stake.[6] Lou Gerstner, the architect of IBM's turnaround throughout the 1990s, understands this principle and applied it liberally during his days at the helm of the corporate giant. He tells the story of an early strategy meeting, convened just after he assumed the role of CEO in 1993. At the appointed time his managers began parading in the room, each followed by legions of paper-toting assistants, and took their assigned seats at the large conference room table. When the meeting got into full swing, Gerstner was bitterly disappointed by the rote slides being presented and the lack of meaningful discussion and debate he knew was necessary to tease out real learning. In what he called the "click heard round the world," he finally jumped from his chair and pulled the plug on the overhead projector, insisting on real dialog and discussion from his team. It set a powerful precedent and laid out his expectations in no uncertain terms.[7]

Meetings are also plagued by what Lencioni has described as a lack of contextual structure, a condition that often leads to the murky mess of "meeting stew."[8] Most management get-togethers lack a focused agenda, with everything from company picnics, to quarterly operational results, to culture being tossed into an agenda bursting at the seams with issues that, while frequently urgent, are rarely important. Paying the ultimate price for this boiling cauldron of meeting stew is the company's strategy; researchers have discovered that, at most companies, just three hours per month is devoted to this critical topic.[9] It should be clear that if we desire to execute our strategy—and an investment in the Balanced Scorecard is a good indication of that intent—we must ceaselessly dissect and analyze the strategy to determine if our efforts are on target. This is best accomplished by letting the Scorecard itself form the heart of the management meeting agenda. Let's now turn our attention to a new type of management meeting, one with strategy squarely at the center of everyone's attention, that uses the Balanced Scorecard to guide frank and progressive discussion of business results.

New Strategy-Centered Management Meeting

To help frame the discussion of the strategy-centered meeting, let's first review a series of questions often raised by newcomers to the approach.

Who Is Invited to Participate at the Meeting?   The progressive and politically correct answer to this question would suggest you toss out the old command-and-control paradigm dictating you invite only senior executives to sit in on strategy meetings, and instead—since strategy should be the responsibility of every employee filling your roster—make attendance a function of strategic contribution, not hierarchical rank. I love the image this change brings to mind, setting free the burdensome mental model that only those in corner offices are qualified to discuss strategy. Pragmatically, however, while they are not always the only qualified contributors, senior executives are frequently the most comfortable at such gatherings. I have witnessed companies that, eager to generate a spirit of esprit de corps and foster collaboration, invite lower-level employees to share results at senior meetings only to have a tongue-tied manager stammer through an obviously rehearsed stanza or two on this month's results. It is truly gut-wrenching to watch as this poor wretch shakes visibly, his body language clearly suggesting he'd rather be enjoying a root canal than presenting to those he normally only sees gracing the pages of the annual report. The intentions may be honorable, but the execution can lead to a long-lasting and foul taste in the mouth of those unaccustomed to such sessions. Thus, feel free to invite managers with a point of view who can contribute, and perhaps call on them with questions of clarification; but at its core strategy execution is the responsibility of the senior management team and they must actively engage in and ultimately own this process.

How Do You Prepare for the Meeting?   Stepping back a bit, before preparation comes scheduling of the meetings, which should be done well before you're sipping coffee at your first review. In fact, given the hectic calendars of most time-starved executives, you will be doing yourself an immense favor by placing these sessions on their calendars months in advance of the actual dates.

Sharing materials in advance of the session is an absolute must should you hope to derive the benefits these meetings are capable of delivering.

Snappy and clever spontaneous dialog is delivered effortlessly in movies and on television, but in the real world, participants will need some help in framing the discussions you hope will lead to creative tension and breakthrough discoveries. That assistance comes in the form of materials delivered approximately one week in advance of the meeting, including your Strategy Map, Balanced Scorecard measure results, commentaries on performance, and updates on key strategic initiatives.

Who Should Facilitate the Meeting?   Practitioners are mixed on this point. Some tap their Balanced Scorecard champion or team leader to guide the review session, and others rotate the assignment among the senior management team. Both options have merit. Using the Scorecard champion ensures the meeting will be led by someone well schooled in the mechanics of the Balanced Scorecard, its principles and functions, thereby helping the group avoid digressing into the weeds of the company's operations and missing the big picture being portrayed by Scorecard results. Having a member of your senior management team conduct the session can also prove beneficial, since one of your aims in pursuing the Balanced Scorecard is to drive ownership and accountability for strategy execution throughout the highest ranks of your organization chart. An additional benefit of employing this option is challenging the senior manager facilitator to step out of his or her usual silo and think broadly about organizational success, engaging in dialog with other business unit leaders, and brainstorming creative solutions to cross-functional challenges.

How Do You Review Results during the Meeting?   Once again you have a menu of options from which to choose when determining how you will actually review Balanced Scorecard results. If your Strategy Map and Scorecard have made good use of cause-and-effect linkages, weaving a powerful strategic story through the four perspectives of the model, you may choose to use these causal paths as your roadmap in reviewing performance. You might begin with the Financial perspective and work through the chain evident in the other perspectives, all the while challenging the hypothesis suggested by the linkages you created when developing the map and measures.

A second method would have you move sequentially through the four perspectives, beginning with Financial and dutifully scanning performance on each objective and measure right on down through the Employee Learning and Growth perspective. This could be called the leave-no-stone-unturned approach, and it is in direct contrast to a final option of examining performance on an exception basis. Those employing this approach look first to measures operating significantly out of a predetermined range of acceptable performance and take a deeper dive to the inner workings of the metrics in an attempt to ferret out their root causes and get things back on track.

As with most things Balanced Scorecard, there is no one right way or absolute method for running your review meetings. In fact, the modus operandi of the session runs a distant second to the actual conversation produced by the investigation itself. Regardless of the tack you use to steer the ship, what really matters is the discussion spawned along the way. The facilitator's primary task is to use the results simply as a spark lighting a flame of intense discussion during which conventional views are challenged, assumptions are exposed, and hypotheses about the strategy are tested. Allow yourself some room for experimentation as you begin to structure your meetings using the Balanced Scorecard as the agenda, making alterations and improvements as you find a style that suits your culture and meets your unique needs.

How Do You Set an Appropriate Tone for the Meeting?   It is here that your commitment to the meaning of the word "balance" is most severely tested, as you attempt to embrace honest and open discussions while shunning a blame culture that inhibits people from saying what is really on their mind. Esteemed leadership expert Warren Bennis has noted, *"Leaders do not avoid, repress, or deny conflict, but rather see it as an opportunity."*[10] No meaningful knowledge or wisdom will bubble to the surface without the ground first being prepared with the enrichment of candor, open and frank discussion of the issues that truly matter. As discussed previously, you must loosen the stifling grip silence holds on true success, encouraging your team to challenge one another, question long-standing assumptions, and ask the questions residing deep in their consciousness, the tough ones most people don't want to hear. Only then can you hope to exploit the full value of what lies within the results supplied by your Balanced Scorecard.

Entrepreneur, inventor, and founder of Polaroid Edwin Land had a small plaque on the wall of his office that read: *"A mistake is an event the full benefit of which you have not yet turned to your advantage."*[11] Organizations are comprised of people, and people have been known to make a mistake or two along the way. However, the strategy-centered meeting is no time to play the I-told-you-so blame game. Rather this gathering must embrace a spirit of learning in which mistakes are transformed into opportunities to improve and inspire greater performance in the future. I once read an account of the management practices at one poorly performing company that excelled in the art of what was known as pigeon management: They dumped all over their employees, left, and then came back in and dumped all over them once again. Not the most charming management metaphor, but it gets the point across pretty effectively. In this environment, no one will be willing to raise the tough issues or pose the challenging questions; doing so may result in a one-way ticket to the unemployment line. Learning, and not blame, must always be the primary goal of the strategy-centered management meeting if you hope to create a culture in which continuous learning about the strategy is truly seen as everyone's job.

How Often Do You Hold Meetings?   I know you want fewer meetings, not more, so I'm risking a good deal of page tearing and muffled expletives when I suggest you hold your strategy-centered meetings *at least* quarterly, but preferably monthly. Before you angrily toss this book across the room shouting "No, not more meetings, please!!" hear me out. Circumstances change so rapidly in our modern business world that you simply cannot afford to let as many as 90 days pass without holding a rigorous review of the results you hope will propel you toward strategy execution. Competitors new and old are undoubtedly plotting aggressive moves to erode your market share, customer preferences may be subtly shifting with new trends on the horizon, and the economic and political landscape in which you operate may be undergoing seismic shifts. Ignoring the warning signs, not to mention the opportunities, in front of you is done entirely at your peril.

The good news is that using the Balanced Scorecard may actually shorten the duration of your review meetings. Where before you launched a painstaking examination of every line on your profit and loss statement and aired as much dirty personnel laundry as you could squeeze in, now your sessions will benefit from the structure of a tool with strategy at its core, with strategy as the guiding force behind your discussion and your exploration of the truth of your business.

How Do You Ensure Accountability?[12]   On the subject of accountability and making the most of time spent in meetings, authors Bossidy and Charan are crystal clear in their excellent book, *Execution*: "*Never finish a meeting without clarifying what the follow-through will be, who will do it, when and how they will do it, what resources they will use, and how and when the next review will take place and with whom.*"[13] Ideas are the currency of the knowledge economy, and during these sessions they will be flowing as freely as promises at a political convention. But as we all know, ideas are only as good as their execution, and they require directed action to reach fruition. Always compile a list of action items flagged during the meeting and ensure updates are provided at the next gathering.

KEEP IN MIND

- As the use of the Balanced Scorecard has evolved from a measurement system to a strategic management system and communication tool, many organizations have looked to technological solutions in an effort to take advantage of advanced Scorecard techniques.

- Software packages provide advanced analytical and decision support tools, allow for wide dissemination of strategic information, and encourage innovation and team problem solving. Choosing a software provider can prove to be one of the most difficult tasks in the entire Scorecard implementation. Elements of the decision include: design and configuration issues, reporting and analysis tools, technical considerations, maintenance and security, and vendor assessments. The latest tools offer human capital modules and the ability to broadcast Scorecard results using wireless applications.

- Despite the many advantages to be gained from a technology solution, it must never take the place of the collaborative effort necessary to craft a Balanced Scorecard describing your specific strategy. Technology is an enabler of the Scorecard, expanding its use and creating unlimited opportunities for knowledge sharing and strategic breakthroughs.

- With the help of desktop publishing tools, those organizations not wishing to pursue a software solution can create polished reports distilling Scorecard information to the entire organization. As a next step, many will use their organization's intranet to communicate Scorecard results and facilitate information sharing and learning.

- The Balanced Scorecard should not contribute to an organization's management reporting burden. In fact, the reporting regimen should be rationalized in light of the Scorecard's presence. Existing reports must be placed under the microscope of strategy to determine whether they own a rightful place in the company's reporting space.

- Most management meetings suffer from a number of critical flaws, including a lack of conflict, no contextual structure, and an absence of strategic discussion and decision making. Using the Balanced Scorecard as the agenda for the management review process can overcome these deficiencies and ensures the organization remains focused at all times on strategy execution.

- Strategy-centered meetings should be held at least quarterly, if not monthly, and be facilitated either by the Balanced Scorecard champion or a member of the senior management team. Materials should be sent to participants (members of the senior management team and others able to contribute to the strategic agenda) in advance and will most likely include the Strategy Map, Balanced Scorecard measures, and updates on key strategic initiatives. Results may be reviewed by examining cause-and-effect linkages, working sequentially through the four perspectives, or on an exception basis. The key to successful meetings is fostering open and candid discussions without allowing blame to creep in. No meeting should end without actions being identified and captured for review at a future session.

Notes

1. Raef A. Lawson, William G. Stratton, and Toby Hatch, "Scorecarding in North America: Moving Toward a Best Practices Framework, Part I," *Cost Management* (July–August 2005): 25–34.

2. Laura M. Downing, "The Global BSC Community: A Special Report on Implementation Experiences from Scorecard Users Worldwide," presented at the *Balanced Scorecard North American Summit,* New Orleans, September 2000.

3. Julia Neyman and Julie Snider, "USA Today Snapshots," *USA Today* (November 15, 2004).

4. Michael C. Mankins, "Stop Wasting Valuable Time," *Harvard Business Review* (September 2004): 58–65.

5. Leslie Perlow and Stephanie Williams, "Is Silence Killing Your Company?" *Harvard Business Review* (May 2003): 110.

6. Patrick Lencioni, *Death by Meeting* (San Francisco: Jossey-Bass, 2004), p. 228.

7. Michael Beer and Russell A. Eisenstat, "How to Have an Honest Conversation About Your Business Strategy," *Harvard Business Review* (February 2004): 82–89.

8. Lencioni, *Death by Meeting,* p. 224.

9. Mankins, "Stop Wasting Valuable Time."

10. Quoted in Stephen R. Covey, *The 8th Habit* (New York: Free Press, 2004), p. 186.

11. Peter Senge, C. Otto Scharmer, Joseph Jaworski, and Betty Sue Flowers, *Presence* (New York: Doubleday, 2005), p. 148.

12. This section drawn from *Paul R. Niven, Balanced Scorecard Diagnostics: Maintaining Maximum Performance* (Hoboken, NJ: John Wiley & Sons, 2005), p. 175.

13. Larry Bossidy and Ram Charan, *Execution* (New York: Crown Business 2002), p. 128.

CHAPTER 11

Maintaining the Balanced Scorecard

Roadmap for Chapter Eleven   When I was writing the first edition of this book, my wife and I were in the middle of a move. After settling into our new home, one of the first things we did was to have our backyard landscaped, nothing extravagant, mostly lawn with some shrubs and trees. Oh, but that lawn — I remember staring at the grass for at least a few moments everyday. It was just so pristine, vibrantly green, and healthy looking. But can you imagine what that same perfect lawn would have looked like after a few weeks with no mowing, watering, or fertilizer? Now consider the condition of your freshly minted Balanced Scorecard without a similar level of ongoing maintenance. To reach its full potential as an integrated strategic management system, the Scorecard must be carefully maintained and nurtured. In this chapter we'll explore the care and feeding of your new performance management system.

The adoption of business rules, processes, and procedures will assist the Scorecard in making the transition from communication tool and measurement system to management tool. Among a host of considerations, organizations must evaluate how the Scorecard fits into long-term strategic planning, how and when new Scorecards will be developed, under what circumstances measure changes will be considered, and how the Balanced Scorecard will ultimately link to management processes like budgeting and compensation. Gathering and reporting data is also central to the Scorecard, and effective techniques must be created to ensure this process is seen as beneficial, not burdensome. Once organizations decide what must be done to make the Scorecard a regular part of ongoing operations, then they must decide who will do what and where the Scorecard function ultimately will reside. The chapter outlines key Scorecard roles and provides guidelines to help you determine who should own the Balanced Scorecard.

THE BALANCED SCORECARD IS NEVER "COMPLETE"

Renowned leadership expert John Kotter has written extensively on the field of organizational change and what it takes to sustain a major transformational initiative. In his book *Leading Change*, he says, *"Major change often takes a long time, especially in big organizations. Many forces can stall the process far short of the finish line: turnover of key change agents, sheer exhaustion on the part of leaders, or bad luck."*[1] The Balanced Scorecard is not a metrics project, it's not a technology project, and it's not a human resources program. More than anything else, the Balanced Scorecard represents a major change initiative, and as such it can fall prey to any of the issues Kotter suggests. Key change agents are critical to the success of any effort but are absolutely vital to institutionalizing the methods of the Balanced Scorecard. Without a person (or team) leading the refinement and continued development of the Scorecard system, it can easily be derailed with managers slipping back into their former practices. We will return to the subject of change agents in the "Key Balanced Scorecard Roles" section of the chapter. Executives who have many important initiatives on their plates can become overwhelmed by change. If executives fail to pay attention or to provide the modeling necessary to set the proper tone throughout the organization, the Balanced Scorecard could pay the price. And yes, even bad luck can victimize Scorecard efforts. Software that simply won't work as guaranteed and inexperienced consultants who promise more than they can deliver are just two examples of circumstances that may conspire to sabotage your carefully planned efforts. Perhaps the single biggest Scorecard pitfall to be avoided, however, is lack of maintenance. The Scorecard, like any major change, must be constantly nurtured for a significant period before it takes root within the culture and ongoing management practices of the organization.

Beyond sustaining momentum, the Balanced Scorecard is never really complete because your business is never really complete. Is there ever a point at which you can stop and say, "Well, this is it, we've done it all, there's nothing left to conquer, looks like smooth sailing ahead"? No, because the environment in which you operate is constantly changing. New competitors enter the marketplace rapidly and from all over the globe; the wide and swift availability of knowledge is causing customers to be more demanding than ever; and employees insist on satisfying and challenging roles that make a real contribution to success while simultaneously providing quality of life. All of these forces will affect your Balanced Scorecard, but fortunately not only is this tool flexible, but flexibility might be its chief identifying characteristic. As conditions change, current strategies will be severely tested, and new strategies may be called into action. Strong relationships thought to exist among measures may prove specious and necessitate the adoption of new indicators. The Scorecard is malleable enough to handle

such changes and will serve as a valuable tool while you navigate the changing course that is your business. The question is: How do you ensure that
the Scorecard remains a viable tool and is fully entrenched in the management system of your organization so that it can be looked to as a guiding
and trusted compass during periods of change? Maintenance, nurturing,
and building on the current Scorecard base are the answers. This care and
feeding is comprised of establishing business rules and processes for effective Scorecarding operations, putting the right people in place to further
the transition to this new method of management, and finding a home
for the Balanced Scorecard. We'll look at each of these items during the chapter. This is critical work, as Kotter reminds us: *"Whenever you let up before the
job is done, critical momentum can be lost and regression may follow."*[2]

MAINTAINING THE BALANCED SCORECARD

Establishing Balanced Scorecard Policies, Procedures, and Processes

The title of this section reminds me of the old command-and-control days
of business that featured a heavy emphasis on rules and process controls
to ensure strict adherence to steadfast procedures. Of course the Scorecard
is more representative of the new business paradigm characterized by open
information sharing, collaboration, empowerment, and team problem solving. Unfortunately, simply developing a Scorecard will not magically transform your organization into a paragon of enlightened management practice. To become part of everyday life in the organization, your Scorecard
will require some business rules, processes, and procedures to ensure smooth
functioning, especially in the early stages of implementation. Here is a list
of specific areas to address once your Scorecard system is up and running.

- *Long-range strategic planning.* What is the role of the Balanced Scorecard
  in the organization's long-term strategic planning efforts? The Scorecard should be at the forefront of strategic planning. However, after initial
  development of a Scorecard, some organizations revert back to their previous methods. Work with your strategic planning team to define the
  Scorecard's role in the process on a go-forward basis, ensuring it will
  remain the key tool in effective execution of strategy.

- *Annual Scorecard development.* The Balanced Scorecard is designed to be
  a flexible and dynamic tool that adjusts easily to the changes occurring
  in your business. At least annually, you should tweak your Balanced
  Scorecard to describe the continuing saga of your strategy. Don't wait until
  the last minute to put together a schedule, surprising the firm's already
  overworked managers. Compose a timeline early in the process, giving

everyone involved ample time to formulate a Balanced Scorecard that thoroughly displays how they contribute to overall success.

- *Reporting dates.* The wide distribution of Scorecard production dates is critical. There is a strong possibility that at least some of your Scorecard data will not come directly from source systems. That data will need to be collected and entered into your reporting system, whether it is automated or not. Those responsible for providing data must be aware of the timelines associated with reporting and the importance of timely and accurate data submission. Your executive team will be relying on the data, so don't be shy about including a veiled threat in any correspondence you produce when on the hunt for data.

- *Terminology.* Does the word "objective" have the same meaning for an executive, midlevel manager, and customer service representative? If you want to use the Scorecard to create a new language of measurement, it should. You'll have to grapple with terminology issues early in your implementation, however. As creatures of habit, people tend to migrate back to earlier definitions.

- *Roles and responsibilities.* Determine who is accountable for administering the Scorecard system in the organization and what their responsibilities are. We'll look at this in greater depth in the "Key Balanced Scorecard Roles" section of the chapter.

- *Thresholds of performance.* When using the Scorecard as a measurement system, organizations compare actual performance against a predetermined benchmark. That comparative may be a budget amount, last year's number, a best-in-class number, or a stretch target. Regardless of the comparative you choose, the relative ranges of performance must be established. Perhaps "green" performance is anything meeting or exceeding the target. "Yellow" may represent an actual amount within 10 percent of the target, and "red" could mean anything greater than a 10 percent variance. Performance thresholds are bound to stir a little controversy. Some people will consider them too strict while others will counter that they are slack and don't promote breakthrough action. My recommendation is to err on the conservative side at least in the first year. Give people the opportunity to become accustomed to this new way of managing before imposing strict thresholds that demand exemplary performance.

- *Changing objectives, measures, and targets.* Under what circumstances will you allow a midyear change in any of these performance indicators? Targets are especially vulnerable because many organizations lack a strong target-setting competence and initial attempts are either too difficult to achieve or too easy. Changes should be permitted only in clear cases of a misguided objective, measure, or target. Perhaps the calculation of a measure is leading to dysfunctional decision making or the target's perceived difficulty is demotivating to employees. In these situations a change may be warranted. We'll examine this topic in greater detail when we discuss "Updating the Scorecard's Core Elements" a little further in the chapter.

- *Timetable for Scorecard linkages to management processes.* During the first year of your implementation, you may or may not wish to cascade the Scorecard and link it to budgeting and compensation. At the very least you should have a plan for future development. Consider it the Balanced Scorecard "master plan" describing where you expect to take the Scorecard in the future and what is required to make that happen. Even if linkages aren't occurring during year 1, the dialog to facilitate future transformation should be taking place.

Gathering Data for the Balanced Scorecard

Gathering and entering data into your Scorecard reporting system often presents unique challenges. The first issue you face is whether the data are even available. One of the strongest benefits of the Scorecard is its ability to highlight the "missing measures" that drive future results. Identifying these indicators is one thing; gathering the supporting data is another. You may not have the systems or tools in place to harvest the data at the outset of your implementation. In fact, estimates vary, but you can probably expect to be missing between 20 and 30 percent of your data as you begin to report results. These absent data should not dictate any delay in reporting the Scorecard. Focus on the measures you do have and spend the necessary time and effort to develop processes for acquiring outstanding data.

Have you ever considered a career in law enforcement? I ask because when you attempt to get Scorecard data from measure owners, you may feel like the Balanced Scorecard Police. Like the highway patrol officer pulling over a contrite speeder, you'll hear every excuse in the book: "The source reports haven't been produced yet," "I'm waiting for one more number from Accounting," "I was on vacation last week and am still catching up!" Some are legitimate and may signal that a redesign of processes is necessary, while others are outrageous. Cajoling, persuading, and even threatening will go only so far. The only reliable method of ensuring a smooth data-gathering process is to make it as painless and simple as possible for those affected. Even if you are using a relatively low-tech reporting solution, you can build automated links into the gathering process, making it easier for those involved to send their much-needed data. Designing and distributing a customized measure template will go a long way toward ensuring data owner compliance. Exhibit 11.1 presents a data collection form you can customize for your performance measures. Develop a form for each owner of Balanced Scorecard measures, and distribute them electronically for completion. In this example, it is assumed that data are requested for

Exhibit 11.1 Balanced Scorecard Data Collection Form

Measure Owner: K. Tobin
Data Owner: S. Chezenko

| Measure Name | Perspective | Description | Actual Results | | | Commentary |
			July	Aug	Sept	
Number of calls received	Customer	Total number of calls logged in the call center during the month	3,000	3,500	3,750	Call volume is increasing steadily as anticipated. Advanced training and the addition of one staff person should enable us to handle up to 5,000 calls per month by year-end.
Number of one-call resolutions	Customer	Number of customers for which all issues were resolved during the first call	50	60	45	Result is deceiving. A lower number of one-call resolutions was logged during September; however, this is a result of callers registering fewer complaints.

the month of September; however, previous submissions are also displayed to provide relevant background and facilitate a performance commentary. Once completed, the form should be sent by e-mail back to the Balanced Scorecard system administrator who will enter the data into the Scorecard reporting tool.

Should you choose an automated solution to report Scorecard results, you may be able to import data directly from the form into the software. Depending on the functionality offered by the program, you may even be able to directly import the narrative supplied in the commentary columns. Using this simple form and taking advantage of your e-mail system for distribution greatly reduces any burden on measure owners. They simply open the e-mail attachment, fill in their performance numbers, and send the form back. Not only does the process make it easier for those responsible to supply data, but Scorecard administrators will also appreciate the existence of just one form of template. Rather than attempting to translate data scribbled on the back of business cards or read barely decipherable faxes, the administrator can easily transfer data from a common form to the reporting tool.

Updating the Scorecard's Core Elements:
Objectives, Measures, and Targets

As discussed, the Balanced Scorecard is designed to be a dynamic tool, flexible and capable of change as necessitated by business conditions. Over time you can expect a number of changes to take place within the realm of your objectives, measures, and targets. At the far end of the possibility spectrum you may decide to abandon a strategy you've pursued based on Scorecard results that disclaim much of your hypothesis. In that extreme case you would likely develop a new strategy for your organization and likewise select new and corresponding objectives, measures, and targets that act as direct translations of the updated strategy. Even with today's shorter strategic shelf lives, you would not expect to make wholesale changes to objectives, measures, and targets each and every year. However, it is a very good idea to critically examine the Scorecard at least annually and determine if its core elements are still appropriate in telling an accurate strategic story. Results of a best practices benchmarking study suggest that a majority of Scorecard practitioners do just that. In the study, 62 percent of participants updated their Balanced Scorecards annually; 15 percent updated every six months, while 23 percent updated every three months.[3] Make the annual Scorecard review process part of the normal planning cycle that occurs at most companies. Organizations engage in strategic planning, budgeting, and business planning every year. The Scorecard can be slotted in with these activities and take its rightful place as a key management process.

Expect many subtle changes to be made to objectives and measures as you gain experience using the Balanced Scorecard system. Objectives may be reworded to more accurately represent their core purpose or to clarify potentially confusing terminology. Similarly, measures could be subject to changes in the method of calculation to better capture the true essence of the event under investigation, or the description may be enhanced to improve employee understanding of operational and strategic significance. You may also change the frequency with which you collect performance data. For example, you may have attempted to track employee satisfaction monthly, but the logistics of gathering the data simply proved too challenging. In that case you wouldn't abandon this important indicator, but you would simply change the reporting period to something more amenable to measurement. Any change in a measure has a potential impact on the corresponding target. This is especially true if you make changes to formulas or calculations.

Updating your performance objectives, measures, and targets is yet another way to tap into the collective knowledge of your organization. Be sure to involve as many employees as possible to ensure that any changes reflect organization-wide interests. Surveying employees is an excellent method of gathering their feedback on Scorecard use and potential improvements. Exhibit 11.2 displays a 10-question survey that can be administered to employees at least annually to ensure the collection of critical feedback and knowledge. Employees should answer the survey questions with their specific group or department in mind. The senior executive team would assess the high-level organizational Scorecard. In addition to asking questions, the survey also includes a space for employee comments and recommendations for Scorecard improvements. In this example, the surveyed employee gives her group's Scorecard 38 out of a possible 50 points. Any total over 35 would be considered positive; however, the composition of the scores provides as much insight as the aggregate. In this case, for example, the Scorecard appears to be working very well in its intended capacity of informing employees about organizational strategy and providing a line of sight. It also appears that this group reviews their results on a regular basis and uses the information to identify future improvement initiatives. However, it is also clear that this employee is not happy with the reporting tool being used, the cause-and-effect linkages aren't clear, and Scorecard results are not stimulating organization-wide discussions. This input is invaluable as managers and employees look to develop future iterations of their Scorecard. Customers and suppliers also have a stake in your performance and would probably be flattered and impressed should you consult them regarding possible updates to the Scorecard.

The caveat regarding changes is this: Don't alter your measures simply because you dislike the current crop or the results aren't what you expected. The Balanced Scorecard is about learning: learning about your strategy, learning about the assumptions you've made to win in your marketplace,

Exhibit 11.2   Balanced Scorecard Employee Survey

Item	Score
Use of the Balanced Scorecard in my group has helped increase my knowledge of the organization's strategy.	5
Our group's Balanced Scorecard measures clearly demonstrate how we contribute to the achievement of overall organizational goals.	5
Our measures represent an appropriate balance among the four Balanced Scorecard perspectives.	4
Our measures are linked in a series of cause-and-effect relationships.	3
My input was sought during the development of our group's Balanced Scorecard.	4
In our group we review Balanced Scorecard results on a regular basis.	4
The reporting tool we use is efficient.	3
Managers and employees are held accountable for achieving Balanced Scorecard results.	4
Analyzing Balanced Scorecard results allows our group to identify potential improvement initiatives.	4
Discussing Balanced Scorecard results with colleagues has increased my knowledge of their function(s).	2
Total Score	**38**

Additional Comments:
I would like to know more about the use of the Scorecard in other groups within the company. How are results reported, and can those results be shared with all employees?

and learning about the value proposition you've put forth. Sometimes you won't enjoy what your measures are telling you, but your challenge is to use these deviations from plan as opportunities for learning, not simply as defects in need of remedy.

Key Balanced Scorecard Roles

Chapter Two introduced the critical roles necessary to make the Balanced Scorecard implementation a success. Let's revisit a number of those roles within a new context—making the Scorecard an ongoing success to maximize your performance and maintain results.

The theme running through this chapter is simple: Balanced Scorecards are not necessarily self-sustaining. Development and progress must be constantly nurtured in order for meaningful results to be derived. The critical player in the Scorecard's ongoing development is the *Balanced Scorecard champion* or *team leader*. Someone in the organization must be equated with the Balanced Scorecard and seen as both its ambassador and thought leader. Everything we've reviewed thus far in this chapter will require leadership. Steering the course of discussions around policies and procedures, evaluating possible measure changes, and providing insight on data acquisition strategies all need a strong leader. The Scorecard champion is that someone. With a unique mix of communication and leadership skills, the champion is the recognized Scorecard subject matter expert, coaching leaders and managers alike on Scorecard concepts and how the tool can best be utilized to achieve breakthrough results. But the Scorecard champion has a bigger role than guiding discussions and setting policies; it's the five-minute conversations in the hallway about last month's Scorecard results, or the distribution of an article about the latest Scorecard techniques, or the presentation to a group of administrative assistants who previously felt out of the Scorecard loop that really make the difference. In a word, it's communication. The champion artfully communicates how the Scorecard is making a difference now and can forge new ground in the future through innovative uses as a strategic management system. The most logical candidate for the role is the individual filling the position during your initial implementation. This person will have already carved inroads in the credibility roadways of the organization and be seen as Mr. or Ms. Balanced Scorecard. Asking the person to assume the role full-time and give up, or at least scale back, former responsibilities probably won't require extensive coaxing. I've been part of a number of implementations during which Scorecard champions so enjoyed their role that they asked to make the position a permanent move. I'm absolutely convinced that the assignment of a full-time Balanced Scorecard champion is a key differentiator of successful Balanced Scorecard implementations. The knowledge, continuity, and constant communication offered by the position can't be beaten.

The other truly indispensable Scorecard role is that of *executive sponsor*. Everything chronicled in Chapter Two regarding this role applies on an ongoing basis as well. The sponsor provides new information on strategy and plans, maintains constant communication with other members of the senior team, and continues to supply enthusiastic support for the Balanced Scorecard. All senior executives must share an ownership interest in the Balanced Scorecard if it is to reach its full potential. The executive sponsor works to make this happen by constantly engaging other members of the senior team in dialog addressing the benefits and future direction of the Scorecard. As the Scorecard program grows and matures, the executive sponsor is counted on to share your enlightened management concepts with colleagues and networks of other executives. Depending on where responsibility for the Scorecard ultimately resides in the organization (see "Who Owns the Balanced Scorecard?" which follows), it would be convenient and beneficial to have the Scorecard champion report directly to the executive sponsor. The clear line of communication resulting from this relationship would ensure that the latest Scorecard developments are funneled to the executive suite where swift action can be taken to leverage opportunities and remove obstacles.

Balanced Scorecard *team members* were integral to the original development of the Balanced Scorecard, but the role of this group changes as the Scorecard develops. Rather than hands-on Scorecard building, the task of the team evolves to information and best practice sharing. Team members must meet on a regular basis to review what the Scorecard has meant in their units or groups. They supply valuable input in the form of tips, effective Scorecard processes, and issue resolution strategies. The team should also be used as a proving ground for your latest Scorecard ideas. When linking the Scorecard to budgeting or compensation, for example, team members are able to provide a unique perspective on what will be necessary to make the transition a success in their business unit or group. Some organizations will migrate from a Balanced Scorecard team to a steering committee comprised of the champion, executive sponsor, other senior executives, and certain members of the original team. This group carries a more formal mandate of establishing Scorecard policies and charting future development.

A role we didn't consider when developing the Balanced Scorecard, but one that is crucial to its long-term success, is that of the *system administrator.* This term is normally associated with the individual administering a packaged software solution but may also apply if you develop your own reporting solution. Depending on the sophistication of your reporting tools, the Balanced Scorecard champion may be able to fill this role competently. However, should you purchase an automated solution, an administrator will most likely be required. System administrators hold the ultimate responsibility of scheduling results reporting and ensuring Scorecard data are gathered on a timely basis and entered accurately into the tool. They also make changes to Scorecard elements (objectives, measures, and targets), provide technical support to users, upgrade to new versions of software, and supply training. Liaising closely with the Balanced Scorecard champion and executive sponsor, the administrator plays an important part in defining the Scorecard's role in management review sessions. Whether it is transparencies displayed on an overhead projector or the latest Scorecard software, the technology that supports Scorecard reviews must function properly to bolster credibility for the new process. Most commercially available software packages provide material spelling out in detail the requirements of a system administrator.

Who Owns the Balanced Scorecard?

We have considered the roles necessary to ensure that the Scorecard is embedded in the management systems of the organization. Now we must find a home for the Scorecard function and more specifically the champion and system administrator. Team members will continue reporting to their business unit head, and the executive sponsor remains in her senior management position, but to whom will the champion and system administrator report? Before we answer that question, let's consider why it is critical to find a home for the Scorecard function. At this point in the process, the Balanced Scorecard may still be viewed as a project and not an ongoing way of managing the business. If the Balanced Scorecard does not have a solid foundation and clear ownership, it will be very difficult to erase this perception, and it may become solidified in the minds of employees. Of course, the word "project" connotes an image of something generally temporary in nature that, over time and with significant effort, is achieved or considered "complete." But as we have seen, the Balanced Scorecard is never really complete since it must flow with the changing tides of your business, helping steer the course as conditions inevitably change. If the Scorecard is thought of as complete, the desire and incentive to report results and use them in making business decisions is greatly reduced, and eventually serious gaps may develop in measurement and reporting. In contrast, providing the Scorecard with a functional home changes the paradigm and shifts the Scorecard to a permanent, legitimate business operation on its way to becoming ingrained in the fabric of everyday organizational life.

The leading candidate in the race for Scorecard custodial rights is the Finance function. In one study, participants were asked which functional area is responsible for managing their company's performance measurement system. Sixty-seven percent replied Finance.[4] My experience echoes this finding. The majority of Scorecard implementations on which I have been engaged concluded with the responsibility for ownership and ongoing development resting with Finance. With its place at the center of the organization's information processing and distribution function, Finance may have always represented a legitimate choice for Scorecard ownership. Recent developments in the field have made its bid for Scorecard ownership even stronger: *"The information age calls for Finance to play a new role —architect of the enterprise . . . . The traditional focus on control and compliance activities must be replaced by strategic, economic, tactical, and performance measurement leadership . . . . Why Finance? Finance has the highest level of access to information, strategy, economic targets, and internal process activities."*[5] It's clear that Finance professionals have begun embracing new roles in the organization, shedding the burdensome, and often nonvalue-added, corporate policeman persona in favor of a powerful and dynamic new look that places strategy and business partnership at its core. The Balanced Scorecard, with its holistic and collaborative nature, fits like a glove in this new Finance paradigm.

Before you rush down the hall and place the Balanced Scorecard Owner sash over the shoulder of your Finance leader, remember that every organization and every Balanced Scorecard implementation is unique. Finance may be a great home for the Scorecard in many organizations, but your Finance function may still be mired in the old control and compliance framework and have yet to experience the benefits of business partnership relationships. If that's the case, you'll probably find that the people-intensive, knowledge-sharing, collaborative features of the Scorecard aren't a great fit for your Finance function. Perhaps the Strategic Planning or Human Resources function fits the bill in your organization. If so, place Scorecard responsibilities there. The bottom line is this: You are looking for a home in which the executive leader believes in the management theory captured by the Scorecard and is willing to actively support, develop, refine, and evangelize the tool. The right person could be in Human Resources, Marketing, Manufacturing, Strategic Planning, or Finance. As always, it's the characteristics of the leader, not the functional title, that really matter.

An Emerging Discipline: The Office of Strategy Management

As organizations and the practice of management have evolved over the past 150 years, we have seen the emergence of a number of disciplines shepherding the ongoing art and science of business. Witness the birth of the chief financial officer (CFO), responsible for the stewardship of money entrusted to management's care and, more recently, a key player at the strategy table of most companies. Similarly, as technology has transformed individual businesses and entire industries alike, we have seen the chief information officer (CIO) rise to prominent heights, charting the technological path necessary to ensure efficient operations, drive innovation, and offer breakthrough customer service.

While most modern organizations employ at least some semblance of a strategic planning group, no single entity within the company has been charged with the joint responsibilities of strategy formation *and* its far more valuable cousin, strategy execution. Unfortunately, most organizations do not actively manage the strategy process in its entirety; bits and pieces of this vital enabler of success are strewn somewhat wildly throughout the vast reaches of the typical enterprise. But help is on the way, with some intrepid pioneers recognizing this deficiency and advocating an entirely new professional function, the Office of Strategy Management (OSM), which marries the strategy formation and execution functions in one coordinated effort. The OSM is a recent phenomenon, championed by Scorecard architects Kaplan and Norton, and holds the hope of bridging the strategy formation and execution gap, thereby making strategy execution a core competency to be wielded at every enterprise.[6] Let's take a closer look at this office and explore how you may use it within your company. As you will discover, the OSM can be considered an umbrella agency for many of the Balanced Scorecard tasks discussed throughout this book.

Functions of the Office of Strategy Management   Fundamentally, the OSM is the guardian of the many processes, which normally cut across organizational boundaries and require significant integration, that are required to execute strategy successfully. As noted, what is new and different here is the fact that one function or office takes responsibility for the complex and coordinated effort required to execute the organization's strategy. Collaboration and integration aren't left to chance but are carefully managed under the auspices of the OSM. Although the art and science of the OSM are nascent fields, early research and practitioner experience has led to a number of key functions falling under the umbrella of the office. An outline of each follows.[7]

- *Change management.* At its very core, strategy is about doing something different: about choosing a different set of activities and processes from your rivals and executing them flawlessly. Therefore, the notions of strategy and change are inextricably linked, since strategy introduces novelty in the form of a new organizational direction. As we all know, change is a difficult concept to operationalize for most organizations. As Machiavelli reminds us in his classic work *The Prince*, *"It ought to be remembered that there is nothing more difficult to take in hand, more perilous to conduct, or more uncertain in its success, than to take the lead in the introduction of a new order of things."*[8] As perilous as the task may be, it must be accomplished if organizations hope to reap the rewards of differentiating strategies. Therefore, among the first responsibilities of the OSM is the challenge of change management. OSM staffers must outline the rationale for the change, discuss how it will be implemented, clarify expectations, and, most vitally, clearly establish what benefits await employees willing to accept the change.

- *Strategy formation and planning.* While the OSM itself is not necessarily responsible for crafting organizational strategy, and in fact probably should not be as strategy is best developed by line managers, it should be accountable for the *process* in which strategy is developed. This process may encompass many duties, including gathering relevant strategy inputs, such as competitive and environmental information; conducting scenario planning; facilitating strategic dialog and debate; and orchestrating the strategy timetable. To execute this responsibility effectively, it is critical that the OSM work closely with the senior executive team.

- *Balanced Scorecard coordination.* An obvious role of the OSM is custodian of the organization's Balanced Scorecard process and its many attendant responsibilities. Members of the OSM team must demonstrate their strategic acumen as they work closely with the executive team in developing the organization's Balanced Scorecard. When the Scorecard is created, much of the OSM's work is still to be done: Scorecard training throughout the enterprise, facilitation of Scorecard result meetings, and guardianship of the information systems used to display and disseminate results, to name but a few.

- *Strategic communication.* Unfortunately, gold stars for communication are not in the immediate future for the vast majority of companies. When it comes to sharing information, the rule of thumb for many organizations appears to be too little, too late, and top down. In the era of scientific management at the turn of the twentieth century, this oversight could be readily ignored. Employees of that epoch generally required little in the form of communication to perform their laborious and repetitive tasks. The knowledge economy of the twenty-first century, however, demands more from our leaders. Should they expect to win both the hearts and minds of their staff, they must engage in virtually constant communication of the building blocks of success: mission, vision, values, strategy, and the necessity of change. Working with other constituents across the organization (Corporate Communications as an example), the OSM should coordinate communication activities centering on strategy. A key tenet of this work is the use of many and varied communication devices, including town hall meetings, presentations, and e-learning opportunities, all segmented by audience.

- *Alignment.* Inconsistency is a ticking time bomb in many organizations, just waiting to explode and destroy any hope of success. Frequently the inconsistencies, while philosophically simple, are profound in their damaging effects. They may include, for example, constantly espousing the value of teamwork but rewarding individual performance or touting the critical nature of innovation but refusing to provide budget dollars for experimentation. Credibility is potentially the most valuable currency possessed by leaders, and when they say one thing and do another, their credibility is substantially eroded, leaving employees wondering why they should expend one ounce of precious energy when they know priorities are as stable as leaves blowing in the wind. The OSM must ensure that all critical organizational processes are in alignment with the strategy, thereby eliminating the possibility of inconsistencies. One of the most vital links is that between strategy and performance management, including personal development planning and compensation. Human capital is the real driver of the knowledge economy, and every organization must ensure this most scarce of resources is aligned with the strategy.

- *Initiative management.* Many organizations receive a high payback on their OSM investment when they actively manage the initiative process. The vast majority of truly "strategic" initiatives are cross-functional in nature, frequently requiring collaboration among business units, IT, and other entities, and thus must be managed in a cross-functional manner. While the OSM will not actively lead strategic initiatives, it supplies the processes to ensure such initiatives are on track and are having the promised strategic impact.

- *Governance coordination.* In the wake of the many scandals that have plagued the business world recently, we have entered a new era of corporate governance. Today our boards require tools that provide an insightful view into the organization's strategy and value-creating mechanisms. The OSM has the opportunity to break new organizational ground in this regard by working with the board and other external stakeholders to proactively determine their information needs and meet them in a timely and efficient fashion.

- *Performance review administration.* Strategy must constantly be monitored and tested in real time to determine its efficacy, and the performance review meeting is the setting for this learning laboratory. The OSM coordinates the overall performance and strategy review process by determining the timetable, developing the agenda, facilitating the discussion, and ensuring that follow-up actions are documented and completed.

Initial Considerations in Establishing a Strategic Management Office
In the field of social psychology, there exists a phenomenon referred to as "diffusion of responsibility," which often manifests itself in scenes of personal tragedy. We've all heard of people suffering from heart attacks on bustling city streets only to be ignored as they cry out for help. That's diffusion of responsibility in action—we all assume that someone else will jump in and lend a hand. In less dramatic fashion, this phenomenon is played out in the halls of organizations each and every day as various functions work independently of one another, often suboptimizing overall results. The OSM can help you overcome this deficiency by acting as connective tissue that binds together the many processes that have a stake in the execution of strategy. But where to begin? Two critical considerations are staffing and areas of emphasis. Let's examine each briefly.

In order to fulfill its vital role, the OSM must have a seat at the executive table or at the very least report to a senior executive within the organization. The office will be called on to work across organizational boundaries. It must have the ability to play the position power card in bringing disparate organizational audiences together. While staff size typically varies depending on the size of the organization, there are some key characteristics to consider when staffing the office. Chrysler Corporation, for example, fills its OSM with what it considers high-potential individuals, each (generally) with five years of experience in multiple areas of the company.[9] Their varied backgrounds provide these individuals with networks throughout the company, while also contributing the diverse viewpoints necessary to fuel creative dissent that often drives breakthrough results.

Creating and managing an OSM where none existed in the past is a significant undertaking, and is best considered from an evolutionary viewpoint. It will prove virtually impossible (given logistical challenges for one) to master all of the functions noted in the last section at the same time. Therefore, organizations must determine where their greatest sources of pain exist and strategically administer aid in the form of OSM interventions. For example, communications may have been nonexistent in your organization in the past, and therefore a first-year imperative of the OSM may be the creation and administration of a strategic communication plan. Of course, in order to make strategy execution a core competency, each of the functions must be attended to. As with all things, it is ultimately a matter of balance.

KEEP IN MIND

- By viewing the Balanced Scorecard as a one-time metrics or systems initiative, some organizations fail to take advantage of the Scorecard's attributes as a strategic management system. Through proper guidance and maintenance, the Scorecard will become the cornerstone of the organization's management system.

- Making this transition requires the consideration of how a number of Scorecard-related tasks will fit into current and anticipated management models. These include the Scorecard's role in long-range strategic planning, annual Scorecard development, reporting dates, terminology, roles and responsibilities for Scorecard development, thresholds of performance, changing Scorecard elements, and linking the Scorecard to management processes.

- Strategies for effectively and efficiently collecting and loading performance data into a Scorecard reporting tool must be developed if the tool is to be accepted and used by employees. Whether an automated Scorecard solution is pursued or not, the data-gathering process is enhanced by the use of customized collection templates.

- A majority of Scorecard practitioners update their Scorecard on an annual basis. As conditions change and Scorecard learning intensifies, many companies will make changes to performance objectives, measures, and targets. The adjustments could reflect a change in strategic direction or a simple clarification to an otherwise confusing indicator.

- All the key players involved in the initial design and development of the Balanced Scorecard have a role to play in its ongoing evolution. The Balanced Scorecard champion's role takes on expanded prominence as this individual uses communication skills and Scorecard knowledge to coach and train executives, managers, and employees alike on the benefits to be derived from an even greater reliance on the Balanced Scorecard methodology. A new function emerges as the Scorecard grows: the system administrator. This individual controls the vital function of ensuring timely and accurate reporting of Scorecard results.

- The Finance function is the predominant home of the Balanced Scorecard in most organizations. As the purveyors of company information and with their unique view into strategy, processes, and economic events, this function often makes a very logical choice. However, the ultimate test for Scorecard ownership is an executive willing to actively use, support, and help shape the future direction of the Scorecard as a key strategy execution tool of the organization.

- As organizations have evolved, new professional disciplines have emerged, such as chief financial officer and chief information officer. In order to cement strategy execution as a core competency, organizations are creating Offices of Strategy Management to bridge the gap between strategy formation and implementation. Among the many functions of the OSM are change management, strategy formation and planning, Balanced Scorecard coordination, strategic communication, alignment, initiative management, governance coordination, and performance review administration.

Notes

1. John Kotter, *Leading Change* (Boston: Harvard Business School Press, 1996).
2. Ibid., p. 133.
3. Best Practices Benchmarking Report, *Developing the Balanced Scorecard* (Chapel Hill, NC: Best Practices, LLC, 1999).
4. Performance Measurement Survey by the American Institute of Certified Public Accountants and Lawrence S. Maisel (2001).
5. Mark J. Morgan, "A New Role for Finance, Architect of the Enterprise in the Information Age," *Strategic Finance* (August 2001).
6. Robert S. Kaplan and David P. Norton, "The Office of Strategy Management," *Harvard Business Review* (October 2005): 73–80.
7. Robert S. Kaplan and David P. Norton, "Strategic Management: An Emerging Profession," *Balanced Scorecard Report* (May–June 2004).
8. Niccolo Machiavelli, *The Prince*, W. K. Marriott, trans., Vol. 23, *The Great Books of the Western World* (Chicago: Encyclopaedia Britannica, 1952), p. 9.
9. Katherine Kane, "Driving Strategy at the Chrysler Group," *Balanced Scorecard Report* (January–February 2005).

CHAPTER 12

Concluding Thoughts on Balanced Scorecard Success

Roadmap for Chapter Twelve Do you remember those college days when you knew you had amassed enough marks to pass a course so you decided to skip the last few classes? Tempting as it may be, let's not have a repeat of history here because we still have some work to do before you get your A in Balanced Scorecard.

Chapter Two introduced the role of an organizational change expert. In this chapter we'll take a much closer look at the important work to be performed by this individual. Following our look at change activities necessary to secure Scorecard success is a review of the "Top 10" Balanced Scorecard implementation issues. Many organizations will determine that building a Scorecard is better done with the assistance of experienced management consultants. The chapter provides a number of criteria to be considered when choosing a consulting partner.

THE IMPORTANCE OF ORGANIZATIONAL CHANGE CONCEPTS

Between 50 and 80 percent of large change initiatives fail to meet expectations. This startling statistic is relevant to us since, as we know, the Balanced Scorecard does not represent a measurement initiative but is instead the very essence of a change effort. Not only does an organization's measurement system change as a result of the Scorecard, but if the implementation is to prove successful, the fundamental management processes guiding the company will be dramatically altered as well. The Balanced Scorecard represents a major departure in performance management for many organizations. Strategy, not financial controls, dictates the firm's direction, and the Scorecard creates a powerful new language for employee change. As is the case with strategy, it's not the change effort itself that tends to cause the failure, it's the execution that always derails the effort.

Effective organizational change is every bit as challenging as successful implementation of a new strategy. Judging by the square footage devoted to the topic at bookstores, most managers would agree with that assessment. Dozens of books and hundreds of articles are devoted to this vexing yet utterly critical management challenge. While cracking the code of change is far beyond the scope of this book, outlining some key change issues that require thought and planning is not. Chapter Two introduced the role of the organizational change expert as a member of the Balanced Scorecard implementation team. Let's now consider some of the key issues that will require the change expert's attention and knowledge as you attempt to develop a Balanced Scorecard system.

- *Why is this change necessary?* Organizations often announce a sweeping change program that will ultimately impact everyone in the organization but neglect to share the necessity of the change and related objectives. Employees will fill any such communication void with rumors, and chances are they won't be overly positive. Not only will the rumors support a negative rationale for the change, but probably they will attribute downright nasty motives to the executives who cooked up the whole scheme. Rationale for the change and associated objectives must be clearly stated at the outset of the implementation if there is any prospect of gaining employee support. Developing a guiding rationale was the very first topic mentioned in Chapter Two. If employees are expected to rally around the Scorecard, they must first recognize the need for a change and the rewards to be achieved by implementing it successfully.

- *What do you expect from me as a result of this change?* Clarity of expectations can be an absolute make-or-break issue when attempting to manage change successfully. What impact will Scorecard reporting have on managers and employees? How does it affect routine processes? Will it disrupt personal relationships? These and several other questions will naturally flow from a review of expectations. Scorecard planners must be proactive in determining what is expected of all employees once the Scorecard is up and running. If certain employees do stand to lose something in the transition to a Balanced Scorecard system, it is very important to honor their past efforts and again promote the rationale for the change.

- *Is the change compatible with the organization's culture and values?* Some organizations have a strong and proud history of managing by measures; others have been content to focus on a few key drivers to monitor their ongoing activities. Introducing the Balanced Scorecard into a culture with no past reliance on or knowledge of advanced measurement techniques may be very difficult.

- *Are support systems in place for completing the change?* When developing a Balanced Scorecard, organizations must ensure resources and support systems are in place to help ensure a successful outcome. Employees will be hesitant to lend their energy and support to any endeavor that lacks the necessary resources to see it through to completion.

- *How confident are employees?* Organizations have long memories, especially for past failures. If previous attempts at change have delivered frustration instead of results, current endeavors may be plagued from the outset by a lack of confidence. Optimism and belief on the part of employees that the change can be wrought is crucial. Confidence tends to boost energy and propel everyone toward achievement, while a lack of belief can lead to organizational apathy. Look to your history for positive examples of change, highlights you can draw on during the Balanced Scorecard implementation.

These are just some of the many issues that affect the success of a change program. There are no easy fixes or answers for any of the issues, as each is a product of the unique culture residing within every organization. However, recognizing that you may have problems and developing potential solutions go a long way toward a smooth Scorecard implementation. At the outset of a Scorecard effort, effective organizational change facilitators can assess staff members across the organization, from executives to managers to front-line employees, in an effort to capture the perceptions held regarding critical success factors. Armed with that knowledge, the facilitator can work with other members of the Scorecard team to develop action plans and programs aimed at mitigating the potentially negative effects associated with the issues identified.

The only way to stack the change deck in your favor is to perform a comprehensive assessment of opinions and perceptions held at all levels of the organization and then take appropriate action based on what you find. Being proactive is always a positive trait, but it is absolutely crucial here. Waiting too long can prove disastrous to your Scorecard efforts. As a final warning, remember it's not technology or methodologies that cause change efforts to fail, it's almost always "people" issues.

TOP 10 BALANCED SCORECARD IMPLEMENTATION ISSUES

In this book I've attempted to provide a comprehensive guide detailing what is necessary to implement the Balanced Scorecard successfully. My optimistic belief is that by following this advice, your organization can evade many of the pitfalls known to be hazardous to your Scorecard's health. Some of the problem areas are so pervasive, however, that they merit further attention and review before you launch your campaign. Here are my top 10 Scorecard implementation issues. It is my sincere hope that your organization can elude the perilous grip of each and every one.

   10. *Premature links to management processes.* The transition from communication tool through the development of a Strategy Map, to measurement, to strategic management system is a natural evolution for

a successful Balanced Scorecard. Embedding the Scorecard into management processes such as budgeting, compensation, and corporate governance allows organizations to tap the full potential of this dynamic framework. However, premature attempts to forge these links may cause a swift decline in Scorecard momentum. A major culprit here is the link of Scorecard measures to compensation. Employee attention and focus are undoubtedly heightened thanks to this powerful lever, but exercising it too soon can produce many unintended side effects. For one thing, the measures linking the Scorecard to compensation may be unproven and lead to dysfunctional decision making on the part of managers looking to cash in. Targets are also an issue, especially for new measures. An aggressive target may be perceived as unattainable and unrealistic, causing employees to lose any motivation they may have had to achieve it. Yet a target easily achieved will do little to foster breakthrough performance. Should the compensation link come under fire, employees, managers, and executives alike may be quick in assigning blame to an inherent shortcoming of the Scorecard system itself rather than shouldering the responsibility for an ill-conceived compensation scheme.

9. *Lack of cascading.* This issue actually warrants a higher placement than number 9 but is positioned here because it doesn't apply to every organization. Some small companies or business units within a larger entity may develop one Balanced Scorecard that is sufficient to guide the actions of the entire workforce. Organizations of any appreciable size, however, must cascade the Scorecard from top to bottom if they hope to gain the advantages offered by this system. Front-line employees are so far removed from organizational strategy that a high-level Scorecard, while providing a modicum of learning and motivation opportunities, will do little to guide daily activities. It is only by cascading the Scorecard to all levels of the organization and allowing all employees to describe how they contribute to the organization's overall success that true alignment can occur.

8. *Ineffective team development.* As I was preparing for a measures workshop with a client recently, my phone rang and the voice on the other end was that of the executive sponsor from this particular organization. After the usual pleasantries she informed me that "Dave" would not be able to attend; he had been called out-of-town for an important customer meeting. It is always amazing to me how many thoughts and emotions a human being can process practically simultaneously. I was at once relieved because Dave was a known skeptic, disappointed because I had prepared group assignments and would now have to replace him, and confused as to why this customer meeting would take precedence over a Scorecard session. When the cognitive dust settled my most resonant feeling was one of disappointment, because

the very fact that Dave was a skeptic made him all the more valuable to the team; his incessant questioning and innate cynicism frequently led to deeper discussions and ultimately better results. In fact, the more I thought of it, the more I concluded that this team had been successful *because of,* not in spite of, the various perspectives brought to bear by different people from different parts of the organization who reflected various viewpoints. Balanced Scorecards thrive in a team environment where backgrounds and functional specialties meld in the alchemy of heated debate and animated discussion aimed at producing a Scorecard reflective of the entire organization.

7. *No new measures.* Taking an existing group of measures and placing them into conveniently predefined perspectives does not a Balanced Scorecard make. Yet the temptation to do just that is sometimes overwhelming for organizations. In an effort to comply with the latest management fiat, groups quickly and easily assemble the same performance measures they've always used and dutifully tuck them into the four perspectives, thinking they've developed a brand new Balanced Scorecard. After several months of reporting, the group will inevitably question the necessity of the Scorecard since results are about the same as always. As we've seen from our discussion of measures in Chapter Five and elsewhere, most often it is the new and "missing measures" and their interplay with other indicators that drive the value of a Balanced Scorecard. Many of the measures needed to tell the story of the strategy may already be present, but in the vast majority of cases they must be supplemented with new and innovative metrics to ensure the execution of strategy.

6. *Inconsistent management practices.* As the name reflects, the Balanced Scorecard represents a new paradigm of balance within an organization: balancing the needs of internal and external stakeholders, balancing short-term opportunities with long-term value creation, balancing lag and lead indicators of performance, and of course balancing financial and nonfinancial indicators. A sure-fire method of promoting premature Scorecard death is to actively promote balanced measures while concurrently rewarding behaviors that reflect decidedly nonbalanced ideals. A good example is attempting to manage by the Balanced Scorecard yet compensating executives solely on short-term financial performance. The message sent with this practice is clear: We may say that nonfinancial indicators are important, but we all know that money really matters most. Many organizations will similarly tout teamwork and collaboration as the critical differentiators of their success while openly promoting individuals based on personal achievements only. Effective use of the Balanced Scorecard dictates a genuine commitment to developing and engaging in

managerial processes that are consistent with the holistic goals inherent in the Scorecard itself.

5. *Not reporting Balanced Scorecard results.* I read in this morning's paper that the Powerball lottery in the United States has ballooned to a record jackpot of over $360 million. I think it's impossible to read a headline like that and not pause for at least a moment to ponder "Hmm, what would I do with $360 million?" Once I transport myself from my private jet, secluded island, or 100-foot yacht back to reality, I realize that it will never happen to me because I probably won't even buy a ticket. In a similar vein, organizations that hope to achieve great success from their investment in the Balanced Scorecard but don't take the time and effort to report and discuss results are hoping to win a lottery without even bothering to buy a ticket; it just won't happen. Scorecard results must be broadcast regularly throughout the organization and, perhaps more important, must frame the agenda of management meetings so that implications and repercussions of results are analyzed, discussed, and debated until the raw material of data is transformed into nuggets of insight and competitive advantage. All it takes to win this prize is the commitment and diligence to pan the potential gold residing in your Balanced Scorecard results.

4. *No guiding rationale for the Balanced Scorecard program.* This issue was discussed in the organizational change section that began the chapter, but it bears repeating. As organizations around the globe experience the multitude of benefits from Balanced Scorecards, the concept has gained wide acceptance and approval as a management tool. With its heavyweight status confirmed, some organizations will adopt the Scorecard simply because it seems like the right thing to do. Certainly it is the right thing to do, but that in no way excuses an executive team from determining the specific rationale it has in mind when turning to the Scorecard. What problem will the Scorecard solve in the organization? If there is no answer to this fundamental question, or worse yet, if it has not even been contemplated, the Scorecard is sure to suffer the ignominious fate of organizational inertia. The lack of a guiding rationale often results from having the Scorecard developed as an add-on to another large-scale change initiative. Perhaps an enterprise resource planning initiative is under way, or a customer relationship management program. Consultants may suggest that the Scorecard is a logical extension of these efforts and should be implemented immediately. With no clearly articulated goal for the program, it can be easily misunderstood and ultimately ignored until it simply fades from view.

3. *No strategy.* It is extremely difficult to implement a strategic management system without a strategy. At the very core of the Scorecard concept is the organization's strategy, which guides all actions and decisions,

and ensures alignment from top to bottom. A Scorecard can be developed without the aid of a strategy, but it then becomes a key performance indicator or stakeholder system, without many of the attributes true Balanced Scorecards offer. Having said that, the processes involved in building a Balanced Scorecard may help a company back into or reverse engineer its strategy as a result of detailed and impassioned discussions surrounding performance measures necessary to stimulate breakthrough performance.

2. *Lack of Balanced Scorecard education and training.* In their haste to build Scorecards, many organizations will sacrifice the up-front effort of providing meaningful and detailed Scorecard training to those expected to use the system. Awareness sessions will be held during which the Scorecard is trumpeted as a measurement system featuring financial and nonfinancial measures, but little information is offered about the many subtleties and complexities of the model. Often the deceptive simplicity of the Scorecard makes people susceptible to the false notion that in-depth training is not required. If it feels that the Scorecard can be mastered simply, the organization may sponsor only high-level training and then trust their employees' business instincts to fuel the development of powerful new performance measures. The cost of this decision will manifest itself in poorly designed Scorecards, lack of use, and weak alignment within the organization. Take the necessary time at the beginning of the implementation to develop a comprehensive Scorecard curriculum that includes background on the concept, your objectives in implementing it, typical problems, success stories, and implementation details.

1. *No executive sponsorship.* Are you surprised by what is in first place? I don't think so. I debated whether lack of education and training should be the number-one issue but concluded that with tenacious leadership and support, a Scorecard project could ultimately succeed despite a lack of training at the outset. Without executive sponsorship, however, the effort is most likely doomed. Chapter Two provides a detailed review of executive sponsorship, including a number of methods for gaining support, and I urge you to review it carefully if you are lacking executive sponsorship for your initiative. Many Scorecard elements will take place in stages: first strategy is deciphered and translated; then objectives, measures, targets, and initiatives are developed; next the Scorecard is cascaded throughout the organization; and finally it becomes embedded in the organization's managerial processes. Executive support and sponsorship is the common thread that connects the entire end-to-end process. Without a strong and vocal leader present at each and every juncture, the effort can quickly stall. Simply put, nothing can take the place of an energetic

and knowledgeable executive willing to work tirelessly toward the cause of advancing the Balanced Scorecard.

USING CONSULTANTS TO DEVELOP THE BALANCED SCORECARD

After reading and digesting this book, I'm sure you'll agree that developing a Balanced Scorecard promises to bring great rewards but is certainly no simple task. Given the complexity of the development process, many organizations will turn to consulting companies for assistance. Even for small organizations, many independent consulting companies and individuals are available to provide assistance. Hiring consultants is often a prudent decision since a quality firm may bring implementation experience, proven methodologies for completing the work in a timely fashion, and objective advice. Consultants also offer a quality that sometimes is in short supply during the implementation period: credibility. Senior management may be more receptive to the Scorecard when it is co-developed by outside "experts." But consulting help doesn't come cheap; in fact, developing even a high-level organizational Scorecard may run into six figures, depending on the scope of the work and the particular consulting organization. And while consulting firms may lend credibility to the Scorecard from a senior management perspective, they may not engender the trust of employees who consider them overpaid and lacking in sufficient organizational knowledge to complete an acceptable work product. The decision of whether to use consultants can be very difficult. Should you feel consulting help would benefit your Scorecard project, here are a number of factors to consider when selecting a firm.

- *Balanced Scorecard experience.* Given the popularity of the Balanced Scorecard, virtually every management consulting firm will suggest it has a performance measurement offering and will boast substantial experience from previous implementations. However, the firm's concept of a Balanced Scorecard and yours may be miles apart. Through presentations and discussions you may discover that what a firm calls a Balanced Scorecard is really an executive information system designed to supply the senior team with important business metrics, but lacking in leading indicators and links to management processes. Be sure the firm you select is able to supply the Balanced Scorecard product you have in mind. This brings us to prior success. Most consulting firms will proudly advertise their past accomplishments at big-name organizations and offer glowing testimonials from satisfied clients. Be sure to perform an appropriate amount of due diligence to ensure those clients really are satisfied with the work performed and the outcome of the consultant's intervention.

- *A range of skills.* As we saw in the review of Balanced Scorecard team members presented in Chapter Two, developing a Scorecard requires a broad range of skill sets. The team assembled by your consulting partner should also have a diverse and complementary array of competencies. The entire team should be comprised of skilled communicators able to liaise easily and comfortably with all levels of staff. Some members should be gifted presenters and trainers to ensure the concepts behind the Scorecard are delivered clearly and cogently. Others should possess strong facilitation skills in order to manage the often (and necessary) conflict-filled Scorecard development sessions. Analytical skills are a must for combing through data and potential measures, and, finally, the team should possess members with enough technical skills to work effectively with your own Information Technology group.

- *Cultural fit.* This is an important and often-overlooked quality when selecting a consulting firm. Your organization has a certain culture, as does each and every consulting company. Cultural fit is often highlighted when two companies are planning a merger; in fact, conflicting cultures sometimes are deal breakers. Although you won't be joined permanently with the consultants you choose, they will be an extremely important part of your organization during the development of your Scorecard. Look past the glitzy sales brochures and testimonials to the real people you'll be dealing with every day. Will they be compatible with the culture of your organization? Will executives and front-line staff alike be willing to work with them? Only you can answer this important question.

- *Knowledge transfer.* A key component of every work plan devised by consulting firms will be sufficient and timely knowledge transfer from the consultants to the employees of the contracting organization. Knowledge transfer implies just that: a passing of knowledge on key concepts and techniques from the consultants to the clients. However, in their zeal to complete their work on time and on budget, consultants may inadvertently sacrifice knowledge transfer activities in favor of more tangible work efforts. Organizations pay a heavy price when this occurs. As the consultants are walking out the door, they leave behind an organization bereft of the skills and knowledge necessary to sustain the momentum that was so difficult to achieve. Ensure that any consultants you work with will devote the necessary time to a comprehensive sharing of Scorecard knowledge.

FINAL THOUGHTS

Since its inception, the Balanced Scorecard has had a profound effect on the practice of management around the world. The transition from antiquated industrial age methods to information age necessities dictated the

emergence of new reporting tools. Heeding the call for new and innovative systems, the Balanced Scorecard ascended the ranks of influential
management tools. As Scorecard practitioners have tinkered with, experimented on, modified, and improved the methodology, it has only become
stronger and more adaptable as a management system. The broad acceptance of the methodology is reflected in recent estimates suggesting that
upward of 60 percent of Fortune 1000 organizations have developed Balanced Scorecard systems. That of course means a corresponding 40 percent
have not. And what of the thousands of small and medium-size enterprises,
government agencies, and not-for-profit organizations spanning the globe?
Clearly the potential for future growth and development of the Balanced
Scorecard is dramatic. Fortunately for all of us the work continues, and
the most exciting breakthroughs are most likely still ahead of us. It is organizations like yours, ready to embark on the Scorecard journey, that will
write the next chapters in the life of this powerful and dynamic system. I
thank you and wish you great success.

KEEP IN MIND

- It seems the only constant in today's organization is, ironically, change.
  The demands of twenty-first-century business dictate that organizations
  constantly adapt to new conditions or risk perishing. Unfortunately, the
  record of successful change in most organizations is dismally low. To
  ensure that the Balanced Scorecard does not suffer the fate of previous
  attempts at change, companies must engage in a number of organizational change activities.

- Rationale for the change must be clearly communicated along with what
  will be expected of employees once the Scorecard system is initiated.
  Organizations must also determine how compatible the Scorecard is with
  current culture and to what extent employees have confidence that the
  tool can be implemented successfully. Change facilitators can assess employee perceptions on key change issues and work with Scorecard team
  members to devise mitigating strategies.

- Many organizations will fall prey to at least one of the Top 10 Balanced
  Scorecard implementation issues. They are: premature links to management processes, lack of cascading, the ineffective development of
  a Balanced Scorecard team, no new measures, inconsistent management
  practices, not reporting Balanced Scorecard results, no guiding rationale
  for the Scorecard, no strategy, lack of training and education, and no
  executive sponsorship.

- Consulting organizations have been quick to develop Scorecard offerings
  in conjunction with the tool's rapid growth. While consulting engagements
  usually are costly and not all employees will relate well with outsiders, they

can provide a number of significant benefits. Proven methodologies, past Scorecard implementation successes, and speedy development times are just a few of the advantages awaiting those organizations that hire consultants. Before deciding whether to hire consultants, organizations should consider the firm's actual implementation experience, skill sets offered, cultural fit, and knowledge-sharing commitment.

Index